Prophets and Prophecy in the Ancient Near East

SBL

Society of Biblical Literature

Writings from the Ancient World

Theodore J. Lewis, General Editor

*Associate Editors*

Billie Jean Collins
Jerrold S. Cooper
Edward L. Greenstein
Jo Ann Hackett
Richard Jasnow
Ronald J. Leprohon
C. L. Seow
Niek Veldhuis

Number 12
*Prophets and Prophecy of the Ancient Near East*
by Martti Nissinen
Edited by Peter Machinist

# PROPHETS AND PROPHECY

# IN THE ANCIENT NEAR EAST

*by*
Martti Nissinen

*with contributions by*
C. L. Seow
*and*
Robert K. Ritner

*Edited by*
Peter Machinist

Society of Biblical Literature
Atlanta

Prophets and Prophecy in the Ancient Near East


**Library of Congress Cataloging-in-Publication Data**

Nissinen, Martti.
Prophets and prophecy in the ancient Near East / by Martti Nissinen with contributions by C. L. Seow and Robert K. Ritner ; edited by Peter Machinist.
p. cm. — (Writings from the ancient world ; no. 12)
Includes bibliographical references and index.
ISBN 1-58983-027-X (paper binding : alk. paper)
1. Prophets—Middle East—History. 2. Prophecy—History. 3. Middle East—Literatures. I. Ritner, Robert Kriech, 1953– II. Seow, C. L. (Choon Leong) III. Machinist, Peter. IV. Title. V. Series: Writings from the ancient world ; no. 12.
BF1762 .N58 2003b
133.3'0939'4—dc21 2003007002

11 10 09 08 07 5 4 3

Printed in the United States of America
on acid-free paper

# Contents

# Series Editor's Foreword

Writings from the Ancient World is designed to provide up-to-date, readable English translations of writings recovered from the ancient Near East.

The series is intended to serve the interests of general readers, students, and educators who wish to explore the ancient Near Eastern roots of Western civilization or to compare these earliest written expressions of human thought and activity with writings from other parts of the world. It should also be useful to scholars in the humanities or social sciences who need clear, reliable translations of ancient Near Eastern materials for comparative purposes. Specialists in particular areas of the ancient Near East who need access to texts in the scripts and languages of other areas will also find these translations helpful. Given the wide range of materials translated in the series, different volumes will appeal to different interests. However, these translations make available to all readers of English the world's earliest traditions as well as valuable sources of information on daily life, history, religion, and the like in the preclassical world.

The translators of the various volumes in this series are specialists in the particular languages and have based their work on the original sources and the most recent research. In their translations they attempt to convey as much as possible of the original texts in fluent, current English. In the introductions, notes, glossaries, maps, and chronological tables, they aim to provide the essential information for an appreciation of these ancient documents.

Covering the period from the invention of writing (by 3000 B.C.E.) down to the conquests of Alexander the Great (ca. 330 B.C.E.), the ancient Near East comprised northeast Africa and southwest Asia. The cultures represented within these limits include especially Egyptian, Sumerian, Babylonian, Assyrian, Hittite, Ugaritic, Aramean, Phoenician, and Israelite. It is hoped that Writings from the Ancient World will eventually produce translations of most of the many different genres attested in these cultures: letters (official and private), myths, diplomatic documents, hymns, law collections, monumental inscriptions, tales, and administrative records, to mention but a few.

Significant funding was made available by the Society of Biblical Literature for the preparation of this volume. In addition, those involved in preparing this volume have received financial and clerical assistance from their respective institutions. Were it not for these expressions of confidence in our work, the arduous tasks of preparation, translation, editing, and publication could not have been accomplished or even undertaken. It is the hope of all who have worked on these texts or supported this work that Writings from the Ancient World will open up new horizons and deepen the humanity of all who read these volumes.

Theodore J. Lewis
Johns Hopkins University

# Abbreviations

The abbreviations follow those of *The SBL Handbook of Style for Ancient Near Eastern, Biblical, and Early Christian Studies* (Peabody, Mass.: Hendrickson, 1999). In addition, the following abbreviations are used:

| | |
|---|---|
| A. | Tablet signature of texts from Mari |
| ABG | Arbeiten zur Bibel und ihrer Geschichte |
| *ABRT* | James A. Craig, *Assyrian and Babylonian Religious Texts.* Leipzig: Hinrichs, 1895. |
| *AD* | Abraham J. Sachs and Hermann Hunger, *Astronomical Diaries and Related Texts from Babylonia.* Vols. 1–3. Vienna: Verlag der Österreichischen Akademie der Wissenschaften, 1988–96. |
| AOTU | Altorientalische Texte und Untersuchungen |
| *ASJ* | *Acta Sumerologica* (Japan) |
| *BB* | Carl Bezold and E. A. Wallis Budge, *The Tell el-Amarna Tablets in the British Museum.* London: British Museum, 1892. |
| *BCSMS* | *Bulletin of the Canadian Society for Mesopotamian Studies* |
| BE | Tablets in the Collections of the Staatliche Museen, Berlin |
| BM | Tablets in the Collections of the British Museum |
| Bu | Tablets in the Collections of the British Museum |
| CRRAI | Comptes rendus de la Rencontre Assyriologique Internationale |
| DMOA | Documenta et Monumenta Orientis Antiqui |
| DT | Tablets in the collections of the British Museum |
| FLP | Tablets in the collections of the Free Library of Pennsylvania |
| IM | Tablets in the collections of the Iraq Museum |
| *JARG* | *Jahrbuch für Anthropologie und Religionsgeschichte* |

| | |
|---|---|
| K | Tablets in the collections of the British Museum |
| *LAS* | Simo Parpola, *Letters from Assyrian Scholars to the Kings Esarhaddon and Assurbanipal.* Vols. 1–2. Kevelaer: Butzon & Bercker; Neukirchen-Vluyn: Neukirchener Verlag, 1970–83. |
| M. | Tablet signature of texts from Mari |
| *NARGD* | J. N. Postgate, *Neo-Assyrian Royal Grants and Decrees.* Rome: Pontificial Biblical Institute, 1969. |
| *NBL* | *Neues Bibel-Lexikon* |
| ND | Tablet signature of texts from Nimrud |
| OAC | Orientis Antiqui Collectio |
| OECT | Oxford Editions of Cuneiform Inscriptions |
| *PNA* | *The Prosography of the Neo-Assyrian Empire.* Vol. 1 edited by K. Radner; vols. 2 and 3/I edited by H. D. Baker. Helsinki: Neo-Assyrian Text Corpus Project, 1998–2002. |
| *RAcc* | François Thureau-Dangin, *Rituels accadiens.* Paris: Leroux, 1921. |
| Rm | Tablets in the collections of the British Museum |
| RS | Tablet signature of texts from Ugarit |
| SFES | Schriften der Finnischen Exegetischen Gesellschaft |
| Sm | Tablets in the collections of the British Museum |
| T. | Tablet signature of texts from Mari |
| TCM | Textes cunéiformes de Mari |
| *TI* | S. Langdon, *Tammuz and Ishtar.* Oxford: Clarendon, 1914. |
| UM | Tablets in the collections of the University Museum, Philadelphia |
| UTB | Uni-Taschenbücher |
| VA | Inscriptions in the collections of the Staatliche Museen, Berlin |
| VAT | Tablets in the collections of the Staatliche Museen, Berlin |
| WdF | Wege der Forschung |
| VS | Vorderasiatische Schriftdenkmäler der Staatlichen Museen zu Berlin |
| W-B | Tablets in the Weld-Blundell Collection in the Ashmolean Museum |
| *4 R* | H. C. Rawlinson, *The Cuneiform Inscriptions of Western Asia.* Vol 4. London: Trustees of the British Museum, 1875. |
| *4 $R^2$* | H. C. Rawlinson, *The Cuneiform Inscriptions of Western Asia.* Vol 4. 2d Edition. London: Trustees of the British Museum, 1891. |
| *5 R* | H. C. Rawlinson, *The Cuneiform Inscriptions of Western Asia.* Vol 5. London: Trustees of the British Museum, 1909. |

# Explanation of Signs

| | |
|---|---|
| [ ] | Brackets enclose restorations. |
| < > | Angle brackets enclose words omitted by the original scribe. |
| ( ) | Parentheses enclose additions in the English translation. |
| . . . | A row of dots indicates gaps in the text or untranslatable words. |
| (?) | A question mark in parentheses follows doubtful readings in the transcriptions and doubtful renderings in the translations. |
| | *Italics* in the English translations indicate uncertain readings. |

# Chronological Table 1: 1850–1500 B.C.E.

| Date | Egypt | Syria | Mesopotamia | | | |
|---|---|---|---|---|---|---|
| | | | Mari | Ešnunna | Babylonia | Assyria |
| 1850 | 12th Dynasty | | | | Sabium | Sargon I |
| | 1991–1783 | | | | 1844–1831 | |
| | | Kings of Yamhad | | Ibalpiel I | | |
| | | ca. 1850–1650 | | Ipiq-Adad | Apil-Sin | Puzur-Aššur I |
| | | | Yaggid-Lim | Naram-Sin | 1830–1813 | Erišum II |
| 1800 | | Yarim-Lim I | Yahdun-Lim | | Sin-muballit | Šamši-Adad I |
| | | | ca. 1810–1795 | Dadusha | 1812–1793 | 1835/30–1777 |
| | | | Sumu-Yamam | | | (king of Ekallatum, |
| | | | 1795–1793 | | | king of Assyria 1807–1775, |
| | | | Yasmah-Addu | | Hammurabi | controlled Mari 1795–1775) |
| | | | 1793–1775 | | 1792–1750 | |
| | | Hammurabi I | Zimri-Lim | Ibalpiel II | | Išme-Dagan |
| | 13th Dynasty | | 1775-1761 | ca. 1779–1765 | | (king of Ekallatum) |
| 1750 | 1783–1640 | Abba-el | | | Samsu-iluna | |
| | | | | | 1749–1712 | |
| | | | | | Abi-ešuh | |
| 1700 | | | | | 1711–1684 | |
| | | | | | Ammiditana | |
| | | | | | 1683–1647 | |
| 1650 | | | | | | |
| | 15th Dynasty | | | | Ammisaduqa | |
| | (Hyksos) | | | | 1646–1626 | |
| | 1640–1532 | | | | Samsuditana | |
| 1600 | | | | | 1625–1595 | |
| 1550 | | | | | | |
| 1500 | | | | | | |

# Chronological Table 2: 1500–1000 B.C.E.

| Date | Egypt | Syria-Palestine | Mesopotamia Mitanni | Babylonia | Assyria |
|---|---|---|---|---|---|
| | 18th Dynasty (New Kingdom) 1550–1307 | | | | |
| 1500 | Thutmosis III 1490–1436 | | Kings of Mitanni ca. 1500–1200 | | Several kings ca. 1550–1362 |
| 1450 | | | | Kassite Kings 1415–1154 | |
| 1400 | Amenophis III 1403–1367 | Kings of Ugarit ca.1400–1180/70 | Šuttarna II<br>Tušratta ca. 1365–1335/22 | | Middle Assyrian Kings 1363–1076 |
| 1350 | Akhenaten 1367–1350<br>Tutankhamun 1347–1339 | Amarna Period 1352–1333 | | | |
| 1300 | 19th Dynasty 1307–1196<br>Ramesses II 1290–1224 | | | | |
| 1250 | | | | Kaštiliaš IV 1232–1225 | Tukulti-Ninurta I 1243–1207 |
| 1200 | 20th Dynasty 1196–1070 | | | | |
| 1150 | | | | | |
| 1100 | Ramesses IX 1080-1070 | | | Marduk-šapik-zeri 1081–1069 | Aššur-bel-kala 1074–1057 |
| 1050 | | | | | |
| 1000 | | | | | |

# Chronological Table 3: 1000–500 B.C.E.

| Date | Egypt | Palestine | | Syria | Mesopotamia | | Persia |
|---|---|---|---|---|---|---|---|
| | | Judah | Israel | | Assyria | Babylonia | |
| 1000 | 21st Dynasty | David | | | Tiglath-pileser II | | |
| | 1070–945 | | | | 966–935 | | |
| 950 | 22d Dynasty | Solomon | | | | | |
| | 945–712 | | | | | | |
| 900 | | Rehoboam | Jeroboam I | | Adad-nirari II | | |
| | | ca. 926–910 | ca. 926–907 | | 911–891 | | |
| | | Jehoshaphat | Omri | | | | |
| 850 | | ca. 868–847 | ca. 878–871 | | Assurnasirpal II | | |
| | | Joram | Jehu | Hazael of Damascus | 883–859 | | |
| | | ca. 847–845 | ca. 845–818 | Bir-Hadad of Damascus | Shalmaneser III | | |
| 800 | | Jehoash | Jehoahaz | Zakkur of Hamath | 858–824 | | |
| | | ca. 840–801 | ca. 818–802 | | Adad-nirari III | | |
| | | | Jeroboam II | | 810–783 | | |
| 750 | | | ca. 787–747 | | Tiglath-pileser III | | |
| | | Ahaz | Hoshea | | 744–727 | | |
| | | ca. 734–725 | ca. 732–724 | | Shalmaneser V | | |
| | | Hezekiah | | | 726–722 | | |
| 700 | 25th Dynasty | ca. 725–697 | | | Sargon II | | |
| | 712–657 | | | | 721–705 | | |
| | | Manasseh | | | Sennacherib | | |
| | | ca. 696–642 | | | 704–681 | | |
| | Neco I | | | | Esarhaddon | | |
| 650 | 671–663 | | | | 681–669 | | |
| | | Josiah | | | Assurbanipal | Šamaš-šumu-ukin | |
| | | ca. 639–609 | | | 668–627 | 668–648 | |
| | | | | | Sin-šarru-iškun | Nabopolassar | |
| | | | | | ca. 623–612 | 625–605 | |
| 600 | | Jehoiakim | | | | Nebuchadnezzar II | |
| | | 609–598 | | | | 604–562 | Cyrus |
| 550 | | | | | | Nabonidus | 559–530 |
| | | | | | | 555–539 | Cambyses |
| | | | | | | | 529–522 |
| 500 | | | | | | | Darius I |
| | | | | | | | 521–486 |

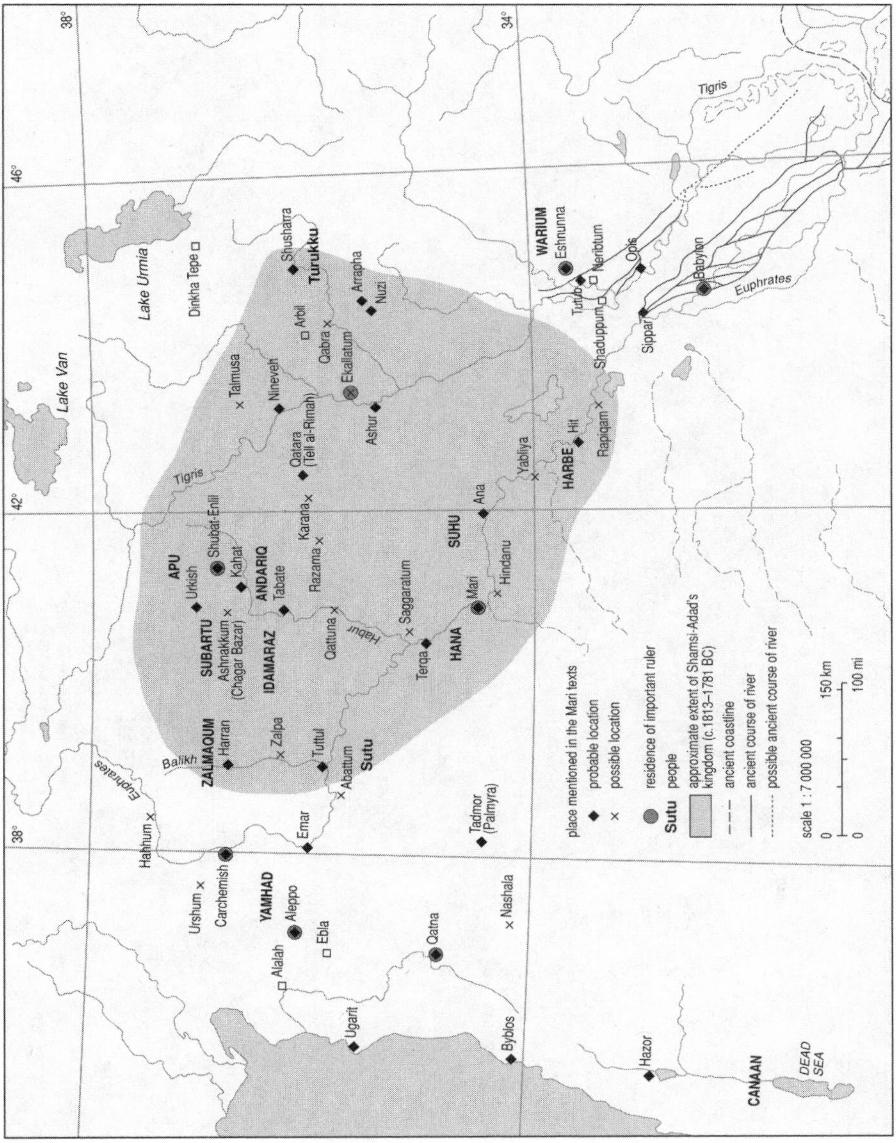


The world of the Mari letters.

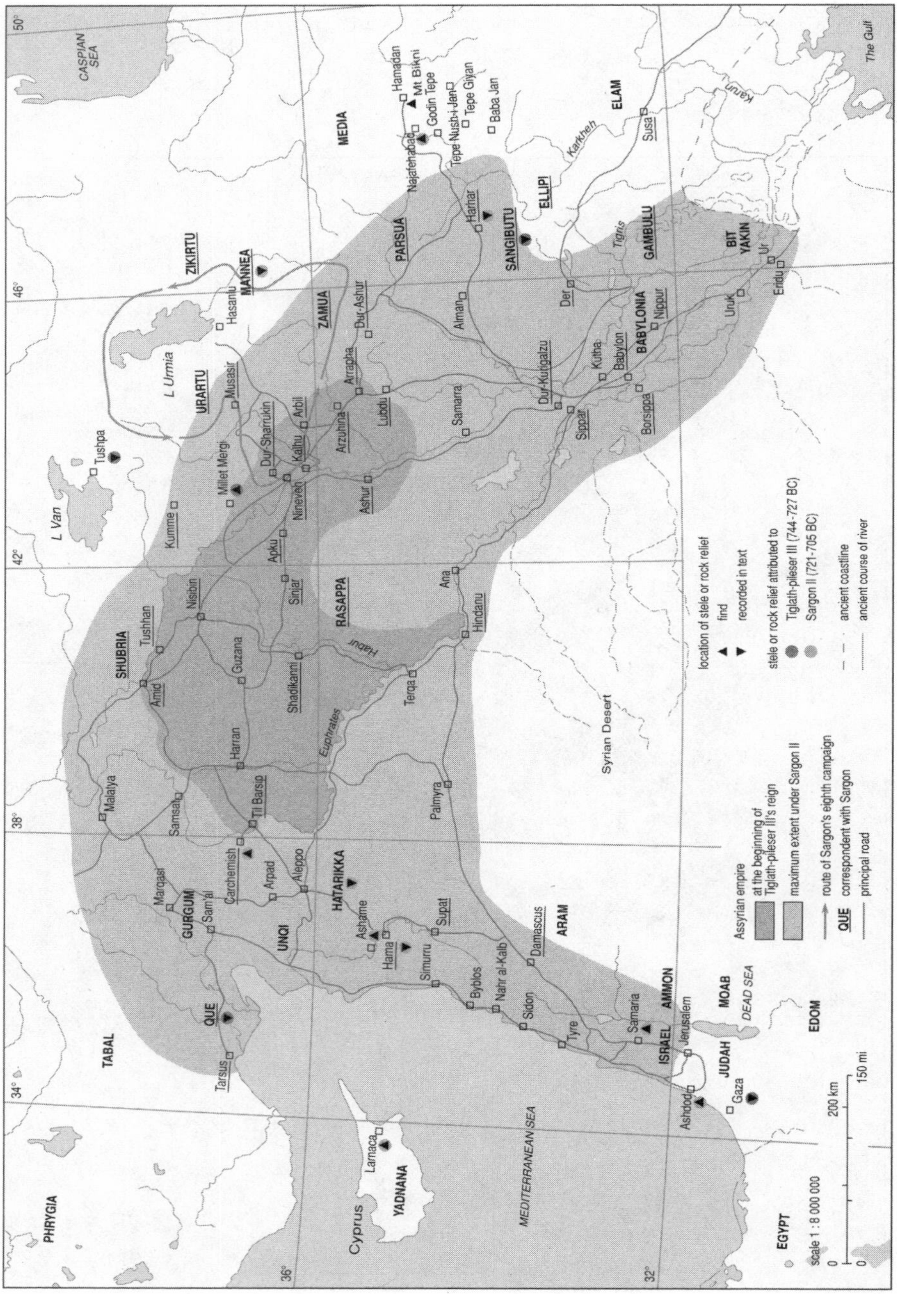


The Assyrian Empire in the late eighth century B.C.E.

# Acknowledgments

It is a great pleasure to offer my acknowledgments to a number of people who devoted their time to working on this book, first of all to Choon-Leong Seow and Robert K. Ritner for their contributions, without which this volume would be seriously incomplete. Peter Machinist was burdened with the task of being my volume editor. He worked on my manuscript with great precision and care, correcting my English as well as my Akkadian and giving editorial advice, for which I am profoundly indebted to him. As always I owe a great debt of gratitude to Simo Parpola, who made a multitude of remarks and corrections to the Assyrian part of the manuscript and helped me out with various difficulties. It is he who first introduced me to the world and spirit of Assyrian prophecy and who has ever since been a never-failing mentor, support, and source of knowledge. In matters concerning Mari, I owe a great deal to the counsel given by Jack M. Sasson, who read the Mari chapters carefully through and gave me valuable linguistic and bibliographical advice. Special thanks are due to Dominique Charpin, who also read my translations of the Mari texts and provided me with important new literature, readings, and sources. I owe to him the possibility of including the texts A. 3760 (no. 3) and M. 9717 (no. 65) in this collection almost simultaneously with their publication. I am also grateful to the series editor Simon B. Parker and the editorial board of the Writings from the Ancient World series for the approval of my manuscript, to Rex D. Matthews, editorial director of the Society of Biblical Literature, for his agreeable cooperation, and to Bob Buller for preparing the manuscript for publication. I have only myself to blame, if all these people have failed in their efforts to improve this book. Leena, Elina, and Kaisa, my wife and daughters, did not even try; they just loved me. *Kiitos!*

# Acknowledgments

# Introduction

## Ancient Near Eastern Prophecy

Ancient Near Eastern sources for prophecy have hitherto been scattered in various publications, often without an appropriate and up-to-date translation and, hence, virtually inaccessible to non-specialist readers. The purpose of this volume is to bring together a representative sample of written documents from a variety of times and places, translated from the newest editions in order to update the present knowledge of the distribution of prophecy in the ancient Near East as well as to provide the reader with a tool for the study of prophecy as an established institution in the ancient Near Eastern world.

Prophecy, as understood in this volume, is human transmission of allegedly divine messages. As a method of revealing the divine will to humans, prophecy is to be seen as another, yet distinctive branch of the consultation of the divine that is generally called "divination." Among the forms of divination, prophecy clearly belongs to the noninductive kind. That is to say, prophets—like dreamers and unlike astrologers or haruspices—do not employ methods based on systematic observations and their scholarly interpretations, but act as direct mouthpieces of gods whose messages they communicate.

This understanding of the term concurs with those definitions of prophecy in which the transmissive or communicative aspect is emphasized as an overall feature that should be found in all phenomena and literary documents that are claimed to represent prophecy (e.g., Overholt 1989; Huffmon 1992; Barstad 1993a; Weippert 1997b; Petersen 2000). Other aspects, like religious and social conditions of the activity, personal qualities of the human beings involved, the possible prediction and other distinctive features of the messages and the means of obtaining them, are subordinate to the basic understanding of prophecy as a process of transmission.

The prophetic process of transmission consists of the divine sender of the message, the message itself, the human transmitter of the message and the recipient(s) of the message. These four components should be transparent in any written source to be identified as a specimen of prophecy.

As a phenomenon, prophecy is cross-cultural, being observable in various cultural environments throughout human history (Overholt 1986; Grabbe 2000). As a term, however, "prophecy," together with its derivatives, has established itself primarily in the language of Jewish, Christian and Islamic cultures. A significant part of the canon of the Hebrew Bible is called *nĕbîʾîm,* the prophets, and the prerequisite for the conceptualization of prophecy by Christians and even Muslims is the biblical idea of prophecy, as developed in early Judaism from the second temple period onwards. Because of the emphatically biblical background of the concept of prophecy, its adaptation to extra-biblical contexts has seldom happened independently from the biblical paradigm and without a comparative purpose. The ongoing debate about the degree of historicity of the Hebrew Scriptures and the quest for authentic prophetic words within the heavily edited prophetic oracles and narratives of the Hebrew Bible have made many scholars seek arguments from related phenomena in the surrounding cultures. On the other hand, the need to study the ancient Near Eastern documents in their own right, independently from the agenda of biblical studies, has been increasingly emphasized.

## The Study of Prophecy in Transition

That prophecy as a phenomenon is not restricted to the early Jewish or Christian realm has never been a secret. It is recognized by the Hebrew Bible, in which the "prophets of Baal" make their appearance (1 Kgs 18). Even for Muhammad, the Prophet of Islam, there were acknowledged precursors in pre-Islamic Arabia (Hämeen-Anttila 2000b). The existence of extra-biblical prophecy has long been an issue for modern scholars as well. Phenomena and written documents related to biblical prophecy were sought in different sources and milieus, ancient and modern, already in the first half of the twentieth century (e.g., Hölscher 1914; Lindblom 1934/1962; Haldar 1945). This quest provided important insights, but was largely impeded not only by definitional unclarity, but also by the uncertainty about the distribution and nature of ancient Near Eastern prophecy because of the lack of pertinent sources.

The situation changed when the first letters with quotations recognized as prophetic words were found in the excavations of the eighteenth-century B.C.E. archives of Mari, an important city-state in the middle Euphrates region. The first two letters were published by George Dossin in 1948 (no.

38) and 1950 (no. 1), and the subsequent volumes of *Archives royales de Mari* (ARM), especially the female correspondence (ARM 10) published by Dossin in 1967, brought more cognate letters to scholarly notice. These sources inspired a lively scholarly involvement that produced a considerable amount of literature (Heintz 1990–2000). For decades, the Mari letters formed the primary extrabiblical evidence for prophecy in scholarly literature, even though the prophetic aspect in them and especially their equivalence to biblical prophecy did not remain unchallenged (e.g., Noort 1977). Since the criteria for classifying texts as prophecy were largely based on the study of the prophetic books of the Hebrew Bible, many would avoid the use of the word "prophecy" outside the biblical context altogether. Moreover, the chronological gap of one millennium and more between Mari and the Bible presented problems for comparison, especially because little material was found outside the two corpora to tie them historically and phenomenologically together. Nevertheless, a few long-known documents of prophecy in West Semitic milieus, like the Egyptian report of Wenamon (no. 142) and the Zakkur Inscription (no. 137), as well as the Balaam Inscription from Deir ʿAllā (no. 138), which became public knowledge in the 1970s, were there to testify that the biblical band of the "prophets of Baal" was not quite without historical foundation.

To be sure, divine messages to the Assyrian kings Esarhaddon and Assurbanipal from the seventh century B.C.E. had already been excavated in the middle of the nineteenth century from the ruins of Nineveh, which by the time of these kings had become the central capital of the Neo-Assyrian Empire. Cuneiform copies and translations of most of these texts, actually referred to as "prophecy" by some contemporary scholars (e.g., Delattre 1889), were published as early as the 1890s. The revival of the comparative study of prophecy generated by the study of Mari letters left the Neo-Assyrian sources at first virtually untouched. The preliminary work done in the 1960s by Karlheinz Deller and Simo Parpola on the Nineveh tablets, which were far from easy to read and interpret, resulted only in the 1970s in scholarly contributions in which they were again recognized as prophecy (Weippert 1972; Dietrich 1973; Huffmon 1976a/b; cf. Merlot 1972: 880–81).

Even in the new phase of study, with two corpora of ancient Near Eastern prophecy from different places and periods, the complicated state of publication was a challenge that could be faced only with a well developed bibliographical sense and a good knowledge of cuneiform sources. Relief for this situation was brought first by Jean-Marie Durand with the edition of the prophetic letters from Mari as a part of the first collection of the Mari correspondence (ARM 26/1, 1988), and finally by Simo Parpola who met a long-felt need with his edition of the Neo-Assyrian prophetic oracles (SAA 9, 1997).

Hence, when it comes to the study of ancient Near Eastern prophecy, the third millennium of our present era begins propitiously with two authoritative editions of the principal text corpora at hand. However, these volumes do not include all evidence of ancient Near Eastern prophecy. Some Mari letters with prophetic content are published or forthcoming in volumes of the ARM series subsequent to the edition of Durand. In addition, there are several ritual and administrative texts from Mari in which prophets are mentioned. As for the Neo-Assyrian sources, the edition of Parpola includes the tablets that are prophetic oracles as such, whereas other texts which refer to prophets or quote prophecy are dealt with in other publications (e.g., Nissinen 1998b; 2000a/b). The two oracles from Ešnunna (nos. 66–67), contemporaneous to those of Mari and published by Maria deJong Ellis (1987), deserve special attention, representing the genre of prophetic oracles outside Mari and Assyria. Finally, the presence of persons with prophetic titles is amply documented in sources from the twenty-first to the second centuries B.C.E. from different parts of the ancient Near East.

## The Nature of the Sources

The existing evidence of prophecy comes from all over the Fertile Crescent, witnessing to the wide distribution of prophets and proving prophecy to be a common cultural legacy which cannot be traced back to any particular society or place of origin. However, the evidence is very fragmentary. Of the many places and periods of time, we can say only that prophets were there, but little can be learned of their activities. Some significant ancient Near Eastern cultures reveal even less: Ugarit leaves us entirely in the dark, the Hittite evidence is equivocal and the Egyptian texts conventionally called prophecies are to be taken as literary predictions rather than the result of a prophetic process of communication (see below). An overall picture of ancient Near Eastern prophecy can be drawn only by filling many gaps with circumstantial reasoning and with the help of comparative material. To use an archaeological metaphor, the sources collected in this volume constitute only the defective set of sherds, of which the badly broken vessel must be restored.

Given the circumstances, the ancient Near Eastern evidence of prophecy consists entirely of written sources, even though it is probable indeed that prophecy was oral communication in the first place. The relatively small number of documents and their haphazard state of preservation for posterity indicate that writing was only exceptionally part of the prophetic process of communication, and that when it was, the written document was not necessarily filed in the archives, at any rate not for long-term preservation. It is certainly not by accident that the majority of the prophetic documents come from Mari and Nineveh, which are in general the two most abundant Mesopotamian archives found thus far. On the other hand, the huge process of collecting, editing, and interpreting prophecy that took place as a part of the formation of the Hebrew Bible is virtually without precedent in the rest of the ancient Near East. Only in Assyria do the collections of prophetic oracles to Esarhaddon document the reuse of prophecy in a new situation, thus bearing witness to the modest beginnings of such a process.

The written sources that comprise the available documentation of ancient Near Eastern prophecy divide into different types. Some of these basically consist of little more than the wording of prophetic utterances, while in others, the words of the prophets—quotations of a known personality or literary paraphrases—are part of the text of another writer, often as one issue among others. In both cases, the way from the spoken word to a written record may be long and twisting, often employing several intermediaries between the prophet and the addressee. The messages transmitted by the prophets are exposed to all the stylistic, ideological and material requirements active in the process of transmission, which may carry beyond the oral stage into the written. Hence, the so-called *ipsissima verba* of the prophets are beyond reach, which only stresses the need to pay attention to the socioreligious preconditions of the whole process instead of the personality of the prophet (Nissinen 2000a).

A great number of texts do not quote words of the prophets but mention them in different contexts and in association with people representing different kinds of professions and social roles. These texts not only give the only available evidence of prophecy in certain periods and places, but also let prophets appear in a variety of social, cultic and lexical contexts. Taken together, these sources yield important insights, however random and scanty, into the socio-religious profile of the prophets—all the more because there are no major discrepancies between the sources in this respect, even though they derive from a time-span of more than one and a half millennia. Many of those from the Mesopotamian or cuneiform realm present prophets in close connection to the goddess Ištar, often associated with persons of distinctive behavior or bodily appearance.

## The Prophets

Who, then, are identified as *prophets* in the written sources? There is no single word for a prophet in any language represented in this book, that is, Akkadian, Egyptian, Hebrew, and other West Semitic. The justification for translating certain appellatives with the English word *prophet* is taken from what the sources inform us about the persons in question. We have already noted that, as a rule, people who transmit divine words that allegedly derive from direct communication with a deity are called by modern interpreters prophets, whatever the original designation may be. All visionaries and dreamers cannot be lumped together as "prophets," though, but the line between prophets and other practitioners of non-inductive divination is difficult to draw and may be partly artificial. As a result, there is no infallible definition of who should be called a prophet in each time, society and situation.

Some designations, nevertheless, have established themselves as prophetic ones. The widest range of attestations belongs to *muḫḫû(m)* (Babylonian)/*maḫḫû* (Assyrian) and the respective feminines *muḫḫūtu(m)*/*maḫḫūtu,* known from Old Akkadian through Old and Middle Babylonian and Middle Assyrian to Neo-Assyrian and Neo-Babylonian. At Mari, *muḫḫûm* is the commonest prophetic title, whereas in Neo-Assyrian documents, *maḫḫû* appears only in literary contexts and in lexical lists. The word is derived from the root *maḫû* "to become crazy, to go into a frenzy," which refers to receiving and transmitting divine words in an altered state of mind. This verb is actually used of the condition in which divine words are uttered (e.g., in nos. 23, 24, 33, 51). Many of the occurrences of this word family reveal nothing of the prophetic capacity of the persons thus designated, but whenever their activities are discernible to some extent, they either assume a cultic role (nos. 51, 52, 103, 118, 122) or convey divine messages (nos. 10, 12, 16, 25, 31, 32, etc.). In Neo-Assyrian inscriptions, prophecies are called *šipir maḫḫê,* "messages of the *maḫḫû*" (nos. 97–99, 101).

At Mari, there is another designation for persons who are involved in prophetic activities. The word in question is *āpilum* (fem. *āpiltum*), from the root *apālu* "to answer." The etymology suggests a transmitter of divine answers to human inquiries, and the *āpilum* actually does convey divine messages in the very same manner as the *muḫḫûm* (e.g., nos. 1, 2, 3, 4, 5, 8). It is difficult to recognize any substantial difference between these two groups of prophets. Durand has suggested that the oracles of an *āpil(t)um* may have been provoked, unlike those of the *muḫḫû(tu)m* which were spontaneous, but the evidence is not unambiguous. In general, the activity of both classes is described in a similar way, although it seems that an *āpil(t)um* could travel from one place to another, whereas the activity of a *muḫḫû(tu)m* was more restricted to the temple to which he or she was affiliated (see Durand 1988: 386–90; 1995: 322–28). In the light of the preserved sources, both groups show themselves to belong to a prophetic institution which had an established position in the society of Mari, although it apparently had a different social and political status from other kinds of divination, above all extispicy. According to the available documentation, the messages of the prophets were transferred to the king by go-betweens, who were often the royal ladies of Mari. This indicates that the relation of the prophets to the king was more indirect than that of the haruspices (*bārû*); nevertheless, even direct contacts are not excluded (see Charpin 2001: 34–41; 2002: 16–22).

Prophetic activity at Mari was not restricted to people called *muḫḫû(tu)m* or *āpil(t)um*. In a number of documents, there are people belonging to neither of these two groups who act as mouthpieces of deities. One of them is called "the *qammatum* of Dagan of Terqa," whose message is reported in two different letters (nos. 7, 9). The word *qammatum* is of unclear derivation—if not a proper name, it may refer to a person with a characteristic hairstyle (Durand 1995: 333-34)—but the role of the female person in question is clearly prophetic. Moreover, a group with the appellation *nabû,* which has been regarded as etymologically related to Hebrew *nābîʾ* "prophet" (Fleming 1993a/b/c; but cf. Huehnergard 1999), is made to deliver an oracle to the king of Mari (no. 26). Even two persons called *assinnu,* a "man-woman" whose gender role is changed from man to a genderless person, appear in prophetic function (nos. 7, 8, 22, 23); this is significant with regard to the undefinable sex of some Assyrian prophets and the repeated appearance of prophets grouped with *assinnu* in lexical and administrative lists (nos. 123, 124, 126, 130).

In Neo-Assyrian sources, the standard word for a prophet is *raggimu,* (fem. *raggintu*), which has replaced the word *maḫḫû* in colloquial use as well as in formal writing. Accordingly, the verb *ragāmu* "to shout, to proclaim" is used of prophesying (nos. 91, 109, 111, 113). Insofar as *raggimu/raggintu* can be taken as a general title of a prophet even in cases when the word is not explicitly used, which is plausible indeed, it is evident that they were devotees of Ištar of Arbela, whose words they usually transmitted. However, their activity was not restricted to the city of Arbela, and they could act as the mouthpieces of other deities, too. In Neo-Assyrian society, prophets seem to have enjoyed a somewhat higher status than their colleagues at Mari, especially in the time of Esarhaddon and Assurbanipal, who not only deposited a selection of their oracles in the royal archives but also were the only Assyrian kings to recognize the significance of prophetic messages in their inscriptions. This was probably due to their personal attachment to the worship of Ištar of Arbela.

The sources documenting prophecy from the West Semitic world add a few items to the list of prophetic designations. The three letters from Lachish (nos. 139–141), which constitute the only extrabiblical evidence of prophets in preexilic Israel, use the standard biblical word *nābîʾ*, whereas the Zakkur Inscription (no. 137) and the Deir ʿAllā inscription (no. 138) know another title well attested in the Hebrew Bible, namely, *ḥzh* "seer, visionary" (Heb. *ḥōzê*). In apposition with this word, the

Zakkur Inscription uses the word *ʿddn,* which, on the other hand, may be related to the Egyptian *ʿḏd ʿȝ* "great seer" or the like, in the Report of Wenamon (no. 142).

## Texts Included and Excluded

It is not always easy to distinguish prophecy from other oracular or divinatory activity and identify a person as a prophet, and the same holds true for recognizing a text as a specimen of prophecy. To be acknowledged as such, a text should reveal the relevant components of the process of transmission. This means that the implied speaker of the words uttered or quoted should be a deity, the implied addressee, respectively, a human being, and the message should be communicated to the addressee or recipient by a human being, the prophet. If this process of communication is only partly or not at all identifiable in the text, its prophetic nature is at issue and often cannot be unequivocally confirmed or denied. This problem is interwoven with the question of the often indefinable and even artificial borderline among prophecy, dreams and other visionary activity. Therefore, an absolutely water-tight set of criteria is difficult to create and the selection of prophetic texts remains debatable.

The texts included in this volume can be divided into three groups:

1. Oracle reports and collections, that is, the Neo-Assyrian oracles to Esarhaddon and Assurbanipal, which are clearly represented as divine words proclaimed by prophets (nos. 68–96), and the oracles to King Ibalpiel II of Ešnunna (nos. 66–67), in which the prophet is not mentioned but the form and content suggest a prophetic origin. The Balaam text from Deir ʿAllā (no. 138), which seems to combine oracles or visions from different sources, as well as the Amman Citadel Inscription (no. 136), may be taken as further representatives of this type.

2. Quotations of prophetic messages in letters and other kinds of literature. This is the main type at Mari (nos. 1–50), and is also represented by an Amarna letter (no. 121), a number of Neo-Assyrian documents (nos. 103, 106, 107, 109, 111–115), Late Babylonian chronographic texts (nos. 134–135), as well as by the Zakkur Inscription (no. 137) and the Report of Wenamon (no. 142). That we have to do with prophecy is in most cases confirmed by the title of the person who speaks. However, this is not always the case, and the prophetic nature of the quotation may then be deduced from the literary context, the comportment of the person in question and the contents of the message.

3. Texts with references to persons having a prophetic title; these make up the miscellaneous group of the remaining sources, comprised of inscriptions (nos. 97–101), literary and religious texts (nos. 51, 52, 64, 118,

122, 133), letters (nos. 105, 108, 119, 139–141), administrative documents (nos. 53–63, 102, 104, 110, 123, 130–132), omen texts (nos. 127-129) and lexical lists (nos. 120, 124–126).

Some texts, more or less frequently presented by other scholars as further representatives of ancient Near Eastern prophecy, are excluded from this volume:

1. Texts that are not compatible with the definition of prophecy as primarily transmissive activity, such as the Egyptian predictive texts referred to as "prophecies" (Lichtheim 1973–80: 1:139–84; Devauchelle 1994), and the literary predictive texts also called "Akkadian Prophecies" or "Akkadian Apocalypses" (Talon 1994: 98–114; cf. Ellis 1989; Nissinen 2001b). These are literary creations that share many elements with prophecies but probably do not go back to actual prophetic activities. However, as a part of the rootage of later apocalypticism (Lambert 1978; Lucas 2000), these texts are not without relevance to the study of prophecy and its learned interpretation.

2. Texts, in which the reference to prophecy is yet to be substantiated. Among these are the texts from Emar mentioning persons with the title *munabbiʾātu* and the like (Fleming 1993a/b/c; Lion 2000). While it is not excluded that the word is etymologically related to Hebrew *nābîʾ* and Akkadian *nabû* attested as a prophetic designation at Mari (see, however, the critique of Huehnergard 1999), the contexts of the attestations do not unequivocally speak for the prophetic interpretation of the word and leave the door open for other possible explanations. This also holds true for the Hittite prayers in which the king seeks relief from plagues with the help of different kinds of divination—eventually, but not certainly, including prophecy of some kind (Weippert 1988: 297–99; Lebrun 1994).

3. References to *āpilu* in three texts from Nuzi (HSS 13 152:16; 14 149:6 and 14 215:16; see Mayer 1978: 140–41; Lion 2000: 23-24) and in a Middle-Babylonian omen from Assur (KAR 460:16; see Lion 2000: 24). In CAD A/2 170, these occurrences of the word *āpilu* are—probably wrongly—separated from those in Mari texts and given a different meaning. In the absence of complete editions, these texts are excluded, even though their relevance to this volume is acknowledged.

In addition, there is an interesting, though enigmatic, document that deserves a special mention. The Aramaic text in Demotic script, Papyrus Amherst 63, still lacks a complete edition and is, therefore, not included in the collection at hand. A full translation of the text is provided by Richard C. Steiner (1997), according to whom the text derives from an Aramaic-speaking community that had been first deported to Samaria by Assurbanipal, and later colonized in Upper Egypt. This long composition of poetry of different kinds (e.g., poems that share a common tradition with the biblical Pss 20 and

75) includes a passage that bears a close resemblance to biblical and extra-biblical prophecies. It presents an oracle of salvation spoken by Mar ("Lord"), the chief god of the community, upon a lament expressed in the first person singular (col. vi, lines 12–18; translation from Steiner 1997: 313):

> Mar speaks up and says to me: "[Be] strong, my servant, fear not, I will save your.... To Marah, if you will ..., to Mar from your shrine and Rash, [I shall destroy your] en[emy in] your days and during your years [your] advers[ary] will be smitten. [Your foes] I shall destroy in front of you; your foot on their necks [you will place. I shall suppo]rt your right (hand), I shall crown you with posterity; your house...."

The relevance of this passage to the study of ancient Near Eastern prophecy is beyond doubt, and it can only be hoped that an edition of Papyrus Amherst 63 will soon evoke scholarly interest in the whole composition.

## Conventions of Transcription and Translation

The transcriptions and translations of Akkadian are my own; those of West Semitic texts and Egyptian were prepared by Choon-Leong Seow and Robert K. Ritner respectively. Since a detailed linguistic analysis is not in place in an anthology like this one, we have purposefully avoided aiming at originality. Therefore, the reader is not likely to find revolutionary new readings and interpretations but will notice that they rarely deviate substantially from the interpretations of Durand (ARM 26/1), Parpola (SAA 9), and other standard editions. Restorations of fragmentarily preserved texts also mostly follow their suggestions.

The West Semitic and Egyptian texts are given in transliteration, whereas the Akkadian texts, according to the policy of the SBLWAW series, are given in transcription rather than in sign-for-sign transliteration of the cuneiform script. This way of presentation is chosen to make the text look like a language rather than a cryptogram, and to give the non-cuneiformist reader, more or less familiar with Akkadian, a better impression of the phonetic structure of the original text. I am fully aware of how hazardous an enterprise this kind of normalization is. In many cases, for example, the length of the vowel or the phonetic form of the plural nouns can only be guessed, and the different conventions of transcription may clash. I have tried to be consistent in following the principles of the Neo-Assyrian Text Corpus Project in Neo-Assyrian texts and those of von Soden (*GAG*) elsewhere. However, uncertain transcriptions and downright mistakes are likely to occur and are all my responsibility.

For these reasons, I cannot stress enough that the transcriptions are prepared for the purposes of this volume and are *not* the original text but an interpretation. Any serious work on them requires consulting the authoritative editions which are always indicated. Two texts (nos. 130, 132), however, are transcribed and translated here for the first time; previously, they were published in cuneiform copies only. All the other texts are adequately edited in other volumes, and the transliterations, which give a more accurate rendering of the cuneiform script, can be found in them.

The translations are not literal reflections of the wording of the original language but strive for modern, idiomatic and readable English. Akkadian phrases are not necessarily translated word for word, and parentheses are generally avoided even though a word in the translation may not have an exact equivalent in the original.

Unfortunately, the transliterations and translations of the Mari prophetic texts by J. J. M. Roberts (*The Bible and the Ancient Near East: Collected Essays* [Winona Lake, Ind.: Eisenbrauns, 2002], 157–253) appeared too late to be taken into account in this book.

# I

# Mari Letters

The ancient city of Mari was the capital of a kingdom that in the second half of the third and the first half of the second millennium B.C.E. was a significant political and economic power in the Near East. The kingdom of Mari occupied large areas on the middle Euphrates and the river Habur and controlled the principal trade routes between Babylonia and Syria. Since 1933, the temples and palaces of Mari have been unearthed in excavations at Tell Ḥarīri in modern Syria, located on the western bank of the Euphrates river only a few kilometers from the Iraqi border. The royal palace of Mari soon turned out to be a treasure trove of written records: more than twenty thousand tablets have been brought to light so far, thousands of which are still unpublished. The overwhelming majority of the tablets date from the time of Yasmaḫ-Addu (ca. 1792–1775) and Zimri-Lim (ca. 1774–1760), the last kings of Mari prior to its destruction by Hammurabi, king of Babylon (for chronology, see Birot 1978; Anbar 1991: 29–37). The texts, published in the series Archives royales de Mari (ARM), include administrative documents of different kinds (expense texts, gift texts, texts concerning provincial administration, etc.), letters, treaties, ritual and omen texts and literary texts (Durand 1992).

Among the hundreds of letters excavated from Mari, a substantial dossier deals with divination. Besides the correspondence between the diviners and the king, dreams, oracles and ominous events are reported to the king by several individuals, mostly by high officials or royal ladies. Even prophetic oracles are frequently reported in letters, which are the only available source of information about the contents of prophetic messages at Mari. For this reason, the prophetic messages from Mari that have more or less intentionally been preserved for posterity present the words of the prophets only to the extent the writers of the letters have considered them worth quoting and bringing to the addressee's knowledge. It was apparently not the standard procedure to communicate prophecies in report format, that is, in tablets containing only the wording of the oracle proper—or if it was, such tablets were thrown away immediately after the messages had come to the notice of the addressee.

The fifty texts collected in this chapter include all letters that have hitherto been identified as prophetic sources, as listed by Heintz (1997a: 214) and complemented in later publications (e.g., Huffmon 1997 and 2000). The selection is, of course, debatable, especially when dreams and visions are concerned. The latter can be seen and reported by prophets, but it is not always easy to distinguish prophecies from dreams and visions seen by people other than prophets. Not every dreamer qualifies as a prophet in Mari society, where the prophets clearly assumed distinctive roles under the aegis of their patron deities. Attempts have been made to separate dreams from prophecies altogether (Nakata 1982), and Durand arranges prophecies and dreams as separate groups in his edition (1988). Since, however, some dream reports—including the first "prophetic" text ever published (no. 38)—are conventionally counted among prophecies, and some of them explicitly mention prophets (nos. 35, 42), the relevant letters are included in this collection, even though the dreamer cannot always be unequivocally called a prophet. Evidently, the writers of the letters were less concerned about the person or social class of the speaker than about the message itself, all the more so because there is no fundamental difference between prophecies and dreams with regard to the contents of the message.

The comparability of prophecy with other oracular utterances is also visible from the fact that there is no single word for "prophecy" in the Mari documents. Instead, prophecies are referred to using words such as *têrtum* (nos. 1, etc.) and *egerrû* (nos. 17, etc.), which are not exclusively prophetic vocabulary but are used of different kinds of oracles. The variety of designations of persons involved in prophetic activity, already dealt with in the general introduction to this volume, demonstrates that there are several words for "prophet" as well. However, *muḫḫûm/muḫḫūtum* and *āpilum/āpiltum* are clearly the most common titles, showing in the letters a distribution of eleven/three and twelve/one, respectively. The *assinnu,* whose role in the light of other Mesopotamian sources is not primarily prophetic (Nissinen 1998c: 28–34), is reported to have transmitted divine messages in four letters that give account of two persons designated with this title, Šelebum (nos. 7, 8, 23) and Ili-ḫaznaya (no. 22). The *qammatum* appears in three letters (nos. 7, 9, 13), two of which quote the same proverb, probably referring to one and the same oracle by the *qammatum* of Dagan of Terqa (nos. 7, 9). Whether the *qammatum* mentioned in number 12 refers to the same person cannot be discerned. The *nabû* appear only once (no. 26); the interpretation of the word as a prophetic designation is suggested by the etymology and the context.

Almost all published letters that are of relevance here date from the time of King Zimri-Lim. Two of them derive, however, from the time of Yasmaḫ-Addu, the predecessor of Zimri-Lim (nos. 3 and 34; see Charpin 2002: 33–38). Furthermore, number 36 is dated to the time of King Yaḫdun-Lim on orthographical grounds (Durand 1988: 469). Most of them are also addressed to Zimri-Lim, with the exception of two letters that mention other persons as addressees (no. 33: Dariš-libur, no. 45: Addu-duri). Even these two pieces of evidence may indicate that it was more common to quote oracles, dreams, and visions in private letters than the preserved documents reveal; the epistolary corpus at our disposal consists mainly of the correspondence of the royal court, eclipsing the private communication outside the court. By the same token, the strong concentration of the royal correspondence on administrative, political and cultic issues overshadows prophecies concerning private matters, which, even though they without doubt were delivered, have left only few traces in the archives (cf. nos. 8, 45).

Most of the letters with divine messages are written in the city of Mari. However, a definite number of them are posted from elsewhere, documenting prophetic activity in different cities and cult centers within the kingdom of Mari. These include Terqa, the second-ranking city of the kingdom and a prominent cult center of Dagan, as well as important provincial cities such as Tuttul, Saggaratum, and Qaṭṭunan. Some letters are sent from abroad, such as from the city-state of Andarig (no. 48). Even Aleppo (nos. 1, 2) and Babylon (no. 47), capitals of the neighbouring kingdoms, appear among the places where prophecies have been received, the divine speakers being Adad of Kallassu/Aleppo and Marduk of Babylon respectively.

In sketching the significance of prophecy and the place of the prophets in the Mari society, we are totally dependent on the more or less distorted and insufficient picture given by the letters written by persons other than prophets (Parker 1993). Among the senders of letters, Queen Šibtu and the royal ladies Inib-šina and Addu-duri, high officials at Mari (Sammetar, etc.) and in provincial cities (Kibri-Dagan, etc.), as well as Zimri-Lim's delegates abroad (Nur-Sîn), assume an important role. This clearly restricts the choice of subjects dealt with in the letters, for the letters refer to prophecies only according to the discretion of the writers, who do not necessarily quote the message word by word but present their own interpretations of what they consider the essential point of the message. In one letter (no. 48) it is reported that a prophet, an *āpilum* of Šamaš, had himself asked for a scribe to write down a divine message to the king. In yet another letter (no. 4), an *āpilum* of Šamaš, presumably the same person, is presented as the sender of the letter, but the impersonal introductory formula—"Speak to Zimri-Lim: thus the *āpilum* of Šamaš" instead of "Speak to my lord: thus NN, your servant"—may suggest that the actual writer of the message is someone else.

On the basis of the existing documentation it is warranted to conclude that prophets formed an established, though not the highest-ranking part of the divinatory apparatus used by the king of Mari (J. M. Sasson 1998: 116–19). Even though prophets seem to have communicated with the king more indirectly than haruspices and some dreamers, prophecies were regarded as significant enough to be reported to the king by others, especially when they dealt with important political matters or presented cultic demands. Some high officials and members of court seem to have regularly lent the prophets an ear. However, the validity of the prophetic oracle was often controlled by extispicy, This did not mean any underrating of prophecy as a divinatory method as such, but was needed to check and exclude the possible misinterpretations and other faults resulting from the vulnerability of the intermediary and the often tangled process of communication. For this purpose, the senders of the letters attached the prophet's hair and garment fringe (*šārtum u sissiktum*) to be used as representing the prophet during the process of authenticating the prophecy by extispicy; the word *sissiktum,* often translated as "hem," probably means just a thin fringe of a garment (Durand 1988: 40). Even dreams were checked in the same way, using different kinds of divinatory methods (cf. no. 36); many times the authors of the letters suggest the "countersignature" of another diviner (nos. 38, 44).

As mouthpieces of deities, prophets were primarily servants of the gods whose words they proclaimed. The Mari prophets tend to be associated with a specific deity. They are often referred to as "NN prophet of DN," for example, Abiya, *āpilum* of Adad (no. 2) and Lupaḫum, *āpilum* of Dagan (no. 9). This indicates the attachment of the prophets to particular deities and temples. In many cases the prophecy is said to have been uttered and dreams to have been seen in the temple of a goddess or god. Among the deities speaking in the prophecies, the god Dagan (thirteen letters) and the goddess Annunitum, a manifestation of Ištar (five letters), most often have the word. In addition, several other goddesses (e.g., Beletekallim, Diritum, Ninḫursag) and gods (e.g., Adad, Šamaš, Marduk) speak through the mouths of the prophets and dreamers.

The outstanding theme of the prophecies, as can be expected of oracles embedded in the royal correspondence, is the well-being and the warfare of the king. Especially in the letters sent by the royal ladies, the king is adviced to protect himself, whether as a part of the prophecies delivered or as the writer's personal message attached to them (nos. 7, 14, 23, etc.). Many prophecies proclaim the victory of the king over his enemies and adversaries in general terms. The enemies in question are often called by name, which connects the prophecies with specific political crises (see Durand 1988: 399–402; Charpin 1992).

The rebellion of the Yaminites, the nomadic groups living on the southern side of the Euphrates, in about the fourth year of Zimri-Lim's reign, is the theme of numbers 10 and 38, and the oracles against the Yaminites are mentioned as a precedent for Zimri-Lim's peace preliminaries with Ibalpiel II, king of Ešnunna, in the sixth year of his reign in number 9. The peace with Ešnunna is explicitly opposed also in number 7 and, implicitly, in numbers 12 and 13—obviously in vain, since Zimri-Lim, despite the prophetic warnings, indeed engaged himself in an alliance with Ešnunna! The enemies mentioned in the prophecies also include Hammurabi, king of Kurdâ (no. 4), and the Elamites (no. 18), against whom Zimri-Lim was at war in his eleventh year. Another enemy was Išme-Dagan, who was of Yaminite origin, son of Šamši-Adad, king of Assyria, and brother of Yasmaḫ-Addu, the predecessor of Zimri-Lim on the throne of Mari. Išme-Dagan was appointed by his father the king of Ekallatum in Assyria. He is mentioned not only as an aggressor against Mari (no. 17; cf. no. 48), but also as a refugee under the protection of Hammurabi, king of Babylon (no. 47). Zimri-Lim's war against Hammurabi is referred to in a number of encouraging oracles (nos. 19, 20, 22), but the hopes inspired by these oracles were dashed, since this war led to the final destruction of Mari.

Besides political and military matters, instructions concerning the maintenance of temples and their cult are well represented in the prophetic oracles transmitted to the king of Mari (nos. 4, 28, 30, 31, etc.). In some cases the king is reproached with neglect or insufficient care of the worship of certain deities (nos. 13, 25, 27, 29). Furthermore, doing the divine will also includes righteousness and social justice, as emphasized in the letters of Nur-Sîn from Aleppo (nos. 1 and 2).

Some prophecies concern individual projects, such as the building of the city gate (no. 32) or a house (nos. 39, 46). Even private affairs, such as the miseries of Šelebum the *assinnu* (no. 8) and the servant girl of Zunana (no. 37), are sometimes reported; a couple of letters deal with the death (no. 33) or the name-giving (no. 44) of a royal child.

## 1. Nur-Sîn to Zimri-Lim

**Text:** A. 1121 + A. 2731.
**Photograph:** Durand 2002: 138.
**Copy:** Lafont 1984: 8.
**Transliteration and translation:** *A. 1121:* Lods and Dossin 1950; von Soden 1950: 403; Schmökel 1951: 55; Ellermeier 1968: 48–53. — *A. 1121 + A. 2731:* Lafont 1984: 7–11; Schart 1995: 80–82; Durand 2002: 137–40.
**Translation:** *A. 1121:* Malamat 1958: 67–70; Huffmon 1968: 106–7; Moran 1969b: 625; Sicre 1992: 243 (lines 13–45); Malamat 1998: 107–111. — *A. 2731:* Dossin 1966: 78; Huffmon 1968: 107; Ellermeier 1968: 52–53;

Malamat 1998: 111. — *A. 1121 + A. 2731:* Dietrich 1986: 85–87; Durand 1994: 67–68; 2000: 130–33 (no. 984).

**Discussion:** *A. 1121:* Malamat 1958; 1962: 148–49; Westermann 1960: 87–91, 112; Wolff 1961: 256; Nötscher 1966: 181–82; Ellermeier 1968: 140–41; Ross 1970: 15–16; Heintz 1971a: 546; Craghan 1975: 47; Huffmon 1976b: 699; Anbar 1981; Durand 1982b: 45–47; Schmitt 1982: 65–72. — *A. 2731:* Ellermeier 1968: 141–42; Anbar 1975: 517. — *A. 1121 + A. 2731:* Dossin 1966: 77–79; Craghan 1974: 47, 54; Wilson 1980: 100–102; Lafont 1984; Ellis 1987: 252–53; 1989: 137; van der Toorn 1987: 84–85; 1998b: 61; Fleming 1993b: 180–81; Gordon 1993: 76–78; Parker 1993: 55, 66–67; J. M. Sasson 1994: 314–316; 1998: 120; Schart 1995: 82–84; Durand 1995: 175–76, 319, 327, 349–50, 526–27; 1997a: 125; Weinfeld 1995: 49; Heintz 1997b: 142; Malamat 1998: 63, 106–121; Pongratz-Leisten 1999: 66–68; Huffmon 2000: 54; Charpin 2001: 28-29, 44-45; 2002: 12, 24, 31; Nissinen 2003: 16–19.

*ana bēlīya qibīma* [2]*umma Nūr-Sîn waradkāma* [3]*ištiššu šinīšu u ḫamšīšu aššum zukrim ana Addi nadā[nim]* [4]*u niḫlatim ša Addu bēl Kallassu* [5]*[ittīn]i irrišu ana bēlīya ašpuram* [6]*[ašš]um zukrim an[a Addi n]adānim Alpān* [7]*maḫar Zū-ḫadnim Abi-šad[î u Z]uḫan* [8]*iqbêm ummāmi zukram alpam* [9]*u liātim idin bēlī maḫar awīlī k[alīšunu]* [10]*zukram nadā[n]am iqbêm ummām[i]* [11]*ana urram šēram lā ibbalakkatan[n]i* [12]*awīlī šībī aškunšum bēlī lū īdi*

Speak to my lord: Thus Nur-Sîn, your servant:[a]

[3]Once, twice, even five times have I written to my lord about the deli[very] of the *zukrum*[b] to Adad and about the estate[c] that Adad, lord of Kallassu, demands [from u]s. Concerning the delivery of the *zukrum* to Adad, Alpan said to me in the presence of Zu-ḫadnim,[d] Abi-šadi and [Zu]ḫan as follows: "Sacrifice the *zukrum* with oxen[e] and cows! My lord, in the presence of a[ll] the people,[f] told me to sacrifice the *zukrum,* saying: 'Never shall he break an agreement with me!' "[g] I have imposed witnesses on him. My lord should know this.

[13]*ina têrētim Addu bēl Kallassu* [14]*[izz]az ummāmi ul anākū* [15]*Addu bēl Kallassu ša ina birit* [16]*paḫallīya urabbûšuma ana kussêm bīt abīšu* [17]*uterrûšu ištu ana kussêm bīt abīšu* [18]*uterrûšu atūrma ašar šubti* [19]*addinšum inanna kīma ana kussê bīt abīšu* [20]*uterrûšu niḫlatam ina bītīšu eleqqe* [21]*šumma ul inaddin bēl kussêm* [22]*eperi u ālim anākūma*

[13]Through oracles,[h] Adad, lord of Kallassu, would stand by, saying: "Am I not Adad, lord of Kallassu, who raised him (scil. the king) in my lap[i] and restored him to his ancestral throne?[j] Having restored him to his ancestral throne, I again gave him a residence. Now, since I restored him to his ancestral throne, I may take the estate away from his

*ša addinū* [23]*atabbal šumma lā kīamma* [24]*erištī inaddin kussâm eli kussêm* [25]*bītam eli bītim eperi eli eperi* [26]*ālam eli ālim anaddinšum* [27]*u mātam ištu ṣītīša* [28]*ana erbīša anaddinšu*

patrimony as well. Should he not deliver (the estate), I—the lord of the throne, territory and city—can take away what I have given! But if, on the contrary, he fulfils my desire, I shall give him throne upon throne, house upon house, territory upon territory, city upon city. I shall give him the land from the rising of the sun to its setting."

[29]*annītam āpilū iqbû u ina têrētim* [30]*ittanazzaz inanna appunamma* [31]*āpilum ša Addi bēl Kallassu* [32]*maskanam ša Alaḫtim ana niḫlatim* [33]*inazzar bēlī lū īdi*

[29]This is what the prophets said, and in the oracles he (scil. Adad) was standing by all the time.[k] Another matter: a prophet of Adad, lord of Kallassu, demands the area[l] of Alaḫtum to be the estate. My lord should know this.

[34]*pānānum inūma ina Māri wašbāku* [35]*āpilum u āpiltum mimma awātam* [36]*ša iqa[bb]ûnim ana bēlīya utār* [37]*inanna i[n]a mātim šanītim wašbāku* [38]*ša ešemmû u iqabbûnim* [39]*ana bēlīya ul ašappar* [40]*šumma urram šēram mimma ḫiṭ[ītu]m ittabši* [41]*bēlī kīam ul iqabbi ummāmi* [42]*awātam ša āpilum iqbikkum u maskanka* [43]*inazzar ammīnim ana ṣērīya* [44]*lā tašpuram anumma ana ṣēr bēlīya* [45]*a[šp]uram bēlī lū ī[d]i*

[34]Previously, when I was still residing in Mari, I would convey every word spoken by a prophet or a prophetess to my lord. Now, living in another land, would I not communicate to my lord what I hear and they tell me? Should anything ever not be in order, let not my lord say: "Why have you not communicated to me the word which the prophet spoke to you when he was demanding your area?" Herewith I communicate it to my lord. My lord should know this.

[46]*[šanī]tam āpilum ša Addi bēl Ḫalab* [47]*[itti Abu]-ḫalim illikamma kīam iqbêm* [48]*ummāmi ana bēlīka šupur* [49]*ummāmi Addu bēl Ḫalab ul anākū* [50]*ša ina suḫātīya urabbûkama* [51]*ana kussêm bīt abīka uterrûk[a]* [52]*[m]imma ittīka ul err[i]š* [53]*inūma ḫablum u ḫabi[ltum]* [54]*išassikkum izizma dī[n]šunu dīn* [55]*[a]nnītam ša ittīka errišū* [56]*annītam ša ašpurakkum teppešma* [57]*ana*

[46][More]over, a prophet of Adad, lord of Aleppo, came [with[m] Abu]-ḫalim and spoke to him as follows: "Write to your lord the following: 'Am I not Adad, lord of Aleppo, who raised you in my lap[n] and restored you to your ancestral throne? I do not demand anything from you, When a wronged man or wo[man] cries out to you, be there and judge their case. This only I

*awātīya taqâlma* [58]*mātam ištu ṣ[ītīš]a ana erbīša* [59]*u māt[ka matt]am anaddinakkum*

have demanded from you. If you do what I have written to you and heed my word, I will give you the land from the r[isi]ng of the sun to its setting, [your] land [greatly in]creased!'"

[60]*[a]nnītam ā[pilum ša] Addi bēl Ḫalab* [61]*maḫar A[b]u-ḫalim iqbêm* [62]*annītam bēlī lū īdi*

[60]This is what the pr[ophet of] Adad, lord of Aleppo, said in the presence of Abu-ḫalim. My lord should know this.

[a] For the historical background of this and other letters of Nur-Sîn, see Durand 2002: 59–97. This letter possibly refers to the oracle of Adad (lines 46–59) that Nur-Sîn quotes in A. 1968 (no. 2) (J. M. Sasson 1994: 314–16).

[b] The word *zukrum* is otherwise unknown; *CAD* Z 153 translates it as "pasture-land (?)" and *AHw* 1536 as "männliches Gesinde"; cf. *CDA* 449: "male personnel". Since the word seems to have a meaning parallel to that of *liātum* (line 9) "cow, cattle" (*CAD* L 218; *AHw* 557–58 sub *lītu*), it is usually translated as "(male) cattle" or "livestock" (Dossin 1966: 78; cf. Ellermeier 1968: 49, 52; Lafont 1984: 11; Dietrich 1986: 85; Malamat 1998: 108). On the basis of the use of the word at Emar, however, it is probable that *zukrum* is a commemorative sacrificial ritual; see Durand 2000: 132–33; Fleming 2000: 120–24.

[c] Dossin 1966: 78 understood the word *niḫlatum* as a name of a city (cf. Ellermeier 1968: 52), as the determinative KI following it on line 32 would suggest. The virtual consensus, however, follows the suggestion of Malamat 1958: 68, 70 (cf. 1962: 148–149; 1998: 109), according to which *niḫlatum* is better translated as "estate, inherited property" (cf. *naḫālum* "inherit" in the Akkadian of Mari, Ug. *nḥl* and Heb. *naḥălâ;* see *AHw* 712 and cf. *CDA* 253: "transferred property"), whereas the KI sign is explained as a scribal error (Lafont 1984: 12).

[d] A high official of Zimri-Lim who acted as his emissary in the West (Birot, Kupper, and Rouault 1979: 244; Durand 2002: 96).

[e] For the reading *zu-uk-ra-[a]m* $\text{GU}_4$.HÁ, see Durand 2002: 140.

[f] For this reading, see Durand 2002: 140.

[g] Dietrich 1986: 86 understands this phrase differently: "In aller Zukunft soll er sich nicht mehr an mich wenden!"; cf. Durand 2000: 131: "À l'avenir, qu'il n'y ait plus de révolte contre moi!"

[h] The word *têrtum* is used of divine messages, in association with both inductive divination (extispicy) and prophecy; see *AHw* 1350–51 and the discussion in Anbar 1981 and Durand 1982: 45–47; 1988: 46, 379; 1997a: 125 who reckon with a double act of divination, performed both by an *āpilum* and by a haruspex (*bārûm*). This assumption, however, is not compulsory, since the phrase *ina têrētim izuzzum* lit. "to stand in oracles", obviously denotes the divine presence in the process of divine-human communication mediated by the diviner, whether a haruspex or a prophet. On the other hand, it would be against the normal hierarchy of divinatory techniques to verify the result of extispicy by prophecy or dreams; see Pongratz-Leisten 1999: 68.

[i] The phrase *ina birit paḫallīya* means literally "between my legs/thighs"; cf. *ina suḫātīya* on line 50.

[j] Lit. "to the throne of his father's house."

[k] The subject of *ittanazzaz,* an iterative Gtn-form of *izuzzum,* is the god Adad rather than *annītam* "this" (Huffmon 1968: 106; Malamat 1998: 110) or the *āpilums* (Moran 1969b: 625), which would require the emendation of the verb into plural.

[k] For the phrase *maskanam nazārum,* see Durand 1982b: 47 n. 15; Lafont 1984: 13. The word *mas/škanum* is also translated as "(tent-)shrine" (Malamat 1998: 110–11; J. M. Sasson 1994: 315; Schart 1995: 82; cf. Heb. *miškān*) and as "threshing-floor" (s. *CAD* M/1: 369; *AHw* 626; thus Ellermeier 1968: 51; Moran 1969b: 625), while the verb is often read as *naṣārum* "to stand guard" (Ellermeier 1968: 51; Moran 1969b: 62; Malamat 1998: 111).

[m] Since the *āpilum* is said to deliver his message in the presence of Abu-ḫalim, the latter, acting as a witness, probably came there along with him (thus translates J. M. Sasson 1994: 315).

[n] The expression *ina suḫātīya* is certainly parallel to *ina birit paḫallīya* on lines 15–16, but the meaning of *suḫātum* is not altogether clear; according to the observation of Lafont 1984: 12, the occurrences of the word refer to the area between the legs and the chest. *CAD* suggests the meaning "armpit" (S 347); *AHw* 1054 that of "(weiches) Unterkinn" ("double chin"). Dietrich 1986: 87 translates idiomatically "Brust".

## 2. Nur-Sîn to Zimri-Lim

**Text:** A. 1968.
**Photograph:** Durand 2002: 133.
**Copy:** B. Lion in Durand 1993a: 44.
**Transliteration and translation:** Durand 1993a: 43–45; 2002: 134–35; Heintz 1997b: 137.
**Translation:** Durand 1994: 67; 1995: 288; 2000: 83–84 (no. 934); J. M. Sasson 1994: 315; Huffmon 1997: 16.
**Discussion:** Charpin and Durand 1985: 297; Durand 1993a; 1995: 288–90, 349, 367; Bordreuil and Pardee 1993a: 69–70; J. M. Sasson 1994: 314–16; Heintz 1997b: 136–50; Huffmon 1997: 16–17; 2000: 51, 54; Fronzaroli 1997: 287; Charpin 1998a; Malamat 1998: 17–18, 151–53, 157–58; J. M. Sasson 1998: 119–20; Wyatt 1998: 841–43; Guichard 1999: 35; van der Toorn 2000: 85; Bauks 2001: 437–38; Annus 2002: 176–77; Nissinen 2003: 19–22.

*ana bēlīya qibīma* [2]*umma Nūr-Sîn waradkāma*

[3]*Abīya āpilum ša Addi bēl Ḫala[b]* [4]*illikamma kīam iqbêm* [5]*ummāmi Adduma mātam kalâša* [6]*ana Yaḫdun-Lim addin* [7]*u ina kakkēya*

Speak to my lord: Thus Nur-Sîn, your servant:

[3]Abiya, prophet of Adad, the lord of Alep[po], came to me and said: "Thus says Adad: 'I have given the whole country to Yaḫdun-Lim.

*māḫiram ul irši* [8]*yâtam īzibma*
*mātam ša addinūšu[m]* [9]*ana*
*Šamšī-Addu ad[di]n* [10]*Šamšī-Addu*


[break]
[1']*lut[ê]rka ana k[ussêm bīt abīka]*
[2']*utêrka kakk[ī]* [3']*ša itti Têmtim*
*amtaḫṣu* [4']*addinakkum šamnam ša*
*namrīrūtīya* [5']*apšuškāma mamman*
*ana pānīka* [6']*ul izz[iz]*


[a]*wātī ištēt šime* [7']*inūma mamman*
*ša dīnim* [8']*išassik<kum> ummāmi*
[9']*ḫ[abt]āku izizma dīnšunu dīn*
[10']*[iša]riš ap[ulšu]* [11']*[an]nītam ša*
*ittīka e[rrišu]*


[12']*inūma girram tu[ṣṣû* [13']*b]alum*
*têrtim lā tu[ṣṣi]* [14']*[i]nūma anāku*
*ina têrtī[ya* [15']*a]zza[zz]u girram taṣi*
[16']*[š]umma [lā k]īamma bābam*
[17']*[lā] tuṣṣi*


*annītam āpilum iqbêm* [18']*anum[ma*
*šārat āpilim]* [19']*u si[ssiktašu ana*
*bēlīya* [20']*uštābilam]*

Thanks to my weapons, he did not meet his equal. He, however, abandoned my cause, so I g[av]e to Šamši-Adad the land I had given to him.[a] Šamši-Adad [. . .]

[break]

[1']. . . let me re[st]ore you! I restored you to the th[rone of your father's house],[b] and the weapon[s] with which I fought with Sea[c] I handed you.[d] I anointed you with the oil of my luminosity,[e] nobody will offer resistance to you.

[6']Now hear a single word of mine: If anyone cries out to <you> for judgment, saying: 'I have been wr[ong]ed,' be there to decide his case; an[swer him fai]rly. [Th]is is what I de[sire] from you.

[12']If you go [off] to the war, never do so [wi]thout consulting an oracle. [W]hen I become manifest in [my] oracle, go to the war. If it does [not] happen, do [not] go out of the city gate."

[17']This is what the prophet said to me. No[w I have sent the hair of the prophet] and a fri[nge of his garment to my lord].

---

[a] This refers to the ousting of Yaḫdun-Lim from kingship of Mari by Šamši-Adad who installed his son Yasmaḫ-Addu at Mari in ca. 1793.

[b] This, again, refers to Zimri-Lim's rise to power in ca. 1775.

[c] I.e., Tiamat, the mythical sea-monster. For parallels in ancient Near Eastern mythology, see Bordreuil and Pardee 1993a (Ugarit); Fronzaroli 1997 (Ebla); Heintz 1997b, 146–50 (Israel) and Wyatt 1998.

[d] This should be understood literally, since such weapons were objects of veneration in Old Babylonian temples in general (van der Toorn 2000: 85), and A. 1858, a letter of Sumu-ila, shows that the very weapons of Adad of Aleppo were brought to the temple of Dagan at Terqa, the religious center of the kingdom of Mari (Durand 2002: 14–15).

[e] This translation derives the word *namrīrūtum* from the root *nwr;* for the alternative translation "the oil of my victory", see Durand 1993: 53–54; 2000: 84, who derives the word from the root *mrr* "to be bitter," or in this case "to be superior."

## 3. La'ûm to Yasmaḫ-Addu

**Text:** A. 3760.
**Photograph:** Charpin 2002: 35.
**Transliteration and translation:** Charpin 2002: 34.

*[an]a bēlī[ya* [2]*qi]bīma* [3]*[um]ma La'û[m* [4]*warad]kā[ma]*
[5]*[aš]šum maturrī ša [Dagan]* [6]*āpilum itbīma* [7]*kīma ištiššu šinīšu awātam ana Bīnim* [8]*u wardīšu ša ina Terqa wašbū* [9]*kīam iqbi ummāmi* [10]*maturr[ū ša Dagan . . .]*
[break]
[1']*warad e[kallim . . .]* [2']*ummāmi [. . .]* [3']*u kaspum ša iš-[. . .]* [4']*eleppum rabûm maturrum [. . .]* [5']*adi Tuttul illakā* [6']*annītam bēlī lū īdi*

[Sp]eak [to my] lord: [Th]us La'ûm, your [servant]:
[5]Concerning the small ships of [Dagan[a]], a prophet arose and, as he had repeatedly said to Binum and his servants, spoke as follows: "The small ship[s of Dagan. . .]
[break]
[1']A servant of the *t[emple . . .]* as follows: "[. . .] and the silver of [. . .]. The big ship and small ship [. . .] must go to Tuttul." My lord should know this.

[7']*šanītam waraḫ Ayyarim* UD.27.KAM *issuḫma* [8']*ṭuppi annêm ina Terqa ana ṣēr bēlīya* [9']*ušābilam waraḫ Niggalim* UD.5.KAM *inassah* [10']*[šip]ir bītim ana pān rugbātim* [11']*[lū i]ggamer ana tamlîm* [12']*[šiprum da]nnum epiri mullîm* [13']*[u abnū ša ina k]išādim zabālim*

[7']Another matter: Today, on the twenty-seventh of the month of Ayyarum (VII),[b] I sent this tablet to my lord to Terqa. By[c] the fifth of the month of Niggalum (VIII), the [wo]rk in the temple [should be co]mpleted up to the roof.[d] It is [ha]rd [work] to fill the terrace with earth [and] to carry [stones to the e]dge.

[14']*[mād M]āri šali[m* [15']*mātum šalm]at*

[14']Mari is well [and the land is we]ll.

[a] Restoration by Charpin 2002: 34 on the basis of other letters of La'ûm (e.g., A. 4487+).

[b] The month names Ayyarum and Niggalum were used only in the time of Yasmaḫ-Addu; hence the dating of the letter to his time; see Charpin 2002: 38.

[c] The durative form of the verb *nasāhum* "to elapse" indicates here a future date, in contrast with line 7', where the preterite form refers to the date of the sending of the letter (hence the translation "today").

[d] The word *rugbum* usually stands for "loft, roof-room;" the plural may in this case denote the roof itself. The unpublished letter A. 4487+:5–7, quoted by Charpin 2002: 36, reports the covering of the temple of Dagan with *rugbātum: šipir bīt Dagan gamer rugbāt[um] ana ṣullulim nadê* "The work at the temple of Dagan is completed; the roof is raised to shelter it."

## 4. An *āpilum* of Šamaš to Zimri-Lim

**Text:** ARM 26 194 (= A. 4260).
**Photograph:** Durand 1988 (microfiche).
**Transliteration and translation:** Durand 1988: 417–19.
**Translation:** Dossin 1966: 85–86 (lines 1–7, 33–42); Huffmon 1968: 107–8; 1997: 12; Ellermeier 1968: 54 (lines 1–7); Durand 1994: 65–66; 2000: 87–89 (no. 940).
**Discussion:** Ellermeier 1968: 142; Ross 1970: 18; Huffmon 1976b: 699; 1997: 12–13; Charpin and Durand 1985: 332; Charpin 1990: 268; 2001: 50–51; 2002: 29–31; Gordon 1993: 78; Durand 1995: 372–73, 526; 2000: 390–91; Weinfeld 1995: 87; Guichard 1999: 42; Pongratz-Leisten 1999: 204; Barstad 2001: 59.

*[an]a Z[i]mrī-L[im q]i[bīma* [2]*u]mma āpilum [š]a [Ša]mšīma* [3]*umma Šamašma bēl māt[im anāku]* [4]*kussêm rabêm ana [š]ubat lal[îya]* [5]*u māratka ša ērišūka* [6]*arḫiš ana Sippar* [7]*[ā]l balāṭim lišaḫmiṭū* [8]*[an]numma šarrū ša ana [pānīka* [9]*izz]izūnikkum u iš[taḫḫiṭ]ūn[ika]* [10]*a[n]a q[āt]īka iknu[šū]* [11]*a[nn]a-n[u]mma gurna[tum in]a mātim* [12]*n[a]dnat[kum]*

S[peak t]o Zimri-L[im]: Thus the prophet of [Ša]maš:

[3]Thus says Šamaš: "[I am] the lord of the lan[d]! Send quickly to Sippar, the [ci]ty of life,[a] a great throne for [my] enjoyable dwelling, and your daughter[b] whom I desired from you! Now the kings who [conf]ronted you and regularly pl[undered you] have submitt[ed] to your p[ow]er.[c] Now the he[ap] (of the enemies' corpses?)[d] is given [to you] in the land!

[13]*u a[šš]um asak Ad[di* [14]*K]ānisānam lāma damdê[m* [15]*ašp]urakkum asakkam kalâšu* [16]*[p]uḫirma* [17]*[ana Ḫ]alab ana bīt Addi* [18]*[li]blū* [19]*[qi]šti Dagan* [20]*[ša āpi]lum iqbêk[um* [21]*annī]tam idi[n]* [22]*[balāṭk]a u napi[štaka* [23]*liš]ārê[kkum]*

[13]Con[cern]ing the portion consecrated to Ad[ad, about which I had wr]itten to you through [K]anisanum[e] before the defe[at],[f] gather all the consecrated portion and [let it] be taken to the temple of Adad [in] Aleppo. As to the [pre]sent for Dagan [about which the pro]phet spoke to y[ou],[g] gi[ve i]t and [may it br]ing [you] your [life] and [your] exis[tence].[h]

[24]*[š]anītam Ner[ga]l* [25]*šar Ḫubšalim* [26]*ina damdêm ana [id]ika* [27]*u idi ummānātika izziz* [28]*mal takrubu u* [29]*namṣaram siparram rabêm* [30]*šupišma ana Nergal* [31]*šar Ḫubšalim liblū*

[24]Another matter: Ner[ga]l, king of Ḫubšalum stood at your and your army's side when you defeated (the enemy)! Have them produce whatever you have vowed, including the large sword of bronze. They should

be delivered for Nergal, king of Ḫubšalum."

[32]*u šanītam umma Šamašma* [33]*Ḫammurabi šar Kurdâ* [34]*[s]arrātim ittīka i[dbub]* [35]*u qāssu ašar šanê[m* [36]*š]aknat qātka i[kaššassu]* [37]*u ina libbi mātī[šu* [38]*a]ndurāram tuwa[ššar]* [39]*u an[u]mma mātum k[alûša]* [40]*ina qātīka nadna[t]* [41]*[k]īma ālam taṣab[batūma* [42]*a]ndurāram tuwaššar[u]* [43]*[akk]êm šarrūtka [d]ari[at]*

[32]Another matter: thus says Šamaš: "Hammurabi, king of Kurdâ, has [talked d]eceitfully with you, and he is contriving a scheme.[i] Your hand will [capture him] and in [his] land you will promu[lgate] an edict of restoration.[j] Now, the land in [its entirety] is given to your hand. When you take con[trol] over the city and promulgate the edict of restoration, [it sho]ws that your kingship is etern[al].

[44]*[u š]anītam Zimrī-Lim šakin Š[amši]* [45]*u Addi ṭu[ppa]m ann[i]am lišmēma [bēl]* [46]*dīnī ana ṣēr Ḫimdiya lišpur[am]*

[44][An]other matter: let Zimri-Lim, governor of Š[amaš] and Adad, listen to what is written on this ta[ble]t and let him send my [adv]ersary to Ḫimdiya."[k]

[a] Reading [URU] *ba-la-ṭim* with Durand 1988: 417. The mentioning of Sippar hardly means that the prophet speaks the words of Šamaš of Sippar (so Malamat 1998: 67–68), since he is to be identified with the *āpilum* who writes to Zimri-Lim from Andarig in ARM 26 414 (no. 48); cf. Charpin 2001: 31; 2002: 14–15.

[b] The daughter in question is probably Erišti-Aya, who lived as a *nadītum* in the temple of Šamaš in Sippar (see Durand 2000: 390–91); her correspondence includes the letters ARM 10 36–43.

[c] Reading *a-[n]a q[a-t]i-ka ik-nu-[šu]* according to the collation of M. Guichard; see Charpin 2002: 30 n. 189.

[d] The reading and translation can be only tentative. Durand 1988: 418–19 reads GIŠ.*gur-na-[tum]* taking it as a variant of *g/qurunnum* "heap" (see *AHw* 930). For a similar idea, cf. ARM 26 217 (no. 27): 25.

[e] Possibly identical with Kanisan, the sender of no. 12 (ARM 26 202).

[f] I.e., the defeat (*damdûm*) of the enemies; cf. line 26.

[g] The beginning of the sentence can also be read as referring to the personal name of the prophet: *[ša Qi]štī-Dagan [āpi]lum iqbêkum* "[As Qi]šti-Dagan, the *[āpi]lum,* spoke to you" (Durand 1988: 419).

[h] Thus according to the restoration of Durand 2000: 88.

[i] Lit. "his hand is busy elsewhere"; for this expression, cf. Durand 2000: 89.

[j] For the practice of exemption (*andurārum*) at Mari, see Charpin 1990; Durand 1995: 526–28; 2002: 80–82; Weinfeld 1995: 86–88.

[k] Lines 44–46 according the new reading of Michaël Guichard; see Durand 2000: 89; Charpin 2002: 31 n. 193. Ḫimdiya ruled as the king of Andarig after Atamrum.

## 5. Addu-duri to Zimri-Lim

**Text:** ARM 26 195 (= A. 3420 = ARM 10 53).
**Copy:** Dossin 1967: pl. 25.
**Transliteration and translation:** Dossin 1978: 88–91, 263; Moran 1969a: 34; Durand 1988: 421–22.
**Translation:** Huffmon 1968: 108; Moran 1969b: 632; Durand 1994: 54; 2000: 280 (no. 1096).
**Discussion:** Moran 1969a: 34–35; Craghan 1974: 46, 52; Durand 1995: 357.

*[ana] bēlīya* 2*[qi]bīma* 3*[um]ma Addu-dūrīma* 4*[ama]tkāma*

[Sp]eak [to] my lord: [Th]us Addu-duri, your [serv]ant:

5*[āp]ilum ina bīt [Ḫ]išamītim* 6*Iṣi-aḫu šumšu* 7*[i]tbī[m]a*

5In the temple of Ḫišamitum,[a] a [pr]ophet called Iṣi-aḫu arose and said:

*ummāmi* 8*[in]a warkīkāma* 9*[aka]l-ka ikkalū* 10*[u k]āska* 11*[iš]attū* 12*[itt]īka lā damqātim* 13*[u le]mnētim* 14*[awīlū b]ēl awātīka* 15*[ušten]eṣṣū* 16*[a]nākūma kabsākšunūti* [. . .]

8"Since your departure, your [foo]d is being eaten [and] your cup [dr]unk. Your [ad]versaries [keep spr]eading evil [and im]proper[b] rumors [abou]t you. But I trample them underfoot [. . .]

[a] For the goddess Ḫišamitum, see Nakata 1974: 210–11 and J. M. Sasson 1979: 132.
[b] Thus according to the collation of Durand 1988: 421.

## 6. Šamaš-naṣir to Zimri-Lim

**Text:** ARM 26 196 (= A. 3719).
**Photograph:** Durand 1988 (microfiche).
**Transliteration and translation:** Durand 1988: 422–23.
**Translation:** Durand 1994: 57; J. M. Sasson 1994: 309; 1995a: 287–88 (lines 5–14').
**Discussion:** Uehlinger 1992: 352–53; Gordon 1993: 72–73; J. M. Sasson 1994: 309; 1995a: 287–92; van der Toorn 1998a; Charpin and Durand 1997: 372; Durand 1993: 56; 1995: 364; 1997a: 131–32; 1998a: 86; Butler 1998: 155; Guichard 1999: 35; Lemaire 1999: 52; Pongratz-Leisten 1999: 71; Barstad 2001: 58–59; Charpin 2001: 50; 2002: 29; Nissinen 2002b: 8–9.

*ana bēlīya* 2*qibīma* 3*umma Šamaš-nāṣir* 4*waradkāma*

Speak to my lord: Thus Šamaš-naṣir, your servant:

[5]*inūma bēlī ana gerrim* [6]*pānē[šu] iškunu kīam uwa’’eranni* [7]*umm[ā-mi] ina āl ilim wašbāt* [8]*ig[e]rrûm ša ina bīt ilim* [9]*i[ba]ššû u tešemmû* [10]*ana ṣērīya šupram* [11]*[iš]tu ū[mi]m šâtu mimma* [12]*[ina bīt ilim ul eštem]me*

[break]

[1']*[ummāmi ana pānīya* [2']*Tišpak lis]sû* [3']*šipṭ[a]m luddin* [4']*Tišpak [i]ssûnimma* [5']*ana Tišpak Dagan kīam* [6']*iqbi ummāmi ištu Šinaḫ* [7']*mātam tebīl inann[a]* [8']*ūtka ittalkam* [9']*ūtka kīma Ekallātim* [10']*tamaḫḫar*

*annītam* [11']*maḫar Dagan u Yakrub-El* [12']*[i]q[b]i umma Ḫanatma* [13']*ana šipṭim ša taddinu* [14']*aḫka lā tanad-din*

[15']*[š]anītam šēm ša epinnī* [16']*ša ekallim* [17']*[š]a ḫalaṣ Terqa* [18']*ana Terqa šurub*

[5]When my lord decided to undertake the campaign, he gave me the following instructions: “You reside in the city of God. Write to me whatever oracle is de[live]red in the temple of God and which you hear.” [Sin]ce that day, [I have not hea]rd anything[a] [in the temple] . . .

[break]

[1']“[Now, let them c]all [Tišpak[b] before me] and I will pass judg-ment.’ So they called on Tišpak for me, and Dagan said to Tišpak as follows: ‘From Šinaḫ (?)[c] you have ruled the land. Now your day[d] has passed. You will confront your day like Ekallatum.”

[10']This is what happened before Dagan,[e] and Yakrub-El said: “Ḫanat[f] says: ‘Be not neglectful of the judg-ment that you passed.’”

[15']Another matter: the grain of the ploughs of the palace of the district of Terqa has been brought into Terqa.

[a] Or: “Whatever [I have hea]rd [in the temple of God]” (without *ul*).

[b] For this deity, see J. M. Sasson 1995a: 289–90. The point is that the “judgment” of Dagan, the principal god of Mari, over Tišpak, the god of Eshnunna, corresponds to Zimri-Lim’s hoped-for victory over Ibalpiel II of Ešnunna. For historical circumstances, see Charpin 1991; 1992: 22–25.

[c] Thus according to the hypothetical reading of J. M. Sasson 1994: 309 n. 39; 1995a: 288 n. 13.

[d] For this interpretation of the unique spelling *ú-ut/d-ka,* see Durand 1988: 423 and cf. the expression *ūmūšu qerbū* ARM 26 212 (no. 22):8' (see Heintz 1971b).

[e] Thus J. M. Sasson 1994: 309; 1995a: 288. If the verb *iqbi* refers to a human speaker of the divine words, possibly mentioned in the destroyed part of the letter, the speaker is a prophet (van der Toorn 1998a; Charpin 2002: 29 n. 177).

[f] A goddess of the town on the Euphrates with the same name (see J. M. Sasson 1995a: 290–91).

### 7. Inib-šina to Zimri-Lim

**Text:** ARM 26 197 (= A. 1047 = ARM 10 80).
**Copy:** Dossin 1967: pl. 35.
**Transliteration and translation:** Dossin 1978: 122–23, 267; Ellermeier 1968: 68–71; Moran 1969a: 52–53; Römer 1971: 21–22, 44–45; Durand 1988: 424.
**Translation:** Huffmon 1968: 115–16; Moran 1969b: 632; Dietrich 1973: 35; 1986: 88; van der Toorn 1987: 77 (lines 11–19); Durand 1994: 59; 2000: 403–4 (no. 1203).
**Discussion:** Ellermeier 1968: 148; Moran 1969a: 53–54; Heintz 1969: 123–25, 130; Ross 1970: 17–18; Dion 1970: 568; Craghan 1974: 45, 49–51, 56; 1975: 41; Anbar 1979; Wilson 1980: 108; Schmitt 1982: 106–12; Ellis 1987: 252; Bodi 1991: 178–79; Charpin 1992: 24; Parker 1993: 54, 58, 62–63; J. M. Sasson 1995; Guichard 1999: 35; Barstad 2001: 59; Nissinen 2003: 28.

*ana Kakkabī* [2]*qibīma* [3]*umma Inib-šināma*

[4]*ina p[ā]nītim Šēlebum assinnu* [5]*têrtam iddi[na]mma ašpurakkum* [6]*inanna qammatum* [7]*ša Dagan ša Terqa* [8]*[i]llikamma* [9]*[k]īam iqbêm* [10]*[u]mma šīma*

[11]*salīmātum ša awīl Ešn[unna]* [12]*dāṣtumma* [13]*šapal tibnim mû* [14]*illakū u ana šētim* [15]*ša ukaṣṣaru akammissu* [16]*ālšu uḫallaq* [17]*u makkuršu* [18]*ša ištu aqdami* [19]*šulputam ušalp[a]t*

[20]*annītam iqbêm* [21]*inanna pagarka* [22]*uṣur balum têrtim* [23]*ana libbi ālim* [24]*lā terru[b]* [25]*kīam ešme ummāmi* [26]*ana ramānīšu ištanarrar* [27]*ana ramānīka la taštanarra[r]*

Speak to my star:[a] Thus Inib-šina:[b]

[4]Some time ago, Šelebum, the *assinnu,* delivered to me an oracle and I communicated it to you. Now, a *qammatum* of Dagan of Terqa came and spoke to me. She said:

[11]"The peacemaking of the man of Ešn[unna][c] is false: beneath straw water runs![d] I will gather him into the net that I knot.[e] I will destroy his city and I will ruin his wealth, which comes from time immemorial."

[20]This is what she said to me. Now, protect yourself! Without consulting an oracle do not enter the city![f] I have heard people saying: "He is always distinguishing himself."[g] Do not try to distinguish yourself!

[a] Pet name for Zimri-Lim, used by the ladies belonging to the most intimate family circle.

[b] Sister (rather than daughter) of Zimri-Lim. According to Durand 2000: 402, she was the high priestess of Adad.

[c] I.e., Ibalpiel II, king of Ešnunna, who himself received prophecies with an opposite message (no. 66). For historical circumstances, see Charpin 1991; 1992: 22–25.

[d] This proverb, quoted also in ARM 26 199 (no. 9) and 202 (no. 12), is usually understood in the meaning "things are not what they seem" (Ross 1970: 17–18; cf. Moran 1969a: 54; 1969b: 632); J. M. Sasson 1994: 306; 1995b: 607, however, remarks that above running water there can only be moving straw which makes the danger even more obvious to the beholder.

[e] Rather than "he knots," which is grammatically possible.

[f] Thus Durand 1988: 424 (*a-na li-ib-bi a-lim*[.KI]).

[g] The Gtn form of the root *šrr* can be translated only tentatively. This translation follows the suggestion of Durand 1988: 424 (cf. Parker 1993, 63), according to whom *šarārum* means here "to shine brilliantly" (cf. *šarūrum* "shine").

## 8. NN to Zimri-Lim

**Text:** ARM 26 198 (= A. 3912).
**Photograph:** Durand 1988 (microfiche).
**Transliteration and translation:** Durand 1988: 425; Barstad 2001: 63; Charpin 2001: 32; 2002: 15; Nissinen 2003: 8–9.

[beginning destroyed]
1′ *u Zimrī-L[im ana Māri]* 2′ *isaḫḫuru šina im[merū liqqû]*

3′ *šanītam Šēlebu[m illikamma]* 4′ *kīam iqbi umma šūma* 5′ *šikāram idatam itti Annu[nītim īkimū]* 6′ *inūma ana išātim qē[mam aḫšiḫū]* 7′ *u ina mušīḫtim bab[assam]* 8′ *kīma qēmim iddin[ūnim]* 9′ *ina pānīya aṭṭu[lma]* 10′ *šinīšu ištu adi nak[rim]* 11′ *akšudu inanna šal[šīšu]* 12′ *bītam ušba u anāku m[ā]di[š]* 13′ *zê u šīnāti wašbāku* 14′ *u [qa]nâm t[i]minim?? akka[l]*

[break]
1″ *[an]a pî Šēlebum i[qbêm ašṭur]* 2″ *[i]nanna anumma šārtam* 3″ *u sissiktam ša Šēle[bim…]*

[rest destroyed]

[beginning destroyed][a]

[...] 1′ that Zimri-L[im] returns [to Mari] and that two sh[eep should be sacrificed].

3′ Another matter, Šelebu[m came to me] and said: "Idatum-beer[b] [has been taken] from Annu[nitum]. When [I desired flo]ur to be thrown to the fire, [they] gave [me] por[ridge](?) in a jar[c] in lieu of flour. [Thus,] I had to depend on myself.[d] Twice after I got into the (territory of) the ene[my],[e] and now the thir[d time], she dwells[f] in a temple, whereas I live amidst an abundance of shit and piss, eating reed of *timinum*.[g]

[break]

1″ [I have written accord]ing to the words that Šelebum sp[oke to me]. Now the hair and a fringe of the garment of Šele[bum...]

[rest destroyed]

[a] The restorations of this fragmentary text are conjectural, following those of Durand. The name of the sender of the letter is destroyed. Durand 1988: 425 holds it possible that this is the letter concerning Šelebum to which Inib-šina refers in ARM 26 197 (no. 7), but this is not really conclusive; see Parker 1993: 54 n. 15.

[b] For this beer, see Birot 1964: 13.

[c] For *mušīḫtum* as a variant of *mašīḫum* "jar," see Durand 1988: 425.

[d] The translation of the expression *ina pāni naṭālum* is conjectural; lit. perhaps: "I looked ahead of me."

[e] This may also mean a hostile environment.

[f] Durand 1988: 425 takes the word *ušba* as an irregular stat. sg. 3. of *wašābu*.

[g] An inexplicable word.

## 9. Sammetar to Zimri-Lim

**Text:** ARM 26 199 (= A. 925 + A. 2050).
**Photograph:** Durand 1988 (microfiche).
**Transliteration and translation:** Durand 1988: 426–29.
**Translation:** Durand 1994: 58–59; J. M. Sasson 1995b: 600–602.
**Discussion:** Charpin 1992: 23–25; Beck 1993; Anbar 1993b/c; 1994: 41–45; 1997; Parker 1993: 54–60, 63; Oliva 1994; Durand 1995: 345–46, 362; Schart 1995: 84–88; J. M. Sasson 1995b; van der Toorn 1998b: 66; Barstad 2001: 58; Charpin 2001: 39, 46–47; 2002: 19–21; Nissinen 2003: 27–28.

*ana bēlīya* [2]*qibīma* [3]*umma Sammētar* [4]*waradkāma*

[5]*Lupaḫum āpilum ša Dagan* [6]*ištu Tuttul ikšudam* [7]*ṭēmam ša bēlī ina Saggarātim* [8]*uwa''erūšu ummāmi ana Dagan ša Ter[q]a* [9]*piqdanni ṭēmam šâti* [10]*ūbilma kīam īpulūšu ummāmi* [11]*ēma tallaku ṭūb libbi* [12]*imtana[ḫḫ]ar[k]a yāšibum* [13]*u [d]imtum [n]adnūnikkum* [14]*ina idīka il[l]akū tappûtka illakū* [15]*ṭēmam annêm ina Tuttul* [16]*īpulūšu*

Speak to my lord: Thus Sammetar, your servant:

[5]Lupaḫum, prophet of Dagan,[a] arrived here from Tuttul. The message that my lord entrusted him in Saggaratum: "To Dagan of Terqa entrust me!"[b]—this message he transmitted and they answered him: "Wherever you go, joy will always find you! Battering ram and siege-tower[c] will be given to you, and they will travel by your side; they will be your companions." With this message they answered him in Tuttul.

*u ištu Tuttul* [17]*kīma kašādīšuma ana Dīr ušērdīma* [18]*sikkūrī ana Dīrītim ūbil* [19]*pānānum šernam ūbil ummāmi* [20]*šernum ul saniqma mû* [21]*iṣuppū šernam dunninī* [22]*inanna sikkūrī ūbil* [23]*u kīam šapir*

[16]On his arrival from Tuttul, I had him taken to Dir and he took my bolt to Diritum. Previously, he had brought a *šernum* [d] saying (to Diritum): "The *šernum* is of no use; it is waterlogged. Reinforce the

24*ummāmi assurri ana salīmim* 25*ša awīl Ešnunna tatakkalīma* 26*aḫki tanaddî* 27*maṣṣarātūki eli ša pānānum* 28*lū dunnunā*

*šernum!*" Now he brought my bolt, and this was his message: "What if you (= Diritum) are negligent, trusting in the peacemaking of the man of Ešnunna? Your guard should be stronger than ever before!"

29*u ayyâšim kīam iqbêm ummāmi* 30*as[s]urri šarrum balum ilim šalim* 31*ana awīl [Eš]nunna napištašu* 32*ilappat kīma ša ina pānītim* 33*inūma m[ār]ē Yamīna urdūnimma ina Saggarātim* 34*ušbū u ana šarrim aqbû umma anākūma* 35*ḫârī ša mārē Yamīna lā taqaṭṭ/ṭṭal* 36*ina Ḫubur rēʾê qinnātīšunu* 37*aṭarrassunūti u nārum ugammarakkum* 38*[in]anna balum i[la]m iš[a]llu* 39*n[apiš]tašu lā ilappat* 40*ṭēmam a[nn]êm Lupaḫum idbubam*

29To me he spoke: "Wh[at] if the king, without consulting God, will engage himself[e] with the man of [Eš]nunna! As before, when the Yamin[ite]s came to me and settled in Saggaratum, I was the one who spoke to the king: 'Do not make a treaty[f] with the Yaminites! I shall drive the shepherds of their clans away to Ḫubur[g] and the river will finish them off for you,'[h] Now then, he should not pledge himself without consulting God." This is the message Lupaḫum spoke to me.

41*warkīšuma ina šanîm [ūm]im* 42*(ištēn) qammatum ša Dagan ša T[erqa]* 43*illikamma kīam iqbê[m ummā]mi* 44*šapal tibnim mû il[lakū]* 45*ana salīmim ištanapp[arūnikkum]* 46*ilūšunu iṭarradū[nikkum]* 47*u šāram šanêmma* 48*ina libbīšunu ikappudū* 49*šarrum balum ilam išallu* 50*napištašu lā ilappat*

41Afterwards, on the following [da]y, a *qammatum* of Dagan of T[erqa] came and spoke [to me]: "Beneath straw water ru[ns].[i] They keep on send[ing to you] messages of friendship, they even send their gods [to you], but in their hearts they are planning something else.[j] The king should not take an oath without consulting God."

51*ištēn ṣubāt laḫarêm u ṣerretam* 52*[ī]rišma ad[dinš]im u wuʾʾurtaša* 53*ina bīt Bēlet-ekallim a[n]a wa[qqurtim In]ib-šina* 54*iddin*

51She demanded a *laḫarûm*-garment[k] and a nose-ring, and I ga[ve them to] her. Then she delivered her instructions in the temple of Belet-ekallim to the high pr[iestess In]ib-šina.

*ṭē[m awātim ša]* 55*idbubūnimma ana ṣēr bēlīya* 56*ašpuram bēlī lištālma ša* 57*šarrūtīšu rabûtim līpuš*

54The repo[rt of the words that] she spoke to me I have hereby sent to my lord. Let my lord consider the matter and act in accordance with his great majesty.

58*u aššum Yanṣib-Dagan beḫrim* 59*awīl Dašrān ša ana qaqqadīšu*

58As regards Yanṣib-Dagan,[l] the *beḫrum* soldier[m] from Dašran,

*nakāsim bēlī išpuram qātam* 60 *ana qātim Abī-Epuḫ ašpur awīlam šâti ul īmurūma bīssu u nī[š]ēš[u]* 61 *a[na wa]rdūti[m i]ddin ina šanîm ūmim ṭuppi Yasīm-Dagan ikš[uda]m* 62 *[u]mmāmi awīlum šū iktašdam inanna annītam lā annītam bēlī lišpura[m]* 63 *nīšēšu luwaššer*

whose head my lord told me to cut off, I immediately sent Abi-Epuḫ. They did not find this man, so he (scil. Abi-Epuḫ) sold his household and his personnel t[o sla]very. On the following day a tablet from Yasim-Dagan arr[ive]d with the following message: "The man has arrived." Now, let my lord write to [me] some indication of whether or not I should release his personnel.

[a] For this person, see also M. 11436 (no. 62) and A. 3796 (no. 53). On the basis of M. 11436, this letter can be dated to Zimri-Lim's fourth year.

[b] In concrete terms, this probably means investigating oracles.

[c] For this expression, see Beck 1993.

[d] The exact meaning of *šernum,* a wooden object, can only be guessed. *CAD* M/2: 30 suggests "log".

[e] Lit.: "touch his throat," designating a symbolic act of validating a treaty.

[f] Lit.: "kill a donkey foal," also referring to an act of treaty-making, for which see Charpin 1993; Lafont 2001: 262–71.

[g] For this reading, see Charpin 2002: 25 n. 149, who reckons with a pun on the names of Ḫabur, a tributary of the Euphrates, and the underworld river Ḫubur. For the interpretation *ḫuburrê qinnātīšunu* ("I shall send them away to their scattered haunts") see Durand 1988: 428, who derives *ḫuburrû* from *ḫabāru* "to leave one's domicile, to be exiled" and translates *qinnu* with "nest." Cf. J. M. Sasson 1995b: 601 n. 7.

[h] Or: "I will stop the river for you," reading ÍD.DA as an accusative (*nāram*).

[i] See no. 7 (ARM 26 197), note d.

[j] The meaning of the expression *šārum šanûm* remains essentially the same, whether *šārum* should be literally translated as "wind" (J. M. Sasson 1995b: 601) or as "enemy" (*AHw* 1193: *šāru* III).

[k] A *hapax legomenon* designating a piece of clothing of unknown kind. Durand 1994: 59 connects the name with the city of Laḫara in southeastern Mesopotamia.

[l] For Yanṣib-Dagan from Dašran in the district of Terqa, see Durand 1988: 429. The same person is probably mentioned also in ARM 13 110 and, possibly, in A. 3796 (no. 53).

[m] The word *beḫrum* can be derived from *beḫērum* "to choose" (*AHw* 117–18), thus designating an elite soldier, or it can be read as *piḫrum,* which means a conscript soldier (Durand 1998b: 362).

## 10. Aḫum to Zimri-Lim

**Text:** ARM 26 200 (= M. 6188).
**Photograph:** Durand 1988 (microfiche).
**Transliteration and translation:** Durand 1988: 429–30.
**Translation:** Durand 1994: 54.
**Discussion:** Charpin and Durand 1986: 151; Durand 1995: 354; Barstad 2001: 57–58.

*[ana] bēlīy[a [2]qi]bīma [3][um]ma Aḫum šangûm ša [Annunītim [4]warad]kāma*

*[5]Ḫubatum muḫḫūtum [6][t]êrtam kīam iddin*

*[7]ummāmi šāru ana māt[im] [8]itebbêm u ka[p]pīš[u] [9]u šitta ta-ak-ka-[...] [10]ašâlšunūt[i] [11]Zimrī-Li[m] [12]u mār Simʾa[l] [13]ebūra[m līpušū] [14][i]štu qā[tīka] [15]Zimr[ī-Lim] [16]mātam [k]alâš[a lā tušēṣi]*

*[17]u itūrma kīa[m iqbi] [18]ummāmi mārē Yamī[na] [19]ammīnim tupalla[s] [20]ašâlka*

*[21]annītam muḫḫūtum šī i[qbi] [22]u anumma šārtam u [23]sissiktam ša sinništim šât[i [24]ana ṣ]ēr bēlīya uštābilam*

[Sp]eak [to m]y lord: [Th]us Aḫum, priest of [Annunitum], your [servant]:

[5]Ḫubatum, the prophetess, delivered the following oracle:

[7]"A wind will rise against the la[nd]! I will test[a] its wings and [its] two ...[...][b]—[let] Zimri-Lim and the Simʾ[al]ite[c] [do] the harvest[ing]! Zimr[i-Lim, do not let] the land in i[ts e]ntirety [slip] from [your] ha[nd]!"

[17]Again she [spoke]: "O Yami[ni]tes, why do you cause wor[ry]? I will put you to the proof!"[d]

[21]This is what this prophetess s[aid]. I have now sent the hair and a fringe of the garment of this woman [to] my lord.

[a] The verb *šâlum* "to ask" seems here to have the meaning "to find out," "to put to the test"; cf. line 20.

[b] An obscure word. Durand 1988: 429 restores *takkā[tīšu]* and translates "its two necks"; another alternative would be *takkā[pīšu]* "its two holes."

[c] "The Simʾalite," whether referring to Zimri-Lim himself or to his tribal backgound (note that the conjunction *u* "and" seems to indicate a difference between the two), marks the opposition of the two groups of Haneans, the Yaminites and the Simʾalites; see Charpin and Durand 1986: 150–51 and cf. no. 38 (ARM 26 233), note c.

[d] See note a.

## 11. Baḫdi-Lim to Zimri-Lim

**Text:** ARM 26 201 (= A. 368 = ARM 6 45).
**Copy:** Kupper 1953: pl. 47.
**Transliteration and translation:** Kupper 1954: 70–71; Malamat 1956: 80; Ellermeier 1968: 38–39; Durand 1988: 430.
**Translation:** Huffmon 1968: 113; Durand 1994: 54–55; 2000: 87 (no. 938).
**Discussion:** Nötscher 1966: 183; Ellermeier 1968: 136; Craghan 1974: 53; J. M. Sasson 1980: 131; Malamat 1998: 72.

*[a]na bēlīya* [2]*qibīma* [3]*umma Baḫdi-Lim* [4]*waradkāma*
[5]*ālum Māri ekallu[m]* [6]*u ḫalṣum šalim*
[7]*šanītam Aḫum šangûm* [8]*šārtam u sissiktam* [9]*[š]a muḫḫūtim u[b]la[m]* [10]*u ina ṭuppim* [11]*ša Aḫum ana ṣēr bē[līya]* [12]*ušābila[m]* [13]*ṭēmša gamrum šaṭer*

[14]*[a]numma ṭuppi Aḫim* [15]*[š]ārtam u sissiktam ša muḫḫūtim* [16]*[ana ṣ]ēr bēlīya* [17]*[uštābi]lam*

Speak [t]o my lord: Thus Baḫdi-Lim, your servant:

[5]The city of Mari, the pala[ce] and the district are well.

[7]Another matter: Aḫum, the priest, has b[ro]ught [me] the hair and the garment fringe [o]f a prophetess, and her complete report is written on the tablet that Aḫum has sent to [my l]ord.[a]

[14][H]erewith I [have conv]eyed the tablet of Aḫum together with the [h]air and a fringe of the garment of the prophetess [to] my lord.

[a] It is possible that Baḫdi-Lim refers here to no. 10.

## 12. Kanisan to Zimri-Lim

**Text:** ARM 26 202 (= M. 11046).
**Photograph:** Durand 1988 (microfiche).
**Transliteration and translation:** Durand 1988: 431.
**Translation:** Durand 1994: 59–60; van der Toorn 1998b: 67.
**Discussion:** Parker 1993: 57–58, 63; Anbar 1994: 45–46; J. M. Sasson 1995b; van der Toorn 1998b, 67; Nissinen 2003: 28–29.

*ana bēlīya* [2]*qibīma* [3]*umma Kānisān* [4]*waradkāma*
[5]*abī Kib[r]ī-D[agan]* [6]*ana Māri [išpuram umma]* [7]*šūma*

Speak to my lord: Thus Kanisan, your servant:

[5]Kibri-D[agan], my father, [wrote to me] in Mari. [This is what] he wrote:

*awātim* [*ša ina bīt Dagan*] 8*in*[*n*]*epšā* [*ešme* 9*k*]*īam i*[*dbubūnim* 10*u*]*mmāmi ša*[*pal tibnim*] 11*mû ill*[*akū*] 12*illikma ilum ša bē*[*l*]*īy*[*a*] 13*awīlê ayyābīšu ana qātīšu* 14*umalli inann*[*a*] 15*muḫḫû*[*m k*]*īma pānānu*[*mm*]*a* 16*irṭub ši*[*t*]*assam*

7"[I heard] the words [that] were uttered [in the temple of Dagan. Th]is is what [they] sp[oke to me]: 'Be[neath straw] water ru[ns].[a] The god of my lord has come! He has delivered his enemies in his hands.' Now, as before, the prophet broke out into constant declamation."

17*annītam Kib*[*rī-Dag*]*an išpur*[*am*] 18*bēlī ana šu*[*lmīšu têr*]*ētim* 19*šūpušim* [. . .]

17This is what Kib[ri-Dag]an wrote [to me]. My lord [*should not be negligent in*] letting [ora]cles be delivered for his [own] goo[d. . .]

[break of four lines]

[break]

24*bēlī lā ulappatam nīqam liqqêmma littalkam*

24Let my lord not tarry, let him perform a sacrifice and let him go!

[a] See no. 7 (ARM 26 197), note d and cf. no. 9 (ARM 26 199). Note that the speaker of this expression is here a *muḫḫûm,* not a *qammatum,* as in the two other instances.

## 13. NN to Zimri-Lim

**Text:** ARM 26 203 (= A. 963).
**Photograph:** Durand 1988 (microfiche).
**Transliteration and translation:** Durand 1988: 431–32.
**Translation:** Durand 1994: 60.

[beginning destroyed]
1*Z*[*imri-Lim. . .*]
[four unreadable lines]
6[. . .] *ūmum* [*kūṣum*] 7*i*[*ttū*]*r u sarabu*[*m*] 8*pānēya idâk* 9*inanna ūm nīqēya* 10*ana bītīya lūrub*

[beginning destroyed][a]
Z[imri-Lim. . .]
[break]
6"[. . .] on the [winter] day it has c[om]e and the ice[b] destroys[c] my face. Today is the day of my sacrifices. I want to return to my temple!"

11[*anu*]*mma šārtam u sissik*[*tam* 12*ša q*]*amma*[*tim*] 13[*ana ṣē*]*r bēlī*[*ya ušābilam*]
14[*šanītam*] *uṭ*[*ba rabû*] 15[. . . *ṣu*]*bātu* [*ana sinništim addin*] 16[*in*]*an*[*na* . . .]
[rest destroyed]

11[No]w [I have sent] the hair and a fringe of the garment [of the *q*]*amma*[*tum* to my] lord.
14[Another matter: I have given a great] *uṭ*[*ba*]-garment[d] [and a . . . gar]ment [to the woman. N]ow [. . .]
[rest destroyed]

[a] The restorations follow those of Durand and, because of the very poor state of preservation of the tablet, are by no means certain.

[b] The word *sarabum* is probably an equivalent of *šar(a)bum* "cold" (Durand 1988: 432).

[c] Lit.: "kills."

[d] On the *uṭba*-garment, see Durand 1983a: 403–6.

### 14. Inib-šina to Zimri-Lim

**Text:** ARM 26 204 (= A. 2264 = ARM 10 81).
**Copy:** Dossin 1967: pl. 35.
**Transliteration and translation:** Dossin 1978: 122–25, 267; Ellermeier 1968: 70–73; Moran 1969a: 33; Römer 1971: 22–23; Durand 1988: 432–33.
**Translation:** Huffmon 1968: 108–9; Durand 1994: 56–57; 2000: 404–5 (no. 1204).
**Discussion:** Ellermeier 1968: 149; Moran 1969a: 33–34; Heintz 1972: 8; Craghan 1974: 41–42, 48, 56; Parker 1993: 63.

| | |
|---|---|
| *ana kakkabī* [2]*qibīma* [3]*umma Inib-šināma* | Speak to my Star: Thus Inib-šina: |
| [4]*Innibana āpiltum* [5]*itbīma kīam idbub* [6]*ummāmi Zimrī-Lim* [7]*adi šarrāqêšu* [8][*u*] *ayyābêšu ša itâtīšu* [9][*i*]*saḫḫurū* | [4]Innibana, the prophetess, arose and spoke as follows: [6]"Zimri-Lim, as long as his thieves [and] enemies who are circling about his borders [. . .] |
| [three unreadable lines] | [break] |
| [13][*lā i*]*ttall*[*a*]*k* [14][. . . *lā*] *išamma* [15]*lā išakkan* | [13]"[He is not to] go anywhere [. . . he is not to] buy, he is not to store up."[a] |
| [16]*anumma šārtī* [17]*u sissiktī addinakkim* [18]*lizakkû* [19]*inanna anumma* [20]*šārtam u sissiktam* [21]*ana kakkabī ušābilam* [22]*k*[*a*]*kkabī têrtam* [23][*lišē*]-*pišma ana zīm* [24]*terêtīšu kakkabī* [25]*l*[*ī*]*puš* | [16]Now I give you my hair and a fringe of my garment. The purification should be performed. I have herewith also sent (another) hair and (another) garment fringe to my Star. My Star [should let] oracles be taken, and according to the oracles my Star should act. |
| *kakkab*[*ī*] [26]*pagaršu liṣṣur* | [26]Let [my] Star protect himself. |

[a] The translation is conjectural because of the fragmentary context.

## 15. NN to Zimri-Lim

**Text:** ARM 26 205 (= ARM 25 816 = M. 7306).
**Photograph:** Durand 1988 (microfiche).
**Transliteration and translation:** Limet 1986: 242; Durand 1988: 433–34.
**Translation:** Durand 1994: 57–58.
**Discussion:** Durand 1995: 356; Huffmon 1997: 10; Charpin 2002: 29.

[beginning destroyed]
[1'] *[u in]a idi b[ēl]ī[ka lizzizū]* [2'] *ina šalšim karā[šim]* [3'] *kāsam liḫpû* [4'] *ana mātim šapil[tim]* [5'] *du'ummatum iš[šakkan]* [6'] *išāt ana tillātim tušeš-š[erši]*

[beginning destroyed][a]
[1'] "[... and let them stand[b]] beside [your] l[or]d. In the third ca[mp] (the people) should break the cup. Darkness will fa[ll] on the Low[er] Land.[c] There will be a confusion,[d] but you will res[tore] order with the help of auxiliaries."[e]

[7'] *Dagan ušāḫiza[nni]* [8'] *um[m]āmi kakkī lupti* [9'] *[wa]rdī Zimrī-Lim* [10'] *[pū]ssu[n]u alputma* [11'] *[wa]rkī[k]a aṭrudam* [12'] *[u]l ikta[šdūma* [13'] *ina* UD].4.KAM *iš[allamū]* [14'] *[warkī]šu šaniš i[...]*

[7'] Dagan made [me] conversant with the following: "Touch[f] the weapons as I have touched the [forehe]ad[g] of the [se]rvants of Zimri-Lim whom I sent away [aft]er you! [If they] have [no]t yet arri[ved], they will be saf[ely there by the] fourth day." There[after] he [...] once more.

[15'] *[umma an]ākūm[a ina pāni]* [16'][UD].4.KAM-*mi lūm[urma ṣābum* [17'] *likš]ud* [...] [18'] *sikkati* [...] [19'] *šanītam ana umma[nātim* ...] [20'] *[u]štābi[l* ...] [21'] *ištēn* [...]
[rest destroyed]

[15'] I [said]: "I want to s[ee the army] com[ing before the] fourth day [...] of the pile [...]."

[19'] Another matter: I have sent [...] to the tro[ops], one [...]
[rest destroyed]

[a] The reconstruction and interpretation of this text are extremely difficult; the interpretations of Durand are followed here.

[b] Or: "let them go" (*lillikū*); the reconstruction is conjectural.

[c] According to Charpin 2002: 29 this may designate the kingdom of Larsa in Southern Babylonia.

[d] The interpretation of *iš-at* is unclear; Durand 1988: 433 reads it as a st. abs. form of *ešītum* "confusion."

[e] On *tillatum,* see Veenhof 1982: 128-33 and cf. ARM 26 207 (no. 17).

[f] Derived from *lapātum* (imp. sg.3.f.) "to touch", following a suggestion of J. M. Sasson; this implies a female author of the letter. Durand 1988: 434 interprets the word as a precative form of *petû* "to open."

[g] For this gesture (*pūtam lapātum*) in taking omens, see Durand 1988: 39.

### 16. [Yaqqim-Addu?] to Zimri-Lim

**Text:** ARM 26 206 (= A. 3893).
**Photograph:** Durand 1988 (microfiche).
**Transliteration and translation:** Durand 1988: 434–35; Heintz 1997a: 204.
**Translation:** Anbar 1993a: 2; Durand 1994: 61; J. M. Sasson 1994: 311 n. 43; Huffmon 1997: 13.
**Discussion:** Astour 1992; Charpin 1992: 22; Anbar 1993a: 2–3; Gordon 1993: 69; Parker 1993: 56; J. M. Sasson 1994: 311–12; Durand 1995: 318, 355; 1997a: 124; Heintz 1997a: 202–12; Huffmon 1997: 13–14; 2000: 55; Malamat 1998: 136–37; van der Toorn 1998b: 62–63; Grabbe 2000: 22; Loretz 2000: 1726; Barstad 2001: 61–62.

*ana [bēlīya]* [2]*qi[bīma] umma [Yaqqim-Addu]* [4]*warad[kāma]* [5]*ištēn muḫḫû[m ša Dagan]* [6]*illikamma kī[ʾam iqbi]* [7]*umma šūma*

Sp[eak] to my [lord]: Thus [*Yaqqim-Addu,*[a] your] servant:

[5]A prophe[t of Dagan] came to me [and spoke as foll]ows. This is what he said:

*w[uddi mīnam]* [8]*ša Zi[mrī-Lim]* [9]*akkal ištēn puḫ[ādam idinm]a* [10]*lūkul*

[7]"V[erily, what] shall I eat that belongs to Z[imri-Lim]? [Give me] one la[mb] and I shall eat it!"

*ištēn puḫādam [addin]šumma* [11]*balṭussuma [in]a [p]ān abullim* [12]*[ī]kulšu* [13]*u šībūtim* [14]*ina pān abullim* [15]*ša Saggarātim* [16]*upaḫḫirma* [17]*kīam iqbi umma šūma* [18]*ukultum iššakkan* [19]*ana <ā>lānē rugumma* [20]*asakkam literrū* [21]*awīl ša rīsam ippušu* [22]*ina ālim lišēṣū* [23]*u ana šalām bēlīka Zi[mrī-Lim]* [24]*ištēn ṣubātam tulabbašanni*

[10][I gave] him a lamb and he devoured it raw[b] [in fr]ont of the city gate. He assembled[c] the elders[d] in front of the gate of Saggaratum[e] and said: "A devouring will take place![f] Give orders to the cities to return the taboo material. Whoever commits an act of violence[g] shall be expelled from the city. And for the well-being of your lord Zi[mri-Lim], clothe me in a garment."

[25]*annītam iqbêmm[a]* [26]*ana šalām bēlī[ya]* [27]*ištēn ṣubātam ulabb[issu]*

[25]This is what he spoke to me. For sake of the well-being of [my] lord, I clothed [him] in a garment.[h]

[28]*anumma tê[rtam ša]* [29]*idbuba[m ašṭurma]* [30]*ana ṣēr [bēlīya]* [31]*aštapra[m]* [32]*u têrtašu ina simmištim* [33]*ul iqbêm ina puḫur šībūtim* [34]*têṛtašu iddin*

[28]Now, [I have recorded] the or[acle that] he spoke [to me] and sent it to [my lord]. He did not utter his oracle in private,[i] but he delivered his oracle in the assembly of the elders.

[a] The name of the author of the letter is broken away. Durand 1988: 435 suggests Yaqqim-Addu who was the governor of Saggaratum. This suggestion, however, is dependent on the assumption that the incident he is reporting actually took place in Saggaratum; see below, note e.

[b] Lit. "alive." This may be a reminiscent of the Sumerian stereotype of the Amorite who "eats uncooked meat" (Huffmon 2000: 55).

[c] Or "I assembled."

[d] For the societal role of the elders, see Anbar 1991: 150–54.

[e] This either means the city gate of Saggaratum or the Saggaratum gate of Terqa (thus van der Toorn 1998b: 62 n. 43); if the latter is true, then there is no specific reason for attributing the letter to Yaqqim-Addu.

[f] The "devouring" (*ukultum*) corresponds to the symbolic act of eating, referring to an epidemic among the cattle or to an even greater catastrophe (cf. Charpin 1992: 22; Heintz 1997a: 209–10; van der Toorn 1998b: 62–63).

[g] This translation of Durand 1988: 434 is based on the only (Late Babylonian) occurrence of the word *rīsu* (cf. *AHw* 989).

[h] Rather than indicating that the prophet was naked (so Astour 1992), this means that he got the garment as a reward for his oracle. Cf. the decrees of expenditures (nos. 55–59 below), which document several prophets as recipients of such garments (Huffmon 1997: 14).

[i] For *simmištum* "secret", see Charpin 1993/94: 18–19. Cf. M. 9717 (no. 65):3 and *samāšum* "to hide" in ARM 26 414 (no. 48):7.

## 17. Šibtu to Zimri-Lim

**Text:** ARM 26 207 (= A. 996 = ARM 10 4).
**Copy:** Dossin 1967: pl. 3.
**Transliteration and translation:** Dossin 1978: 24–27, 252; Moran 1969a: 46–48; Römer 1971: 50–53; Durand 1988: 435–437.
**Translation:** Moran 1969b: 629–30; Weippert 1972: 472 (lines 3–12); Dietrich 1986: 84–85; Durand 1994: 66; 2000: 322–23 (no. 1144).
**Discussion:** Moran 1969a: 48–50; von Soden 1969; Heintz 1971a: 547; J. M. Sasson 1974; 1994: 307–8; Durand 1982b; 1984: 150–55; 1995: 329–30, 347; Veenhof 1982: 124–133; Wilcke 1983; Parker 1993: 60–62, 64–65; Rowlett 1996: 54–55; Malamat 1998: 72–73, 149; Butler 1998: 153–55; Grabbe 2000: 21; Charpin 2001: 40–41; 2002: 21; van Koppen 2002: 318.

| | |
|---|---|
| *ana bēlīya qibīma* [2]*umma Šibtu amatkāma* | Speak to my lord: Thus Šibtu,[a] your servant: |
| [3]*aššum ṭēm gerrim* [4]*ša bēlī illakū ittātim* [5]*zikāram u sinništam* [6]*ašqi aštālma igerrûm* [7]*ana bēlīya mādiš damiq* [8]*ana Išme-Dagan qātamma* | [3]Concerning the campaign my lord is planning, I gave drink to male and female persons to inquire about signs.[b] The oracle[c] is |

*[9]zikāram u s[i]nništam [10]aštālma egerrûšu [11]ul damiq [12]u ṭēmšu šapal šēp bēlīya [13]šakin*

extremely favorable to my lord. Likewise, I inquired of male and female about Išme-Dagan. The oracle is unfavorable to him. The report concerning him goes: "He will be placed under the feet of my lord."

*umma šunūma bēlī ḫumāšam i[šši] [14]ana Išme-Dagan ḫumāšam iššīma [15]umma ina ḫumāšim ele''ika [16]šitpuṣum šitpaṣma [17]ina šitpuṣu ele''ika*

[13]They said: "My lord ha[s raised] a *ḫumāšum*![d] Raising the *ḫumāšum* against Išme-Dagan he says: 'I will beat you with the *ḫumāšum*! Wrestle as much as you can, I shall win the match!'"

*[18]umma anākūma bēlī ana kakki [19]iṭeḫḫe umma šunūma [20]kakku [21]ul inneppešu [22]kīma kašādimma [23]tillātū[š]u [24]issappa[ḫ]ā [25]u qaqqa[d Išme]-Dagan inakkisūma [26]šapal šēp [b]ēlīya [27]išakkanū ummāmi [28]ṣābum ša I[šm]e-Dagan [29]mād u šumma ṣ[ābūšu m]ād [30]tillātūšu issapḫāšu [31]tillātī yattūm Dagan [32]Šamaš Itūr-Mer u Bēlet-ekallim [33]u Adduma bēl purussêm [34]ša ina idi bēlīya ill[akū]*

[18]I said: "Will my lord come near to a conflict?" They answered: "There will be no armed conflict! For as soon as his (Zimri-Lim's) auxiliaries[e] arrive they[f] will be scattered. The he[ad of Išme]-Dagan will be cut off and placed under the feet of my lord, saying: 'The army of I[šm]e-Dagan is large, but even if [his] a[rmy is la]rge, his auxiliaries have scattered it. My auxiliaries are Dagan, Šamaš, Itur-Mer, Belet-ekallim and Adad, the Lord of Decisions, who g[o] beside my lord.'"

*[35]assurri bēlī kêm i[qabbi] [36]ummāmi ina belāni u[šadbibš]unūti [37]mimma ul uš[a]dba[būšunūti] [38]šunūma idabbabū šunū[ma] imtaḫḫa[ṣū] [40]umma šunūma tillāt Išme-[Dagan] [41]asīrū ina sarrātim[ma [42]u] dīṣāti[m] ittīšu ittanaššū [43][awā]ssu ul ileqqû [44][an]a pāni bēlīya ṣābūšu [45][is]sappaḫ*

[35]Perhaps my lord would s[ay] this: "She has [made them speak] by fraudulent means."[g] But [I did] not make [them] speak anything. They speak voluntarily — they could resi[st] as well![h] They say: "The auxiliaries of Išme-[Dagan] are prisoners. When they fall into deceit and distress[i] with him, they will not take heed of his [word]. Before my lord's arrival, his army will be dissipated."

[a] On Šibtu, the queen of Mari, wife of Zimri-Lim and daughter of Yarim-Lim, king of Aleppo, and her extensive correspondence with her husband, see (Artzi and) Malamat 1998: 175–91; Ziegler 1999: 54–56.

[b] Lit. "The signs, male and female, I gave to drink, making an inquiry," reading the beginning of line 6 as *aš-qi* with Durand 1982b: 43–44. The two verbs *ašqi aštālma* constitute an asyndetic construction, indicating that the inquiry is made by giving drink to the persons in question (Wilcke 1983). The grammatical object of this hendiadys is somewhat unclear. While Durand 1982b; 1984b takes *ittātim zikāram u sinništam* as the object, thus interpreting the male and female persons as signs, J. M. Sasson 1994: 308 reckons with a double accusative: "I gave male and female the signs to drink," thus assuming that the drink itself contains the signs to be rendered into understandable oracles by the ones who drink it (cf. ARM 26 208 [no. 18]:11'–25'). The divinatory technique, mentioned also in ARM 26 212 (no. 22):2' (cf. M. 9717 [no. 65] r. 3'), remains obscure. Well imaginable as it would be, it is not certain whether the drink is alcoholic (so Durand) or otherwise intoxicating; in any case, the men and women in question are affected by it (or by the hospitality of Šibtu; thus Wilcke) to the extent that they utter the inquired oracles. —Butler 1998: 153–54, following Finet 1982: 51–52, translates "I have asked for omens from the male and female ecstatic(s)," reading the beginning of line 6 as MAH, and interpreting it as an ideogram for *muḫḫûm*.

[c] The word *egerrûm* "speech omen" has been perceived a "chance-heard remark or sound which is perceived as portentous by its hearer" (Cryer 1994: 160; cf. Oppenheim 1954/56). According to Butler 1998: 152, an *egerrûm* "may derive from a wider spectrum of auditory experiences, which are deemed to be ominous, possibly by hindsight." In this case, *egerrûm* is clearly an answer to an oracle query. The analysis of Durand 1988: 385 shows that, at least at Mari, it is one of the terms for prophetic discourse. Cf. also ARM 26 196 (no. 6).

[d] The meaning of the word *ḫumāšum* can only be guessed; for a survey of its occurrences, see von Soden 1955: 142. Since it is the object of the verb *našû* "to lift," it probably means a conrete object (Moran 1969a: 47 n. 4). Dietrich 1986: 84 translates "Ringkampfklammer" (= *umāšum,* see *AHw* 1412; cf. J. M. Sasson 1974), whereas Durand 1988: 436 (cf. 1984: 154; 2000: 323) interprets the word as "rod, cane."

[e] On *tillatum,* see Veenhof 1982: 128–33.

[f] I.e., Išme-Dagan's army.

[g] For this interpretation of *ina belāni,* see Durand 1987: 180 n. 27. Moran 1969a: 48 reading *ina tillâni* (*tillû* cf. *bēlu* II *AHw* 120), translates "by means of arms."

[h] Reading *imtaḫa*[*ṣū*] with Durand 1988: 435, who translates: "Certains parlent, d'autres résistent." The alternative reading *imtaḫa*[*rū*] is represented by Moran 1969a: 47 ("On their own they speak, on their [own] they agre[e]") and Dietrich 1986: 85 ("Sie sprechen aus freien Stücken, sie sind an mich herangetreten").

[i] The word *dīṣtum* "distress" is derived from *dâṣum* "to plague, harass."

### 18. Šibtu to Zimri-Lim

**Text:** ARM 26 208 (= A. 2233 = ARM 10 9).
**Copy:** Dossin 1967: pl. 6.
**Transliteration and translation:** Dossin 1978: 34–37; Moran 1969a: 50–51; Durand 1988: 437–38; J. M. Sasson 1982: 153–54 (lines 1'–26').
**Translation:** Huffmon 1968: 108 (lines 1–15); Moran 1969b: 632; J. M. Sasson 1982: 151 (lines 1–15); 1995a: 286 (lines 1'–26'); Durand 1994: 64; 1995: 192, 371; 2000: 319–21 (no. 1142).
**Discussion:** Dossin 1978: 253–25; Moran 1969a: 51–52; Heintz 1971a: 547; 1972: 9; J. M. Sasson 1982; 1995a: 286–87; Durand 1984: 152–53; 1995: 192, 354; 1997a: 132; Uehlinger 1992: 351–52; Gordon 1993: 72; Oliva 1994; Heimpel 1999; Pongratz-Leisten 1999: 71; Charpin 2001: 35; 2002: 16–17; Nissinen 2002b: 7–8.

*ana bēlīya* [2]*qibīma* [3]*umma Šibtu* [4]*amatkāma*
*ekallum šalim*
[5]*Qīšti-Dīrītim* [6]*āpilum ša Dīrītim* [7]UD.2.KAM *ana bāb ekall[im illikam]* [8]*[k]īam išpuram [ummāmi]* [9]*ana pāni kussî Mā[ri]* [10]*mammām ul i[llêm]* [11]*ana Zimr[ī-Limma]* [12]*alaʾitum nad[nat]* [13]*šukur awīl El[amtim išebbir]* [14]*annītam iqbêm*

Speak to my lord: Thus Šibtu, your servant:
[4]The palace is well.
[5]On the second day, Qišti-Diritim, a prophet of Diritum,[a] [came] to the gate of the pala[ce] and sent to me the following message: "Nobody will r[ise] against the throne of Ma[ri]. It is Zimr[i-Lim] to whom the Upper Country[b] is giv[en]. [He will break] the lance of the El[amite[c]]. This is what [he spoke].

[15]*šanītam [. . .]*
[break]
[1']*umma [Ēama . . .]* [2']*kimt[um . . .]* [3']*nī[š ilim i niḫsus]* [4']*ašar m[û ibaššû]* [5']*nīš ilim ni[ḫsus]*
[6']*Asumêm iš[tassi]* [7']*Asumûm arḫ[iš illik]* [8']*awātam ana Ēa [iqbi]* [9']*ša Asumûm [iqbû]* [10']*ul ešme it[bīma Ēa]* [11']*iqbi ummāmi [kīma nīš ilim]* [12']*nizakkarū rū[šam]* [13']*u sippam ša bāb [Māri]* [14']*lilqūnimma nīš ilim [i niḫs]us*

[15]More[over, . . .]
[break]
[1']Thus says [Ea:[d] ". . .] the family [. . . let us mind] the oath![e] Where [there is] wa[ter][f] we mi[nd] the oath."
[6']He ca[lled] the god Asumûm,[g] and Asumûm [came] quick[ly, saying] a word to Ea. What Asumûm [said], I did not hear. [Ea] ro[se] and said: "[Because] we shall declare [an oath], let door-jamb di[rt][h] from the gate of [Mari] be brought to us, and [we shall mi]nd the oath."

[15']*rūšam u sippam ša bā[b] Māri* [16']*ilqūnimma ina mê imḫuḫūma* [17']*ilū u ilātum i[š]tê* [18']*umma Ēama*

[15']Door-jamb dirt from the ga[te] of Mari was brought and dissolved in water. The gods and the

*ana ilī* [19'] *tibā ša ana libitti* [20'] *Māri u rābiṣ* [21'] *[Māri u]gallalū* [22'] *[il]ū u ilāt[um iqbênim* [23'] *umm]āmi ana libitti* [24'] *[Mā]ri u rābiṣ* [25'] *Māri* [26'] *ul nugalla[l]*

goddesses drank it[i] and Ea said to the gods: "Stand up,[j] those of you who intend harm to the brickwork of Mari or to the protective guardian [of Mari]!" The [god]s and the goddes[ses said]: "We intend no harm to the brickwork of [Ma]ri or to the protective guardian of Mari!"

[a] The goddess Diritum is the patron deity of the town called Dir, probably the local manifestation of Ištar (as the sequence Ištar–Ištar Diritum–Annunitum in ARM 24 263 suggests; cf. Talon 1980). The goddess enjoyed in the time of Zimri-Lim an extensive veneration at Mari, but the location of Dir is disputed. It is hardly identifiable with the Transtigridian religious center with the same name, but should be sought in the vicinity of Mari. See the discussion in Birot 1972: 134–36; Nakata 1974: 152–160; J. M. Sasson 1979: 131; 1982: 151–52; Lambert 1985: 529; Oliva 1994.

[b] This translation of Durand 1988: 438 understands the word *alaʾitum* in a meaning similar to *(mātum) elītum*. For other interpretations, cf. Huffmon 1968: 108 ("woman citizen"; cf. *CAD* A/1 391); Dossin 1978: 253 ("tout ce qui relève de la ville"; cf. *AHw* 36 sub *ālīum*); J. M. Sasson 1982: 152 (Alaḫtum).

[c] This reading is based of the collation and reconstruction of Durand 1988: 437.

[d] Only the remains of the determinative of a divine name is readable here; the reconstruction is based on the role of the god Ea in the following lines of this letter.

[e] For the phrase *nīš ilim ḫasāsum,* used in ARM 14 89 and 106 besides *nīš ilim zakārum,* see Birot 1974: 237 and Heimpel 1999, who makes a distinction between "declaring" (*zakārum*) and "minding" (*ḫasāsum*) an oath.

[f] Thus according the reconstruction of Moran 1969a: 50.

[g] On this god, probably identical with Usumu, the Janus-faced vizier of Ea, see J. M. Sasson 1982: 155 n. 2 with further references.

[h] For this hendiatical translation, s. J. M. Sasson 1995a: 286 n. 9. Cf. Stol 1991: 627–28, who opts for "grease".

[i] Cf. ARM 26 207 (no. 17) and 212 (no. 22).

[j] Thus according to the interpretation of J. M. Sasson 1995a: 286 n. 10, reading *ti-ba-a* and interpreting it as a contracted imperative 2. pl. of *tebûm* (for *tibiā*). Durand 1988: 438 reads *ṭì-ba-a,* interpreting it as a stat. pl. 3. f. of *ṭiābum* and connecting *ana ilī* with it, hence the translation "Est-il agréable aux dieux. . . ? "

### 19. Mukannišum to Zimri-Lim

**Text:** ARM 26 209 (= A. 4996 = ARM 13 23).
**Transliteration and translation:** Bottéro in Dossin et al 1964: 42–43; Ellermeier 1968: 40–42; Durand 1988: 438–39.
**Translation:** Huffmon 1968: 109; Moran 1969b: 625; Weippert 1972: 474–75 (lines 4–14); Durand 1994: 69; 2000: 87 (no. 939); Malamat 1998: 90.
**Discussion:** Schult 1966: 228–31; Ellermeier 1968: 136–37; Hayes 1968: 84–85; Heintz 1969: 126, 131; Ross 1970: 18; Craghan 1974: 48, 51; 1975: 37, 48; Huffmon 1976b: 699; Schmitt 1982: 50–55; Bodi 1991: 179; Durand 1995: 348; Laato 1996: 172; Malamat 1998: 70, 90–94; Lafont 1999: 70; Grabbe 2000: 30; Charpin 2002: 20.

*[a]na bēlīya* [2]*qibīma* [3]*umma Mukannišum* [4]*waradkāma nīqam ana Dagan* [5]*ana balāṭ bēlīya aqqīma*

Speak to my lord: Thus Mukannišum,[a] your servant:

[4]I have made the offerings for Dagan for the sake of the life of my lord.

[6]*aplûm ša Dagan ša Tutt[ul]* [7]*itbēma kīam iqbi* [8]*ummāmi Bābilu mīnam* [9]*tettenēpeš ana pûgim u ša-ka-ri-im* [10]*upaḫḫarka* [11]*bītāt sebet awīlī atḫî* [12]*u makkuršunu* [13]*a[n]a [q]āt Z[i]mrī-L[im]* [14]*lumallêm*

[6]A prophet[b] of Dagan of Tutt[ul] arose and spoke as follows: "Babylon, what are you constantly doing?[c] I will gather you into a net and. . . .[d] The dwellings of the seven accomplices and all their wealth I give in the hand of Zimri-L[im]."

[15]*u ap[l]ûm ša Bēlet-ekallim* [16]*i[tb]ē[ma* [17]*k]ī'a[m] i[qbi] [ummā-mi]* [18]*Ḫamm[ura]b[i . . .]*

[15]Also, a prophet[e] of Belet-ekallim arose and sp[oke]: "O Hamm[ura]bi [. . .]"

[rest broken away]

[rest broken away]

[a] Mukannišum is well known from administrative documents, including ARM 22 326 (no. 58) and ARM 25 15 (no. 60) in which prophets are mentioned. On him and his activities, see Rouault 1977: 110–258; Lafont 2002.

[b] A variant form *aplûm* (LÚ.*a-ap-lu-ú-um*) of *āpilum*.

[c] A phonetic variant of the Gtn form *tēteneppeš*.

[d] The reading is based on the collation of Durand 1983b: 145; however, the translation of *ša-ka-ri-im* is unclear. Durand suggests a word *šakarû* "couteau" ("spear") on the basis of *šukurrum* "lance" (cf. *AHw* 1139 sub *šak/g/qarum*). Alternatively, the word could be related to *šikru/šakru* II "handle, grip" (see *AHw* 1141, 1235).

[e] See note b.

## 20. Kibri-Dagan to Zimri-Lim

**Text:** ARM 26 210 (= M. 13843 = ARM 13 114).
**Transliteration and translation:** Kupper in Dossin et al 1964: 120; Ellermeier 1968: 46–49; Durand 1988: 439–40.
**Translation:** Moran 1969b: 624; Durand 1994: 69; 2000: 86 (no. 937); Malamat 1998: 94.
**Discussion:** Schult 1966: 231–32; Ellermeier 1968: 140; Hayes 1968: 85; Heintz 1969: 121–22; Dion 1970: 568–69; Ross 1970: 19; Craghan 1974: 47, 52; Durand 1995: 348; Rowlett 1996: 97–98; Malamat 1998: 70, 94–96; Charpin 2001: 29; 2002: 12.

*[ana bēlīya* [2]*q]ibīma* [3]*umma Kibrī-D[agan]* [4]*waradkāma*
[5]*ūm ṭuppi annêm ana ṣēr bēlīya* [6]*ušābilam* [7]*lām[a] tirik šadîm* [8]*ištēn awīltum aššat awīlim illikamma* [9]*aššum ṭēm Bābili* [10]*kīam iqbêm*

[Sp]eak [to my lord]: Thus Kibri-D[agan], your servant:
[5]When I sent this tablet to my lord, before the mountains cast their shadow,[a] a woman, spouse of a free man, came to me and, concerning Babylon, spoke as follows:

*ummāmi* [11]*Dagan išpuranni* [12]*šupur ana bēlīk[a* [13]*l]ā iḫâš u mā[tum]ma* [14]*[lā] iḫâš* [15]*[Ḫa]mmurabi* [16]*[šarru š]a Bābili* [unreadable line]

[11]"Dagan has sent me. Write to your lord that he should not be anxious, and [neither] should the la[nd] be anxious. [Ha]mmurabi, [king o]f Babylon [. . .]

[1']*[. . .] ana ḫalāqīšu* [2']*[iḫamm]uṭ*

[1'][is ru]shing[b] to his complete undoing."

[a] I.e., by nightfall. For the expression *tirik šadîm,* see Kupper 1964: 111 n. 1; Durand 2000: 86.
[b] Or "I will precipitate (*[aḫamm]uṭ*) his complete undoing," both suggested by Durand 1988: 440.

## 21. Šibtu to Zimri-Lim

**Text:** ARM 26 211 (= A. 3178).
**Photograph:** Durand 1988 (microfiche).
**Transliteration and translation:** Durand 1988: 440.
**Translation:** Durand 1994: 71; 1995: 355.

*ana bēlīya* [2]*qibīma* [3]*umma Šibtu* [4]*amat[k]ām[a]*
[5]*[Išḫa]ra-[. . .] num*

Speak to my lord: Thus Šibtu, your servant:
[5][The lady Išḫa]ra-[. . .](?)

[one unreadable line]
7*[ša Bēlet-e]kallim* 8*izzi[zma]* 9*kīam iqbêm*
10*umma šīma Zimrī-Lim* 11*ašar illiku* 12*ul ibâš* 13*ḫaddânšu ikaššad*
14*kinnikêm araʾʾub* 15*u ina lītim azzaz*

[one unreadable line]
7[of Belet-e]kallim(?) sto[od and] said:
10"Zimri-Lim—wherever he had gone, he cannot come to shame. He will catch his ill-wisher.[a] There[b] I will rage and stand in victory."

[a] Lit. "his malicious one"; for *ḫaddânu/ḫādiānu,* see *AHw* 307.
[b] For the meaning of *kinnikêm,* see Durand 1988: 440.

## 22. Šibtu to Zimri-Lim

**Text:** ARM 26 212 (= A. 3217 = ARM 10 6).
**Copy:** Dossin 1967: pl. 4.
**Transliteration and translation:** Dossin 1978: 28–31; Ellermeier 1968: 54–57; Moran 1969a: 35; Römer 1971: 24–25; Durand 1988: 440–41.
**Translation:** Huffmon 1968: 111; Moran 1969b: 630; Durand 1994: 69–70; 2000: 326 (no. 1146).
**Discussion:** Ellermeier 1968: 142–43; Moran 1969a: 36–38; Heintz 1971b; Craghan 1975: 48; Durand 1982b; Schmitt 1982: 101–6; J. M. Sasson 1994: 308; Durand 1995: 348; Malamat 1998: 149–50; Butler 1998: 154.

*ana bēlīya* 2*qi[bī]ma* 3*umma Š[i]btu amatkām[a]*
4*ekall[um] šalim*
5*I[lī-ḫa]znāya a[ss]inn[u]* 6*ša An[nunītim il]lika[m]* 7*ina l[ibbi bīt Annunītim* 8*...]-ma* 9*[ṭēmum aššum Bābil]i* 10*[ana bēlīya išš]aprāššu* 11*[ummāmi Ḫammu-r]abi* 12*[...]-ku*
[one-third of the tablet broken away]
1'*[aššum ṭē]m Bāb[ili]* 2*ittātim ašqi aštalm[a]* 3'*awīlum šū mādātim ana mātim annītim* 4'*ušām ul ikaššad* 5'*bēlī immar ša ilum awīlam šâti* 6'*ippešu takaššassu* 7'*u elīšu tazzaz* 8'*ūmūšu qerbū ul iballuṭ* 9'*bēlī annītam lū ī[d]e*

Speak to my lord: Thus Šibtu, your servant:
4The pala[ce] is well.
5I[li-ḫa]znaya,[a] *a[ss]innu* of An[nunitum ca]me [to me]. I[n the temple of Annunitum, ... the following message about Baby]lon [was s]ent [to my lord:[b] "Hammur]abi [...]"
[break]
1'[Concern]ing Babyl[on] I inquired about the matter[c] by giving signs to drink.[d] This man unsuccessfully tries to determine many things against that country. My lord will see what God will do to this man: You will capture him and stand over him. His days are running short,[e] he will not live long. My lord should know this.

[10'] *lāma ṭēm Ilī-ḫaznā[y]a* [11'] *ša Annunītum išpuraššu* [12'][UD].5.KAM *anāku aštā[lm]a* [13'][*ṭē*]*mum ša Annunī*[*tum* [14'] *išp*]*urakkum* [15'] *u ša ašālu* [16'] *ištēnma*

[10']I myself inquired five days before the message of Ili-ḫaznaya, which Annunitum sent to him. The [mes]sage which Annuni[tum se]nt to you and the one I inquired for are identical.

[a] The *assinnu* Ili-ḫaznaya is attested also in M. 11299:13; see Durand 1988: 399.
[b] Assuming that the suffix sg. 3. in *iššapraššu* refers to the king.
[c] Possibly in response to the letter of Zimri-Lim to Šibtu ARM 26 185 bis (Charpin 2002: 22 n. 125).
[d] Cf. ARM 26 207 (no. 17): 6 with note b.
[f] For the phrase *ūmūšu qerbū,* see Heintz 1971b; J. M. Sasson 1993.

## 23. Šibtu to Zimri-Lim

**Text:** ARM 26 213 (= A. 100 = ARM 10 7).
**Copy:** Dossin 1967: pl. 5.
**Transliteration and translation:** Dossin 1978: 30–33, 253; Ellermeier 1968: 56–59; Römer 1971: 19–20; Moran 1969a: 29–30; Durand 1988: 441–42.
**Translation:** Dossin 1966: 82; Huffmon 1968: 111; Moran 1969b: 63; Dietrich 1973: 34; 1986: 92–93; Durand 1994: 70; 2000: 315–16 (no. 1137).
**Discussion:** Ellermeier 1968: 143; Heintz 1969: 125–26; Moran 1969a: 30–31; Ross 1970: 19; Craghan 1974: 52, 56; Huffmon 1976b: 699; Wilson 1980: 106–7; Schmitt 1982: 34–37; Ellis 1987: 254; van der Toorn 1987: 77.

*ana bēlīya* [2]*qi*[*bī*]*ma* [3]*umma Šibtu* [4]*amatkāma*
*ekall*[*um*] *šalim*
[5]*ina bīt Annunītim* UD.3.KAM [6]*Šēlebum* [7]*immaḫḫu*

*umma Annunītumma* [8]*Zimrī-Lim* [9]*ina bārtim* [10]*ilattakūka* [11]*pagarka uṣur* [12]*wardē* <*l*>*ibbīka* [13]*ša tarammu* [14]*itâtīk*[*a*] [15]*šukun* [16]*šuzissunūtima* [17]*liṣṣurūk*[*a*] [18]*ana ramānīka*[*ma*] [19]*lā tattana*[*lla*]*k* [20]*u awīlū ša ila*[*ttakūk*]*a* [21]*ana qātīka a*[*wīlī*] *šunūti* [22]*umal*[*lam*]

Spe[ak] to my lord: Thus Šibtu, your servant:
[4]The pala[ce] is well.
[5]In the temple of Annunitum, three days ago, Šelebum[a] went into trance and said:

[7]"Thus says Annunitum: Zimri-Lim, you will be tested in a revolt! Protect yourself! Let your most favored servants whom you love[b] surround you, and make them stay there to protect you! Do not go around on your own! As regards the people who would tes[t you]: those pe[ople] I deli[ver up] into your hands."

23 *inanna a[numma]* 24 *šā[r]ta[m u sissiktam]* 25 *ša assi[nnim]* 26 *ana ṣ[ēr bēlīya]* 27 *ušābilam*

23 Now I am sending the hai[r and the fringe of the garment] of the *assi[nnu]* to [my lord].

[a] For Šelebum, *assinnu* of the temple of Annunitum, see Durand 1988: 399 and cf. ARM 26 197 (no. 7) and 198 (no. 8).

[b] Thus according to the emendation *<li>-ib-bi-ka* (cf. Ellermeier 1968: 58; Durand 1988: 442). Without emending the text, the word *ebbu* has been interpreted in a similar sense (cf. *CAD* E 4; Bottéro in Dossin et al. 1964: 160; Finet 1966: 21).

## 24. Šibtu to Zimri-Lim

**Text:** ARM 26 214 (= A. 671 = ARM 10 8).
**Copy:** Dossin 1967: pl. 5.
**Transliteration and translation:** Dossin 1978: 32–35, 253; Ellermeier 1968: 58–61; Moran 1969a: 31–32; Römer 1971: 20–21; Durand 1988: 442–43.
**Translation:** Dossin 1966: 82; Huffmon 1968: 114–15; Moran 1969b: 630; Dietrich 1973: 34–35; 1986: 93; Durand 1994: 70–71; 2000: 316 (no. 1138).
**Discussion:** Ellermeier 1968: 143–45; Heintz 1969: 126; Moran 1969a: 32; Weippert 1972: 474; Craghan 1974: 52–53; 1975: 35, 43, 49; Huffmon 1976b: 699; Durand 1995: 363; Nissinen 2003: 4–5.

*ana bēlīya* 2 *qibīma* 3 *umma Šibtu* 4 *amatkāma*
5 *ina bīt Annunītim ša libbi ālim* 6 *Aḫātum ṣuharat Dagan-Malik* 7 *immaḫḫima kīam iqbi*

Speak to my lord: Thus Šibtu, your servant:

5 In the temple of Annunitum in the city, Aḫatum,[a] a servant girl of Dagan-Malik went into trance and spoke:

8 *ummāmi Zimrī-Lim* 9 *u šumma atta mišâtanni* 10 *anāku elīka* 11 *aḫabbuṣ* 12 *nakrīka* 13 *ana qātīka* 14 *umalla* 15 *u awīlī šarrāqīya* 16 *aṣabbatma* 17 *ana karāš Bēlet-ekallim* 18 *akammissunūti*

8 "Zimri-Lim: Even though you are neglectful about me, I will massacre on your behalf.[b] Your enemy I will deliver up into your hand. The people that steal[c] from me I will catch, and I will gather them into the camp of Belet-ekallim."[d]

19 *ina šanîm ūmim* 20 *Aḫūm sangûm ṭēmam* 21 *annêm šārtam* 22 *u s[i]ssiktam* 23 *ublamma ana bēlīya* 24 *ašpuram šārtam* 25 *u sissiktam* 26 *aknukamma* 27 *ana ṣēr bēlīya* 28 *uštābilam*

19 On the day following, Aḫum the priest delivered to me this message together with the hair and the fringe of the garment. I have now written to my lord. I have sealed the hair and the fringe of the garment and sent them to my lord.

[a] Possibly the housekeeper belonging to the palace staff and mentioned in ARM 8 88:2 (Moran 1969a: 32).

[b] Thus according to the collation of Durand 1988: 443 (*a-ḫa-ab-bu-uṣ*$_4$), even though the verb *ḫabāṣu* is difficult to combine with *elīka,* translated here as "on your behalf." Many have read *a-ḫa-ab-bu-ub,* which is understood as a gesture of love (Ellermeier 1968: 60–61; Moran 1969a: 31; Dietrich 1986: 93 and cf. *CAD* Ḫ 2–3 sub *ḫabābu* B).

[c] For this translation, see Berger 1969: 209; Römer 1971: 55.

[d] Thus Dossin 1966: 82; Huffmon 1968: 115; Ellermeier 1968: 61; Durand 1988: 443. The alternative translations include "to the destruction of Belet-ekallim" (*karāšu* II; see *AHw* 448; thus Moran 1969a: 31; Dietrich 1986: 93); "im Bauch der Belet-ekallim" (von Soden 1969: 198; cf. Durand 1984: 70).

## 25. Lanasûm to Zimri-Lim

**Text:** ARM 26 215 (= A. 455).
**Photograph:** Durand 1988 (microfiche).
**Transliteration and translation:** Durand 1988: 443–44.
**Translation:** Dossin 1966: 79–80 (lines 5–24); Huffmon 1968: 112–13 (lines 1–24); Ellermeier 1968: 53 (lines 5–24); Durand 1994: 53.
**Discussion:** Huffmon 1976b: 699; Gordon 1993: 68–69; Parker 1993: 55; J. M. Sasson 1994: 311; Durand 1990: 51, 58; 1995: 355; 1997a: 124; van der Toorn 2000: 81–82; Nissinen 2003: 6–7.

| | |
|---|---|
| *ana bēlīya* [2]*qibīma* [3]*umma Lanasûm* [4]*waradkāma* | Speak to my lord: Thus Lanasûm, your servant: |
| [5]*bēlī kīam išpuram* [6]*umma bēlīma anumma nīqam* [7]*ana Dagan ušerrem* [8]*ištēn alpu u šeššet immerī [bi]l* | [5]My lord has written to me: "I have just consigned an offering for Dagan. [Bri]ng one bull and six sheep!" |
| [9]*inanna nīqum ša bēlīya* [10]*ina šalāmim ana ālim ikšudam* [11]*u pān Dagan innaqi* [12]*u mātum iptun* [13]*u ālum kalûšu ana nīqim ša bēlīya* [14]*[m]ādiš ḫadi* | [9]Now, the offering of my lord has arrived safely in the city and was performed before Dagan. The land ate the sacrificial meal[a] and the whole city was overjoyed by the offering of my lord. |
| [15]*u muḫḫûm pān Dagan* [16]*[i]tbīma kīam iqbi* [17]*u[m]māmi šūma* [18]*admati mê zakūtim* [19]*ul ašatti* [20]*ana bēlīka šupurma* [21]*u mê zakūtim lišqenni* | [15]Also, a prophet arose before Dagan and spoke: "How much longer will I not drink pure water? Write to your lord that he may provide me with pure water!" |
| [22]*inanna anumma* [23]*etqam ša qaqqadīšu* [24]*u sissiktašu ana ṣēr* | [22]Now I have sent a lock of his head[b] and his garment hem to my |

*bēlīya* [25]*ušābilam bēlī l[i]zakki*

lord; let my lord perform the purification offering.

[26]*šanītam aššum sīrim ša bēlīya* [27]*ina wardī ša bēlīya ištēn awīlum taklum* [28]*lillikamma u sīram* [29]*ša bēlīya itti mārē ālim* [30]*[l]ilqi* [31]*u mārē ālim balūya* [32]*šitta dalāti ana Dagan* [33]*issuḫū*

[26]Another matter, concerning the tax[c] of my lord, let a trusted man among the servants of my lord come and take the tax of my lord from the inhabitants of the city. The inhabitants of the city have, without my permission,[d] detached two doors for Dagan.

[a] The verb *patānum* may be used here elliptically for *naptanam patānum* "to eat a meal" (cf. ARM 6 32:23).

[b] The word *etqum* is used here instead of the usual *šārtum*; cf. ARM 234 (no. 39): 13. According to Durand 1988: 444; 1997a: 124, the word, also used of the hirsute appearance of Enkidu in Gilgameš I ii 37, designates the fur of an animal rather than human hair. This may be taken as a hint of the bizarre image of a *muḫḫûm;* cf. Gordon 1993, 68.

[c] The word used here is neither *sīrum* I "plaster" nor *sīrum* II "roof of reed" (see *AHw* 1050; *CAD* S 319–20) but designates "taxe prélevée sur le croît des animaux et sur la récolte" (Durand 1990: 58–60; cf. Charpin 1993/94: 18).

[d] Or "without me being there."

## 26. Tebi-gerišu to Zimri-Lim

**Text:** ARM 26 216 (= A. 2209).
**Photograph:** Durand 1988 (microfiche).
**Transliteration and translation:** Durand 1988: 444–45.
**Translation:** Anbar 1993a: 1; Durand 1994: 55; Huffmon 1997: 14.
**Discussion:** Anbar 1993a: 1–2; Durand 1995: 314–15; 1997a: 119–20; Fleming 1993a: 219–21; 1993b: 179–81; 1993c; Gordon 1993: 65–66; Parker 1993: 66; Heintz 1997a: 198–202; Huffmon 1997: 14–15; Pongratz-Leisten 1999: 69–70; Charpin 2001: 38–39; 2002: 19.

*ana bēlīya* [2]*qibīma* [3]*umma Tebī-gērīšu* [4]*waradkāma*

[5]*ūm ana ṣēr Ašma[d]* [6]*akšudu ina šānim ūm[im]* [7]*nabî ša Ḫanê upaḫ-ḫ[ir]* [8]*têrtam ana šalām bēlīy[a]* [9]*ušēpiš umma anākūma* [10]*šumma bēlī inūma ramā[kšu]* [11]*ippešu* UD.7.KAM *ina ka[wātim* [12]*u]š[š]abma ina šulmi[m* [13]*ana āl]im [iturram]*

Speak to my lord: Thus Tebi-gerišu,[a] your servant:

[5]On the d[ay] following the day I arrived in Ašmad's presence, I asse[mbl]ed the *nabûs*[b] of the Haneans,[c] and I had them deliver an oracle for the well-being of my lord. This is what I said: "Will my lord, when performing [his] ablution rite

and [st]aying seven days ou[tside the city walls], [return] safe[ly to the ci]ty [. . .]

[break]

[1'][. . . *ū*]*m* [*ana Annunītim*] [2']*ša kawātim* [*bēlī illakū*] [3']*bēlī paga*[*ršu*] [4']*liṣṣur* [*ṣābum*] [5']*ina rēš bēlī*[*ya lizziz*] [6']*u maṣṣarāt* [*ālim*] [7']*lū dan*[*nā*] [8']*ana naṣār pagrī*[*šu*] [9']*bēlī aḫšu lā inaddi*

[break]

[1'][. . . On] the day [my lord goes to (the temple of) Annunitum] outside the city walls,[d] let my lord protect him[self! The troops should stand ready] to assist [my] lord, and the [city] watches should be stre[ngthened]. Let my lord not be neglectful about protecting him[self]."

[a] On this person, see Birot 1993: 40.

[b] For this designation, etymologically comparable to the Hebrew *nābîʾ*, see Durand 1988: 377–78; Fleming 1993a/b/c; Heintz 1997a: 198–202 and, for a more sceptical view, Huehnergard 1999.

[c] According to Charpin and Durand 1986, "Haneans" is the common designation of the (semi-)nomadic tribes on both sides of the Euphrates: the Yaminites and the Simʾalites. Cf. also Anbar 1991: 80–88; Fleming 1998: 54–56.

[d] Cf. no. 36 (ARM 26 229), note c.

## 27. Itur-Asdu to Zimri-Lim

**Text:** ARM 26 217 (= M. 8071).
**Photograph:** Durand 1988 (microfiche).
**Transliteration and translation:** Durand 1988: 445–46.
**Translation:** Durand 1994: 72.
**Discussion:** Parker 1993: 64; J. M. Sasson 1994: 314; Barstad 2001: 61; Charpin 2001: 31; 2002: 15.

[ten lines from beginning destroyed]
[11][*i*]*na lib*[*b*]*i bītīya* . . . [. . .] [12]*iddinamma daltu š*[*a* . . .]*-mi an*[*a ṣērīya*] [13]*šupur* [. . .] . . .
[14]*ištu ṣuḫrīka u*[*k*]*ānakkama* [15]*u ēm šalmātim attanabbalka* [16]*u irištī īriškama* [17]*ul tanaddinam* [18][*in*]*anna ana Naḫur* [19][*šūl*]*êmma irištī* [20][*ša aqb*]*ikkumma idnašši* [21][*ša išt*]*u pānānum ana qā*[*t* [22]*abbēka*] *ašruku* [23][*inanna an*]*a kâšum aša*[*rrak*] [24][*nakrum ša*] *ibaššû*

[beginning destroyed][a]

[11]"[. . .] inside my temple [. . .] he gave. The door of [. . .] send t[o me]. [. . .]

[14]Since your childhood I have taken care of you, I am constantly taking you where there is safety. However, if I desire something from you, you do not give it to me. Now [se]nd an ex-voto to Naḫur and give me [what I requ]ested from you! [For what] I have bestowed on

*25[šapa]l šēpīka ukamma[r] 26[māt]ka ana nuḫšim u ḫega[ll]im 27[utā]r*

[your fathers] in the past, I will [now] bes[tow o]n you. [Whatever enemies] there may be, I will pile them up [unde]r your feet. [I will retu]rn your [land] to prosperity and abundance."

*sinništum šī annêtim idbubamma 28[aw]āt pīša ana bēlīya ašpuram 29anumma sārassa u sissiktaša 30ana bēlīya ušābilam bēlī têrētim 31lišēpišma ana kī ilu bēlī ippalu lī[p]uš*

27This is what this woman said, and I have written her [wor]ds to my lord. I have herewith sent her hair and a fringe of her garment to my lord. My lord should let oracles be taken. Let my lord act according to what the god answers.

*32šanītam aššum êm ana bēlīya aštanapparamma 33ûm ul ublūnim anumma inanna 34Yapṭur ištu Sārim adi Buš*ʾ*ān 35ibb[a]lkit nikūrtašunu uweddû 36u [n]aṣrum uṣṣêmma 37[kīam idb]ubam ummā-mi [šūma] 38[itti erbet l]īmi ḫamšat līmi ṣābim [...] 39[ana Naḫu]r nisanni[q] 40[... -š]unu ana Naḫu[r]*

32Another matter, concerning the grain about which I have been writing to my lord: The grain has not been brought to me. Now Yapṭur has rebelled from Sarum[b] to Bušʾan, making their hostility plain. A man secretly[3] came to me [and to]ld me: [With four th]ousand or five thousand men [...] we approached [Naḫu]r [...]

[rest destroyed]
s.1[... *u]šēṣi*

[rest destroyed]
s. 1[... I/he] brought out.

[a] The author of this letter has been identified by Michaël Guichard as Itur-Asdu on the basis of the handwriting (see Charpin 2002: 12 n. 51). Earlier suggestions include Baṣṣum, an official in Ida-maraṣ (Durand 1988: 446), and Šaknum, an officer functioning in Naḫur (J. M. Sasson 1994: 314).

2. Identified with Wadi Sarum, east of Ida-maraṣ.

3. For the word *naṣrum,* see Charpin 1988: 133 ad ARM 26 357:7.

## 28. NN to Zimri-Lim

**Text:** ARM 26 218 (= M. 14836).
**Photograph:** Durand 1988 (microfiche).
**Transliteration and translation:** Durand 1988: 446–47.
**Translation:** Durand 1994: 72–73.

*[ana bēlīya 2qibīma 3umma ... 4waradkāma]*

[Speak to my lord: Thus NN, your servant:]

[5]*[ina pānītim ... iqb]i* [6]*[ummāmi Zimrī-Lim]* [7]*ḫumūsam in[a ... liḫmis]* [8]*u šumšu ana dārīti[m] uš[zaz] u* [9]*nīqu ša ḫumūsi[m]* [10]*šêtu ul naqi u bēlī kīam* [11]*iqbêm ummāmi ina Māri* [12]*saparram lušābilakkum* [13]*ina ḫumūsim šêtu šukun*

[[5]Before, *the god DN* spo]ke [as follows: "Let Zimri-Lim erect][a] a commemorative monument[b] in [...], and I will es[tablish] his name for ev[er]." However, the sacrifice for this commemorative monument has not been offered, and my lord has said to me as follows: "In Mari I shall deliver to you a *saparrum*.[c] Place it in this commemorative monument!"

[14]*[ina]nna bēlī Māri ik[šud]* [15]*[sapa]rram ul ušāb[ilam]*

[14][No]w, my lord has ar[rived] in Mari, but has not deliv[ered] the *saparrum*.

[break]

[r.1']*[... b]ēlī ša šarrūtīšu [līpuš]*

[r.1'][Let] my [lo]rd [act] according to his kingship [...]

[rest destroyed]

[a] Reconstruction according to Durand 1988: 447.
[b] For *ḫumūsum,* see Durand 1995: 297–98; Durand and Guichard 1997: 33.
[c] A word of unknown meaning; Durand 1988: 447 gives "chariot" as the best, but not the only possible alternative.

## 29. NN to Zimri-Lim

**Text:** ARM 26 219 (= M. 13496 + M. 15299).
**Photograph:** Durand 1988 (microfiche).
**Transliteration and translation:** Durand 1988, 447–48.
**Translation:** Durand 1994: 60–61; Nissinen 2003: 9–10.

[beginning destroyed]

[1']*akkīma sebe mêtim ṣāb[am ...]* [2']*u ālum kal[ûša an]a [b]ēlīya i[krub]* [3']*u damiqt[i bēlī]ya iq[bi]*

[1']... as seven hundred sold[iers...]. The who[le] city has p[rayed for] my [l]ord and spo[ken] in favo[r of] my [lord].

[4']*šanītam ūm nī[qe in]a bīt [N]inḫur[sagga]* [5']*āpilum š[a Nin]ḫursagga it[bīma]* [6']*kīam idbu[b um]māmi šū[ma]* [7']*ištiššu šinīšu u šalāšī[šu] pān Zim[rī-Lim]* [8']*ēristī ē[ri]šma u [m]i[mma]* [9']*ul iddin[am ...*

[4']Another matter: On the day of the sacri[fice i]n the temple of [N]inḫur[sag], a prophet o[f Nin]ḫursag ar[ose] and spo[ke] as follows: "Once, twice, even three [times] have I ex[pr]essed my request

10' *u]mma anāku[ma* ...

before Zim[ri-Lim], but he did not give [me any]th[ing ...] I said [...] [break]

[lines 11'–16' destroyed or unintelligible]
17' *u šanītam [itbīma* ...] 18' MUNUS.TE.BAR *ša* MU *lā* [...] 19' *tammaram šan[ītam* ...] 20' *damqam ša šumka [šaṭram]* 21' *šūbilam*

17' Another matter: [He arose] a ...[a] that did not [...] you find.

19' More[over], deliver to me a good [... inscribed] under your name."

*annêtim ā[pilum]* 22' *idbub u anumma š[ārtam u sissiktam]* 23' *ša āpilim ana bēlīya u[šābilam]* 24' *bēlī ša epēšīšu līpu[š* ...]

21' This is what the pr[ophet] said. I have now s[ent] the h[air and a fringe of the garment] of the prophet to my lord. My lord may do what he deems best.[b]

25' *[u šanīta]m Ṣūra-ḫammu* [...] 26' [... *išt]anappa[r* ...]
[rest destroyed]

25' [Moreov]er, Ṣura-ḫammu [...] keeps sending [...]
[rest destroyed]

[a] The ideogram suggests a female animal.
[b] Lit. "do his deed."

### 30. Kibri-Dagan to Zimri-Lim

**Text:** ARM 26 220 (= A. 4865 = ARM 2 90).
**Copy:** Jean 1941: pl. 108–9.
**Transliteration and translation:** Jean 1945: 162–65; von Soden 1950: 399–400; Schmökel 1951: 55; Ellermeier 1968: 28–31; Durand 1988: 448–49.
**Translation:** Malamat 1956: 76–77; Huffmon 1968: 116; Moran 1969b: 624 (lines 13–25); Durand 1994: 52; 2000: 123 (no. 978).
**Discussion:** Kupper 1957: 64; Ellermeier 1968: 134; Schmitt 1982: 88–91; Durand 1995: 356.

*ana bēlīya* 2 *qibīma* 3 *umma Kibrī-Dagan* 4 *waradkāma*
5 *Dagan u Ikrub-El šalmū* 6 *ālum Terqa u ḫalṣum [š]alim*

Speak to my lord: Thus Kibri-Dagan, your servant:

5 Dagan and Ikrub-El[a] are well, the city of Terqa as well as the district is [s]afe.

7 *šanītam <ina> aḫarātim immerū nawûm* 8 *[ša mār]ē [Y]amīna ana kišādi Puratti* 9 *[urdānim]ma itti immerī nawêm* 10 *[ša Ḫanāyāni] rîtam ikkala* 11 *[mimma ḫiṭī]tum ul*

7 Another matter: On the West Bank[b] the flocks [of the Y]aminites [have come down[c]] to the bank of the Euphrates and are pasturing with the flocks of the clans [of the

*ibašši* [12]*[libbi bēlīya l]ā ina*ʾʾ*id*

Haneans[d]]. Nothing is [out of pla]ce, [my lord has no]thing to worry about.

[13]*[ūm ṭuppi an]nêm* [14]*[ana ṣēr] bēlīya* [15]*[ušābilam* [16]*muḫḫû]m* [17]*[š]a Dagan aw[ātam kīam iqbi]* [18]*um-māmi aššum nīqe [pagrāʾi]* [19]*epēšim Dagan išpu[ranni]* [20]*ana bēlīka šupurma* [21]*warḫum ēribam ina* UD.14.KAM [22]*nīqu pagrāʾi linnēpiš* [23]*mimma nīqu šêtu lā ušetteqū*

[13][When I sent th]is [tablet to] my lord, [a prophe]t of Dagan [spoke the following] wo[rds]: "Dagan has sen[t me] to deliver a message concerning the execution of the [*pagrāʾum*] offerings:[e] 'Send to your lord the following message: The new month has now begun, and on the fourteenth day, the *pagrāʾum* offerings should be executed. Not a single offering may be neglected.'"

[24]*annītam awīlum šū iqbêm* [25]*inanna anumma ana bēlīya* [26]*aštapram bēlī ana kīma* [27]*muštālūtīšu* [28]*ša elīšu ṭābat līpuš*

[24]This is what the man spoke to me. Now I have communicated it to my lord. Let my lord do what he deems appropriate according to his own deliberation.

[a] Possibly a manifestation of the god Adad.
[b] In the Akkadian of Mari, *aḫarātum* means the west bank of Euphrates.
[c] Thus according to the restoration of Durand 2000: 123.
[d] Thus according to the conjecture of Durand 1988: 448–89, who considers "the Simʾalites" another possibility.
[e] For these offerings, see no. 38, note h.

## 31. Kibri-Dagan to Zimri-Lim

**Text:** ARM 26 221 (= A. 2030 = ARM 3 40).
**Copy:** Kupper 1948: pl. 44.
**Transliteration and translation:** Kupper 1945: 64–65; von Soden 1950: 399; Schmökel 1951: 54; Malamat 1956: 75–76; Ellermeier 1968: 32–34; Durand 1988: 449–50.
**Translation:** Huffmon 1968: 113; Moran 1969b: 624 (lines 7–23); J. M. Sasson 1984a: 118; Dietrich 1986: 87–88; Sicre 1992: 242; Durand 1994: 51–52; 2000: 89–90 (no. 941).
**Discussion:** Ellermeier 1968: 135; Craghan 1974: 47; 1975: 35; Huffmon 1976b: 699; Schmitt 1982: 91–92; Durand 1995: 339, 355–56; Pongratz-Leisten 1999: 65; Charpin 2001: 29; 2002: 12.

*[ana] bēlīya* [2]*[q]ibīma* [3]*umma Kibrī-Dagan* [4]*waradkāma*

[S]peak [to] my lord: Thus Kibri-Dagan, your servant:

5 *[D]agan u Ikrub-El [š]almū* 6 *ālum Te[rq]a u ḫalṣu<m> [š]alim*

5[D]agan and Yakrub-El are [w]ell, the city of Te[rq]a as well as the district is [s]afe.

7 *šanītam ūm ṭuppi annêm* 8 *ana [ṣ]ēr bēlīya u[š]ā[b]ilam* 9 *[m]uḫḫûm ša [D]agan* 10 *illi[ka]mma* 11 *awātam kīam [i]qbê[m]* 12 *ummāmi* 13 *ilum išpuranni* 14 *ḫumuṭ ana šarri* 15 *šupurma* 16 *kispī ana eṭemm[im]* 17 *ša Yaḫdun-Lim* 18 *likrubū*
19 *annītam muḫḫûm šū* 20 *iqbêm ana bēlīya* 21 *aštapram* 22 *bēlī [š]a el[ī]šu ṭābat* 23 *līpuš*

7Another matter: When I sent this tablet to my lord, a [p]rophet of [D]agan ca[m]e and [s]poke to [me]: "The god has sent me, saying: 'Hurry up and deliver a message to the king that a *kispum* offering[a] be performed for the spirit of Yaḫdun-Lim!'"

19This is what the prophet spoke to me and I have herewith communicated it to my lord. Let my lord do what he deems appropriate.

[a] This offering, for which see, e.g., J. M. Sasson 1979: 126–28; Birot 1980; Tsukimoto 1985; Charpin and Durand 1986: 163–70; Schmidt 1994: 28–39; Durand and Guichard 1997: 28, 63–70 and Jacquet 2002, is comparable to, though not identical with, the *pagrāʾum* offering in other letters (see no. 38, note h). In this instance, the *kispum* is dedicated to the late Yaḫdun-Lim, the royal father of Zimri-Lim.

## 32. Kibri-Dagan to Zimri-Lim

**Text:** ARM 26 221bis (= A. 4934 = ARM 3 78).
**Copy:** Kupper 1948: pl. 73–74.
**Transliteration and translation:** Kupper 1945: 100–103; von Soden 1950: 399; Malamat 1956: 78–79; Ellermeier 1968: 34–37; Durand 1988: 450–51.
**Translation:** Huffmon 1968: 113; Moran 1969b: 624 (lines 7–30); Sicre 1992: 243 (lines 10–28); Durand 1994: 73; 2000: 90–91 (no. 942).
**Discussion:** Ellermeier 1968: 135–36; Parker 1993: 55–56; Durand 1995: 342–43; Huffmon 2000: 53.

*[ana] b[ēl]īya* 2 *[qi]bīma* 3 *[umma] Kibrī-Dagan* 4 *[warad]kāma*
5 *[D]agan u Ikrub-El šalmū* 6 *[āl]um Terqa u ḫalṣum šalim*

[Sp]eak [to] my l[ord]: [Thus] Kibri-Dagan, your [servant]:

5[D]agan and Yakrub-El are well, the [ci]ty of Terqa as well as the district is safe.

7 *ana êm ša ḫalṣīya eṣēdim* 8 *[u] ana maškanātim nasākim* 9 *[aḫa]m ul nadêku*
10 *[šanītam] aššum abullim eššetim* 11 *[epēš]im ina pānītim* 12 *[. . .]*

7I am not [id]le[a] about the harvest of the wheat of the district [and] its threshing on the threshing floors.

10[Another matter], concerning the [build]ing of a new city gate, *muḫḫûm* [13]*[illika]mma* [14]*[itašš]aš* [15]*[umma šū]ma* [16]*[ana šipir ab]ullim šāti* [17]*[qātka šuk]un*

the prophet [NN cam]e to me some time ago [full of an]xiety,[b] [sayin]g: "[You[c] shall be]gin [the building of] this [city ga]te!"

[18]*[inanna ūm] ṭuppi annêm* [19]*[ana ṣē]r bēlīya ušā[b]ilam* [20]*[muḫ]ḫûm šū itūramma* [21]*[kīam] iqbêm* [22]*[u da]nnātim iškunam ummāmi* [23]*[šumma] abullam šâti* [24]*ul teppešā* [25]*[kur]ullum iššakkan* [26]*[u] kašdātunu*

[18][When] I sent this tablet [to] my lord, this [pro]phet once more spoke to me [and] gave me [str]ict orders as follows: "[If] you[d] do not build this city gate, there will be a [dis]aster[e] and you will [n]ot succeed."

[27]*[annī]tam muḫḫûm šū* [28]*[iqb]êm u ana eb[ū]r[im* [29]*pul]lusāku suḫḫu[r]* [30]*[wa]rdīya ul elê[m]* [31]*[šumma] bēlī iqabbi* [32]*[neḫrārum lill]ikam[m]a*

[rest destroyed]

[27][Th]is is what the prophet [sp]oke to me. I am now [in]volved in the harv[est] and cannot[f] dive[rt] my [ser]vants. [If] my lord could give an order for [help to co]me here...

[rest destroyed]

[a] The expression *aḫam nadûm* (lit. "let the arm hang down") means "to be idle, remiss"; see *AHw* 706 (sub *nadû* 12a).

[b] Thus according to Durand 1988: 451, who interprets the broken word as a form of *ašāšum* "to be worried"; cf. ARM 26 350:18. The restored Gt form is otherwise attested only in Old Assyrian.

[c] The remaining signs of the imperative verbal form indicate a 2.p.sg. form.

[d] Here the verbal forms are in plural; thus the prophet is described as addressing a larger audience (Parker 1993: 55 n. 19).

[e] For this meaning of *kurullum,* see *CAD* K 573 ("calamity, catastrophe"); cf. the translation "dead bodies" (Durand 1988: 451, 561). Cf. also ARM 26 259:11; 263:12.

[f] Thus Durand 1988: 451, who interprets the partially broken verb as *le'ûm* "to be able."

## 33. Ušareš-hetil to Dariš-libur

**Text:** ARM 26 222 (= ARM 10 106 = A. 3724).
**Copy:** Dossin 1967: pl. 48.
**Transliteration and translation:** Dossin 1978: 158–61; Durand 1988: 451–52.
**Translation:** Durand 1994: 73; 2000: 425–26 (no. 1220); Huffmon 1997: 10–11; Malamat 1998: 122–23.
**Discussion:** Dossin 1978: 272; Durand 1995: 353; Huffmon 1997: 10–11; Malamat 1998: 122–24; Charpin 2002: 27.

*ana Dāriš-lībūr* [2]*qibīma* [3]*umma Ušareš-ḫetil* [4]*[mār]kāma*

Speak to Dariš-libur: Thus Ušareš-ḫetil, your [son]:

5*[aššum ṣebertim š]a bēltim* 6*[imma-ḫ]êm* 7*[mārat b]ēlīya* 8*[ul ibluṭ* 9*inanna i]mtū[t* 10UD].4/6.KAM *wal-dat* 11[. . .]

5[Concerning the daughter o]f the queen, [he[a] went into tran]ce. [The daughter of] my [l]ord [did not survive; now she] is de[ad]. She was born on the fourth/sixth[b] day [. . .]

12*[ūmīšum]a Irra-gamil* 13*[imma]ḫêm* 14*[umma š]ūma* 15*[ul iball]uṭ*

12[On that same day] Irra-gamil [went into tr]ance. [This is what] he said: "[She will not li]ve."

16*[lāma ša]rrum ana Māri* 17*[i]kaš-šadam* 18*kīma mārtum šī mītat* 19*qibišumma lū ide* 20*[a]ssurri ana Māri* 21*ina erēbīšu* 22*mūt mārtim šāti šarrum* 23*išemmēma* 24*iṣabba[t]* 25*ītaš-šušša[m]*

16[Before the ki]ng enters Mari, tell him that this daughter is dead—he should know it. Otherwise, if the king hears about the death of that girl upon entering Mari, he will become grief-stricken.

[a] I.e., Irra-gamil, the prophet, also known from administrative documents ARM 21 333 (no. 55) and ARM 23 446 (no. 59), as well as from the report M. 9717 (no. 65).
[b] The cuneiform sign is either 4 or 6 (Durand 1988: 451).

## 34. La'ûm (?) to Yasmaḫ-Addu (?)

**Text:** ARM 26 223 (= M. 9601).
**Photograph:** Durand 1988 (microfiche); Charpin 2002: 37.
**Transliteration:** Durand 1988, 452.
**Transliteration and translation:** Charpin 2002: 36-37.

[beginning destroyed]
1'*ina* [. . .] 2'*ina pānītimma* [. . .]
3'*ištēn maturru ina ḫal[āṣ* . . .] 4'*u ištēn maturru ina T[uttul* . . .]
5'*u āpilum šū ill[ikam kīam iqbêm]*
6'*ummāmi ana elep[pī* . . .] 7'*qirsê* . . . [. . .]
8'*annītam iqb[êm* . . .] 9'*enūtam mal īri[šanni addin]* 10'*têrētim ša mā[t* . . .] 11'*ul* [. . .]

[break of at least three lines, one unreadable line]
2''*inanna a[nnumma]* 3''*ša āpilum an[a Bīnim iqbû]* 4''*ummāmi*

[beginning destroyed]
. . . in [. . .] before [. . .]
3'One small ship in the dist[rict of . . .] and one small ship in T[uttul. . .]
5'This prophet ca[me and said] as follows: "For the shi[ps. . .] the *qirsus*[a] of [. . .]
8'This is what he spo[ke. . .]. [I shall give him] all the equipment he des[ires from me]. Oracles of the lan[d. . .] not [. . .]' "
[break]

2''Now, since the prophet [has spoken] to [Binum[b]]: "Thus says

*Dag[an ammīnim eleppū]* [5"]*lā illakā[ma]* [6"]*ana kirî ša bīt* [...] [7"]*asuḫī rabā[tim* ...] [8"]*u naḫlaptu* [...] [9"]*ana* ... [...]

Dag[an: 'Why are the ships] not on their way? For the garden of the temple of [DN...] the gre[at] *asuḫu* trees [...] and the garment [...] to [...]"

[10"]*annīta[m āpilum iqbi]*

[10"]This is [what the prophet said]

[a] The word cannot be translated with certainty; the determinative GIŠ designates a wooden object, e.g., in this case, the mast of a ship.

[b] Binum is the recipient of prophetic words in the letter of La'ûm A. 3760 (no. 3). This restoration assumes that this letter belongs together with the present one as suggested by the common subject matters ship and temple (Charpin 2002: 38).

## 35. Addu-duri to Zimri-Lim

**Text:** ARM 26 227 (= M. 9576).
**Photograph:** Durand 1988 (microfiche).
**Transliteration and translation:** Durand 1988: 467.
**Translation:** Durand 1994: 52; Huffmon 1997: 15.
**Discussion:** Huffmon 1997: 15–16.

*[ana bēlīya* [2]*qibīma* [3]*umma] Addu-dūrīma*

[4]*[... b]ilā'u šuttam* [5]*[iṭṭ]ulma umma šīma* [6]*[ina šu]ttīya* [7]*[Ḫa]dnu-El* [8]*[u] Iddin-kūbi* [9]*[m]uḫḫû* [10]*i[b]l[uṭ]ūnimma* [11]*ana [l]ēt Abba* [12]*īrubūma* [13]*kīam iqbū* [14]*umma šunūma* [15]*ana kūbīkina* [16]*qibêma* [17]*ebūr šulmim* [18]*Zimrī-Lim* [19]*līpuš* [20]*[Z]im[rī-L]im* [...]

[rest destroyed]

[Speak to my lord: Thus] Addu-duri:

[4][(The woman) ...-b]ila'u has [had] a dream. This is what she said: "[In my dr]eam the [p]rophets [Ḫa]dnu-El [and] Iddin-Kubi were a[li]ve.[a] They went in before the cows[b] of Abba[c] and said: 'Speak[d] to your still-born calves,[e] and let Zimri-Lim make a harvest of well-being. [Z]im[ri-L]im [...]'"

[rest destroyed]

[a] Obviously, then, the *muḫḫûms* were dead by the time the dream was seen.

[b] Interpreting *lētu* as "cow" (= *lītu*). Durand 1988: 467 takes *ana lēt* as a prepositional expression (< *lētu* "side").

[c] For this god, see Nakata 1974: 11–14.

[d] The verb is a feminine imperative; thus the miscarried cows are addressed. The fetuses are used as omens for good harvest (J. M. Sasson, private communication).

[e] For *kūbum*, see *AHw* 498.

## 36. Report of Ayala

**Text:** ARM 26 229 (= A. 222).
**Photograph:** Durand 1988 (microfiche).
**Copy:** Dossin 1975: 28.
**Transliteration and translation:** Dossin 1975: 29–30; Durand 1988, 468–69.
**Translation:** J. M. Sasson 1983: 291 (lines 4–13); Durand 1994: 50; 2000: 78–79 (no. 932); Malamat 1998: 77.
**Discussion:** J. M. Sasson 1983: 291; Malamat 1987: 46–47; 1998: 77–78; Durand 1995: 343–44; 1997b: 273; Pongratz-Leisten 1999: 104.

*Ayala* [2]*ina šuttīša* [3]*kīam iṭṭul*

Ayala,[a] in her dream, saw the following:

[4]*ummāmi ištēn awīltum Šeḫrītum* [5]*ištēn awīltum Mārītum* [6]*[in]a bāb Annunītim* [7]*ša kawātim* [8]*iṣṣillā* [9]*umma awīltum Šeḫrītum* [10]*ana awīltim Mā[r]ītim* [11]*enūti terrêm* [12]*ūlū atti šibi* [13]*ūlūma anāku lūšib*

[4]A woman from Šeḫrum[b] and a woman from Mari had a quarrel a[t] the gate of Annunitum-beyond-the-walls.[c] The woman from Šeḫrum said to the woman from Mari: "Give me back my business![d] Either you sit down or I will be the one who will sit down!"

[14]*ina iṣṣurē ḫurrim* [15]*warkassa aprusma* [16]*naṭlat* [17]*anumma šārassa* [18]*u sissiqta[š]a* [19]*ušābilam* [20]*bēlī warkassa* [21]*liprus*

[14]By means of bird divination[e] I inquired about her, and the dream was really seen. Now I send her hair and a fringe of h[er] garment. Let my lord inquire about her.

[a] An otherwise unknown woman. The author and the addressee of the report are anonymous; according to the observation of Dossin, the orthography of the tablet dates it to the Yaḫdun-Lim period.

[b] A locality close to the city of Mari; see Wilcke 1979: 48.

[c] This probably refers to the temple of Annunitum other than the one in the city proper referred to in ARM 26 214 (no. 24): 5; cf. J. M. Sasson 1983: 291 n. 41; Durand 1987b, 91.

[d] Or "utensils" (cf. Durand 1988: 469; J. M. Sasson 1983: 291 n. 42), rather than "the position as high priestess" (Dossin 1975: 28; Malamat 1987: 46; 1998: 77).

[e] For *iṣṣur ḫurrim,* see Durand 1988: 38; 1997b.

## 37. Zunana to Zimri-Lim

**Text:** ARM 26 232 (= A. 907 = ARM 10 100).
**Copy:** Dossin 1967: pl. 45.
**Transliteration and translation:** Finet in Dossin 1978: 150–53, 271; Ellermeier 1968: 72–75; Moran 1969a: 54; Römer 1971: 62–63; Durand 1988, 471–72.
**Translation:** Moran 1969b: 631; Durand 2000: 494–95 (no. 1262).
**Discussion:** Ellermeier 1968: 150; Moran 1969a: 54–56; Craghan 1975, 37; J. M. Sasson 1983, 292; Durand 1995: 337; Malamat 1998, 63–64; Butler 1998: 219–20.

*ana bēlīya [2]qibīma [3]umma Zunāna amatkāma*

Speak to my lord: Thus Zunana,[a] your servant:

*[4]inūma ina Ganibātim ušbu [5]Kittum-šimḫīya ana Rubbên ašpurma [6]ina alākīša itbalūši [7]u D[aga]n bēlka uṣall[i]lamma [8]mamman ul ilputanni [9][D]agan kīam iqbêm umma šū[m]a*

[4]When I was still living in Ganibatum, I sent Kittum-šimḫiya to Rubbân. On her way, she was kidnapped. D[aga]n, your lord, appeared to me in a dream,[b] even though nobody had performed an incubation ritual[c] on me. Dagan spoke to me:

*[10]pānūki eliš šap[l]iš [11]umma anākūma šapli[š]ma [12]allikamma [13]amtī ul āmur [14]inūma ana Andarig [15]bēlī illiku [16]zimzimmu ša amtīya [17]itti Sammētar [18]īlêmma [19]allikšumma annam īpula[nni] [20]itūrma ibbalkitannima [21]amtī ul [i]ddinam*

[10]"Are you heading up or down?"[d] I answered: "Down! I went there but could not find my servant girl. When my lord had gone to Andarig, rumors[e] concerning my servant girl came to me through Sammetar. I went to look for him and he answered me, 'Yes!'[f] But then he changed his mind and took back his words, and he did not give me my servant girl."

*[22]Dagan kīam iqbêm umma šūma [23]adi itti Zimrī-Lim amtaki [24]lā ušeṣṣêm mamman [25]ul u[w]aššarā[ki]š*

[22]Dagan answered me with the following words: "Until Zimri-Lim gets involved, he will not bring out your servant girl, and no one will release her to you."

*[26]inanna kīma qibīt Dagan [27]amtī bēlī lā ikalla*

[26]Now, according to the order of Dagan, my lord should not withhold my servant.

[a] An otherwise unknown woman, whose name was previously read as Yanana; the present reading is due to the collation of Durand 1988: 461 n. 38; 471.

[b] Deriving *ṣullulum* from *ṣalālum* "to lie down, to sleep" (Durand 1988: 472). Moran 1969a: 54 n. 3 takes the word as a denominative of *ṣillum* "shade, protection."

[c] For this ritual (*liptum*), see Durand 1988: 461.

[d] Lit. "Is your face up or down?" This rather means direction of motion (so J. M. Sasson, private communication) than the mood ("are you happy or sad?"; thus Durand 1988: 471) of Zunana.

[e] For this meaning of *zimzimmum,* see Durand 2000: 493-94. This interpretation is due to thed use of the word in an unpublished letter A. 630: 20 and replaces his earlier suggestion "shallot" (1988: 472).

[f] The answer of Sammetar probably confirms that the rumors had come from him.

### 38. Itur-Asdu to Zimri-Lim

**Text:** ARM 26 233 (= A. 15).
**Photograph:** Durand 1988 (microfiche).
**Copy:** Dossin 1948: 128, 130.
**Transliteration and translation:** Dossin 1948: 129, 131; von Soden 1950: 398–99; Schmökel 1951: 53; Ellermeier 1968: 24–29, Durand 1988: 473–47.
**Translation:** Oppenheim 1956: 195; Malamat 1956: 81–83; Huffmon 1968: 117; Moran 1969b: 623; Dietrich 1986: 91–92; Durand 1994: 55–56; 2000: 78–83 (no. 933); van der Toorn 1998b: 58 (lines 9–39).
**Discussion:** Dossin 1948; Malamat 1956; Westermann 1960: 84–87; Nötscher 1966: 180; Ellermeier 1968: 133–34, 197–200; Ross 1970: 17; Heintz 1969: 125, 129–30; 1971a: 544–45; Craghan 1974: 43, 45, 51; 1975: 49; Schmitt 1982: 16–23; J. M. Sasson 1983: 290–91; Bodi 1991: 177–78; Gordon 1993: 73; Durand 1995: 317, 338–39, 345; van der Toorn 1998b: 58; 2000: 81; Nissinen 2000a: 255; 2003: 25–26; Pongratz-Leisten 1999: 104–5, 110–11, 205–7; Barstad 2001: 57.

*ana bēlīya* [2]*qibīma* [3]*umma Itūr-Asdū* [4]*waradkāma*

[5]*ūm ṭuppi annêm ana* [*ṣ*]*ēr* [6]*bēlīya ušābilam* [7]*Malik-Dagan awīl Šakkâ* [8]*il*<*li*>*kamma kīam iqbêm* [9]*ummāmi*

*ina šuttīya anāku u ištēn awīlum ittīya* [10][*iš*]*tu ḫalaṣ Saggarātim* [11]*ina ḫalṣim elîm ana Māri ana alākim* [12]*pānūya šaknū* [13]*ina pānīya ana Terqa ērumma kīma erēbīyama*

Speak to my lord: Thus Itur-Asdu, your servant:

[5]When I sent this tablet to my lord, Malik-Dagan, a man from Šakkâ came to me and spoke to me as follows:

[9]"In my dream I, as well as another man with me, was planning a travel [fr]om the district of Saggaratum, through the upper district,[a] to Mari. [13]Before (reaching

*[14]ana bīt Dagan ērumma ana Dagan [15]uškên ina šukênīya [16]Dagan pîšu iptēma kīam iqbêm [17]ummāmi*

Mari)[b] I entered Terqa. Having entered (the city), I went into the temple of Dagan and prostrated myself before Dagan. During my prostration, Dagan opened his mouth and spoke to me thus:

*šarrānu ša mārē Yamīna [18]u ṣābūšunu [19]itti ṣābim ša Zimrī-Lim [20]ša īlêm [21][i]slimū [22][u]mma anākū<ma> ul islimū [23]ina pāni waṣîya kīam iqbêm [24]ummāmi mārē šipri [25]ša Zimrī-Lim [26]kayyāniš maḫrīya ana m[ī]nim [l]ā wašbūma [27]u ṭēmšu gamram maḫrīya ammīnim [28]lā išakkan [29]ullāman ištu ūmi mādūtim [30]šarrānu ša mārē [Ya]m[ī]na [31]ana qāt Zimrī-Lim umtallišunūti [32]inanna alik aštaparka [33]ana Zimrī-Lim kīam taqabbi umma attāma [34]mārē šiprīka ana ṣērīya [35]šu[pr]a[mm]a u ṭēmka gamram [36]ma[ḫrī]ya [š]ukunma [37]u šarrā[ni ša mār]ē Yamīna ina sussul [38]bāʾer[im luša]pšilšunūtīma [39]maḫrīka [lušk]unšunūti*

[17]'Have the kings of the Yaminites[c] and their troops made peace with the troop of Zimri-Lim who has gone up there?'[d] I answered: 'No, they have not made peace.' [23]Before I left, he spoke to me as follows: 'Why do the messengers of Zimri-Lim not stay before me regularly, and why does he not provide me with a full account[e] of his undertakings? Had it been otherwise, I would have delivered the kings of the [Ya]minites into the hands of Zimri-Lim a long time ago! [32]Now go, I have sent you to speak to Zimri-Lim as follows: S[en]d your messengers to me and provide me with a full account of your undertakings, and I [will make] the king[s of the] Yaminites flounder[f] in a fisherman's chest[g] and [pl]ace them before you.' "

*[40]annītam awīlum šū [in]a šuttīšu iṭṭulma [41]u a[yyâ]šim idbūbam [42]inanna anumma ana ṣēr bēlīya aštapram [43]warkat šutti<m> annītim bēlī [44]liprus [45]šanītam šumma libbi bēlīya [46]bēlī ṭēmšu gamram [47]pān Dagan liškun [48]u mārē šipri ša bēlīya [49]ana ṣēr Dagan lū kayyānu*

[40]This is what the man saw in his dream and what he told me. I have now written to my lord. Let my lord check on this dream. [45]Further, if it pleases my lord, let my lord provide Dagan with a full account of his undertakings. Let the messengers of my lord come regularly before Dagan.

*[50]awīlum ša šuttam annītam [51][iqb]êm pagram ana Dagan [52]inaddinma ul aṭrudaššu [53]u aššum awīlum šū taklu šārassu u sissi<k>tašu [54]ul elqi*

[50]The man who to[ld] me this dream will bring a *pagrum* offering[h] for Dagan. I have not sent him. Moreover, since this man is reliable,[i] I have not taken his hair and a fringe of his garment.

[a] The expression *ḫalṣum elûm* designates an area upstream from Mari. It may mean the city of Saggaratum itself, situated on the lower course of the river Ḫabur (thus Dietrich 1986: 91), but, since it would hardly be necessary to explain the location of Saggaratum to the recipient of the letter, it more likely refers generally to the area on the way from Saggaratum to Terqa; cf. van der Toorn 1998b: 58 and the translation of Durand 1988: 474: "venant du district de Saggarâtum, (et me trouvant) dans le district d'amont."

[b] *ina pānīya* is an idiom for "before my doing something" (Durand 1988: 474–75); thus, it is not necessary to interpret it as a West Semitism, as Malamat 1956: 81 and Moran 1969b: 623 have done. Their translation "on my way", however, renders essentially the same idea.

[c] For "Yaminites" and "Simʾalites," see Charpin and Durand 1986; Anbar 1991: 80–88; Fleming 1998: 54–56. For the reading of DUMU as *mārū Yamīna,* instead of the Hebraistic *binî Yamīna* (hence "Benjaminites"), see Weippert 1967: 110–12; however, Fleming 1998: 60–62 is in favor of the reading *binî Yamīna*. For the leaders ("kings") of the Yaminites, see Anbar 1991: 120–23.

[d] I.e., in the upper district, upstream from Mari. The Yaminites lived in the area toward the west and southwest from Mari and seem to be encountering with the troops of Zimri-Lim in that area.

[e] *ṭēmum gamrum* is a written report that is compared with the so-called "letters to gods," in which the kings give account of their military activities and which are placed (*šakānum*) before the gods in the temple. In this case, however, it is clearly to be understood as an interim report, because the conflict with the Yaminites is still unresolved; see Pongratz-Leisten 1999: 204–7.

[f] Thus according to von Soden 1950: 398 (cf. *AHw* 841b sub *pašālu*), followed, among others, by Ellermeier 1968: 26; Heintz 1971a: 544; Durand 1988: 473, 475. The alternative reading *[luša]bšilšunūtīma* "[I will have] them cooked," suggested by Malamat 1956: 83, derived from *bašālu* "cook", is followed, among others, by Moran 1969b: 623.

[g] For *sussullum* "box, chest" see *AHw* 1063; *CAD* S 418; Heintz 1969: 133 n. 1; Salonen 1970: 79.

[h] This offering belongs to the *pagrāʾum* ritual, probably associated with the cult of the dead, for which see J. M. Sasson 1979: 131; Durand 1982a: 160 n. 20; Birot 1993: 156; Schmidt 1994: 28–39; Durand and Guichard 1997: 35–36, and cf. the *pgr* offering in Ugarit (see Dietrich and Loretz 1980; Bordreuil and Pardee 1993b: 25–28).

[i] Reading *ták-lu,* as first suggested by Oppenheim 1952: 131 and followed a.o. by Malamat 1956: 83; 1998: 100 n. 40; Moran 1969b: 623; Durand 1988: 474, 476. The reading *kal-lu* of Dossin 1948: 131 is preferred by Ellermeier 1968: 29, who translates "Schnellbote" (cf. *AHw* 426 sub *kallû*). The translation of von Soden 1950: 399 "geringer Herkunft" is followed by Dietrich 1986: 92 ("ein Minderer").

## 39. Kibri-Dagan to Zimri-Lim

**Text:** ARM 26 234 (= M. 13841 = ARM 13 112).
**Transliteration and translation:** Kupper in Dossin et al 1964: 118–19; Ellermeier 1968: 42–45; Durand 1988: 476.
**Translation:** Moran 1969b: 623–24; Durand 1994: 62; 2000: 85 (no. 935); Malamat 1998: 98.
**Discussion:** Schult 1966: 231–32; Ellermeier 1968: 138; Craghan 1974: 53; Ishida 1977: 87; Wilson 1980: 109; J. M. Sasson 1983: 290; Malamat 1998: 75–76, 96–101; Pongratz-Leisten 1999: 109.

*ana bēlīya* [2]*qibīma* [3]*umma Kibrī-Dagan* [4]*waradkāma*
[5]*D[agan] u Ikrub-El šalmū* [6]*āl[um Terqa u] ḫalṣum šalim* [7]*ši[prum ša] bēlī [uwa⁾⁾er]anni*

[break]
[1']*kīam i[ṭ]ṭul ummā[mi ilumma]* [2']*bītam annêm ḫarībam lā te[ppešā]* [3']*bītu šū inneppišma* [4']*ana nārim ušamqassu* [5']*ina ūmi[m š]a šuttam šâti* [6']*[i]ṭṭulū [ana] mamman ul iq[bi]*

[7']*šanêm ūmam itūr šuttam* [8']*iṭṭul ummāmi ilumma* [9']*bītam annêm lā teppešā* [10']*teppešāšumma ana nārim* [11']*ušamqassu*

*inanna* [12']*anumma sissikti ṣubātīšu u* [13']*etqam ša qaqqadīšu* [14']*ana ṣēr bē[l]īya* [15']*uštābi[l]am* [16']*ištu ūm[im š]âtu* [17']*māru š[ū]* [18']*maruṣ*

Speak to my lord: Thus Kibri-Dagan, your servant:

[5]D[agan and] Ikrub-El are well; the ci[ty of Terqa as well as] the district is well. The t[ask which] my lord [assigned] to me [. . .]

[break]

[1']This is what he saw: "Thus sa[ys God]: You (pl.) may not bu[ild] this ruined house again! If this house is rebuilt, I will make it fall into the river." On the da[y] he had this dream, he did not te[ll] it [to] anybody.

[7']The next day, he had the same dream again: "Thus says God: You may not rebuild this house! If you rebuild it, I will make it fall into the river."

[11']Now I have sent a fringe of his garment and a lock[a] of his head to my lord. From that day on, the servant[b] has been ill.

[a] The word *etqum* is used here instead of the usual *šārtum*. See no. 25 (ARM 26 215) note b.
[b] Or "the youth."

## 40. Kibri-Dagan to Zimri-Lim

**Text:** ARM 26 235 (= M. 13842 = ARM 13 113).
**Transliteration and translation:** Kupper in Dossin et al. 1964: 119; Ellermeier 1968: 44–47; Durand 1988, 476–77.
**Translation:** Huffmon 1968: 119–20; Moran 1969b: 624; Durand 1994: 74; 2000: 85–86 (no. 936).
**Discussion:** Kupper 1964: 110–11; Schult 1966: 231–32; Ellermeier 1968: 138–140; J. M. Sasson 1983, 290; Durand 1995: 319, 353; Malamat 1998: 96–97; Nissinen 2000a: 256–57.

| | |
|---|---|
| *[ana bēl]ī[ya]* [2]*[qi]bīma* [3]*um[m]a Kibrī-Dagan* [4]*waradkāma* | [Sp]eak [to] m[y lord]: Thus Kibri-Dagan, your servant: |
| [5]*[Da]gan u Ik[rub]-El šalmū* [6]*[ālum] Terqa [u] ḫ[alṣum ša]lim* | [5][Da]gan and Ik[rub]-El are well. [The city] of Terqa [and] the d[istrict are] well. |
| [7]*[šan]ītam ištēn awīlum šut[tam īmu]rma* [8]*[u] Aḫum ušan[ni]* | [7][More]over, a man [has se]en a dre[am and] Aḫum repeated it [to me as follow]s: |
| [9]*[ummām]i ṣābum [nakrum* [10]*in]a ālāni dann[atim* [11]*Mā]ri Terqa* [12]*[u Sa]ggarātim* [13]*[erbu m]imma išt[aḫ-ḫiṭū* [14]*u ina] dannat bē[līya* [15]*waš]bū* | [9]"The [hostile] army [has entered] the fortif[ied] cities of [Ma]ri, Terqa [and Sa]ggaratum. They have taken plun[der], and have [occup]ied the fortifications of [my] lord." |
| [16]*[Aḫum] šuttašu annītam* [17]*[ušan-n]imma arnam elīya* [18]*[ut]ērma ummāmi šupur ana ša[rri]* [19]*u aššum kī[am] ana b[ēl]īya* [20]*ašpu[r]a[m]* | [16][Aḫum repeated to] me this dream of his and [sh]ifted the responsibility on me,[a] saying: "Write to the ki[ng]!" Therefore, I have written to my lord. |

[a] For the expression *arnam turrum,* see J. M. Sasson 1983: 285 n. 12; Durand 1988: 477.

## 41. Šibtu to Zimri-Lim

**Text:** ARM 26 236 (= A. 2437 = ARM 10 10).
**Copy:** Dossin 1967: pl. 7.
**Transliteration and translation:** Dossin 1978: 36–37; Ellermeier 1968: 62–63; Moran 1969a: 45–46; Römer 1971: 25–26; Durand 1988: 477–78.
**Translation:** Dossin 1966: 83; Huffmon 1968: 118–19; Moran 1969b: 630–31; Dietrich 1986: 89; Durand 1994: 71; 2000: 316–17 (no. 1139).

**Discussion:** Ellermeier 1968: 145; Moran 1969a: 46; Heintz 1972: 8–9; Dossin 1978: 254; J. M. Sasson 1980: 132; 1983: 290; Durand 1984: 155–56; 1995: 354–55; Ellis 1987: 252.

*[ana bēlīya* [2]*qibī]m[a* [3]*u]mma Šibtu amatkā[ma]*
[4]*bītāt ilī ekallum* [5]*u nēparātum šalmā*
[6]*šanītam Kakka-līdi* [7]*ina bīt Itūr-Mēr īmur* [8]*ummāmi šina eleppū mallû* [9]*rabbûtum narâm parkūma* [10]*šarrum u awīlī redûm* [11]*ina libbīšina rakib ša imittim* [12]*[an]a šumēlim* [13]*[i]šassû* [14]*[um]ma šunūma šarrūtum* [15]*[ḫa]ṭṭum kussûm* [16]*palûm mātum elītum u* [17]*šaplītum* [18]*ana Zimrī-Lim* [19]*na[d]nat u awīlī redûm* [20]*kalûš[u] ippal* [21]*ana Zimrī-Limma* [22]*nadnat* [23]*eleppū m[a]llû šunu* [24]*ana [b]āb ekallim* [25]*[raksū]-ma* [26]*[. . .]-šu*

[Speak to my lord: T]hus Šibtu, your servant:

[4]The temples, the palace, and the workhouses are in order.

[6]Another matter: Kakka-lidi[a] had the following vision in the temple of Itur-Mer: "Two big cargo ships were crossways on the river (blocking it). The king, together with his entourage, was on board.[b] The people on the right were shouting to those on the left and this is what they said: 'The kingship, the scepter, the throne, the dynasty,[c] and the Upper and Lower land are given to Zimri-Lim!' And the whol[e] entourage answered: 'It is given to Zimri-Lim!' Then, those c[a]rgo ships [docked[d]] at the [g]ate of the palace [. . .]"

[a] An otherwise unknown female person.
[b] Reading ŠÀ.BA (*ina libbi* + suff.) with J. M. Sasson 1980: 132; Durand 1988: 478.
[c] *pa-lu-um* according to the collation of Durand 1988: 477.
[d] Restoration according to J. M. Sasson 1983: 290 n. 32.

## 42. Addu-duri to Zimri-Lim

**Text:** ARM 26 237 (= A. 994 = ARM 10 50).
**Copy:** Dossin 1967: pl. 24.
**Transliteration and translation:** Dossin 1978: 84–87; Ellermeier 1968: 64–67; Moran 1969a: 38–39; Römer 1971: 23, 26–27; Durand 1988: 478–79; Schart 1995: 77–78.
**Translation:** Dossin 1966: 84; Huffmon 1968: 114; Moran 1969b: 631; J. M. Sasson 1983: 286 (lines 1–21); 1984a: 112; Dietrich 1986: 89–90; Durand 1994: 51; 2000: 278–79 (no. 1094).
**Discussion:** Ellermeier 1968: 145–47; Moran 1969a: 39–40; Dossin 1978: 262; Heintz 1972: 7–8; 1979: 430–31; Craghan 1974: 43, 48–50, 56; 1975: 38;

Huffmon 1976b: 698–99; Schmitt 1982: 37–41; J. M. Sasson 1983: 286–87; 1994: 306–7; Durand 1984: 157; 1995: 344–45; Bodi 1991: 206–7; Gordon 1993: 70; Parker 1993: 54; Schart 1995: 78–80; Pongratz-Leisten 1999: 110; Barstad 2001: 62.

*ana bēlīya qibīma* [2]*umma Addu-dūrī amatkāma*
[3]*ištu šulum bīt abīka* [4]*matīma šuttam annītam* [5]*ul āmur ittātūya* [6]*ša pānānum* [7]*[an]nittān*

Speak to my lord: Thus Addu-duri, your servant:

[3]Since the destruction[a] of your father's house, I have never had such a dream. My earlier signs are [th]ese two:

[8]*ina šuttīya ana bīt Bēlet-ekallim* [9]*ērubma Bēlet ekallim* [10]*ul wašbat u ṣalmū* [11]*ša maḫrīša ul ibaššū* [12]*u āmurma arṭup bakâm* [13]*šutti annītum ša barartim* [14]*atūrma Dādâ šangûm* [15]*[š]a Ištar-Bišra* [16]*[i]na bāb Bēlet ekallim* [17]*izzazma pīu nakrum* [18]*[kī]am ištanassi* [19]*ummāmi t[ūr]a D[ag]an* [20]*tūra Dagan kīam* [21]*ištanassi*

[8]In my dream I entered the temple of Belet-ekallim, but Belet-ekallim was not present nor were there images in front of her. When I saw this, I began to weep. This dream of mine took place during the evening watch. When I returned,[b] Dadâ, the priest of Ištar of Bišra,[c] was standing at the gate of Belet-ekallim, and an eerie voice[d] kept calling out: "Co[me ba]ck, O Dagan! Come back, O Dagan!"[e] This is what it kept calling out over and over.

*šanītam* [22]*muḫḫûtum ina bīt Annu-nītim* [23]*[i]tbêma ummāmi Zimrī-Lim* [24]*ana gerrim lā tallak* [25]*ina Māri šibma* [26]*u anākūma ātanappal*

[21]Another matter: a prophetess arose in the temple of Annunitum and spoke: "Zimri-Lim, do not go on campaign! Stay in Mari, and I shall continue to answer."

[27]*ana pagrīšu naṣārim* [28]*bēlī aḫšu lā inaddi* [29]*anumm[a] šārtī* [30]*u si[ss]iktī* [31]*a[nāku] aknukamma* [32]*ana ṣēr bēlīya* [33]*ušābilam*

[27]My lord should not be negligent in protecting himself. Now I [myself] have hereby sealed my hair and a fringe of my garment and I have herewith sent them to my lord.

[a] There are two possibilities to interpret the word *šulmu* here: either in the meaning "peace, restoration" referring to the restoration of the dynasty of Zimri-Lim (Ellermeier 1968: 65; Moran 1969a: 38; Schart 1995: 78), or as "destruction" (Dietrich 1986: 89; Charpin and Durand 1985: 327 n. 51; Durand 1988: 392, 478), i.e., the defeat of Yaḫdun-Lim in Šamši-Adad's conquest. Both interpretations make sense, and the semantic ambiguity, whether or not intentional, remains (cf. J. M. Sasson 1983: 286; 1984: 111).

[b] I.e., when Addu-duri, in her dream, returns from the temple; the oneiric experience is still going on in the following scene.

[c] Probably a manifestation of the goddess Ištar in Bišra (modern Jebel Bishri); see Durand 1983a: 18 n. 4; Lambert 1985: 527 n. 3. The name was previously read as "Ištar-pišra" (e.g., Moran 1969a: 38; Ellermeier 1968: 64) or "Ištar-Qabra" (von Soden 1969: 198).

[d] The "eerie voice" probably comes from the mouth of Dadâ. It is not quite clear whether he is presented as a living person or as a ghost of the already deceased priest, but the strangeness of his voice points to the latter alternative; cf. Isa 29:4 and see Hoffner 1967: 398.

[e] The Akkadian words have also been interpreted as a personal name Tura-Dagan; a king with this name ruled Mari a century before Zimri-Lim (Kupper 1971: 118 n. 3; Durand 1985). If he is mentioned here, the purpose is probably to remind Zimri-Lim of the fate of one of his predecessors. J. M. Sasson 1983: 289; 1984: 111 holds it for probable that the semantic dilemma of *tūra Dagan* was intentional and likely perplexed Zimri-Lim himself.

## 43. Addu-duri to Zimri-Lim

**Text:** ARM 26 238 (= A. 122 = ARM 10 51).
**Copy:** Dossin 1967: pl. 24.
**Transliteration and translation:** Dossin 1978: 86–89, 263; Ellermeier 1968: 66–69; Moran 1969a: 41, 56; Römer 1971: 28; Durand 1988: 478–79.
**Translation:** Huffmon 1968: 120; Moran 1969b: 631; Dietrich 1986: 90–91; Durand 2000: 279–80 (no. 1095).
**Discussion:** Ellermeier 1968: 147–48; Moran 1969a: 41–43; Heintz 1972: 9–10; Craghan 1974: 43, 56; J. M. Sasson 1983: 285–86; Pongratz-Leisten 1999: 108–9; Barstad 2001: 60–61.

*ana bēlīya* [2]*qibīma* [3]*umma Addu-dūrī*

Speak to my lord: Thus Addu-duri:

[4]*Iddin-ilī šangû* [5]*ša Itūr-Mēr* [6]*šuttam iṭṭul* [7]*umma šūm[a]* [8]*ina šuttīya* [9]*Bēlet-bīri izzizzamma* [10]*kīam iqbêm* [11]*umma šīma* [12]*šarrūtum nalba[n]ass[u]* [13]*u palûm dūršu* [14]*ana dimtim* [15]*ana mīnim ītenelle* [16]*pagaršu l[i]ṣṣur*

[4]Iddin-ili, the priest of Itur-Mer has had a dream. He says: [8]"In my dream Belet-biri[a] stood by me. She spoke to me as follows: 'The kingdom is his brick mould[b] and the dynasty is his wall! Why does he incessantly climb the watchtower? Let him protect himself!'"

[17]*inanna bēlī ana naṣar* [18]*pagrīšu* [19]*lā igge*

[17]Now, my lord should not fail to protect himself.

[a] The name of the goddess is often translated "The Lady of Divination," by analogy to *Bēl-bīri* "The Lord of Divination" used of Šamaš and Adad (cf. Nakata 1974:

100–101). Recently, Durand (1995: 187–88) has suggested the translation "The Lady of the Wells" (derived from **bērum* "well").

[b] Thus according to the collation of Durand 1988: 479.

## 44. Šimatum to Zimri-Lim

**Text:** ARM 26 239 (= A. 2858 = ARM 10 94).
**Copy:** Dossin 1967: pl. 42.
**Transliteration and translation:** Dossin 1978: 142–45, 270; Moran 1969a: 43–44; 1969b: 631; Römer 1971: 28–29; Durand 1984a: 127–29; 1988: 480–81.
**Translation:** Durand 2000: 430–31 (no. 1221).
**Discussion:** Moran 1969a: 44–45; Craghan 1974: 41; 1975: 42; J. M. Sasson 1983: 291; Pongratz-Leisten 1999: 103–4.

| | |
|---|---|
| *ana bēlīya [qibīma]* $^{2}$*umma Šīmat[um amatkāma]* $^{3}$*ištu ūmīm ša iš[tu Māri ušēṣūni]* $^{4}$*mādiš alta[ssum]* $^{5}$*u ālāni kalâšunu ā[mur]* $^{6}$*ša kīma šubat bēlīya[ma]* $^{7}$*u ša kīma bēlīya ī[murūni]* | [Speak] to my lord: Thus Šimat[um,[a] your servant]: $^{3}$Since [I departed] fr[om Mari] I have been run[ning about][b] a lot. I have seen all the cities, in which there are dwellings of my lord[c] and the representatives of my lord have s[een me]. |
| $^{8}$*inanna šumma bēlī ana [Ilān-ṣurā]* $^{9}$*an[a] alākim pānūšu ša[knu]* $^{10}$[. . .] | $^{8}$Now, if my lord is plan[ning] to go to [Ilan-ṣura[d] . . .] |
| [break] | [break] |
| $^{1'}$[. . .] *ana pān [b]ēl[ī]ya* $^{2'}$[. . .] *uṣabba[t]* $^{3'}$*u pān bēlīya uṣabba[t]* | [lines 1'–3' unintelligible] |
| $^{4'}$*u aššum mārtim [š]a Tepā[ḫim]* $^{5'}$*ina šuttīy[am]a awīlum* $^{6'}$*izzizma u[mm]a šum[a]* $^{7'}$*ṣeḫertu mārat Tepaḫimm[a]* $^{8'}$*Tagīd-nawê li[štasû]* | $^{4'}$As regards the daughter of Tepa[ḫum], in my dream a man stood there, saying: "The little daughter of Tepaḫum shall [be called] Tagid-nawûm." |
| $^{9'}$*annītam iqbêm inanna* $^{10'}$*bēlī warkatam mār bārî* $^{11'}$*lišaprisma šumm[a š]utt[um šī]* $^{12'}$*naṭlat bēlī mārtam T[ag]ī[d-nawê lissi]* $^{13'}$*kem[m]a liššasi* $^{14'}$*u šulum bēlīya lū [k]a[yy]ā[n]* | $^{9'}$This is what he said to me. Now, my lord should let a diviner check on this. If [this dr]eam was really seen, [let] my lord [give] the girl [the name] T[ag]i[d-nawûm], so she shall be called by this name, and may my lord enjoy permanent well-being. |

[a] Daughter of Zimri-Lim and, beside her sister Kirûm, wife of Ḫaya-Sumu, who was king of Ilan-ṣura and vassal of Zimri-Lim (see J. M. Sasson 1973b: 68–72; Durand 1984: 162–72; Charpin 1988, 44–45).

[b] Durand 1988: 481 reconstructs a Gtn form of the verb *lasāmum* "to run."

[c] "My lord" probably refers here to Ḫaya-Sumu.

[d] Nothing is left from the destination of "my lord," who can be either Ḫaya-Sumu or Zimri-Lim, but Ilan-ṣura is the best alternative (see Durand 1984: 127–29).

## 45. Timlû to Addu-Duri

**Text:** ARM 26 240 (= A. 3424 = ARM 10 117).
**Copy:** Dossin 1967: pl. 53.
**Transliteration and translation:** Dossin 1978: 174–75; Moran 1969a: 45; Römer 1971: 29; Durand 1988: 481–82.
**Translation:** Moran 1969b: 63; J. M. Sasson 1983: 284; Durand 2000: 282–83 (no. 1101).
**Discussion:** Heintz 1971a: 547–48; J. M. Sasson 1983: 284; Butler 1998: 220.

*ana Addu-dūrī bēltīya* 2*qibīma* 3*umma Timlû amatk[īma]* 4*lū ittumma ša inūma* 5*ina libbi Kasapâ* 6*Yar*ʾ*ip-Abba ušēṣe[nni* 7*u a]na ṣērīki allika[mma* 8*kīam] aqbêki ummā[mi* 9*šutt]am āmurrakki[m* 10*u ina š]uttīya Bēlet-[ekallim* 11*kīam išp]uranni* 12*[ummāmi . . . ]*

[break]

4'*[. . . šeššet] mārē Dūrum-labīrum* 5'*[ša ṭuppātim i]naššû šeššet awīl[ī* 6'*šunūti] qīpīšimma tú-ur-[da-ši* 7'*ù šu]-uš-qi*

*šanītam* 8'*[ištēn . . . ] . . .* 9'*[u ištēn] par-šīgu [š]a qaqqadīki* 10'*šūbilim* 11'*erīš bēltīya* 12'*luṣṣenma* 13'*libbī mītu* 14'*libluṭ*

Speak to Addu-duri, my lady: Thus Timlû,[a] yo[ur] servant:

4It was certainly a sign that when Yarʾip-Abba sent [me] away from Kasapâ[b] [and] I came to you, I said to you the [following]: "I had a [dre]am in your behalf,[c] [and in] my [dr]eam Belet-ekallim [se]nt me to say [as follows]: "[. . . ]

[break]

4'[. . . six] men from Durum-labirum[d] [who] carry [the tablets]. Trust [these] six men to her and se[nd them [dow]nstream [to her]!"[e]

7Another matter: send me [one . . . and one] headgear of your own. I want to smell the scent of my lady to revive my dead heart.

[a] An otherwise unknown female subject of Addu-duri.

[b] A town to the north of Mari.

[c] This translation follows the interpretation of J. M. Sasson 1983: 284. Moran 1969a: 45 (cf. Durand 1988: 482) translates: "I had a dream concerning you."

[d] A fortress near Mari on the left bank of the Euphrates; see Durand 1988: 339–40.
[e] Restorations according to Durand 2000: 283

## 46. NN to Zimri-Lim

**Text:** ARM 26 243 (= A. 4400).
**Photograph:** Durand 1988 (microfiche).
**Transliteration and translation:** Durand 1988: 499–500.
**Translation:** Durand 1994: 62–63.
**Discussion:** Charpin 1992: 27; Durand 1995: 342; Malamat 2000: 632–33.

*[ana bēlīya* [2]*qibīma]* [3]*umm[a* . . .] [4]*waradkā[ma]*

[5]*aššum bīt Sammē[tar]* [6]*ša ina pānītimma qiddū[tam illik]u* [7]*muḫḫû ša D[agan]* [8]*kayyantam ida[b]b[ub]ūni[m]* [9]*ummāmi libnātim ša bītim šâtu* [10]*ilum irrur* [11]*libbi m[a]yy[ā]lim u ušše libn[ātim]* [12]*epire lišpuk[ū]*

[13]*annītam m[uḫḫ]û ša D[agan]* [14]*idabbubūnim* [15]*[i]nanna anumma* [16]*ana bēlīya aštap[par]* [17]*bēlī lištālma* [18]*akkīma [mu]štal[ūtim]* [19]*ša bēlī ištal[lu]* [20]*meḫer ṭuppīya lilli[kam]* [21]*šumma bēlī iqab[bi]* [22]*libnātim ša bītim šâtu luša[šši]* [23]*ana muḫḫi dūrim lu[šābilam]* [24]*u epire* [. . .] [25][. . .]

[rest largely destroyed]

[Speak to my lord]: Thu[s NN], your servant:

[5]Concerning the house of Samme[tar] that was for some time sa[ggi]ng,[a] the prophets of D[agan] keep s[a]y[in]g to m[e]: "God has cursed the bricks of that house! Earth should be deposited within its inner r[oo]m and on its bri[ck] foundation."[b]

[13]This is what the p[rophet]s of D[agan] are saying to me. I have now writ[ten] to my lord. Let my lord reflect upon it and, according to the [dis]cre[tion] my lord will exerc[ise], let him answer my letter. If my lord say[s] so, I will have the bricks of that house car[ried away] and [taken] to the city wall, and the earth [. . .]

[rest largely destroyed]

[a] The word *qiddūtum* is a *hapax* probably to be derived from *qadādum* "to bend down" (Durand 1988: 500); cf. *qiddatum* (*AHw* 920). This may refer to the abandonment of the house after the death of Sammetar, a high official whose house could not be in such condition while he was alive. For the background of this letter, see van Koppen 2002.

[b] Or "It should be demolished to the ground down to its innermost parts and foundation."

## 47. Yarim-Addu to Zimri-Lim

**Text:** ARM 26 371 (= A. 428).
**Copy:** Charpin et al 1988 (microfiche).
**Transliteration and translation:** Charpin 1988: 177–79.
**Translation:** Charpin 1992: 28 (engl.), 29 (fr.) (lines 9–33); J. M. Sasson 1994: 312; Durand 1994: 64–65.
**Discussion:** Charpin 1992: 28–29; 2001: 48–49; 2002: 27–28; Gordon 1993: 78–79; J. M. Sasson 1994: 312; Durand 1995: 328, 346–47; 1997a: 125–26; van der Toorn 1998b: 63; Pongratz-Leisten 1999: 64; Nissinen 2000b: 103.

*[ana bēlīya qibīma* [2]*umma] Yarīm-[Addu* [4]*waradkāma]*

[3]*aššum ṭēm elê Išme-[Dagan]* [4]*ana Ekallātim* [5]*[š]a bēlī ištenemmû mim[ma]* [6]*ana Ekallātim ul ī[lê]* [7]*awātūšu ittabšêma* [8]*itâtīšu irṭupū saḫāram*

[9]*āpilum ša Marduk ina bāb ekallim* [10]*izzizma kīam ištanassi* [11]*umma šūma Išme-Dagan ina qāt Marduk* [12]*ul uṣṣi šaḫarram* [13]*ikaṣṣar* [14]*u iḫḫabbassim* [15]*annētim ina bāb ekallim* [16]*ištassima* [17]*[mamm]an mimma ul iqbīšum*

[18]*kīma pānīšunūma ina bāb Išme-Dagan* [19]*izzizma ina puḫur mātim kalîša* [20]*kīam ištanassi ummāmi* [21]*ana salīmim u damqātim šakānim* [22]*ana ṣēr sukkal Elamtim tallikma* [23]*kīma damqātim šakānim* [24]*niṣirti Marduk u ālim Bābili* [25]*[a]na sukkal Elamtim tušēṣi* [26]*[kā]rē u nakkamātīya tagmurma* [27]*[g]imillī ul tutêr* [28]*u ana Ekallātim tattallak* [29]*[š]a kīma niṣirtī ušēṣû* [30]*[ta]rdissa lā išallan[ni]* [31]*[kīma ann]ētim ina puḫur m[ātim* [32]*kalîša išt]anassû* [33]*[mamman] ul iqbīš[um]*

[Speak to my lord: Thus] Yarim-[Addu, your servant:]

[3]Concerning the report of Išme-[Dagan]'s going up to Ekallatum,[a] which my lord has heard repeatedly: he in no way we[nt up] to Ekallatum. It is a product of rumours about him that keep circulating around him.

[9]A prophet of Marduk stood at the gate of the palace,[b] proclaiming incessantly: "Išme-Dagan will not escape the hand of Marduk. That hand will tie together a sheaf and he will be caught in it." This is what he kept proclaiming at the gate of the palace. [Nobo]dy said anything to him.

[18]Directly he stood at the gate of Išme-Dagan,[c] proclaiming incessantly in the midst of the whole citizenry as follows: "You went to the ruler[d] of Elam to establish peaceful relations; but when there was a peaceful relationship, you had the treasures of Marduk and the city of Babylon delivered to the ruler of Elam. You exhausted my [ma]gazines and treasuries without returning my favors. And now you are going off to Ekallatum? He who dissipates my treasures must not demand from [me mo]re!" [As he]

[four unreadable lines]
[38][... *ana Ek*]*allātim* [39]*iṭṭarad u awīlum šū* [40]*murṣam rabêm* [41]*maruṣ balāssu* [42]*ul kīn*

kept [pro]claiming [this] in the midst of [the whole] ci[tizenry, nobody] said anything to h[im].

[break]

[38][...] sent [to Ek]allatum. The man[e] is very seriously ill; his life is in danger.

[a] Išme-Dagan, king of Ekallatum (in Assyria), was in asylum with Hammurabi, king of Babylon.
[b] I.e., the palace of Hammurabi, the king of Babylon.
[c] I.e., the lodging of Išme-Dagan in Babylon.
[d] The word *sukkallu* is used of the Elamite rulers; cf. Charpin and Durand 1991.
[e] I.e., Išme-Dagan.

## 48. Yasim-El to Zimri-Lim

**Text:** ARM 26 414 (= ARM 2 108 = A. 431 + A. 4883).
**Copy:** Charpin et al 1988 (microfiche).
**Transliteration and translation:** Jean 1945: 186–87 (A. 4883); Durand in Joannès 1988: 294–95.
**Translation (lines 29–42):** Durand 1988: 391; 1998b: 253–55 (no. 595); Charpin 1992: 25; Huffmon 1997: 11; Malamat 1998: 129.
**Discussion:** Durand 1988, 391–92; 1995: 320, 370; Charpin 1992: 24–25; 2001: 31; 2002: 14–15; Huffmon 1997: 11–12; 2000: 55–56; Malamat 1998: 128–30; van der Toorn 1998b: 62; Pongratz-Leisten 1999: 64–65; Nissinen 2000a: 245–46.

[*ana*] *bēlīya* [*qi*]*bīma* [2]*umma Yasīm-El waradkāma*
[3]*Yaqqim-Lim warad bēlīya* [4]*ša ina Qaṭṭarâ wašbū kīam išpuram* [5]*ummāmi mārē šipri Ekallatāyu* [6][*i*]*štu* UD.10.KAM [*i*]*na libbi Qaṭṭarâ* [7][*w*]*ašbūm*[*a ana bē*]*līya usammašūšunūti* [8]*a*[*d*]*i ša* [...]

[Sp]eak [to] my lord: Thus Yasim-El, your servant:

[3]Yaqqim-Lim, a servant of my lord who lives in Qaṭṭarâ, wrote to me the following message: "The messengers of Ekallatum have resided in Qaṭṭarâ for ten days, and they have been hidden[a] [from] my [lo]rd until [...]"

[two unintelligible lines]
[11]*warki na*[*špartīšu Ekallat*]*āyum* [12]*ina* UD.3.KAM [...] [13]*ana ṣērīy*[*a* ...] [14]*kīam ublam* [*ummām*]*i ṣābum* [15]*Eka*[*ll*]*atāyum āl*[*am*]

[break]

[11]After his me[ssage], on the third day, the [Ekallat]ean [...] to me [...]. This is the message that was conveyed to me: "The troops of

*Nusar* [16]*išḫiṭma alpī u immerī itbal* [17]*ṭēmam ša ubarrūnim ana bēlīya* [18]*ašpuram u anumma salāšā wardī rabûti* [19]*u šalāšā wardī ṣeḫrī ištu Andarig* [20]*ana Māri iraddū* [21]*wardū šunūti lū ana ek[a]ll[im]* [22]*iraddû-šunūti ul īde* [23]*ūlūma ana (awīlī) wēdûtim paqā[dim]* [24]*ereddišunūti ul īde*

Eka[ll]atum have plundered the ci[ty] of Nusar[b] and taken away cattle and sheep." I have informed my lord about the matter that came to my knowledge. Now, thirty adult slaves and thirty young slaves are being transferred from Andarig to Mari. I do not know whether these slaves will be brought to the pala[ce]; I do not know either whether I should commit them to the keep[ing] of the principal authorities.

[25]*aššum narē'am ša gabā'i na-pālim* [26]*ša bēlī išpuram anumma narâm šêti* [27]*appulamma ana ṣēr bēlīya* [28]*ušābilam*

[25]As to the quarrying a stele from the cliffs[c] about which my lord wrote to me, I have now quarried this stele and sent it to my lord.

[29]*šanītam Atamrum āpilum* [30]*ša Šamši illikamma kīam iqbêm* [31]*um-māmi ištēn mār bīt ṭuppi naṣram* [32]*ṭurdamma ṭēmam ša Šamši* [33]*ana šarri išpuranni lušašṭer* [34]*annītam iqbêm Utu-kam aṭrudma* [35]*ṭuppam šêtu išṭur u awīlum šū* [36]*(awīlī) šībī ušzizamma* [37]*kīam iqbê[m u]m-mām[i]* [38]*ṭuppam annêm arḫ[iš]* [39]*šubilma ša pî ṭuppim* [40]*līpuš annītam iqbêm* [41]*anumma ṭuppam šêtu* [42]*ana ṣēr bēlīya uštābilam*

[29]Another matter: Atamrum, prophet of Šamaš, came to me and spoke to me as follows: "Send me a discreet[d] scribe! I will have him write down the message which Šamaš has sent me for the king." This is what he said to me. So I sent Utu-kam and he wrote this tablet. This man brought witnesses[e] and said to [me a]s follows: "Send this tablet quic[kly] and let the king act according to its words." This is what he said to me. I have herewith sent this tablet to my lord.

[a] Derived from *samāšum* II "to hide" (*CAD* S 114); cf. ARM 26 420:51 and *simmištum* ARM 26 206 (no. 16):32; M. 9717 (no. 65):3.

[b] For this locality, see Lafont 1988: 476 (cf. ARM 26 514; 515).

[c] Translation of J. M. Sasson (private communication). For *gabā'u/gab'u,* see also Birot 1974: 239; Charpin 1988: 216 ad ARM 26 388:12.

[d] For this translation of *naṣrum,* see Charpin 1992: 31 n. 18. For the alternative translation "competent," see Durand 1988: 391 n. 80. Malamat 1998: 129 assumes a double translation: "Send me a competent and discreet scribe." Durand 1998b: 254 translates "Envoie-moi un scribe très soignuex," whereby the "carefulness" of the scribe is understood as a part of the secure transmission of the letter to its destination.

[e] It is not clear whether Atamrum or Utu-kam is meant here. The witnesses are not necessarily aware of the content of the letter; they are just there to certify that

the letter is written on the request of the prophet and forwarded to the king by Yasim-El, who, then, must take care of its transportation to the king. That letter—presumably ARM 26 194 (no. 4; cf. Charpin 2001: 31; 2002: 14–15)—probably accompanied the present one.

### 49. Zakira-Ḫammû to Zimri-Lim

**Text:** ARM 27 32 (= M. 13741).
**Copy:** Birot 1993: 89.
**Transliteration and translation:** Birot 1993, 88–90.
**Discussion:** Durand 1993b; Malamat 2000: 633–34.

*[ana b]ēlīya* [2]*[qi]bīma* [3]*umma Zakira-Ḫamm[û]* [4]*waradkāma* [5]*ālum Qaṭṭunān u ḫa[lṣum šalim]*

[6]*erba awīlī Yamūt-Bālī awīlū* [. . .] [7]*muḫḫû ša Ami-Ḫubšalim* [8]*šībūtum Gaššim ša an[a ṣēr]* [9]*bēlīya illakū* [10]*awīlī šunūti iṣbatūnimma* [11]*ana ṣēr Ibâl-El* LÚ [. . .]

[break]
[six fragmentary lines]
[r.7']*an[a] n[ā]rim nire[ddīma]* [8']*amtu šâti išriqūma* [9']*itti amti šâti* [. . .] [10']*šībūtum Gaššim* [11']*erba awīlī [Yamū]t-Bāl imḫ[aṣūma]* [12']*uš[ār]êmma ṭēm awīlī šu[nūti]* [13'][. . .] *šībūtum Gaššim* [14']*[ana ṣ]ēr bēlīya ittalkū-[nim]*
[15']*[šanītam] ina pānītimma aššum ṭēm* [. . . [16']. . .] *ana ṣēr bēlīya* [17']*[ašpur]am ḫurpī u uplītam* [18']*[š]ēm ša ḫalṣim erbum īku[l]* [19']*ištu Teḫrān adi Raḫatim* [20']*erbum rakib*

[Sp]eak [to] my lord: Thus Zakira-Ḫammû, your servant:

[5]The city of Qaṭṭunan and the dis[trict are well].

[6]Four Yamutbaleans [. . .] The prophets of Amu of Ḫubšalum,[a] elders of Gaššum,[b] who have been coming t[o] my lord, have seized these men and [brought them] to Ibâl-El,[c] the [. . .]

[break]

[r.7']We were mo[ving] to the river, when that slave-girl was stolen [. . .] with that slave-girl [. . .] The elders of Gaššum be[at] the four [Yamu]t-baleans,[d] they have been delivered up to me. The report about these men [. . .] the elders of Gaššum have come t[o] my lord.

[15'][Another matter]: concerning the issue of [. . . *about which* I wro]te to my lord earlier, that is, the early and the late harvest, the locusts have devou[red] the grain of the district. The locusts have spread[e] all over from Teḫran to Raḫatum.[f]

[a] The god Amu of Ḫubšalum, a locality in Yamutbal, may be identifiable with Nergal of Ḫubšalum in ARM 26 194 (no. 4) (Charpin and Durand 1985: 333).

[b] For this locality, probably in the western part of Ida-maraṣ, see Birot 1993: 90. It seems that the *muḫḫûms* are represented as the elders of Gaššum, but this is not altogether clear because of the break at the end of line 6.

[c] Probably identical with Ibalpiel, the chief of the Haneans functioning in the western part of Ida-maraṣ; cf. Birot 1993: 16–17, 90; Durand 1988: 143.

[d] Or (less likely): "The four Yamutbaleans beat the elders of Gaššum."

[e] The verb *rakābum* means literally "to ride"; for the present translation, see Durand 1993b; Lion and Michel 1997: 711 n. 15.

[f] This expression means the whole area of the province of Qaṭṭunan (Birot 1993: 7–8).

## 50. Manatan to Zimri-Lim

**Text:** M. 9451.
**Copy:** Ozan 1997: 303.
**Transliteration and translation:** Ozan 1997: 303.
**Discussion:** Huffmon 2000: 52.

*ana bēlīya* [2]*qibīma* [3]*umma Manatān* [4]*warad[kā]ma*
[5]*ḫamšat [muḫ]ḫû ša Addi*
[break]
[1']*[ana ālim Māri ekallim* [2']*bītī ilī nēparātim* [3']*u maṣṣarātīya]* [4']*šulmu[m]*

Speak to my lord: Thus Manatan, your servant:
[5]Five [pro]phets of Adad [...]
[break]
[1'][The city of Mari, the palace, the temples, the workhouses and the guard][a] are well.

[a] Restoration by analogy of the other letters of Manatan.

# II

## Other Documents from Mari

While the letters are the only documents from Mari that give information about the contents of the prophetic oracles and other sayings of the prophets, there are scattered mentions of prophets in a number of other sources of different kinds. An assortment of such texts is represented in this chapter, but the selection is hardly exhaustive; most of them are referred to and quoted by Durand in his introduction to the prophetic letters (1988: 377–412). Forthcoming editions of yet unpublished documents are likely to contain more of such references.

Most of the texts other than letters in which prophets (*muḫḫûm/muḫḫūtum* or *āpilum*) make an appearance are administrative documents listing outlays delivered to differents classes of people. The reason for the delivery is usually not indicated, but it is discernible from number 61 that prophets and other people who brought good news or otherwise weighty messages to the king were rewarded for their services with more or less precious gifts. The articles delivered to the prophets are often pieces of ordinary clothing (nos. 54–59), but some of them are granted even more valuable items such as lances (no. 60), silver (nos. 61–63) or a donkey (no. 53). It is conceivable from the extant letters, that the prophets could request these gifts themselves (nos. 9, 16).

With the exception of the anonymous *muḫḫûm* of Adad in number 61, the prophets are always mentioned by name, expanding the prosopography of Mari prophets by six proper names: Annu-tabni *muḫḫūtum* (no. 58), Ea-maṣi, *muḫḫûm* of Itur-Mer (nos. 55, 59), Ea-mudammiq, *muḫḫûm* of Ninḫursag (nos. 56, 57), Ili-andulli, the *āpilum* (no. 54), Išḫi-Dagan, *āpilum* of Dagan of Ṣubatum (no. 63) and Qišatum, *āpilum* of Dagan (no. 60). In addition, two prophets are known from the letters: Irra-gamil, *muḫḫûm* of Nergal, (nos. 55, 59, 65), who predicts the death of the royal child in no. 33, and Lupaḫum, *āpilum* of Dagan (nos. 53, 62), whose message upon his arrival from Tuttul—possibly the one he is rewarded for in number 61—is quoted in number 9. Moreover, Qišatum could be identical with the *āpilum* of Dagan referred to by Mukannišum in number 19.

A different kind of information is provided by the two cultic texts, which reveal some interesting features of the prophets' involvement in the ritual of Ištar, the most important festival in the ritual calendar of Mari (Lafont 1999: 67). The prophets, together with the musicians, turn out to play an important role in this royal ceremony involving a great number of cult functionaries, as described in no. 51 (Durand and Guichard 1997). It appears that, after elaborate preparations described in the first column, the emblems of the goddesses are brought in and the king enters together with his courtiers. This is the moment when the chanters strike up a canonical lamentation song—provided that the prophet acquires the condition that enables him to fulfill his task. If the prophet fails to get into a frenzy, the lamentation is not performed. The interplay of prophecy and music becomes apparent also in no. 52; this text indicates what the musicians sing in the case that the prophetesses are not able to prophesy. In both cases, the comportment of the prophets, interpreted as a sign of divine inspiration, is presented as a decisive part of the ceremony.

The only literary reference to prophets from Mari is to be found in the so-called Epic of Zimri-Lim (no. 64), a hitherto unpublished text, the relevant passage of which is quoted by Durand (1988: 393). In this text, an *āpilum* appears as a "sign" for Zimri-Lim. The words that follow, assuring the support of Adad and Erra for him, are best interpreted as a prophetic oracle of encouragement.

## 51. Ritual of Ištar, Text 2

**Text:** A. 3165.
**Photograph:** Durand and Guichard 1997: 72–73.
**Copy:** Dossin 1938: 2–3; Durand and Guichard 1997: 53, 56.
**Transliteration and translation:** Dossin 1938: 4–13; Durand and Guichard 1997: 52–58.
**Translation:** J. M. Sasson 1973a: 152–53 n. 9; Durand 1995: 284–85.
**Discussion:** Nötscher 1966: 175, 177; Renger 1969: 220; Huffmon 1976b: 698; J. M. Sasson 1979: 132–33; R. R. Wilson 1980: 104; Durand 1988: 386–87; 1995: 286, 323; 1997b: 273; Durand and Guichard 1997; Groneberg 1997: 146–48; Lafont 1999: 67–69; Nissinen 2000b: 92.

**Lines ii 1'–27'**

[beginning destroyed]
*ana šumēlim ša [Ištar]* 2' *Latarak* 3' *u ilū dingirgubbû uššabū* 4' *šurīnī ša ilātim* 5' *ištu bītīšunu innaššûnimma* 6' *ina bīt Ištar imittam u šumēlam* 7' *iššakkanū*

8' *ištu annûm kunnu šarrum lullumtam iltabaš* 9' *warki kalê* 10' *ina kussîm malāḫim uššab*

11' *ištēn ina wardī šarrim* 12' *ša eli šarrim ṭābu* 13' *ina kussîm šap[i]ltim* 14' *a[n]a idi šarrim ušša[b]* 15' *ina rēš šarrim mamm[a]n* 16' *ul izzaz*

17' *gerseqqû imittam* 18' *u šumēlamma izzazzū* 19' *kalû* ú.ru am.ma.da.ru.bi 20' *[r]ēš warḫi iz[a]mmur[ū]*

21' *šumma ina rēš war[ḫim]* 22' *muḫḫûm ištaqa[lma]* 23' *an[a] maḫḫēʾi[m] ul i[reddû]* 24' *ištu* mà.e ú.re.m[én *šēram]* 25' *iktašdū waklū n[ārī]* 26' *uwaššarūma im[maḫḫima]* 27' mà.e ú.re.m[én *izammarū]*

[beginning destroyed]
On the left side of [Ištar], Latarak and the standing gods[a] sit down. The emblems of the goddesses are brought from their shrines and placed on the right and on the left in the temple of Ištar.

8When this position is taken, the king, dressed in the *lullumtum*-cloak,[b] (walks) after the chanters and sits down on the shipper's chair.

11One of the king's servants of the king's own choice sits do[wn] on the lo[w]er chair b[e]side the king. The king may not be served by any[o]ne.

17The *gerseqqû*-courtiers stand on his right and left side. The chanters st[r]ik[e] up the "ú-ru am-ma-da-ru-bi"[c] of the [e]nd of the month.

21If by the end of the mo[nth] the prophet maintains his equili[brium][d] and is not a[ble] t[o] prophes[y] when it is time for [the chant] "mà-e ú-re-m[én],"[e] the temple officials let the m[usicians] go. If he pr[ophesies, they strike up] "mà-e ú-re-m[én]".

**Lines s. ii 1–3:**

[Col. s. i completely destroyed]
*ina našappī išakkanū mê ina karpatim* 2 *u erbet me[ḫs]û uktannūma ana erešti* 3 *muḫḫê ukallû*

[Col. s. i completely destroyed]
... they place in the baskets.[f] Water in a container and four *meḫsû*-jars[g] are installed; they are always at the disposal of the prophets.

[a] For Latarak and the "standing gods" (*dingirgubbû*), see Durand and Guichard 1997: 48. This is the only occurrence of Latarak, possibly associated with Nergal and assisted by the "standing gods" who, judged from their position, play the role of servants.

[b] A garment of unspecified quality; probably a cloak worn on specific ritual occasions (Durand and Guichard 1997: 27–28).

[c] Civil 1974: 95 identifies this with the Sumerian canonical lamentation ú-ru àm-ma-i-ra-bi "The Plundered City".

[d] For this reading and interpretation of *šaqālum* Gt, see Durand 1988: 386–87.

[e] Thus according to the reading of Durand and Guichard 1997: 54 who suggest this song to be identical with another Sumerian canonical lamentation, me-e ur-re-mèn (p. 50). Note the substantial difference from the earlier reading of Durand 1988: 386.

[f] For *našappum* "basket", see AHw 758. Durand and Guichard 1997: 58 translate "sur le plat".

[g] Probably jars provided with a lit (< *ḫesû* "to cover").

## 52. Ritual of Ištar, Text 3

**Text:** A. 1249b + S. 142 75 + M. (unnumbered).
**Photograph:** Durand and Guichard 1997: 74–75.
**Copy:** Durand and Guichard 1997: 59, 61.
**Transliteration and translation:** Durand and Guichard 1997: 59–63.

### Lines iii 1'–23'

[beginning destroyed]
*lā irrub[u/ū* ...] $^{2'}$*muḫḫû[m* ...] $^{3}$*ša itebbû* [...]

$^{4'}$*inūma ana me[ḫertīša]* $^{5'}$*mārū īter[bū]* $^{6'}$*muḫḫâtum* [...] $^{7'}$*u mārē nā[rī* ...]

$^{8'}$*inūm[a muḫḫâtum]* $^{9'}$*išta[qqalū]* $^{10'}$*šina mār[ē nārī* ...] $^{11'}$*ana* [... *irrubūma]* $^{12'}$*pāni [iltim ana Enlil?]* $^{13'}$*eršemmakk[am izammurū]*

$^{14'}$*ištēn gābi[štum]* $^{15'}$*igabbi[š]* $^{16'}$*kīma* ud.da.ab *[šēram iktašdū]* $^{17'}$*uṣṣû* [...] $^{18'}$*mārū iza[mmurūma]* $^{19'}$*ištu šub[at iltim uṣṣû]*

$^{20'}$*sebe gābi[šātum maḫar* ...] $^{21'}$*igabbišā i[štu igdabšā]* $^{22'}$*usaḫ-ḫarām[a* ...] $^{23'}$*igabbišā* [...]

[beginning destroyed]
... [do/does)] not enter [...] the prophe[t ...] who arise(s) [...].

$^{4}$When the musicians[a] have entered before her,[b] the prophetesses[c] [...] and the mu[sicians].[d]

$^{8}$Whe[n the prophetesses] main[tain their equilibrium],[e] two m[usicians ... enter] the [...]. [They sing] an *eršemmakkum*[f] before [the goddess for *Enlil*[g]].

$^{14}$A *gābištum*[h] does her service. When [it is time for the chant] "ud-da-ab", they go out [...]. The musicians[i] si[ng and go out] from the dwell[ing of the goddess].

$^{20}$Seven *gābi[štum* women] do their service [...]. Wh[en they have finished], they turn and [...] do their service [...]

[a] DUMU.MEŠ probably refers to the "musicians" DUMU.MEŠ NA[R] (line 7'; if that reading is correct), and may be understood as an abbreviation or haplography. The word *māru* (DUMU) "son" may refer to the age of the musicians (Durand and

Guichard 1997: 62: "petits-musiciens") but does not necessarily do so, since the word is also used of representatives of a profession.

[b] I.e., Ištar.

[c] The word, written syllabically MÍ.*mu-ḫa-tum,* is probably a plural of *muḫḫūtum* (cf. the Assyrian plural genitives *maḫḫuʾāte* VS 19 1 [no. 125]:38; *maḫḫâte* SAA 12 69 [no. 110]:29).

[d] Durand and Guichard 1997: 60 n. 212 suggest GUDU$_4$.U (*luḫšum,* a cult functionary) as an alternative reading.

[e] Cf. above, Ritual of Ištar, Text 2 (no. 51):22'.

[f] A lamentation song (*AHw* 1554; cf. 246).

[g] Restoration according to Durand and Guichard 1997: 60.

[h] For this female functionary, see Durand and Guichard 1997: 51–52. If the word *gābištum* is related to *kāpištum*/*ḫabbištu* = TÚG.TÚG-bal, it refers to changing of cloths or appearance (cf. Heb. *ḥpš* hitp.). Groneberg 1997: 147 translates accordingly "die Verkleiderinnen."

[i] Cf. note a.

## 53. Assignment of a Donkey

**Text:** A. 3796.
**Transliteration and translation:** Durand 1988: 396–97.

*[imērum]* [2]ZI.GA [3]*ana Lupāḫim* [4]*[āp]ilim* [5]*[ša] Dagan* [6]*ina imērī* [7]*ša šallat* [8]*Ida-Maraṣ* [9]*ša māt Šudê* [10]*ša qāt Yanṣib-Dagan*

One [donkey], outlay to Lupaḫum, [pr]ophet [of] Dagan,[a] (taken) from the donkeys of the booty from Ida-Maraṣ in the land of Sudâ, (carried out) under the authority of Yanṣib-Dagan.[b]

[11]*waraḫ Ḫibirtim* [12]*šanat Zimrī-Lim* [13]*kussâm rabâm ana [Dagan]* [14]*ša Terqa uš[ellû]*

[11]Month of Ḫibirtum (V), the year of Zimri-Lim (11') when the great throne is of[fered] to [Dagan] of Terqa.[c]

[a] Probably the same person as in ARM 26 199 (no. 9).

[b] Cf. ARM 26 199 (no. 9):58-63.

[c] Each regnal year of Zimri-Lim has a title; the numbers in brackets indicate the order of the years. On the year-counting of Mari, see J. M. Sasson 1984b: 249–50; Charpin and Durand 1985: 305–6; Anbar 1991: 30–37; Charpin and Ziegler 2002.

## 54. Outlay of Garment

**Text:** ARM 9 22.
**Copy:** Birot 1960a: pl. 6.
**Transliteration and translation:** Birot 1960b: 11–12.

| | |
|---|---|
| 18 *ṣubātū* [2]*ša ana Māri illeqû* | Eighteen garments that were taken to Mari; |
| [3]5 *ṣubātū ana lubušāt* 5 *ṣuḫārē* [4]1 *Yantinim* [5]1 *Šamaš-rabî* [6]1 *Iludayyān* [7]1 *Eḫlip-šarri* [8]*u Kasap-Šamaš* | [3]five garments for clothing of five apprentices:[a] one for Yantinum, one for Šamaš-rabû, one for Iludaian, one for Eḫlip-šarri and for Kasap-Šamaš; |
| [9]4 *ṣubātū* [10]*ša ana* [. . .] [11]*ša elippim išša[k]nū* [12]*ana Māri ub[l]ū[šun]ūti* [13]*šēp Ilī-tūra* | [9]four garments that were [*taken*] to [. . .] that were set on a boat and brou[gh]t to Mari; supervision[b] of Ili-tura; |
| [14]1 *ṣubātum Ilī-andu[l]li āpilum* [15]1 *ṣubātum Ana-Šamaš-anaṭṭal* [16]1 *ṣubātum Šimgina* [17]1 *ṣubātum Š[a]maš-dumqi* | [14]one garment for Ili-andu[l]li, the *āpilum*, one garment for Ana-Šamaš-anaṭṭal, one garment for Šimgina, one garment for Š[a]maš-dumqi. |
| [18]*napḫar* 31 *ṣubātū* [19]*iškar Šamaš-mutapli* | [18]Thirty-one garments total, work quota of Šamaš-mutapli. |
| [20]*waraḫ Kinūnim* UD.28.KAM [21]*šanat Zimrī-Lim* [22]*tillūt Bābili illiku* | [20]Month of Kinunum (VII), twenty-eighth day, the year of Zimri-Lim (10') when he went to the aid of Babylon.[c] |

[a] Lit.: "young ones."
[b] The sign GÌR for *šēpum* "foot" probably refers to Ili-tura as the supervisor of the transaction.
[c] See above, no. 53 (A. 3796), note c.

## 55. Outlay of Garment

**Text:** ARM 21 333.
**Copy:** Durand 1982a: pl. 110–11.
**Transliteration and translation:** Durand 1983a: 442–49.
**Discussion:** Durand 1988: 398; Malamat 1987: 39; Charpin 1998b: 86; 2001: 36; 2002: 17.

**lines 33'–44'**

[33']1 *ṣubātum kitīt ḫuššî ana Admu* [34']1 *ṣubātum išārum tardennum Irra-gāmil muḫḫû ša Nergal* [35']1 *ṣubātum Yamḫadû rēštum* [36'] *Warad-ili-šu rab nārim*

[33']One red cloth of linen for the god Admu; one ordinary garment of second quality for Irra-gamil prophet of Nergal;[a] one Yamhadean garment of prime quality for Warad-ili-šu the chief chanter;

[37']2 *patinnū uṭublū rēštum* [38']2 *kaballū* [39']1 *mešēn šuḫuppim rēštum* [40'] *ana Ḫāya-Sūmū*

[37']two *uṭublum* belts[b] of prime quality, two pairs of shoes,[c] one pair of *šuḫuppum* sandals of prime quality for Ḫaya-Sumu;[d]

[41']1 *ṣubātum išārum tardennum Ḫabdu-Malik ša ištu Šubat-Enlil illikam* [42']1 *ṣubātum išārum Yadīda lillatum* [43']1 *ṣubātum išārum Ēa-maṣi muḫḫû Itūr-Mēr* [44']1 *ṣubātum išārum Šarrum-dâri nārum*

[41']one ordinary garment of second quality for Ḫabdu-Malik who has come from Šubat-Enlil; one ordinary garment for Yadida "the crazy woman";[e] one ordinary garment for Ea-maṣi prophet of Itur-Mer; one ordinary garment for Šarrum-dâri the chanter.

[a] This prophet predicted the death of the royal child in ARM 26 222 (no. 33) and is mentioned as a potential witness in a report of crimes committed in the house of Sammetar in M. 9717 (no. 65).

[b] For *uṭublum,* see Durand 1983a: 403–6, according to whom the word designates the material (Durand 1983a: 445: "serge") rather than the form of the clothing in question; cf. no. 58 (ARM 22 326).

[c] For *kaballum,* see Durand 1983a: 423 ("chausson"); CAD K 2-3.

[d] May or may not be identical with Ḫaya-Sumu, king of Ilan-ṣura, who was Zimri-Lim's vassal and son-in-law. He is mentioned in ARM 25 15 (no. 60):5; cf. no. 44 (ARM 26 239), note a.

[e] The word *lill(at)um* means basically "crazy, idiot" (see Durand 1995: 458), but may also designate ecstatic behavior in the same sense as *muḫḫûm*. Note that the lady is accompanied by a prophet and a chanter in this list.

## 56. Outlay of Garment

**Text:** ARM 22 167.
**Transliteration and translation:** Kupper 1983: 282–85.
**Discussion:** Durand 1988: 398; Bardet et al. 1984: 347.

### lines r. 2'–8'

[2']2 *paršigū ḫam[d]û tardennum ana* [. . .] [3']1 *ṣubātum išārum tardennum Iddin-Ya[k]rub-I[l]* [4']1 *mešēnu tardennum Šuḫalān* [5']*awīlum Qata-nim* [6']1 *ṣubātum išārum tardennum Yatāḫum* [7']1 *ṣubātum išārum Ḫiddum* 2 *Sutû* [8']1 *ṣubātum išārum Ēa-mudammiq muḫḫû ša Ninḫursagga*

Two *ḫamdûm*-turbans of second quality for [. . .]; one ordinary garment of second quality for Iddin-Ya[k]rub-I[l]; one pair of sandals of second quality for Šuḫalan a man[a] from Qatnu; one ordinary garment of second quality for Yataḫum; one ordinary garment for Ḫiddum—two Suteans; one ordinary garment for Ea-mudammiq, prophet of Ninḫursag.[b]

[a] The transliteration of Kupper has LUGAL *Qa-ta-nim*.KI. Since, however, there is no such king of Qatnu, the reading LUGAL is probably an error for LÚ (Dominique Charpin, private communication).

[b] "The Lady of the Mountain," one of the Mesopotamian mother goddesses; for her attestations at Mari, see Nakata 1974: 398–409.

## 57. Extract from a Decree of Expenditures

**Text:** A. 4676.
**Transliteration and translation:** Durand 1988: 381.
**Discussion:** Charpin 2001: 36; 2002: 17.

*Yatāḫum* [2]*[Ḫ]iddum* [3]2 *Sutû*

[4]*Ēa-mudammiq* [5]*muḫḫû* [6]*ša Ni[nḫursa]gga*
[7][ZI.GA] [8]*ana a[wīlī š]a* [9]*š[i]pr[ī]*

Yatahum and Ḫiddum, two Suteans;

[4]Ea-mudammiq, prophet of Ni[nḫursa]g.[a]

[7][Outlay to] pe[ople w]ho deliver m[es]sage[s].

[a] The names Yatahum, Hiddum, and Ea-mudammiq are identical with those mentioned on lines r. 6'–8' of the previous document (ARM 22 167), from which this text may have been extracted. For Ninḫursag, see no. 56 (ARM 22 167), note b.

## 58. Outlay of Garment

**Text:** ARM 22 326.
**Transliteration and translation:** Kupper 1983: 510–13.
**Discussion:** Durand 1988: 398; Malamat 1987, 39.

1 *ṣubātum uṭublu tardennum* [2]1 *tilpānu* [3]*ana Abdu-Malik* [4]*sugāgim* [5]*awīl Šakka*

One *uṭublum* garment[a] of second quality and one bow for Abdu-Malik, a sheikh[b] from Šakka;

[6]1 *ṣubātum uṭublu tardennum* [7]2 *paršigū šutî* [8]*ana Annu-tabni* [9]*muḫ[ḫ]ūtim* [10]*ša Annun[ītim]*

one *uṭublum* garment of second quality and two woven turbans for Annu-tabni, prophetess of Annunitum.

[11]ZI.GA *ša [qāt Muka]nnišim*

[11]Outlay, under [the authority of Muka]nnišum.[c]

[12]*waraḫ Lilâtim* [13]UD.6.KAM [14]*šanat Zimrī-Lim* [15]*dawidâm* [16]*ša mārē Yamīna idūku*

[12]Month of Liliatum (IX), sixth day, the year of Zimri-Lim (2') when inflicted a defeat on the Yaminites.[d]

[a] See no. 55 (ARM 21 333), note b.
[b] For *sugāgum,* see Kupper 1957: 16-17.
[c] This official, for whom see Rouault 1977, reports a prophetic appearance in ARM 26 209 (no. 19).
[d] See above, no. 53 (A. 3796), note c.

## 59. Outlay of Garment

**Text:** ARM 23 446 (= M. 5858 + ARM 22 171). (cf. ARM 21 333 = no. 55)
**Transliteration and translation:** Soubeyran in Bardet et al. 1984: 392–95.
**Discussion:** Durand 1988: 398.

### lines 8'–20' (= ARM 21 333:33'–44')

[8']*[1] ṣubātum kitīt ḫuššî ana [Admu]*
[9']1 *ṣubātum išārum tardennum Irr[a-gāmil muḫḫû ša Ne]rgal*
[10']1 *ṣubātum Yamḫadû [rēštum]* [11']*ana Warad-ili-[šu nārum rabûm]*
[12']2 *patinnū u[ṭublū rēštum]* [13']2 *[kab]allū*
[14']1 *[mešēn šuḫuppim]* [15']*ana Ḫ[āya-Sūmū]*
[16']1 *ṣubātum išārum tardennum*

[This section of a tablet summarizing various disbursements resumés no. 55 above, where a translation may be found; see Soubeyran in Bardet et al. 1984: 344–46.]

*Ḫabdu-Malik ša išt[u Šubat-Enlil]* [17']*illikam* [18']1 *ṣubātum išārum tardennum Yadīda lillatum* [19']1 *ṣubātum išārum Ēa-maṣi muḫḫû ša Itūr-Mēr* [20']1 *ṣubātum išārum Šarrum-dâri nārum*

## 60. Donation of Lances

**Text:** ARM 25 15 (= A. 4675).
**Transliteration and translation:** Limet 1986: 5.
**Discussion:** Durand 1988: 397; Charpin 1992: 28.

1 *šukurrum kaspim* [2]10(?) *šukurrū siparrim* [3]2/3 *manûm* [4]*šūbultum* [5]*ana Ḫāya-Sūmū* [6]*šar Ilān-ṣūrāya* [7]2 *zamrātū siparrim* [8]*ana Qīšatim* [9]*āpilim ša Dagan* [10]ZI.GA *ša qāt Mukannišim*

[11]*waraḫ Uraḫim* [12]UD.28.KAM [13]*šanat Zimrī-Lim* [14]*kussâm rabâm ana Šamši* [15]*ušellû*

One lance of silver, ten[a] lances of bronze, 2/3 of a mina each; gift for Ḫaya-Sumu, king of Ilan-ṣura;[b] [7]two lances[c] of bronze, for Qišatum, prophet of Dagan.[d] [10]Outlay, under the authority of Mukannišum.

[11]Month of Uraḫum (I), twenty-eighth day, the year of Zimri-Lim (4'), when he offered a great throne to Šamaš.[e]

[a] Thus according to the translation of Limet 1986: 5; the number is missing from the transliterated text.

[b] For this person, son-in-law and vassal of Zimri-Lim, possibly mentioned also in ARM 21 333 (no. 55):40', see Charpin 1988: 43–46.

[c] For *zamrātum,* see Durand 1987a: 187.

[d] Note that Mukannišum reports an appearance of an *āpilum* of Dagan in ARM 26 209 (no. 19).

[e] See above, no. 53 (A. 3796), note c.

## 61. Donation of Silver Rings

**Text:** ARM 25 142 (= A. 4674).
**Transliteration and translation:** Limet 1986: 46–47; Durand 1988: 380–81.
**Discussion:** Durand 1988: 380–81; Malamat 1998: 125; Gordon 1993: 75; Charpin 2001: 35; 2002: 17.

1/2 *manâ kaspum* [2]*ša Yaḫmusim* [3]*ana ḫišeḫ[ti e]kallim* [4]*ana Bābi[lim* . . .] [5]*ana* 3 *ḫ[ullī kaspim]* [6]*šūpušim*

Half a mina of silver belonging to Yaḫmusum for the use of the palace, [to be delivered] to Baby-[lon], for making of three *ḫ[ullum* rings[a] of silver],

[7]*ina libbīšu* 1 *ḫullu kaspim* [8]*ana mār Ubdalān*

[7]including one *ḫullum* ring of silver for the servant of Ubdalan;

[9]1 *ḫullu kaspim* [10]*ana mār Ḫāya-Sūm[ū] š[a]* [11]*bussurtam ublam*

[9]one *ḫullum* ring of silver for the servant of Ḫaja-Sum[u] wh[o] brought here good news;

[12]1 *ḫullu kaspim* [13]*ana muḫḫîm ša Addu* [14]*inūma têrtam ana šarrim* [15]*iddinu*

[12]one *ḫullum* ring of silver for the prophet of Adad, when he delivered an oracle to the king.

[16]*napḫar* 1/2 *manâ kaspum* [17]ZI.GA *awīlī ša šipri*

[16]Total: half a mina of silver, outlay to people who deliver messages.

[18]*waraḫ Uraḫim* [12]UD.25.KAM [s. 1]*šanat Zimrī-Lim* [2]*ṣalam Ḫatta ušellû*

[18]Month of Uraḫum (I), twenty-fifth day, the year of Zimri-Lim (7') when he presented a statue to (the god) Ḫatta.[b]

[a] Restoration by Durand 1988: 380.
[b] See above, no. 53 (A. 3796), note c.

## 62. Outlay of Silver

**Text:** M. 11436.
**Transliteration and translation:** Durand 1988: 396.
**Discussion:** Charpin 2002: 20

1 *šiqil kaspum* [2]*ina aban maḫīrim* [3]*ana Lupāḫim* [4]*āpilim ša Dagan* [5]*inūma ana Tuttuli* [6]*illiku*

One shekel of silver, according to the market weights, to Lupaḫum, prophet of Dagan, when he went to Tuttul.[a]

[7]*waraḫ Dagan* UD.7.KAM [8]*šanat Zimrī-Lim* [9]*kussâm rabâm ana Šamši* [10]*ušellû*

[7]Month of Dagan (VIII), seventh day, the year of Zimri-Lim (4') when he offered a great throne to Šamaš.[b]

[a] Lupaḫum's returning from Tuttul is mentioned in ARM 26 199 (no. 9).
[b] See above, no. 53 (A. 3796), note c.

## 63. Deed of Donation

**Text:** T. 82.
**Transliteration and translation:** Durand 1988: 380.
**Discussion:** Charpin 1992: 28.

### Lines ix 2–4:

| | |
|---|---|
| [2]1 *šewerum kaspim Išḫi-Dagan* [3]*āpili ša Dagan* [4]*ša Ṣubātim* | One silver ring: Išḫi-Dagan, *āpilum* of Dagan of Ṣubatum. |

## 64. The Epic of Zimri-Lim unpublished[a]

**Transliteration and translation:** Durand 1988: 393 (lines 137–42).
**Discussion:** Durand 1988: 393; 1995: 329–30; Guichard 1999: 36; Nissinen 2000a: 263–64.

### Lines 137–142

| | |
|---|---|
| [137]*Zimrī-Lim zikruš Dagan eṭilma* | [137]Zimri-Lim is heroic like an image of Dagan. |
| [138]*tuklassu Itūr-Mēr uršānu* | [138]His protection is Itur-Mer, the warrior. |
| [139]*īmurma ittašu āpilam eṭel māti*[*m*] | [139]The hero of the land[b] saw his sign, the prophet:[c] |
| [140]*šarru libbašu danānam uṣbam* | [140]"The king goes forth with forceful heart![d] |
| [141]*illak Addum ina šumēlīšu* | [141]Adad goes at his left side, |
| [142]*Erra dapinumma ina imnīšu* | [142]Erra, the mighty one, at his right side." |

[a] Only excerpts of this text, an edition of which is announced by Michaël Guichard (*NABU* 1994 § 105), have been quoted in transliteration and translation, without museum numbers, in Charpin and Durand 1985: 325, 328, 333–34; Durand 1988: 57, 393, 428; Guichard 1999.

[b] I.e., Zimri-Lim; cf. note c.

[c] Both *ittum* "sign" and *āpilum* are objects of *īmur* "he saw."

[d] Literally, "The heart of the king goes vigorously forth."

## 65. Report of Criminal Acts

**Text:** M. 9717
**Transliteration and translation:** van Koppen 2002: 356–57.
**Discussion:** van Koppen 2002: 316–18.

5 *šewirū* 1 *ḫullu ša kaspim* $^{2}$*šewirū qīštum u ḫullu* $^{3}$*ina simmištimma* $^{4}$*ina bīt mayyāli ša Sammētar imḫur*

$^{6}$1 *šewiru* 1 *ṣubātu* 10 *šamnu ṭābu inūma pagrê ilqe*

$^{7}$3 *ṣubātū ša ina bīt Sammētar* $^{8}$[. . .] *x x* [*imḫ*]*uru*

[break of approximately ten lines]

$^{r. 1'}$[. . . *iṣab*]*bat* $^{2'}$[. . . . . . -*k*]*um ša* [. . . $^{3'}$*Irra*]-*gamil išatti* $^{4'}$[*u*] *kussûm ša ina abūsim* $^{5'}$[*ša bīt*] *Sammētar* $^{6'}$[*maḫar*] *Šamši nadīma* $^{7'}$[*ina li*]*bbīšu Ir*<*ra*>*-gamil wašibma* $^{8'}$[*ina p*]*lān šapīṭim* $^{9'}$[*u*] *rabênim ša mātim* $^{10'}$[. . .] *x-i dibbī* $^{11'}$[*ina*] *ṣilli Sammētar* $^{l. e. 1}$[*mi*]*mma ša ina ṭupp*[*im annîm* $^{2}$*šaṭ*]*ru ša bīt* [*Sammētar*]

He received secretly in the bedroom of Sammetar five rings and one *ḫullum* ring of silver; the rings, as well as the *ḫullum* ring, were a gift.

$^{6}$He took one ring, one garment and ten (liters) of choice oil on the occasion of the *pagrā'um* ritual.[a]

$^{7}$Three garments that he had [rec]eived in the house of Sammetar [. . .]

[break]

$^{r. 1'}$[. . . he shall ta]ke [. . .] of [. . . Irra]-gamil shall drink.[b] [Then] the chair that is to be found in the storage room [of the house] of Sammetar shall be placed [before] Šamaš and Irra-gamil shall sit [on] it. [Bef]ore the governor [and] the magnates of the country[c] [he shall say: . . .] "My declaration is [in] the shade of Sammetar.[d] [Wh]atever is [reco]rded in [this] tabl[et] belongs to the house [of Sammetar]."

[a] For the *pagrā'um* ritual, see no. 38, note h.

[b] Giving drink to a person to obtain an oracle is mentioned in ARM 26 207 (no. 17).

[c] For the unique expression *rabênum ša mātim,* see van Koppen 2002: 357.

[d] According to van Koppen 2002: 317–18, this refers to necromancy, i.e., invocation of the spirit of Sammetar, the deceased majordomo of Mari; this text probably belongs to the same context as ARM 26 243 (no. 46). Irra-gamil is presented as a prophet of Nergal, the god of underworld, in ARM 21 333 (no. 55) and ARM 23 446 (no. 59).

# III

## Ešnunna Oracles

The evidence of prophetic oracles from the Old Babylonian period, mostly coming from Mari, is amplified by two tablets in the Free Library of Pennsylvania, deriving from the Old Babylonian city and state of Ešnunna and published by Maria deJong Ellis (1987). Each tablet, one of which is badly damaged, contains an oracle of the goddess Kititum, a local manifestation of Ištar, to King Ibalpiel II of Ešnunna. He was a contemporary of King Zimri-Lim of Mari, reigning approximately 1779–1765, and is well known from Mari documents—including the quotations of prophecy, in which he is called "the man of Ešnunna," with whom Zimri-Lim should not ally himself (nos. 7, 9).

The two Kititum oracles show that the divine words Ibalpiel received were in many respects similar to those delivered to his contemporary Zimri-Lim and the later Assyrian kings. Even though the texts make no mention of human intermediaries, they are likely to be based on prophetic performances in the temple of Kititum, in the archive of which they probably have been deposited. The plain style and the quality of the language suggest the involvement of a competent scribe recording an oral performance (Moran 1993: 257). As regards the form and content, the better-preserved text (no. 66) represents the type of a letter from a deity to the king called *šipirtu,* which contains only divine words without further authorship indications (Pongratz-Leisten 1999: 204). Otherwise it is analogous to the Assyrian prophecy reports. It begins with indications of the divine speaker and the addressee, followed by the actual message written in highly polished style, with many reminiscences of literary works and divination texts.

The fully preserved oracle to Ibalpiel presents the type of the oracle of well-being—*šulmu* or *Heilsorakel*—well known from the Hebrew Bible as well as from the documents from Mari and Assyria. The goddess promises to reveal to the pious king the "secrets of the gods," in other words, the decisions of the divine council, by which the country is given to his rule. The stability of the throne and the well-being of the country are guaranteed by this divine support. As such, the Kititum oracle is a purebred specimen of ancient Near Eastern royal prophecy.

## 66. Oracle of Kititum to Ibalpiel

**Text:** FLP 1674.
**Photograph:** Ellis 1987: 260.
**Copy:** Ellis 1987: 259.
**Transliteration and translation:** Ellis 1987: 240, 258; Moran 1993: 253.
**Discussion:** Ellis 1987: 240–41, 258–66; 1989: 138–40; Huffmon 1992: 480; Moran 1993; Nissinen 1993: 223–24; 2000a: 242–43; 2002b: 9–10; Laato 1996: 256–59; Malamat 1998: 20; van der Toorn 1998b: 64; Pongratz-Leisten 1999: 204–5; Grabbe 2000: 24–25; Charpin 2001: 42; 2002: 22.

*šar Ibâl-pî-ēl* [2]*umma Kitītumma* [3]*niṣrētum ša ilī* [4]*maḫrīya šaknā* [5]*aššum zikrum* [6]*ša šumīya ina pîka* [7]*kayyānu niṣrēt ilī* [8]*aptanattiakkum*

O king Ibalpiel, thus says Kititum: [3]The secrets of the gods are placed before me. Because you constantly pronounce my name with your mouth,[a] I constantly disclose the secrets of the gods to you.

[9]*ina milki* [10]*ša ilī ina šipṭi* [11]*ša Anim mātum* [12]*ana bēlim* [13]*nadnatkum* [14]*šīn mātim elītim* [15]*u šaplītim tapaṭṭar* [16]*makkūr mātim elītim* [17]*u šaplītim tepedde* [18]*maḫīrka ul imaṭṭi* [19]*ayyim mātim ša qātka* [20]*ikšudū akal* [21]*tanēḫtim ikā[niššum]*

[9]On the advice of the gods and by the command of Anu, the country is given you to rule. You will ransom[b] the upper and lower country, you will amass[c] the riches of the upper and lower country. Your commerce[d] will not diminish; there will be a perm[anent[e]] food of peace[f] [for] any country that your hand keeps hold of.

[22]*išdi kussîka* [23]*anāku Kitītum* [24]*udannan lamassam* [25]*nāṣertam aštaknakkum* [26]*[u]zunka libaššiam*

[22]I, Kititum, will strengthen the foundations of your throne; I have established a protective spirit for you. May your [e]ar be attentive to me!

[a] Literally, "Because you constantly have the memory of my name in your mouth"; for the expression *zikir šumim,* see Kraus 1971.

[b] The reading (*ši-in* … *ta-pa-ṭa*$_3$*-ar*) and translation of lines 14–15 according to Ellis 1987: 261–63, who interprets the "loosening of the sandals" (*šēnam paṭārum*) as an idiom; cf. Moran 1993: 255. For *šēnum* "sandal", see Salonen 1969: 16–17, 27.

[c] If the word *te-pé-ed-de* may be derived from *pedû* "to ransom/redeem" (Ellis 1987: 263), the lines 16–17 form a parallelism with the lines 14–15. Moran 1993: 255 opts for *bedûm,* translating "you will have at your disposal."

[d] Literally, "your market price."

[e] Thus according to the restoration of Ellis 1987: 264.

[f] The expression *akal tanēḫtim* is not attested elsewhere but can be compared with, e.g., *aklu taqnu* and *mê taqnūti* in the Neo-Assyrian prophetic oracle SAA 9 1.10 (no. 77) vi 22–23.

## 67. Oracle of Kititum to Ibalpiel

**Text:** FLP 2064.
**Photograph:** Ellis 1987: 239.
**Copy:** Ellis 1987: 239.

*šar Ibâl-pî-ēl* [2]*umma Kitītumma*
[3][. . .] *ukannišakkum*
[remaining eighteen lines very fragmentary]

O king Ibalpiel, Thus says Kititum:
[3][. . .] I have subjugated to you.
[rest too fragmentary for translation]

IV

# Nineveh Oracles

The second biggest corpus of ancient Near Eastern prophetic texts outside the Hebrew Bible comes from the royal archive of Nineveh, which is the main source of our knowledge of the Neo-Assyrian empire (see Parpola 1995). This archive, destroyed by the Babylonians and Medes in the year 612 B.C.E. and discovered by Sir Austen Henry Layard in 1848–1850, also functioned as the royal library. It is the most prolific repository of cuneiform documents found thus far: the Nineveh excavations unearthed almost 30,000 clay tablets now deposited in the British Museum. About 24,000 of them belong to the so-called Library of Assurbanipal, the remaining approximately 6,000 texts forming the archival corpus which, supplemented by the less numerous texts from other Neo-Assyrian archives, is being published in the series State Archives of Assyria (SAA) by the Neo-Assyrian Text Corpus Project in Helsinki.

The Neo-Assyrian archival corpus consists of documents of different kinds: royal correspondence, administrative records (lists of persons, legal transactions, decrees and gifts etc.), treaties, religious and literary texts, divination texts like astrological reports and oracle queries—and prophetic oracles: words of deities to humans, transmitted by a human intermediary, the *raggimu,* or his female counterpart, the *raggintu*. These oracles, consisting of the eleven tablets published by Simo Parpola (1997), are included in this chapter. In addition to the actual oracles, there is further evidence of prophecy in other Neo-Assyrian sources collected in the next chapter.

The Neo-Assyrian prophetic oracles are written on two kinds of tablets. Some of them (nos. 90–96) are recorded individually each on its own tablet, while others (nos. 68–89) are collected on larger tablets composed of several oracles. This roughly corresponds to two basic tablet formats: the horizontal report format used for disposable documents which only occasionally were deposited in the archives, and the vertical format, often consisting of several columns and used for letters, lists, treaties and other documents meant for long-term preservation (Parpola 1997: liii; cf. Radner 1995). The two tablet types give a clue to the transformation of oral prophetic communications into literature. The reports of individual oracles are the most immediate records of a prophetic performance. They may be taken as scribal formulations of the substance of the divine message spoken by the prophet. The reports are not written according to a strict formal standard, and they were probably composed only to preserve the message until it had reached its destination; only very few of them ended up in the archives. Sometimes, however, there was a need to make a selection of individual oracles and subsequently rewrite them in a collection edited by the scribes. In this phase, not only editorial selection and stylization of the oracles takes place, but prophecy is reused in a new situation and finally becomes a part of written tradition transcending specific historical situations and retaining its relevance in changing circumstances (van der Toorn 2000; Nissinen 2000a).

The fact that the extant documentation of Neo-Assyrian prophecy consists of no more than twenty-nine individual oracles, only seven of which have been preserved on their original tablets, gives reason to conclude that in Assyria, as at Mari, it was not the standard procedure to preserve prophetic messages for the posterity. The reports may have been produced on a much larger scale than the extant copies suggest; if so, they were probably disposed of soon after their use. To the best of our knowledge, Esarhaddon and Assurbanipal were the only kings of Assyria who purposefully let prophecies be filed away, and all the preserved collections derive from Esarhaddon's time. This, together with the fact that these two kings are the only ones to mention prophets in their inscriptions, makes it probable that they were more attentive to prophecy than any of their predecessors. Their special appreciation of prophecy is possibly due to their demonstrably close relationship with the cult of Ištar of Arbela, the principal divine speaker of the prophetic oracles (Parpola 1997: xxxix–xl).

In general, the socioreligious status of the Assyrian prophets was bound to their fundamental and well documented affiliation with the temples of Ištar. Their communication with the king was enabled by their position as servants of the goddess whose words they were believed and supposed to transmit. When delivering oracles, they, in fact, impersonated the deity speaking. Hence, the divine authority of their messages, guaranteed by the proper context of the proclamation, weighed more than their personalities. Functionally, the proclamation of the divine will by the prophets is comparable to the study of omens by the ancient scholars, and prophecy was indeed regarded as one branch of divination among the others in Assyria. However, the divinatory method, the education and the social position of the prophets were clearly different from those of the scholars. As successors of the antediluvian sages, the astrologers, haruspices and exorcists were versed in traditional literature, whereas the prophets' expertise was in becoming possessed by the god(dess) rather than literary skills. The communication of the prophets with the king was obviously less direct than that of the scholars who carried on a correspondence with him and belonged to his closest advisory board. To this should be added that the Assyrian prophets known to us are predominantly women, which cannot be said of the scholars, all of whom are male. While the prophets, hence, clearly represent a class different from the scholars, the function and purpose of prophecy was not regarded as different from that of divination in general. All divination was supposed to share the theological and ideological foundation of the Neo-Assyrian empire and to work for its goals.

The Neo-Assyrian prophetic oracles are most illustrative specimens of prophecy, as they almost without exception name the main components of the prophetic process of communication: the divine speaker, the human addressee and the prophet who mediates.

With regard to the socioreligious affiliation of the prophets to the temples of Ištar it is not surprising that this goddess in her various aspects appears more often than not as the divine speaker in prophetic oracles. Among the manifestations of the goddess, Ištar of Arbela and Mullissu (who in the Neo-Assyrian era was equated with Ištar of Nineveh) most frequently have the word, but she may also appear in hypostases like Banitu (no. 78) and Urkittu (no. 83)—even as "the goddesses" (*ištarāti*) of Babylon (no. 78). However, Ištar is not the only divine speaker in Neo-Assyrian prophetic oracles, and nothing prevented the prophets from speaking on behalf of different deities. One oracle (no. 71) is presented as the word of three deities, Bel, Ištar and Nabû, and in numbers 84–88, the prophet La-dagil-ili proclaims the word of both Aššur and Ištar. This is probably due to an aspectual—rather than "polytheistic"—concept of the divine, that is, a concept according to which the individual deities represent different aspects of one universal divinity. This makes the prophecies an important source for the study of Assyrian religion (Parpola 1997: xviii–xxvi; cf. Parpola 2000).

The addressee of the Neo-Assyrian prophetic oracles is usually the king of Assyria, either Esarhaddon (681–669) or Assurbanipal (668–627), both of whom received prophecies already as crown princes. In a few oracles the deity speaks to Esarhaddon's mother, Naqia (nos. 75, 78; probably also nos. 74, 83), and one is proclaimed to the people of Assyria as a whole (no. 85), but even these texts deal with matters concerning Esarhaddon. The strong concentration on the king and the royal family is not surprising, given that the texts derive from archives of the two kings who showed a special predilection for prophets and the worship of their patroness Ištar. Whether the same was also true for Assyrian prophecy during the reigns of their predecessors, cannot be said because of the lack of evidence, even though there is no doubt that the kings in general were the most prominent addressees of prophetic oracles. However, the most immediate context of the prophets was the temple rather than the court, and some of the texts collected in the next chapter show that prophecies could be delivered to other persons as well, for example to temple officials and even to private persons.

With the exception of number 93, the sources—both reports and collections—are careful to mention the name and gender of the transmitter of each oracle, usually also the city in which the prophet is based. This indicates that the personalities of the prophets and prophetesses were not altogether indifferent, even though subordinate to the divine authority. The purpose of the colophons indicating the provenance of the oracles is probably to confirm that the oracle in question was really spoken in an appropriate context. For the study of Neo-Assyrian prophecy, again, they reveal many important features. First, the names of the prophets are highly theological, themselves carrying a message relevant to the worship of Ištar, such as, *Ilūssa-āmur* "I have seen her divinity"; *Issār-bēlī-da''ini* "Ištar, strengthen my lord!"; *Issār-lā-tašīyaṭ* "Do not neglect Ištar!"; *Sinqīša-āmur* "I have seen her distress." Secondly, they show the predominance of women among the prophets: eight out of thirteen prophets whose personalia have been preserved in the oracles are women, and more prophetesses are known from other Neo-Assyrian documents (nos. 105, 109–111, 113–114). To be noted is that in two or three cases (nos. 71, 72 and possibly no. 68) the gender of the prophet is not clear due to incongruent personal details. It is possible that these persons assumed an undefinable gender role, comparable to that of the *assinnu*s. Thirdly, Arbela appears as the most important base of the prophets (Nissinen 2001a). Seven prophets are located in that city, the Ištar temple of which was doubtless the cradle of Neo-Assyrian prophecy; even prophets that are indicated to come from elsewhere speak on behalf of Ištar of Arbela (nos. 70, 81). Other localities mentioned as domiciles of the prophets include Assur (nos. 72, 78), Calah (no. 81) and the otherwise unknown Dara-aḫuya (no. 70). In addition, nonprophetic Neo-Assyrian sources document prophetic activities elsewhere in Mesopotamia, e.g., in Babylon (no. 103), Akkad (no. 109) and Harran (no. 115).

In accordance with the royal context of the extant prophetic oracles, their contents are entirely focused on the king, his rule and his relationship with the divine world. The prophecies delivered to Esarhaddon and Assurbanipal represent a very distinctive royal theology based on the idea of a close relationship of the king with the goddess, the king serving as her son and chosen one (Parpola 1997: xxxvi–xliv). Most of the prophecies can be characterized as oracles of well-being (*šulmu*), proclaiming the reconciliation of the king with the gods. This reconciliation guarantees the equilibrium of heaven and earth, as demonstrated by the stable rule of the Assyrian king, his superiority over all enemies and adversaries and the legitimate succession. The divine reconciliation is effected by the intercession of Ištar who protects the king and fights for him; this is described by rich metaphorical language, that employs maternal images side by side with metaphors for destruction, often taken from nature (Weippert 1985).

Most of the prophecies are easily datable and can be more or less firmly associated with historical events. The ten oracles of the first collection (nos. 68–77) are proclaimed during Esarhaddon's victorious war against his brothers before his rise to power in the year 681; this is the most probable historical background of number 90, too. The third collection (nos. 84–88) is composed of oracles and cultic commentaries attached to Esarhaddon's enthronement ritual in Ešarra, the temple of Aššur in Assur, which took place in Adar (XII), 681. The prophecies collected in the second collection (nos. 78–83) deal with the stabilization of Esarhaddon's rule and the reestablishment of the cult of the gods of Babylon; they are likely to have been uttered at the outset of his reign. Of the prophecies addressed to Assurbanipal, one presents him as the crown prince (no. 92); however, this part of the tablet may be a quotation from an earlier oracle. Tablet 93, which is formally somewhat different from the others, contains divine words concerning one of Assurbanipal's Elamite campaigns, most probably that of the year 653. The latest datable prophecy (no. 94) is connected with Assurbanipal's war against his elder brother Šamaš-šumu-ukin, the ruler of Babylonia; this can be verified by the date in the colophon (Nisan 18, 650).

As for the dates of the collections, it is important to note the temporal difference between the proclamation of the oracles and their subsequent compilation. This is especially noteworthy in the case of the first collection, which is probably drawn up at the same time and for the same purpose as Esarhaddon's Nineveh A inscription (no. 97), dated to Adar (XII), 673 (see the introduction to the following chapter). The re-actualization of oracles delivered seven years earlier by rewriting and compiling them lifted them from specific historical situations and turned them into a part of written tradition that could be used and reinterpreted by posterity.

## 68–77. First Collection of Prophecies<br>Different Prophets to Esarhaddon

**Text:** SAA 9 1 (= *4 R*$^2$ 61 = K 4310).
**Photograph:** Mattila (ed.) 1995: 162 (obv.); Parpola 1997: pls. I–III.
**Copy:** Smith 1875: 68; Pinches in Rawlinson 1891: 61.

**Transliteration and translation:** Delattre 1889; Pinches in Sayce (ed.) 1891: 129–40; Banks 1898: 267–77; Schmidtke 1916: 115–23; Parpola 1997: 4–11.
**Translation:** Gray in Harper (ed.) 1904: 414–19; Jastrow 1912: 158–65; Langdon 1914: 128–33; Ebeling in Greßmann (ed.) 1926: 281–83; Luckenbill 1927: 238–41; Pfeiffer 1955: 449–50; Biggs 1969: 605; Hecker 1986: 56–60; Talon 1994: 121–22; Mattila (ed.) 1995: 163–66.
**Discussion:** Greßmann 1914: 289–90; Harner 1969: 419–21; Ishida 1977: 90–92; Parpola 1997: il–lii, lv–lvi, lxviii–lxix; Nissinen 2000a: 248–54; Huffmon 2000: 57–59; van der Toorn 2000: 74–75; Weippert 2001; 2002: 40–42; Steymans 2002.

## 68. SAA 9 1.1 (lines i 4'-29')
## Issar-la-tašiyaṭ to Esarhaddon

**Translation and/or discussion:** Labat 1939: 257; Westermann 1964: 362; Labat in Labat et alii 1970: 257; Ramlot 1972: 881; Weippert 1972: 473–74; 1981: 81–84, 98; 1985: 67–68; 2001: 41, 43; Dijkstra 1980: 160; Nissinen 1991: 120; 1993, 225, 244; 1998b: 25, 94; Sicre 1992: 239; Laato 1992: 62–65; 1996: 186–87; Rowlett 1996: 117; Fales and Lanfranchi 1997: 109; Villard 2001: 71–72; Steymans 2002: 192–97.

4' *[Aššūr-aḫu-]iddina šar mātāti* 5' *[lā t]apallaḫ* 6' *[a]yyu šāru ša idibakkāni* 7' *aqappušu lā aksupūni* 8' *nakarūtēka* 9' *kî šaḫšūri ša Simāni* 10' *ina pān šēpēka ittangararrū*

11' *Bēltu rabītu anāku* 12' *anāku Issār ša Arbail* 13' *ša nakarūtēka* 14' *ina pān šēpēka akkarrūni* 15' *ayyūte dibbīya ša* 16' *aqqabakkanni* 17' *ina muḫḫi lā tazzizūni*
18' *anāku Issār ša Arbail* 19' *nakarūtēka ukāṣa* 20' *addanakka anāku* 21' *Issār ša Arbail* 22' *ina pānātūka* 23' *ina kutallīka* 24' *allāka*
*lā tapallaḫ* 25' *atta ina libbi muggi* 26' *anāku ina libbi ū'a* 27' *atabbi uššab*

4'[Esarh]addon, king of the lands, fear [not]! What is the wind that has attacked you,[a] whose wings I have not broken? Like ripe apples[b] your enemies will continually roll[c] before your feet.

11'I am the great Lady, I am Ištar of Arbela who throw your enemies before your feet. Have I spoken to you any words that you could not rely upon?

18'I am Ištar of Arbela, I will flay[d] your enemies and deliver them up to you. I am Ištar of Arbela, I go before you and behind you.

24'Fear not! You have got cramps, but I, in the midst of wailing, will get up and sit down.[e]

[28']*ša pî Issār-lā-tašīyaṭ* [29']*mār Arbail*

[28']By the mouth of Issar-la-tašiyaṭ, a man[f] from Arbela.

---

[a] The word *idibakkāni* is derived from *tabû* "to rise"; see Parpola 1997: 4 and Nissinen 1991: 120 n. 145.

[b] Literally, "like apples of Siman (III)," i.e., the month in which apples mellow in Assyria.

[c] Derived from the four-radical verb *nagarruru* "to roll." Cf. Fales and Lanfranchi 1997: 109, who derive the word from *q/garāru* "to bend": "Your enemies bend at your feet like branches of the apple-tree in the spring."

[d] The collations of Hecker 1986: 57 and Parpola 1997: 4 confirm the reading *ú-ka-a-ṣa* instead of the erroneus *ú-ka-a-a,* adopted from Pinches by earlier editions and translations.

[e] The "getting up" and "sitting down" is probably an expression for the whole action of the goddess, who rises to the king's rescue, fights for him, and finally returns to her place.

[f] The masculine determinative of the PN is written over an erased feminine determinative; this either indicates an error of the scribe or his uncertainty about the gender of the prophet; cf. no. 71, note f.

## 69. SAA 9 1.2 (lines i 30'–ii 10')
## Sinqiša-amur to Esarhaddon

**Translation and/or discussion:** Nissinen 1993: 247; 1998b: 20, 153; Laato 1996: 177–78; Pongratz-Leisten 1999: 94; Weippert 2002: 40.

[30']*šar māt Aššūr lā tapallaḫ* [31']*nakru ša šar māt Aššūr* [32']*ana ṭabaḫḫi addana* [33']*[ina] bēt rēdūtēka* [34']*[utaqq]anka* [35']*[urabb]akka*

[30']King of Assyria, fear not!

[31']The enemy of the king of Assyria I will lead to the slaughter. [In] the Palace of Succession[a] [I prote]ct you and [rai]se you.

[36']*[Bēltu rab]ītu anāku* [37']*[anāku Issār š]a Arbail* [38']*[... is]su libbīšu* [39']*[...] -šu*

[36']I am [the gr]eat Lady, [I am Ištar o]f Arbela! [... fr]om it. [...]

[break of about six lines]

[break]

ii [1']*[...]* [2']*a[yy]u [...]* [3']*lā ašmēk[a] [nakarūti]* [4']*ina sigar[āti salmūti]* [5']*ina madda[nāti ...]* [6']*nakarka ina lib[bi qarābi]* [7']*ēdānīe akt[ašad]*

[1'][...] w[ha]t [...] I did not hear y[ou]? [I will bring enemies] in necksto[cks, allies] with tribu[te]. I have de[feated] your enemy in a single [combat]!

[8']*utakkilka lā ušbā[ku]*

[8']I have inspired you with confidence, [I] do not sit idle.

| | |
|---|---|
| 9' *ša pî Sinqīša-āmur* 10' *mar᾽at Arbail* | 9'By the mouth of Sinqiša-amur, a woman from Arbela. |

[a] When the crown prince of Assyria was chosen, he entered the Palace of Succession (*bēt rēdūti*) in which he not only was prepared for his future kingship, but also took part in the administration of the empire. Note that Esarhaddon is already addressed as the king, even though he, at the time of the proclamation of the oracle, still seems to dwell in the Palace of Succession. This may seem contradictory (Weippert 2002: 40), but the oracle may have been proclaimed after the death of Sennacherib, reflecting the conviction of the prophetic circles that Esarhaddon was predestined to kingship.

## 70. SAA 9 1.3 (lines ii 11'–15')
## Remut-Allati to Esarhaddon

**Translation and/or discussion:** Sicre 1992: 239; Nissinen 1998b: 28; 2001a: 206-7.

| | |
|---|---|
| 11' *rīšāk issi Aššūr-aḫu-iddina* 12' *šar-rīya rīši Arbail* | 11'I[a] rejoice over Esarhaddon, my king! Arbela rejoices![b] |
| 13' *ša pî Rēmūt-Allati* 14' *ša Dāra-aḫūya* 15' *ša birti šaddâni* | 13'By the mouth of the woman Remut-Allati from Dara-aḫuya[c] in the mountains. |

[a] Even though there is no self-presentation formula, the speaker is certainly Ištar of Arbela (rather than the prophetess).

[b] Or, "Rejoice, Arbela!"

[c] An otherwise unknown locality; geographical position unknown (cf. Nissinen 2001a: 206–7).

## 71. SAA 9 1.4 (lines ii 16'–40')
## Bayâ to Esarhaddon

**Translation and/or discussion:** Wolff 1961: 256; Nougayrol 1968b: 68; Dietrich 1973: 41; Dijkstra 1980: 160; Tadmor 1982: 458; Nissinen 1991: 285; 1993: 226; 1998b: 19, 94, 121; 2002b: 15-16; Sicre 1992: 239; Laato 1996: 177; Rowlett 1996: 117; Parpola 2000: 174, 205; van der Toorn 2000: 83; Weippert 2001: 42; 2002: 14-15; Villard 2001: 70.

[16']*lā tapallaḫ Aššūr-aḫu-iddina* [17']*anāku Bēl issīka* [18']*adabbūbu* [19']*gušūrē ša libbīka* [20']*aḫarrīdi kî ummaka* [21']*tušabšûkāni* [22']*šūš ilāni rabûti issīya* [23']*ittitissū ittaṣarūka* [24']*Sîn ina imittīka Šamaš ina šumēlīka* [25']*šūš ilāni rabûti ina battibattīka* [26']*izzazzū qabalka irtaksū*

[16']Fear not, Esarhaddon! I am Bel, I speak to you! I watch over the supporting beams of your heart. When[a] your mother gave birth to you, sixty Great Gods stood[b] there with me, protecting you. Sîn stood at your right side, Šamaš at your left. Sixty Great Gods are still standing[c] around you; they have girded your loins.

[27']*ina muḫḫi amēlūti lā tatakkil* [28']*mutuḫ ēnēka* [29']*ana ayyāši dugulanni* [30']*anāku Issār ša Arbail* [31']*Aššūr issīka ussallim* [32']*ṣeḫerāka attaṣakka* [33']*lā tapallaḫ na''idanni* [34']*ayyu šū nakru* [35']*ša idibakkanni* [36']*anāku qālākūni* [37']*urkīūte lū kî pānīūte* [38']*anāku Nabû bēl qarṭuppi* [39']*na''idāni*

[27']Do not trust in humans! Lift up your eyes and focus on me! I am Ištar of Arbela. I have reconciled Aššur to you. I protected you when you were a baby. Fear not; praise me!

[34']Is there an enemy that has attacked you, while I have kept silent? The future shall be like the past![d] I am Nabû, the Lord of the Stylus.[e] Praise me!

---

[40']*ša pî* MÍ.*Bayâ mār Arbail*

[40']By the mouth of the woman Bayâ, a man[f] from Arbela.

---

[a] The past tenses of the following verbs imply that the particle *kî* should be understood here in its temporal rather than comparative meaning ("Like the mother"; thus Biggs 1969: 605; Hecker 1986: 57), referring to the very childhood of the king nursed in the temple of Ištar; see Parpola 1997: xxxix-xl and cf. Assurbanipal's hymn to Ištar SAA 3 3 13:13-15: "I knew no father or mother, I grew up in the lap of my goddesses. As a child the great gods guided me, going with me on the right and the left."

[b] The word *ittitissū* is G perf. sg.3. of *uzuzzu;* see Hämeen-Anttila 2000a: 99.

[c] Unlike the other verbs on lines 19'-26', the verb *uzuzzu* is in present form here. This indicates that from line 25' on, the oracle refers to the present (cf. the translation of Dietrich 1973: 41). Cf. the same expression by the same prophet in SAA 9 2.2 (no. 79) i 21.

[d] Cf. SAA 9 2.2 (no. 79) i 17–18.

[e] The epithet "Lord of the Stylus" refers to Nabû as the writer of the "tablet of destiny" of mankind.

[f] The gender of the prophet is ambiguous: Bayâ is called a "son" (DUMU) of Arbela, but the determinative before the PN is feminine: MÍ.*ba-ia-a* DUMU URU.*arba-ìl* Cf. the correction of the determinative before the name of Issar-la-tašiyaṭ (line i 28'; see no. 68, note f). Bayâ possibly belonged to those with undefinable gender role, like the *assinnus* (see Nissinen 1998c: 28-34), among whom there were

prophets at Mari. It is noteworthy that the name Bayâ is used as male and female name alike (see *PNA* 1/II: 253), which makes it possible that the writing here reflects a lapse of the scribe (thus Weippert 2002: 34).

## 72. SAA 9 1.5 (lines iii 1'-6')
## Ilussa-amur to Esarhaddon

| | |
|---|---|
| [beginning {about fourteen lines} destroyed] | [beginning destroyed] |
| [three lines too fragmentary for translation] | |
| 2' *anāku* [. . .] 3' *atta tal-*[. . .] 4' *anāku Mu[llissu . . .]* | 2' I [. . .] you shall [. . .] I am Mu[llissu . . .] |
| 5' *ša pî* MÍ.*Ilūssa-ām[ur]* 6' *Libbālā[yu]* | 5' By the mouth of the woman Ilussa-am[ur][a] of Assur.[b] |

[a] This name, probably referring to the same person, appears also in the provisions list *KAV* 121.

[b] In the prophetic oracles, the city of Assur is always called *Libbi-āli* (*Libbāli*), "Inner City." Note that in spite of the female determinative MÍ, the gentilic adjective *Libbālāyu* is masculine; the feminine equivalent would be *Libbālītu* (see *PNA* 2/II: 661). Cf. no. 71 note f.

## 73. SAA 9 1.6 (lines iii 7'–iv 35)
## NN to Esarhaddon

**Translation and/or discussion:** Zimmerli 1953: 194–95; Labat in Labat et alii 1970: 257–58; Dijkstra 1980: 154, 161; Weippert 1981: 84–87; 1985: 58–60, 63, 68–70; 2002: 40–42; van der Toorn 1987: 86; Bodi 1991: 91; Nissinen 1991: 286; 1993: 231–32; 1998b: 24, 29, 94; 2001a: 186–87; Sicre 1992: 239–40; Rowlett 1996: 117; Pongratz-Leisten 1999: 93; van der Toorn 2000: 85–86; Villard 2001: 73; Steymans 2002: 192–97.

| | |
|---|---|
| 7' *anāku Issār ša [Arbail]* 8' *Aššūr-aḫu-iddina šar māt A[ššūr]* | 7' I am Ištar of [Arbela]! Esarhaddon, king of A[ssyria]! |
| 9' *ina Libbi-āli Nīnu[a]* 10' *Kalḫi Arbai[l]* 11' *ūmē arkūt[e]* 12' *šanāte dārāt[e]* 13' *ana Aššūr-aḫu-iddina šarrīya* 14' *addanna* | 9' In Assur, Ninev[eh], Calah and Arbe[la] I will give endle[ss] days and everlasti[ng] years to Esarhaddon, my king. |

15' *sabsubtak[a]* 16' *rabītu anāku* 17' *mušēni[q]taka* 18' *deʾiqtu anāku* 19' *ša ūmē arkūte* 20' *šanāte dārāte* 21' *kussīka ina šapal šamê* 22' *rabûte uktīn*

15'I am yo[ur] great midwife, I am your excellent wet nurse. For endless days and everlasting years I have established your throne under the great heavens.

23' *ina massiki ša ḫurāṣi* 24' *ina qabassi šamê aḫarrīdi* 25' *nūr ša elmēši* 26' *ina pān Aššūr-aḫu-iddina šar māt Aššūr* 27' *ušanamāra* 28' *kî agê ša kaqqidīya* 29' *aḫarrissu*

23'I keep watch in a golden chamber in the middle of heaven, I let a lamp of amber[a] shine in front of Esarhaddon, king of Assyria, I guard him like the crown on my own head.[b]

30' *lā tapallaḫ šarru* 31' *aqṭibak* 32' *lā aslīk[a]* iv 1 *utakki[lka]* 2 *lā ubâš[ka]* 3 *nāru ina tuqunni* 4 *ušēbar[ka]*

30'Fear not, king! I have spoken to you, I have not slandered yo[u]! I have inspi[red you] with confidence, I have not caused [you] to come to shame! I will lead [you] safely across the River.[c]

5 *Aššūr-aḫu-iddina aplu* 6 *kēnu mār Mullissi* 7 *ḫangaru akku* 8 *ina qātēya* 9 *nakarūtēka* 10 *uqatta* 11 *Aššūr-aḫu-iddina šar māt Aššūr* 12 *kāsu ša mallû qīlte* 13 *kalappu ša šinā šiqli*

iv 5Esarhaddon, legitimate heir, son of Mullissu! With a sharp dagger[d] in my hand I will put an end to your enemies. Esarhaddon, king of Assyria—cup filled with lye, axe of two shekels![e]

14 *Aššūr-aḫu-iddina ina Libbi-āli* 15 *ūmē arkūti* 16 *šanāti dārāti* 17 *addanakk[a]* 18 *Aššūr-aḫu-iddina ina libbi Arbai[l]* 19 *arītka deʾiqtu a[nāku]*

14Esarhaddon, in Assur[f] I will give yo[u] endless days and everlasting years! Esarhaddon, in Arbe[la] I [will be] your effective shield!

20 *Aššūr-aḫu-iddina aplu k[ēnu]* 21 *mār Mul[lissi]* 22 *ḫissat[ka]* 23 *ḫassā[ku]* 24 *artāmk[a]* 25 *adan[niš]* 26 *ina kizirtīk[a]* 27 *ina šamê rabûti* 28 *ukâlka*

20Esarhaddon, leg[itimate] heir, son of Mul[lissu]! [I] keep thinking of [you], I have loved yo[u] great[ly]! I hold you by yo[ur] curl[g] in the great heavens.

29 *ina imittīka* 30 *qutru uqatt[ar]* 31 *ina šumēlīk[a]* 32 *išātu ušaḫ[ḫaz]* 33 *šarrūtu ina muḫḫi* [. . .]

[two lines too fragmentary for translation; rest {about fourteen lines} destroyed]

30I make smoke go up on your right, I light a fire on your left. The kingship upon [. . .]

[rest destroyed]

[a] For the meaning "amber" of the word *elmēšu* (Heb. *ḥašmal* Ez 1:4, 27; 8:2), see Bodi 1991: 82–94 and Heltzer 1999, who demonstrates its Baltic origin.

[b] Lines 23–29 are reminiscent of the mystical commentary SAA 3 39:30–32: "The middle heaven of *saggilmud* stone is of the Igigi gods. Bel sits there in a

high temple on a dais of lapis lazuli and has made a lamp of amber (*elmešu*) shine there."

[c] Besides mythical allusions, the "River" may have a concrete reference here, since the crossing of the river Tigris was the final effort before invading Nineveh and gaining the victory in the civil war against his brothers (Nin A i 84–86; cf. no. 97); see already Banks 1898: 273 and cf. Nissinen 1998b: 21.

[d] Because of the ambiguous meaning and etymology of the words *ḫangaru akku,* the translation is tentative. While *ḫangaru* can be derived from Syr. *ḥangrā* "dagger" (von Soden 1977: 18; Parpola 1997: 8), *akku* yields a twofold interpretation. The above translation takes it as a verbal adjective of *akāku/ekēku* "scratch," while the translation "angry" (Parpola 1997: 8) equates it with *aggu* "angry" (cf. Syr. *ʾakketā,* von Soden 1977: 184).

[e] The point of these curious metaphors may be that the cup and the "axe" of two shekels (only 32 gr.!), harmless as they seem, contain destructive power.

[f] See no. 72, note b.

[g] The meaning of *kizirtu* is not altogether clear; the translation "curl" is based on *kezēru* and its derivatives, which refer to a characteristic hairdo. In *ABL* 1277:3 (*pillurtu kizirtu ša Nabû šī* "the cross is the *kizirtu* of Nabû") the word seems to mean an emblem of the god.

## 74. SAA 9 1.7 (lines v 1–11) Issar-beli-da››ini to the Queen Mother

**Translation and/or discussion:** Nötscher 1966: 184; R. R. Wilson 1980: 114–15; Weippert 1985: 66–67; Nissinen 1998b: 23, 75.

[beginning destroyed]
[1]*. . . issu pānīšu* [2]*lā imaḫḫar* [3]*kakkišāti* [4]*pušḫāti* [5]*ša idabbabūni* [6]*ina pān šēpēšu* [7]*ubattaqšunu* [8]*atti attīma* [9]*šarru šarrīma*

---

[10]*ša pî Issār-bēlī-da››ini* [11]*šēlūtu ša šarri*

---

[beginning destroyed]
[1][. . .] He will not receive [. . .] from him! The conspiring polecats and rats[a] I will cut in pieces before his feet! You[b] are who you are, the king is my king!

---

[10]By the mouth of Issar-beli-da››ini, a votaress of the king.[c]

---

[a] The words *kakkišu* (cf. Syr. *karkuštā*) and *pušḫu* (equated with *ḫulû* "shrew" in *STT* 402 r. 20) are names of rodents, mustelids, or insectivores, here used for the adversaries of Esarhaddon. *Kakkišu* is used in a similar meaning in SAA 10 352 (no. 109) and, possibly, in SAA 9 4 (no. 89; see Nissinen 1998b: 74–75).

[b] The feminine pronoun indicates that the queen mother Naqia (rather than the prophetess; cf. Hecker 1986: 59) is addressed; cf. the next oracle.

[c] I.e., a person who has been donated by the king to the temple of Ištar.

## 75. SAA 9 1.8 (lines v 12–25)
## Aḫat-abiša to the Queen Mother

**Translation and/or discussion:** Dietrich 1973: 41–42; Dijkstra 1980: 155; Parpola 1980: 178–79; Weippert 1981: 96; Nissinen 1991: 304; 1993: 231; 1998b: 22, 87; Laato 1996: 178; Villard 2001: 67.

| | |
|---|---|
| [12]*anāku Bēlet Arbail*<br>[13]*ana ummi šarri* [14]*kî taḫḫurīninni* [15]*mā ša imitti* [16]*ša šumēli* [17]*ina sūnīki tassakni* [18]*mā īyû* [19]*ṣīt libbīya* [20]*ṣēru tussarpidi* | [12]I am the Lady of Arbela!<br>[13]To the king's mother, since you implored me, saying: "The one on the right and the other on the left[a] you have placed in your lap. My own offspring you expelled to roam the steppe!"[b] |
| [21]*ūmâ šarru lā tapallaḫ*<br>[22]*šarrūtu ikkû* [23]*danānu ikkûma* | [21]Now, king, fear not! Yours is the kingdom, yours is the power! |
| [24]*ša pî Aḫāt-abīša* [25]*mar'at Arbail* | [24]By the mouth of Aḫat-abiša, a woman from Arbela. |

[a] This refers to the rebelling brothers of Esarhaddon, who at the time of the proclamation of this oracle had the upper hand; see Parpola 1980: 175; Nissinen 1998b: 22. For later references to the position of the crown princes on the right and left side of the king, cf. SAA 10 185: 12–13: "You have placed the first on your right and the second on your left side," and the reliefs on the Zencirli stele of Esarhaddon, which has the two princes on the each side of the monument (see, e.g., Parpola and Watanabe 1988, 20).

[b] This not only alludes to Gilgameš's desperate roaming the steppe after the death of Enkidu (Gilg. ix 2–5; cf. Zimmern 1910), but also refers to the expatriation of Esarhaddon to the Western provinces during the rebellion of his brothers.

## 76. SAA 9 1.9 (lines v 26–36)
## NN to Esarhaddon

**Translation and/or discussion:** Nissinen 1991: 291–92; 1998b: 28–29; 2001a: 184.

| | |
|---|---|
| [26]*šulmu ana Aššūr-aḫu-iddina šar māt Aššūr*<br>[27]*Issār ša Arbail* [28]*ana ṣēri tattūṣi* [29]*šulmu ana mūrīša* [30]*ana birit āli* | [26]Peace[a] to Esarhaddon, king of Assyria!<br>[27]Ištar of Arbela has left for the steppe.[b] She has sent an oracle of |

*tassapra* 31 *ana uṣê[ša . . .]*

[five lines too fragmentary for translation; rest {about eight lines} destroyed]

peace[c] to her calf[d] in the city.[e] At [her] coming out [. . .]

[rest destroyed]

[a] The word *šulmu* (like the Heb. *šālôm*) has the general meaning "peace, well-being" but may also designate a greeting of peace or an "oracle of salvation" (*Heilsorakel*); cf. line 29.

[b] Ištar's "going to the steppe" refers to the temporary sojourning of the goddess in the "Palace of the Steppe" in Milqia, outside the city of Arbela; cf., no. 90 (SAA 9 5) note d.

[c] See above, note a.

[d] A verbal equivalent to the iconographic "cow-and-calf" motif in which the goddess, represented as a cow, suckles her calf, the king; see Nissinen 1991: 290, 294; Parpola 1997: xxxvi–xxxviii.

[e] Since Esarhaddon has entered the "city" (either Nineveh or Arbela) but the goddess is still in Milqia, the oracle must have been proclaimed after the conquest of Nineveh but before the triumphal return of the goddess and the enthronement of Esarhaddon.

## 77. SAA 9 1.10 (lines vi 1–32)
## La-dagil-ili to Esarhaddon

**Translation and/or discussion:** van der Toorn 1987: 86–87; 2000: 75; Nissinen 1991: 304; 1993: 232–33; 1998b: 29-30, 153; Laato 1996: 178–79.

---

2 *[anāku Bēlet Arb]ail* 3 *[Aššūr-aḫu-iddina ša] ina ṭābti* 4 *[Issār] ša Arbail* 5 *ḫabūnšu* 6 *tumal lûni* 7 *dabābu pāniu* 8 *ša aqqabakkanni* 9 *ina muḫḫi lā tazzīzi* 10 *ūmâ* 11 *ina muḫḫi urkî* 12 *tazzazma*

13 *na*<sup></sup>*ʾʾidanni* 14 *kî ūmu* 15 *išīṣūni* 16 *zīqāti* 17 *lukillū* 18 *ina pāni naʾʾidanni*

19 *[n]irriṭu* 20 *[is]su libbi ekallīya* 21 *ušēṣa* 22 *aklu taqnu takkal* 23 *mê taqnūti* 24 *tašatti* 25 *ina libbi ekallīka* 26 *tataqqun* 27 *maraʾka mār marʾīka* 28 *šarrūtu* 29 *ina burki ša Inurta* 30 *uppaš*

---

2[I am the Lady of Arb]ela!

3[Esarhaddon], whose bosom [Ištar] of Arbela has filled with favor: You could rely upon the previous word I spoke to you, couldn't you?[a] Now you can rely upon the later words, too!

13Praise me! When the daylight declines, let torches flare! Praise me before them![b]

19Fear and trembling I will banish [fr]om my palace. You shall eat safe food; you shall drink safe water; you shall live in safety in your palace.[c] Even your son and grandson will exercise kingship in the lap of Ninurta.[d]

---

[31]*ša pî Lā-dāgil-ili* [32]*mār Arbail*

[31]By the mouth of La-dagil-ili, a man from Arbela.

---

[a] Perhaps an allusion to similar words in the first oracle in this collection (lines i 15–17).

[b] Or "before me"; this refers to an unceasing worship of the goddess by day and by night.

[c] The word family *tuqqunu* indicates physical security, political stability as well as the equilibrium of heaven and earth (see Nissinen 1998b: 153); cf. SAA 9 2.5 (no. 82) iii 33–34.

[d] For the god Ninurta, son of Marduk, as the "heavenly crown prince" and the paragon of the king, see Annus 2002; Parpola 1997: xli, ci nn. 196, 197. Lines vi 19–30 cf. the oracle spoken by the same prophet SAA 9 2.3 (no. 80) ii 11–14.

## 78–83. Second Collection of Prophecies Different Prophets to Esarhaddon

**Text:** SAA 9 2 (= *TI* pl. 2–3+ = K 12033 + 82-5-22, 527).
**Photograph:** Parpola 1997: pls. IV–V.
**Copy:** Langdon 1914: pls. 2–3 (K 12033 only).
**Transliteration and translation:** Parpola 1997: 14–19.
**Translation:** Langdon 1914: 138–40.
**Discussion:** Parpola 1997: il–lii, lviii, lxix–lxx; Weippert 2002: 42–44.

## 78. SAA 9 2.1 (lines i 1'–14') [Nabû]-hussanni to Esarhaddon and to the Queen Mother

**Translation and/or discussion:** Nougayrol 1956, 159 (lines 10'–12'); Nissinen 2001a: 196–97; Weippert 2002: 42.

[beginning {about five lines} destroyed; four lines too fragmentary for translation]
[5'][... *anāku*] *Banītu* [6'][...] *utaqqan* [7'][*kussiu ša Aššūr-aḫu*]*-iddina ukâna*
[8'][...] *anīnu ištarāti* [9'][... *i*]*na Esaggil*

[beginning destroyed]

[5'][... I am] Banitu,[a] [...] I will put in order. I will establish [the throne of Esarh]addon.

[8'][...] We are the goddesses [... i]n Esaggil![b]

*10'[. . .] Aššūr-aḫu-iddina šar māt Aššūr 11'[nakarūtēka] usappak 12'[ina šēpēya] ukabbas 13'[lā tapa]lliḫi ummi šarri 14'[issu pî Nabû]-ḫussanni Libbi-ālāya*

10'[. . .] Esarhaddon, king of Assyria! I will catch [your[c] enemies] and trample them [under my foot]. 13'[Fe]ar [not], queen mother! 14'[By the mouth of Nabû]-ḫussanni[d] of Assur.

---

[a] Banitu is a designation of the creation goddess Belet-ili (Deller 1983), here appearing as an aspect of Ištar (see Parpola 1997: xviii).

[b] It is noteworthy that the goddesses or "Ištars" (*ištarāti*) of Esaggil, the main temple of Marduk in Babylon, appear as speakers in an oracle spoken by a prophet from Assur, when Babylon still lay in ruins after its destruction by Sennacherib in 689.

[c] Or "his," if the queen mother is addressed (Weippert 2002: 42).

[d] For the restoration of the name, see Parpola 1997, li.

## 79. SAA 9 2.2 (lines i 15'–35')
## Bayâ to Esarhaddon

**Translation and/or discussion:** Villard 2001: 73; Weippert 2002: 42.

*15'[lā tapal]laḫ Aššūr-aḫu-iddina 16'[akī m]allāḫi damqi ina kāri ṭābi 17'[eleppu uk]alla akī ša pānīti 18'[lū ina u]rkīti ina batbattīka 19'[asaḫḫu]r maṣṣartaka anaṣṣar*

15'[Fe]ar not, Esarhaddon! 16'[Like] a skilled [p]ilot [I will s]teer [the ship] for a good harbor.[a] [Let the f]uture be like the past![b] [I will circl]e around you; I will stand guard for you.

*20'[maṣṣartu ša] mātāti dannat adanniš 21'[šūš ilāni rabûti ina imittī]ya šūš ilāni rabûti ina šumēlīya 22'[izzazzū]*

20'The countries are [watched over] very closely. [Sixty gods are standing at] my [right], sixty gods at my left.[c]

*Aššūr-aḫu-iddina šar māt Aššūr 23'[nakarūtēk]a akaššad 24'[. . .] bēlšunu anāku 25'[. . . issu qā]tēya maḫrū 26'[. . .] uda''ināninni 27'[. . .] Aššūr-aḫu-iddina 28'[. . .] ša šamê 29'[...] paršamūtu 30'[. . .] ušallakšu 31'[. . .] ukāna 32'[. . . uša]nmar 33'[. . . š]ulmi ša [Aššūr-aḫu]-iddina 34'[. . .]*

22'Esarhaddon, king of Assyria! I will defeat yo[ur enemies]. [. . .] I am their lord [. . . .] received [from] my [ha]nd [. . .] gave me strength. 27'[. . .] Esarhaddon [. . .] of the heavens [. . .] old age [. . .] I will send him away [. . .] I will establish [. . . I will let] shine [. . . the w]ell-being of [Esarh]addon [. . .]

*35'[issu pî* MÍ.*Bay]â mār Arbailāya*

35'[By the mouth of the woman Bay]â, a man[d] of Arbela.

[a] For the occurrences of this metaphor in Mesopotamian and classical literature, see Parpola 1997: cvii n. 296, 14.
[b] Cf. SAA 9 1.4 (no. 71) ii 37.
[c] Cf. SAA 9 1.4 (no. 71) ii 22, 25.
[d] For the ambiguous gender of Bayâ, see no. 71, note f.

## 80. SAA 9 2.3 (lines i 36'–ii 28')
## La-dagil-ili to Esarhaddon

**Translation and/or discussion:** Nougayrol 1956: 159 (lines 24'–27'); Ishida 1977: 91; Weippert 1985: 64–65; 2001: 44–45; 2002: 42-44; van der Toorn 1987: 86; Nissinen 1998b: 29–30, 41–42, 101; 2001a: 197–98; 2003: 12–13.

| | |
|---|---|
| 36' *[anāku B]ēlet Arbail* 37' *[Aššūr-aḫu-iddina šar] māt Aššūr* 38' *[lā tapallaḫ* ...] [break of about six lines] ii 1' *nakarūtēka mar* [*šunūni* ...] 2' *ina libbi ekallīka lū* [*kammusāka*] | i 36' [I am the L]ady of Arbela! [Esarhaddon, king] of Assyria, [fear not! ...] [break] ii 1' Your enemies, whatever [they are, *I will defeat. You shall stay*] in your palace. |
| 3' *māt Aššūr issīka u*[*sallam*] 4' *ša kal ūme kallamār*[*i maṣṣartaka*] 5' *anaṣṣar agûka u*[*kāna*] 6' *akī iṣṣūr akappi ina mu*[*ḫḫi marʾīšu*] 7' *ina muḫḫīka aṣabbur ina batbat*[*tīk*]*a* 8' *alabbi asaḫḫur* 9' *akī murāni damqi ina ekall īka* 10' *adūal nakarūtēka uṣṣāna* | 3' I will [reconcile] Assyria with you. Throughout the day and by dawn I will stand [guard over you]; I will [establish] your crown. Like a winged bird ov[er *its fledgling*] I will twitter above you, going aroun[d yo]u, surrounding you. Like a faithful cub[a] I will run around in your palace, sniffing out your enemies. |
| 11' *ina ekallīka utaqqanka* 12' *nikittu nirriṭu ušanṣāka* 13' *maraʾka mār marʾīka* 14' *šarrūtu ina pān Inurta uppaš* 15' *taḫūmāni ša mātāti* 16' *ugammar addanakka* | 11' I will protect you in your palace, I will make you overcome fear and trembling. Your son and your grandson shall exercise kingship before Ninurta.[b] I will do away with the boundaries of the countries and give them to you. |
| 17' *amēlūtu ṭullumâ* 18' *anāku šî qābītu ēpissu* 19' *marʾutu ḫubburtu anāku* 20' *uṣṣāna ubāra adda*[*nak*]*ka* | 17' Mankind is treacherous,[c] but I am the one whose words and deeds are reliable.[d] I am the one who sniffs out and captures the riotous people[e] and gi[ves] them to you. |

21' *atta ana ayyāši na᾿᾿idanni* 22' *dibbīya annūti issu libbi Arbail* 23' *ina bētānukka esip* 24' *ilāni ša Esaggil ina ṣēri lemni balli* 25' *šarbubū arḫiš šittā maqaluāti* 26' *ina pānīšunu lušēṣiū lillikū* 27' *šulamka liqbiū*

28' *issu pî ša Lā-dāgil-ili Arbailāya*

21' You praise me! Take to heart these words of mine from Arbela: The gods of Esaggil are languishing in an evil, chaotic wilderness.[f] Let two burnt offerings be sent before them at once; let your greeting of peace be pronounced to them![g]

28' From the mouth of La-dagil-ili of Arbela.

---

[a] The word *murānu* can be used of cubs of different animals. While some translations opt for a dog (e.g., Weippert 1985: 65) as a pet animal, Parpola 1997: 15 pays attention to the fact that the animal appears as a mortal danger to the king's enemies and suggests "lion," which also is an emblematic animal of Ištar.

[b] Lines ii 11–14 cf. the oracle spoken by the same prophet SAA 9 1.10 (no. 77) vi 19–30.

[c] For *ṭullumâ* (cf. Syr. *ṭolûm*), see von Soden 1968: 261.

[d] Literally, "I am the one who says and does," i.e., who gives orders and puts them into effect. The emphasis here is on the contrast between the goddess and mankind

[e] Literally, "the noisy daughter," a unique metaphor that may refer to mankind as the "noisy" creation of the gods in the Atrahasis Epic (Lambert and Millard 1969: 72: 106–21). Weippert 2001: 44–45; 2002: 42–44 interprets line 19 differently, interpreting *ḫubburtu* as "active" and translating "Ein tatkräftiges Mädchen bin ich!"

[f] This refers to the exile of the gods of Esaggil after the destruction of Babylon. According to the Babylon inscription of Esarhaddon (Borger 1956 [§ 11]:11–29) it was Marduk himself who, together with the other gods, abandoned Babylon in his anger at the negligent and treacherous people.

[g] Literally, "Let them go and pronounce your well-being," meaning those in the previous sentence who take the offerings to the gods. This meaning presumes that the three precative verbs in these sentences all have the same subject. If, on the other hand, *lillikū* and *liqbiū* refer to the gods of Esaggil, then the *šulmu* ("well-being") is to be understood as their oracle of salvation for Esarhaddon.

## 81. SAA 9 2.4 (lines ii 29'–iii 18')
## Urkittu-šarrat to Esarhaddon

**Translation and/or discussion:** Nougayrol 1956: 159 (lines 9'–18'); Huffmon 1976b: 70; Dijkstra 1980: 153; Nissinen 1991: 137; 1993: 248; 1998b: 54, 104; 2001a: 193–94; Laato 1996: 177.

29' *akī tappala lā kēnūti*

ii 29' This is how she answers[a] to the disloyal ones:

30' *abat Issār ša Arbail abat šarrati Mullissi*

30'The word of Ištar of Arbela, the word of Queen Mullissu:[b]

31' *adaggal assanamme* 32' *uḫayyāṭa lā kēnūti* 33' *ina qāt šarrīya ašakkan*

31'I will watch, I will listen carefully! I will search out[c] the disloyal ones and deliver them into the hands of my king.

34' *adabbub ana maʾ[dūti]* 35' *sitammeā napāḫ [Šamši]* 36' *rabā Šamši* [. . .] 37' *abanni* [. . .]

34'I will speak to the mul[titude]: Listen carefully, [sun]rise and sunset! [. . .] I will create [. . .]

38' *abat Issār [ša Arbail]* 39' *ana* [. . .]

38'The word of Ištar [of Arbela] to [. . .]

[break of about four lines]

[break]

iii 1' *lū etk[āka* . . .] 2' *dāgil iṣṣurāti* [. . .] 3' *anākūma* [. . .] 4' *agallal maʾd[ūti* . . .] 5' *abīar ub[ā]r[a* . . .] 6' *anāku* [. . .]

iii 1'Be on the al[ert . . .] the augur[s[d] . . .]. I [. . .] I will roll lot[s of . . .], I will choose and cat[ch . . .], I [. . .]

7' *akê akê ša ana [ṣābē]* 8' *maʾdūti ussanaʾʾū[ni]/ussannaʾū[ni]* 9' *mā immati mātu nakkuru ibbašši* 10' *mā ina Kalḫi Nīnua lū lā nūšab*

7'How, how (to respond) to those who . . .[e] to many [people], saying: "When will the change in this country come about?[f] Let us not stay in Calah and Nineveh!"

11' *atta lū qālāka Aššūr-aḫu-iddina* 12' *ṣīrāni Elamāya* 13' *Mannāya abīar Urarṭāya* 14' *šiṭrīšu abarrim* 15' *igib ša Mugalli ubattaq*

11'You, Esarhaddon, keep silent! I will select the emissaries of the Elamite king and the Mannean king; I will seal the messages of the Urartean king; I will cut off the heel[g] of Mugallu.[h]

16' *mannu ēdu mannu ḫablu* 17' *lā tapallaḫ ina ṣilli Aššūr-aḫu-iddina šar māt Aššūr*

16'Who is now lonely, who is now wronged? Fear not! Esarhaddon, king of Assyria, is in my protection.[i]

18' *issu pî Urkittu-šarrat Kalḫītu*

18'From the mouth of the woman Urkittu-šarrat of Calah.

---

[a] Or, "This is how you answer." It is even possible that *akī* (= *akê*) is an interrogative particle "how?" (cf. line iii 7).

[b] Ištar and Mullissu merge here into one and the same divine being, and Mullissu is equated with Ištar of Nineveh; cf., e.g., SAA 9 7 (no. 92) r. 6 and SAA 3 7:11: "The Lady of the Lands comes out, Queen Mullissu, who dwells in [. . .]. At the coming out of the Lady of Nineveh all the gods rejoice!"

[c] Literally, "weigh out"; the idea is the same as in *uṣṣunu* "to sniff out" in the previous oracle (lines ii 10, 20).

[d] It is very atypical to refer another method of divination (i.e., to bird diviners) in a prophetic oracle; cf. no. 36 (ARM 26 229).

[e] The word in question is difficult to read, and its meaning can only be guessed. A translation such as "tramp all around" would take it as *ussanaʾʾū*[*ni*], an otherwise unattested Dtn-form of *šaʾû* "run" (cf. *AHw* 1205; *CAD* Š/2 243–44 sub *šâʾu*); this verb, however, is not attested in Neo-Assyrian. Another possibility would be *ussannaʾū*[*ni*] (*šanāʾu* Dt "be obstructive").

[f] Literally, "When will there be a change in the country?"

[g] The word is interpreted in the same meaning as *eqbu* "heel" (see *AHw* 231).

[h] Lines iii 12–15 manifest the rule of Esarhaddon over the surrounding lands. "The Elamite," "the Mannean," and "the Urartian" mean the kings of the southeastern, eastern, and northern neighbors and potential enemies of Assyria. Mugallu is the king of Melid in Anatolia (cf. SAA 4 1–12).

[i] Literally, "in the shadow."

## 82. SAA 9 2.5 (lines iii 19'–36')
## [Sinqiša-amur[a]] to Esarhaddon

**Translation and/or discussion:** Ishida 1977: 91; Dijkstra 1980: 151–53; Weippert 1985: 62; van der Toorn 1987: 78; Nissinen 1991: 288–89; 1998b: 100, 119–20, 153; Parpola 2000: 192.

[19'] *Aššūr-aḫu-iddina lā tapallaḫ māt Aššūr utaqqan* [20'] *ilāni zenûti* [*is*]*si māt Aššūr usal*[*l*]*am*
[21'] *ṣipputu ša nakarūtēka anassaḫ* [22'] *dāme ša nakarūti ša šarrīya atabbak* [23'] *šarrī anaṣṣar nakarūti ina sigarāti* [24'] *salmūti ina maddanāti* [25'] *ina pān šēpēšu ubbāla*

[19'] Esarhaddon, fear not! I will keep Assyria in order; I will reconcile the angry gods [wi]th Assyria.
[21'] I will pull the orchard of your enemies up by the roots;[b] I will shed the blood of my king's enemies. I will guard my king; the enemies I will bring in neckstocks and the allies with tribute before his feet.

[26'] *anāku abūka ummaka* [27'] *birti agappīya urtabbīka* [28'] *nēmalka ammar*
[29'] *lā tapallaḫ Aššūr-aḫu-iddina* [30'] *birti izirîya ammātēya* [31'] *ašakkanka ina libbi ūʾa* [32'] *nakarūti ša šarrīya aka*[*šša*]*d*
[33'] *māt Aššūr utaqqan šarr*[*ūtu ša*] [34'] *šamê utaqqa*[*n* . . .] [35'] [*na*]*pāḫ Šamš*[*i* . . . [36'] *rabā Šamš*]*i* [. . .]

[rest {about five lines} destroyed]

[26'] I am your father and mother.[c] I brought you up between my wings; I will see how you prosper.
[29'] Fear not, Esarhaddon! I will place you between my arm and forearm. In the midst of distress, I will va[nqu]ish the enemies of my king.
[33'] I will put Assyria in order; I will put the king[dom of] heaven in orde[r . . .][d] the sunri[se . . ., the sunse]t [. . .]

[break]

[a] The similarity with SAA 9 1.2 (no. 69) suggests that the prophet who uttered this oracle is Sinqiša-amur.

[b] Thus the translation of van der Toorn 1987: 78, equating *ṣipputu* with *ṣippatu* "orchard"; for the destruction of orchards as a method of warfare, see Cole 1997. Cf. the translation of Parpola 1997: 17, who explains *ṣipputu* with the help of Syr. *ṣipptô* "a mat" and rabbinic *ṣippĕtā* "covering, mat": "I will pull away the cover of your enemies."

[c] For the goddess parenting the king, see no. 71, note a. For the double-gender role of Ištar, see also Groneberg 1986 and Nissinen 1998c: 30–31.

[d] Cf. no. 77, note c.

## 83. SAA 9 2.6 (lines iv 1'–31')
## NN to Esarhaddon

| | |
|---|---|
| [beginning {2–3 lines} destroyed] 1'[. . . 2'. . .] *Aššūr* 3'[. . .] *atta* 4'[. . . *Esaggi*]*l Bābili* 5'[. . . *e*]*tkāku* 6'[. . .] *ša*[*rru*] 7'[. . .] *attidin* | [beginning destroyed] 1'[. . .] Aššur [. . .] you [. . . Esaggi]l, Babylon [. . .] I am on the [a]lert [. . .] the ki[ng . . .] I gave [. . .]. |
| 8'[*anāku Urk*]*ittu na*<sup></sup>*ʾʾidanni* 9'[*bēt tallak*]*ūni anaṣṣarka* 10'[. . . 11'. . .] *naʾʾidanni* 12'[. . .] *adanniš* 13'[. . . *d*]*aʾattu atta* 14'[. . . *l*]*ā tapallaḫ* 15'[. . . *ē*]*nāka* 16'[. . . *š*]*aknā* 17'[. . . 18'. . .] 19'[. . . *u*]*sallam* 20'[*lā tapallaḫ*] *mūrī* | 8'[I am Urk]ittu—praise me! [Wherever you g]o, I will guard you. [. . .] Praise me! [. . .] greatly [. . . s]trong. You [. . .] fear [n]ot! [. . .] Your [e]yes [. . .] are set [. . .] 19'[I will re]concile [. . . Fear not], my calf![a] |
| 21'[. . .] *gattaka ašīal* 22'[*birti iz*]*irîya* 23'[*ammātēya an*]*aṣṣarka* 24'[. . .] *kēni* 25'[. . . *tub*]*aʾʾāni* 26'[. . .] *ina pānīya* 27'[. . . *š*]*arruttaka utaqqan* | 21'I will cover your entire body[b] [. . . I will pr]otect you [between] my [a]rm [and my forearm].[c] [. . .] loyal [. . . you s]eek me [. . .] before me. [. . .] I will put your [k]ingdom in order. |
| 28'[*ummi šarri l*]*ā tapalliḫi* 29'[. . . *t*]*ukulti Aššūr* 30'[. . . *l*]*ā tapallaḫ* 31'[. . .] [rest {about six lines} destroyed] | 28'[F]ear not, [mother of the king![d] . . . the s]upport of Aššur [. . .] Fear [n]ot! [. . .] [rest destroyed] |

[a] Cf. no. 76, note d.

[b] The word *gattu* means "stature" ("Gestalt"); cf. Asb B v 71-72 (no. 101): *ina kirimmīša ṭâbi taḫṣinkāma taḫtina gimir lānīka* "She (= Ištar) sheltered you in her sweet embrace; she protected your entire body."

[c] Cf. the previous oracle (lines iii 30–31).

[d] The person addressed is a female, most probably the mother of the king.

## 84–88. Third Collection of Oracles
## La-dagil-ili to Esarhaddon

**Text:** SAA 9 3 (= ABRT I 22–23 = K 2401).
**Photograph:** Mattila (ed.) 1995: 167 (obv.); Parpola 1997: pls. VI–VII.
**Copy:** Strong 1893: 637–43 (cols. ii–iii); Craig 1895: pls. 22–25.
**Transliteration and translation:** Strong 1893: 627–30; Martin 1902: 88–97; Parpola 1997: 22–27.
**Translation:** Scheil 1897: 206; Jastrow 1912: 166–70; Langdon 1914: 134–37; Hecker 1986: 60–62; Mattila (ed.) 1995: 166–69.
**Discussion:** McCarthy 1978: 419–20; Laato 1996: 179–80; 272–76; 1998: 95–99; Parpola 1997: l, lviii–lix, lxx; Otto 1998: 56–59; 1999: 80–84; 2000: 74–75; Nissinen 2000a: 251–53; Villard 2001: 79–80; Weippert 2002: 15–19, 44–47; Steymans 2002.

## 84. SAA 9 3.1 (lines i 1–26)

**Translation and/or discussion:** Nissinen 2001a: 189–90.

[four unintelligible lines]
⁵[...] *ṭābtu* ⁶[...] *dina* ⁷[... i]*ḫtiṣin* ⁸[... -šun]*u ussēlia*

⁹[*šulmu a*]*na šamê kaqqiri* ¹⁰[*šulm*]*u ana Ešarra* ¹¹[*šulmu*] *ana Aššūr-aḫu-iddina šar māt Aššūr* ¹²[*šulm*]*u ša Aššūr-aḫu-iddina* ¹³[*iškun*]*ūni ina muḫḫi šēpē lillik*

¹⁴[*isinnu ina*] *Ešarra Aššūr issakan* ¹⁵[...] *ša Libbi āli* ¹⁶[... *Aš*]*šūr-aḫu-iddina* ¹⁷[... ¹⁸... in]*ašši* ¹⁹[...] *mātāti*
²⁰[...] *ina pān Aššūr* ²¹[...] *issi Aššūr-aḫu-iddina* ²²[...] *illakūni* ²³[...] *išarrupū* ²⁴[... a]*na garinnīšu* ²⁵[...] *šalāšat timmē* ²⁶[... ēn]*āšu ušētaq*

[four unintelligible lines]
⁵[...] favor[a] [...] give [... he] has taken care of [...] he has made [the]ir [...] rise.

⁹[Peace be] with heaven and earth! [Peac]e be with Ešarra! [Peace] be with Esarhaddon, king of Assyria! May the [peac]e [established] by Esarhaddon become stable and prosper![b]

¹⁴Aššur has arranged [a festival[c] in] Ešarra. [...] of Assur [... E]sarhaddon [... l]ifts up [...] the lands.

²⁰[...] before Aššur [...] with Esarhaddon [...] they come [...] is burnt [... t]o his mother [...] three pillars [...] he casts his [ey]e over [...]

---

[a] Or, "covenant."
[b] Literally, "go on its feet" or "get on to its feet."

[c] Thus according to the restoration of Parpola 1997: 22. What follows is probably a description of a procession leading to Esarhaddon's enthronement festival in Ešarra, the Aššur temple of Assur.

## 85. SAA 9 3.2 (lines i 27–ii 9)

**Translation and/or discussion:** Dietrich 1973: 42; Ishida 1977: 91; Nissinen 1991: 137; 1998b: 76–77, 94; Ivantchik 1993a: 184–85.

*27 [sitam]meā mar'ē māt Aššūr 28 [šarru na]karšu iktašad 29 [šarrakun]u nakaršu 30 [ina šapal šē]pēšu issakan 31 [issu rab]ā Šamši 32 [adi napā]ḫ Šamši 33 [issu napā]ḫ Šamši 34 [adi ra]bā Šamši*

27 [Lis]ten carefully, O Assyrians! [The king] has vanquished his [e]nemy! [From] sun[set to] sun[ris]e, [from] sun[ris]e [to] sun[se]t [you]r [king] has trod his enemy [underf]oot!

*35 [Melīd]i aḫappi 36 [... aḫa]ppi 37 [...] ii 1 Gimirrāya ina qātēšu ašakkan 2 išātu ina Ellipi ummad*

35 I will destroy [Meli]d,[a] [... I will de]stroy. I will deliver the Cimmerians[b] into his hands; the land of Ellipi[c] I will set on fire.

*3 kippat erbetti Aššūr ittannaššu 4 issu bēt inappaḫanni 5 bēt irabbûni 6 šarru miḫiršu laššu 7 akī ṣēt Šamši namir*

ii 3 Aššur has given him the whole world.[d] From the place where the sun rises to where it sets there is no king to set beside him. He is bright like sunshine!

*8 anniu šulmu ša ina pān Bēl-tarbiṣi 9 ina pān ilāni šakinūni*

8 This is the oracle of peace placed before Bel-Tarbaṣi and before the (other) gods.[e]

---

[a] Cf. SAA 9 2.4 (no. 81) iii 15, referring to Mugallu, king of Melid. In the present text, the destroyed lines i 36–37 probably mention other neighboring countries and potential enemies of Assyria.

[b] A people who moved from Caucasus or Central Asia to Anatolia, invaded large areas north and northwest of Assyria (Urartu, Lydia and Phrygia) in the Neo-Assyrian period and were a constant problem for Esarhaddon (see Lanfranchi 1990; Ivantchik 1993a).

[c] A kingdom southeast of Assyria, between Elam and Mannea.

[d] Literally, "the four regions," meaning the totality of the world surrounding Assyria, illustrated by the previously mentioned country names. Esarhaddon has the title "king of the four regions," e.g., in the prologue of the Nin A inscription (no. 97), line i 3.

[e] The word *šulmu* refers to lines i 27–ii 7 as an "oracle/greeting of peace/well-being" (cf. no. 76, n. 1); hence, lines ii 8–9 do not belong to the oracle but describe

a ritual taking place at the courtyard of Ešarra, the placing of the oracle before Bel-Tarbaṣi ("Lord of the Pen") and other courtyard gods. This implies that the oracle was not only proclaimed by the prophet to the people, but it was also written down and placed before the statues of the gods.

### 86. SAA 9 3.3 (lines ii 10–32)

**Translation and/or discussion:** Scheil 1897: 206; Weippert 1972: 481–82; 1981: 93–96; 1997a: 157–60; Huffmon 1976b: 700; 1992: 481; Ishida 1977: 115–16; R. R. Wilson 1980: 117–18; Dijkstra 1980: 157–59; Ellis 1989: 143–44; Nissinen 1991: 146; 1993: 240, 243; 1998b: 26–28, 76–77; Talon 1994: 123; Lewis 1996: 407; Pongratz-Leisten 1999: 78–81; Huffmon 2000: 59–60; van der Toorn 2000: 85; Köckert 2001: 218; Villard 2001: 79–80.

[10]*annūrig sarsarrāni annûti* [11]*ussadbibūka ussēṣûnikka* [12]*iltibûka atta pīka* [13]*taptitia mā anīna Aššūr*

[10]Now these traitors[a] conspired against you, expelled you and surrounded[b] you.[c] You, however, opened your mouth, crying: "Hear me, O Aššur!"[d]

[14]*anāku killaka asseme* [15]*issu libbi abul šamê* [16]*attaqallalla* [17]*lakrur išātu lušākilšunu*

[14]I heard your cry and appeared as a fiery glow[e] from the gate of heaven,[f] to throw down fire and have it devour them.

[18]*atta ina birtuššunu tazzaz* [19]*issu pānīka attiši* [20]*ana šadê ussēlīšunu* [21]*abnāti aqqullu ina muḫḫīšunu azzunun* [22]*nakarūtēka uḫtattip* [23]*dāmēšunu nāru umtalli*

[18]As you were standing in their midst, I removed them from your presence, drove them up the mountain and rained fire and brimstone[g] upon them.[h] I slaughtered your enemies and filled the River[i] with their blood.

[24]*lēmurū lūna''idūni* [25]*akī Aššūr bēl ilāni anākūni*

[24]Let them see it and praise me, for I am Aššur, lord of the gods!

[26]*annû šulmu ša ina pān ṣalmi* [27]*ṭuppi adê anniu ša Aššūr* [28]*ina muḫḫi ḫa'ūti ina pān šarri errab* [29]*šamnu ṭābu izarriqū* [30]*niqiāti eppušū* [31]*riqiāti illukū* [32]*ina pān šarri isassiū*

[26]This is the oracle of peace placed before the statue. This covenant[j] tablet of Aššur enters the king's presence on a cushion.[k] Fragrant oil is sprinkled, sacrifices are made, incense is burnt and (the tablet) is read out before the king.[l]

---

[a] The word *sarsarrāni* is interpreted as pl. of *sarsarru,* a pejorative *paspass* formation from *sarru* "criminal" (see Parpola 1997: 23; cf. Weippert 1972: 481; 2002:

45–46: "Aufrührer, Rebell"). Other interpretations include the likewise disparaging *šaršarrāni* "would-be-kings" (*AHw* 1191; Weippert 1981: 94) and *šar šarrāni* "kings of kings" (Hecker 1986: 60).

[b] Derived from *law/bû* "surround" (Parpola 1997: 24).

[c] Lines ii 10–12 cf. Nin A (no. 97) i 23-28.

[d] Lines ii 12–13 cf. Nin A (no. 97) i 32-37, 53-62. The word *anīnu* is interpreted as an interjection similar to *anīna* or *annû* "behold" (cf. Hebrew *hinnê*); cf. SAA 16 59 (no. 115 note a) and *ABL* 1250 r. 7.

[e] The four-radical verb *naqallulu* is a denominal formation, denoting the appearance of *anqullu* "glow," which is used of sunset as a bad portent for the enemy in SAA 10 79:20; cf. next note.

[f] "The gate of heaven" means the two spots of the sunrise and the sunset in the horizon.

[g] The "fire and brimstone" is translated from *abnāti aqqullu* "stones of the fiery glow," which alludes to *attaqallalla* (line ii 16; cf. note e).

[h] Lines ii 19–21 cf. Nin A (no. 97) i 82–84.

[i] See above, no. 73 note c, and cf. Nin A (no. 97) i 86.

[j] I.e., the document of the covenant between the supreme god and the king (see Ellis 1989: 144; Lewis 1996: 406–8; Otto 1999: 81, n. 365).

[k] The exact meaning of *ḫaʾūtu* is unclear; this translation connects it with *ḫawû* "seat cover for thrones" (see *CAD* Ḫ 163). Judged from the context, the word is used of an object on which (*ina muḫḫi*) the tablet of the covenant is transported (Weippert 1981: 95 n. 54).

[l] Lines ii 26–32 are not part of the oracle but contain two ritual descriptions. The first one (line 26) is comparable to lines ii 8–9: the *šulmu* (i.e., the tablet on which the oracle is written) is now placed before the statue of Aššur in the throne room of the temple. The second one (lines 27–32) describes the ceremonial transport of *ṭuppi adê* "tablet of the covenant" (not necessarily identical with the previously mentioned tablet) and its recitation to the king.

## 87. SAA 9 3.4 (lines ii 33–iii 15)

**Translation and/or discussion:** Huffmon 1976b: 700; 1992: 481; Ishida 1977: 115–16; van der Toorn 1987: 92–93; Nissinen 1991: 136, 181–82; 1993: 237–38; 2002b: 14–15; Weippert 2002: 18–19.

33 *abat Issār ša Arbail* 34 *ana Aššūr-aḫu-iddina šar māt Aššūr*
35 *ilāni abbēya aḫḫēya alkāni* 36 *ina libbi ad*[*ê* . . .]
[break of two lines]
iii 2 *ina muḫḫi* [*taml*]*ê ḫirṣ*[*u* . . .] 3 *mê ṣarṣāri tassiqīšunu* 4 *massītu ša issēn sūt* 5 *mê ṣarṣāri tumtalli*

33 Word of Ištar of Arbela to Esarhaddon, king of Assyria.

35 Come, gods, my fathers and brothers! [Enter] the cove[nant[a] . . .]

[break]

iii 2 On the [terra]ce [ . . . ] a slic[e of . . . ]. She[b] gave them[c] water from a cooler[d] to drink. She filled a pitcher

[6]*tatannaššunu*

[7]*mā taqabbiā ina libbīkunu* [8]*mā Issār pāqtu šî* [9]*mā tallakā ina alānīkunu* [10]*nagiānīkunu kusāpu takkalā* [11]*tamaššiā adê annûti* [12]*mā issu libbi mê annûti* [13]*tašattiā taḫassasāni* [14]*tanaṣṣarā adê annûti* [15]*ša ina muḫḫi Aššūr-aḫu-iddina aškunūni*

of one seah[e] with water from the cooler, gave it to them and said:

[7]"You say to yourself: 'Ištar—she is small beer!'[f] Then you go into your cities and your districts, eat your own bread and forget this covenant. But every time when you drink this water, you will remember me and keep this covenant which I have made on behalf of Esarhaddon."

---

[a] The covenant (*adê*) now refers to the treaty of the king with the citizens and vassals of Assyria, whose gods act as the witnesses of the treaty. What follows is a description of the meal of the covenant that was served on the temple terrace.

[b] With regard to iii 12–15, the verbal forms are to be understood as third-person feminines, referring to Ištar, not as second-person forms (thus Hecker 1986: 61; Nissinen 1991: 181; 1993: 237).

[c] It is conceivable that the meal of the covenant is served, not only to the aforementioned gods (Laato 1996: 273–74; 1998: 96), but also, and quite concretely, to the vassal kings and the representatives of the citizens of Assyria (Otto 1999: 81–82).

[d] Parpola 1997: 25 arrives at this translation of the word *ṣarṣāru* by comparison with the rabbinic *ṣarṣūr*, which means a stone vessel used as a cooler, and with regard to the fact that cooled water played a prominent part in libations to gods. The word is used in a similar function in Šurpu iii 62, which mentions an oath taken by drinking water from a *ṣarṣāru*.

[e] Otto 1999: 82 translates: "ein Trinkgefäß hat sie zur Hälfte … gefüllt," interpreting the sign BÁN as *mišlu* "half."

[f] An idiomatic translation of *pāqtu*, derived from *piāqu* "to be narrow" (see *AHw* 861, 865) and referring to Ištar's restricted power.

## 88. SAA 9 3.5 (lines iii 16–iv 35)

**Translation and/or discussion:** Dietrich 1973: 42–43; Dijkstra 1980: 165–66; Weippert 1981: 87–89; 2001: 43–44; Perroudon 1993; Nissinen 2001a: 187–88; 2003: 10–12.

[16]*abat Issār ša Arbail* [17]*ana Aššūr-aḫu-iddina šar māt Aššūr*

[18]*akī ša memmēni lā ēpašūni* [19]*lā addinakkanni* [20]*mā erbet sippī ša māt Aššūr* [21]*lā akpupâ lā addinakkâ* [22]*nakarka lā akšūdu* [23]*giṣṣiṣīka*

[16]Word of Ištar of Arbela to Esarhaddon, king of Assyria.

[18]As if I had not done or given to you anything![a] Did I not bend and give to you the four doorjambs of Assyria?[b] Did I not vanquish your

*ayyābīka* 24*[akī gu]rṣipti lā alqūtu*

enemy? Did I not gather your foes and adversaries [like but]terflies?

25*[att]a ana ayyāši mīnu taddina* 26*[ak]āli ša qarīti* 27*l[aššu] ša ak lā bēt ili* 28*a[kkall]i akālī* 29*akk[a]lli kāsī* 30*mā ina pāni adaggal* 31*ēnu ina muḫḫi aktarar*

25What have [yo]u, in turn, given to me? The [fo]od for the banquet is no[t there], as if[c] there were no temple at all! My food is wi[thhe]ld from me, my drink[d] is with[he]ld from me! I am longing for them, I have fixed my eyes upon them.

32*mā kettumma issēn sūt akāl aṣūdi* 33*issēn sūt massītu ša šikāri ṭābi* 34*ke᾽᾽in urqī akussu* 35*laššīa ina pīa laškun* 36*lumalli kāsu ina muḫḫi lassi* 37*lalâya lutirra*

32Verily, see to it that there is a bowl of one seah of food and a pitcher of one seah of best beer! Then I will take and put vegetables and soup in my mouth, fill the cup and drink from it. I want to restore my charms![e]

[break][f]

iv 1[. . .] 2[. . .] 3*lašši* 4*[. . . la]llik* 5*[. . .] ētalia* 6*[. . . isin]nu assakan* 7*[akī ina libbi] anākūni* 8*[mā nūda] akī Issār* 9*[ša] Arbail attīni*

iv 3[. . .] let me lift up [. . . let m]e go [. . .] I went up [. . .] I arranged [a banq]uet. [While] I was [there, they said: "We know] that you are Ištar [of] Arbela!"

10*[ana māt Aš]šūr uttammeša* 11*[nēmalk]a lāmur šadâni* 12*[ina šēpēya] lakbus* 13*[ladb]ub ina muḫḫi Aššūr-aḫu-iddina*

10I set out [for As]syria to see yo[ur success], to tread the mountains [with my feet, to spe]ak about Esarhaddon.

14*[ūm]â rīš Aššūr-aḫu-iddina* 15*[erbet sipp]ī ša māt Aššūr* 16*[aktapp]a attanakka* 17*[nakar]ka aktašad* 18*[nīšī š]a issīka izzazzūni* 19*[ṭēnšun]u nabalkut* 20*[ina libbi annīt]i tammar* 21*[akī Issār ša] Arbail anākūni*

14[Theref]ore, rejoice, Esarhaddon! [The four doorjamb]s of Assyria[g] [I have ben]t and given to you! I have vanquished your [enemy]! [The people th]at stand by your side— [the]ir [mind] is completely changed! [From thi]s you see [that] I am [Ištar of] Arbela.

22*[kīma parriṣū u]ssaddidūni* 23*[ša imitti] ša šumēli* 24*[šipṭu] naṣṣū izzazz[ū]* 25*[manzāz] eka[lli* 26*urdu] ekalli šunu* 27*[ša ina muḫḫī]ka isīḫūni* 28*[alti]bia ina muḫḫi šinnīšunu* 29*[ana] zaqībāni* 30*[as]sakanšunu*

22[When the conspirators] have been hauled up, [those at the right] and those at the left[h] will be there and suffer [the punishment]. [The cour]tiers and [servants] of the palace, those who rebelled [against] you, [I have sur]rounded and fixed them to the stake by their teeth.

[31][*Lā-dāgil-i*]*li raggimu* [32][*Arbail*]*āya* [33][...] *Issār* [34][...] [35][...]

[31][La-dagil-i]li, a prophet from [Arbe]la [...] Ištar [...].

[a] Or, "As if I had not given to you things that nobody else can give!" (cf. Otto 1999: 82).

[b] This probably refers to the four major cities of Assyria: Assur, Nineveh, Calah, and Arbela; cf. SAA 9 1.6 (no. 73) iii 9–14 and see Nissinen 2001a: 186–95.

[c] For the *hapax* expression *ša ak lā,* see Parpola 1997: 26.

[d] Literally, "my cup."

[e] Cf. SAA 9 9: 8–15.

[f] Lines iv 3–4 seem to be a continutation of the cluster of precative forms in lines iii 35–37. Restorations of the very fragmentary column iv according to Parpola 1997: 27.

[g] See note b.

[h] This refers to the rebelling brothers of Esarhaddon and their accomplices; cf. SAA 9 1.8 (no. 75) v 15–16.

## 89. Fragment of a Collection of Prophecies NN to Esarhaddon

**Text:** SAA 9 4 (= 83-1-18, 839).
**Photograph:** Parpola 1997: pl. VIII.
**Transliteration and translation:** Parpola 1997: 30.
**Discussion:** Parpola 1997: lix–lx, lxx; Nissinen 1998b: 75.

[beginning destroyed]
[...] [2'][*Aššūr-aḫu-iddi*]*na šar māt Aššūr* [...] [3'][*kakki*]*šāti u*[*bāra* [4] *ina pān*] *šēpēka a*[*karrar*]
[5'][*att*]*a lā tap*[*allaḫ* ...] [6'][...] *urkīūte ak*[*aššad* ...] [7'][... *-k*]*a taptan*-[...] [8'][...] *aša*[*kkan* ...]

[one unintelligible line; rest destroyed]

[beginning destroyed]
[2'][... Esarhadd]on, king of Assyria [...] I will [catch the polec]ats,[a] I will [cast them before] your feet.
[5'][Yo]u fe[ar] not! [...] I will va[nquish] the later [...] You will ... your [...] I will pu[t ...]
[rest destroyed]

[a] For *kakkišu,* see no. 74 (SAA 9 1.7), note a and cf. SAA 10 352 (no. 109) r. 2–3.

## 90. A Prophecy Report
## NN to the Queen Mother

**Text:** SAA 9 5 (= *TI* pl. 4 = K 6259).
**Photograph:** Parpola 1997, pl. VIII.
**Copy:** Langdon 1914: pl. 4.
**Transliteration and translation:** Parpola 1997: 34.
**Discussion:** Parpola 1997: lx, lxx; Nissinen 1998b: 23; 2001a: 183; Weippert 2002: 47.

*abat Issār ša Arbail* [*ana ummi šarri*] [2]*kinṣāya kanṣā an*[*a Aššūr-aḫu-iddina šarrīya*] [3]*Mullissu ana killi* [*ša mūrīša tasseme*]

[4]*qablīki ruksī* [...] [5]*ša Aššūr-aḫu-iddina šar māt Aššūr* [...] [6]*Inurta imittu u šumēlu š*[*a šarrīya illak*] [7]*ayyābīšu ina šapal šēpē*[*šu ukabbas*]

[8]*ina ekal ṣēri u*[*ṣṣa* ...] [9]*tuqqun ana A*[*ššūr-aḫu-iddina šar māt Aššūr* [10]*a*]*ddan n*[*akarūtēšu*] [r. 1]*ina libbi* [...] [2][...] [3]*nakru š*[*a* ...] [4]*nakru ša* [... *ina pān šēpēšu*] [5]*nikrur ni*[*llik* ...]

[6]*Mullissu dulla* [...] [7][*š*]*a Šamši šina adi abūa uza-*[...]

[1]Word of Ištar of Arbela [to the king's mother]:[a] [2]My knees are bent fo[r Esarhaddon, my king]![b] Mullissu has [heard] the cry [*of her calf*].

[4]Gird your[c] loins! [...] of Esarhaddon, king of Assyria [...] Ninurta [goes] at the right and the left o[f my king. He treads] his enemies under [his] foot.

[8]I will [go] to the Palace of the Steppe[d] [...] I will give protection to [Esarhaddon, king of Assyria. His] e[nemies] in [...] The enemy of [...] The enemy of [...] we will cast [before his feet]; we will g[o ...]

[6]Praise[5] Mullissu! [...o]f Šamaš they are until my father [...]

[a] The restoration is conjectural, but the addressee is most likely the queen mother; see note c.

[b] A likewise conjectural restoration, supported by the fact that the victory and kingship of Esarhaddon are the subject matter of the oracle. For the intercessory role of the goddess, see, e.g., SAA 9 9 (no. 94) 20–25 and cf. SAA 3 13.

[c] The feminine addressee of *qablīki ruksī* indicates that the oracle is spoken to the queen mother Naqia. It certainly belongs historically to the same background as the other oracles addressed to her (SAA 9 1.7 and 1.8 [nos. 74 and 75]).

[d] The "Palace of the Steppe" is a shrine of Ištar in Milqia, a locality near Arbela, where she dwelled during the absence of the king, in anticipation of a triumph after his return from a victorious campaign (see Pongratz-Leisten 1994: 79–83; Nissinen 2001a: 183–86). Cf. SAA 9 1.9 (no. 76).

[e] Plural form.

## 91. A Prophecy Report
## Tašmetu-ereš to Esarhaddon (?)

**Text:** SAA 9 6 (= Bu 91-5-9,106 + Bu 91-5-9,109).
**Photograph:** Parpola 1997: pl. VIII.
**Transliteration and translation:** Parpola 1997: 35.
**Discussion:** Nissinen 1993: 225; Parpola 1997: lii, lx, lxx.

*Issār ša Arbail* [*mā* . . .] [2]*mā utaqqa*[*n* . . .] [3]*utaqqan* [. . .] [4][. . .] [5]*mā* URU.[. . .] [6][. . .] [7]*ētarbū* [. . .] [8]*ša šarri* [. . .] [9]*iddūk*[*ū* . . .] [10][. . .] [r. 1][*m*]*ā lā* [. . .] [2]*usutu* [. . .] [3]*asseme* [. . .] [4]*nakarūtēka* [. . .]

[5]*annî* [. . .] [6]*irgumūni* [. . . [7]*ina l*]*ibbi* [. . .] [8]*ša irgum*[*ūni* . . .] [9]*ina pan kudu*-[. . .] [10]*a*[*d*]*i nakar*[*ūtēka* . . .]

[11]*Tašmētu-ēreš* [*raggimu annītu*] [12][*ina lib*]*bi Arbail irt*[*ugum*]

Thus [says] Ištar of Arbela:

[2]I will put in orde[r . . .] I will put in order [. . .] The city [. . .] they entered [. . .] of the king [. . .] they killed [. . .] Do not [. . .] help [. . .] I have heard [. . .] your enemies [. . .]

[r. 5]This [is how . . .] he/they prophesied [. . . i]n [. . .] he/they prophesi[ed . . .] before [. . .] u[nt]il [your] enem[ies . . .]

[11]Tašmetu-ereš, the p[rophet], prop[hesied this i]n Arbela.[a]

[a] Lines r. 11–12 are a colophon written on the upper edge of the tablet. The title *raggimu* is conjectural; only the determinative of professional titles (LÚ) is preserved. It is probable, however, in view of the multiple occurence of the verb *ragāmu* in this oracle.

## 92. A Report of Prophecies
## Mullissu-kabtat to Assurbanipal

**Text:** SAA 9 7 (= ABRT I 26–27 = K 883).
**Photograph:** Mattila (ed.) 1995: 169 (obv.); Parpola 1997: pls. IX, XIII.
**Copy:** Strong 1893: 645; Craig 1895: pls. 26–27.
**Transliteration and translation:** Strong 1893: 633–35; Martin 1902: 100–105; Ivantchik 1993b; Parpola 1997: 38–39.
**Translation:** Scheil 1897: 206–7; Jastrow 1912: 171–72; Langdon 1914: 143–45; Pfeiffer 1955: 451; Castellino 1977: 458–59; Hecker 1986: 62–63.
**Discussion:** Streck 1916: clxx–clxxv; Ramlot 1972: 881; R. R. Wilson 1980: 117; Dijkstra 1980: 156; Weippert 1985: 62–63, 65–66, 84; 1997a: 153–57; 2001: 39–41; 2002: 13–14, 47–51; van der Toorn 1987: 85–86; 2000: 76; Nissinen 1991: 287–88; 1993: 225, 242–43; 1998b: 59; 2000a: 243; Ivantchik 1993a: 101–2, 275–77; Laato 1996: 183; Rowlett 1996: 118; Parpola 1997: li, lx, lxx.

*Mullissu-kabtat raggintu*
²[m]ā abat šarrati Mullissu šî mā lā
tapallaḫ Aššūr-bāni-apli ³[m]ā adi
kî ša aqbûni eppašūni addanak-
kanni ⁴[m]ā adi ina muḫḫi mar'ē
ša ša-ziqnāni ina muḫḫi ḫalpiti ša
ša-rēšāni ⁵[att]a šarrūtu ina muḫ-
ḫišunu tuppašūni ⁶[aḫaṣ]ṣinka ina
bēt rēdūti ⁷[abīka] pitūtu irakkas

⁸[mā ... šarr]āni ša mātāti ana
aḫē'iš iqabbūni ⁹[mā alkāni n]illik
ina muḫḫi Aššūr-bāni-apli šarru
šībī raši x ¹⁰[mā mīnu ša il]āni ana
abbēni ab abbēni išīmūni ¹¹[mā
ūmâ š]û ina birtunni liprus

¹²[mā Mull]issu taqtibi mā [šarrā]ni
ša mātāti ¹³[tapīa]l taḫūmāni tukal-
lamšunu [ḫūl]āni ina šēpēšunu
tašakkan

¹⁴[m]ā šanītu laqbâkka kî Elamtu
Gimir agammar ʳ·¹[m]ā talla gišṣu
ašabbir mā murdinnu ana nipši
anappaš ²adammumāti ana sarbi
utâra

³ḫallalatti enguratti ⁴atta taqabbi
mā mīnu ḫallalatti enguratti ⁵ḫal-
lalatti ina Muṣur errab enguratti
uṣṣâ
⁶mā ša Mullissu ummašūni lā
tapallaḫ ša Bēlet Arbail tārīssūni lā
tapallaḫ
⁷mā kî tārīti ina muḫḫi giššīya
anaššīka ⁸mā armannu ina birit
tulêya ašakkanka ⁹ša mūšīya ērāk
anaṣṣarka ša kal ūme ḫilpaka
addan ¹⁰ša kallamāri unnānika
uṣur uṣur uppaška

Thus the prophetess Mullissu-kabtat:
²This is the word of Queen[a]
Mullissu: Fear not, Assurbanipal!
Until I have done and given to
you what I promised, until [yo]u
yourself exercise kingship over
the descendants of the bearded
courtiers and over the successors
of the eunuchs,[b] [I will take ca]re
of you in the Palace of Succession,[c] [your father] will gird the
diadem.[d]

⁸[The king]s of the countries
shall say to one another: "[Come,
let us] go to Assurbanipal! The king
has got witnesses.[e] [Whatever the
god]s[f] decreed to our fathers and
forefathers, [now] let [hi]m pass
judgment between us!"

¹²[Mullis]su has said: [You shall
reig]n over [the king]s of the countries! You shall show them their
boundaries; you shall determine
the [ro]ads they take.

¹⁴Moreover, let me speak to you:
Like Elam, I will finish off the land
of the Cimmerians![g] ... I will hew
down the thorn; I will pluck the
bramble as a tuft of wool; the
wasps I will turn into a mash.[h]

ʳ·³ḫallalatti enguratti! You ask:
"What means ḫallalatti enguratti?"
ḫallalatti I will enter Egypt, enguratti I will go out![i]

⁶You whose mother is Mullissu,
fear not! You whose nurse is the
Lady of Arbela, fear not![j]

Like a nurse I will carry you on
my hip. I will put you, a pome-
granate, between my breasts. At
night I will be awake and guard
you; throughout the day I will give
you milk, at dawn I will hush you.[k]

[11]*mā atta lā tapallaḫ mūrī ša anāku urabbûni*

[11]Fear not, you, my calf whom I rear.

---

[a] The cuneiform sign here is LUGAL "king," whence the translation "a word for the king" (a.o., Weippert 1981: 77 and Hecker 1986: 62). Since *abat šarri* means a message sent by the king and not to him (e.g., SAA 1 1:1; 5:1; 10:1; 11:1), it is more probable that *a-bat* LUGAL [d]NIN.LÍL is a formula comparable to *a-bat šar-ra-ti* [d]NIN.LÍL "word of Queen Mullissu" in SAA 9 2.4 ii 30. If this is true, LUGAL stands here for *šarratu* "queen" (Parpola 1997: 38). Cf. also Weippert 2001: 39; 2002: 48–50, who has recently translated: "Eine Appellation der Mullissu ist dies," taking *abat šarri* as a technical term of juridical proceedings corresponding the Roman *appellatio*.

[b] The bearded courtiers and the eunuchs designate the totality of the palace officials, and the descendants and followers (eunuchs could not have descendants) refer to the government of the future king.

[c] For the Palace of Succession, see no. 69 (SAA 9 1.2), note a.

[d] Cf. SAA 10 185: 7–9: "You (Esarhaddon) have girded a son of yours (Assurbanipal) with diadem and entrusted to him the kingship of Assyria." This refers to the investiture of Assurbanipal as crown prince in the year 672.

[e] This may refer to the gods as the witnesses of the succession treaty (SAA 2 6) that was concluded on the occasion of the investiture of Assurbanipal.

[f] Restoration by Parpola 1997: 38: [*ma-a mi-i-nu šă* DINGIR].MEŠ *a-na* AD.MEŠ-*ni* AD—AD.MEŠ-*ni i-ši-mu-u-ni;* cf. the restoration of Weippert 2002: 50–51: [*ša* AD.MEŠ NAM.ME]Š *a-na* AD.MEŠ-*ni* AD—AD.MEŠ-*ni i-ši-mu-u-ni* "[whose fathers] decided [the destinie]s of our fathers and forefathers."

[g] Elam was not actually "finished" by Esarhaddon. After the death of the Elamite king Ḫumban-ḫaltaš, who invaded Babylonia in 675, Esarhaddon concluded a treaty with his follower Urtaku in 674. For Cimmerians, see no. 85 (SAA 9 3.2), note b.

[h] Or, "I will make the wasps fall down like a shower [*sarbu*]."

[i] The words *ḫallalatti enguratti* may be names of insects, but they cannot be translated with any certainty and may be intentionally obscure; for possible explanations, see Parpola 1997: 39. The prophecy certainly concerns the conquest of Egypt which Esarhaddon tried in 674/3 and finally accomplished in 671. For a similar expression connected with peaceful intentions, see EA 23 (no. 123): 14–16: "I want to go to Egypt, the country that I love, and then return."

[j] For the equation of Ištar and Mullissu, cf. no. 81 (SAA 9 2.4), note b.

[k] "Hush you" is not a direct translation but an attempt to express the more or less probable meaning of the words *unnānika uṣur uṣur uppaška,* which may be understood as prattling to a baby or as singing a nursery rhyme (Ivantchik 1993b: 41). For another interpretation, see Weippert 1985: 62: "Jeden Morgen merke ich mir deine Gebete, merke (sie) mir und erfülle (sie) dir"; cf. Weippert 2001: 40; 2002: 51: "Jeden Morgen erfülle ich dir dein Flehen 'merke dir! merke dir!'" The latter translation assumes that *uṣur uṣur* alludes to the appeals in prayers, e.g., [*M*]*arduk uṣur teslītī* "Marduk, take heed of my prayer!" *KAR* 26 r. 30.

## 93. A Report of Prophecies
## NN to Assurbanipal

**Text:** SAA 9 8 (= ABL 1280 = K 1545).
**Photograph:** Parpola 1997: pl. X, XIII.
**Copy:** Waterman 1912: 16; Harper 1913 (XII): no. 1280.
**Transliteration and translation:** Klauber 1914: 254; Waterman 1930 (II): 388-89; Parpola 1997: 40.
**Translation:** Dietrich 1973: 40.
**Discussion:** Waterman 1931 (III): 337; Weippert 1981: 73, 96; 2002: 51–52; Laato 1996: 184; Parpola 1997: lxi, lxx; Nissinen 1998b: 59–60; 2000a: 249; Villard 2001: 74, 76–77.

*dibbī [ša Elam]āyi*
[2]*kî an[nî ilu] iqabbi* [3]*mā att[alak at]talka*
[4]*ḫamšīšu šiššīšu iq[ṭib]i iddāti* [5]*mā issu muḫḫi [nar]ʾanti attalka* [6]*mā ṣerru ša ina libbīša assadda* [7]*abtataq*
*u mā narʾantu* [8]*aḫtepi*
*u mā Elamtu* [9]*aḫappi aḫūšu issi kaqqir* [r. 1]*isappan*
*mā kî annî* [2]*Elamtu agammar*

[1]Words[a] [concerning the Elam]ites:[b]
[2]Thus says [the god[c]]: "I have go[ne, I ha]ve come!"
[4]Five, six times he s[ai]d (this). Then he said: "I have come from[d] the [m]ace. The snake in it I have hauled out and cut in pieces."[e]
[7]And: "I have crushed the mace."
[8]And: "I will crush Elam! Its army shall be levelled to the ground."
[r. 1]And: "This is how I will finish off Elam."

---

[a] The plural indicates that the tablet is a compilation of quotations from several oracles, the historical context of which is most probably Assurbanipal's campaign against Teumman, the king of Elam, in 653; cf. Prism B v 15–vi 16 (no. 101).

[b] Weippert 2002: 51 interprets the gentilic ending *–a-a* as belonging to a personal name.

[c] The restoration is conjectural, but there is no room for the determinative (DINGIR) and the divine name proper. Weippert 2002:51 restores [*šu-ú*] "he," referring to the speaker (see note b).

[d] Weippert 2002: 52: "Zu der *narʾantu* bin ich hineingegangen," interpreting TA* as *issi* "with."

[e] The metaphor is not quite intelligible, but the "mace," being a weapon (or a cultic symbol), probably denotes a war, whereas the "snake" is obviously used of the Elamites. Snake is a prominent symbol in Elamite religion and art.

## 94. A Report of a Prophecy
## Dunnaša-amur to Assurbanipal

**Text:** SAA 9 9 (= ZA 24 169+ = K 1292 + DT 130).
**Photograph:** Parpola 1997: pls. XI–XII.
**Transliteration and translation:** Zimmern 1910; Parpola 1997: 40–41.
**Discussion:** Zimmern 1910; Streck 1916: clxx–clxxv; van der Toorn 1987: 84; Nissinen 1991: 282–84, 290; 1993: 225–26; 1998b: 57, 59; 2000a: 96–97; 2002b: 12; Laato 1996: 183; Parpola 1997: il–l, lxi, lxxi; Weippert 2002: 14, 52–53.

*[kidin]nu ša Mullissu 2[...] ša Bēlet A[r]bail 3[šinām]a ina ilāni dannā 4[ira]ʾʾamā u raʾāmšina 5[ana] Aššūr-bāni-apli binūt qātīšina 6iltanapparā ša balāṭīšu 7[uša]škanāšu libbu*

[An oracle of protec]tion[a] of Mullissu, a [...] of the Lady of Arbela!

3[They] are strongest of all gods. They [lov]e and incessantly bestow their love [upon] Assurbanipal, the creation of their hands. For the sake of his life they [encou]rage his heart.

*8[balā]ṭaka eršākūma arappuda ṣēru 9[ē]tanabbir nārāti u tâmāti 10ētanattiq šadê ḫursāni 11ētanabbir nārāti kalīšina 12ētanakkalāni yāši 13ṣē[t]āte sarabāte 14iltanappatā banû lānī 15anḫā[k]ūma šaddalupūka lānīya*

8Desiring your [li]fe I roam the steppe,[b] continually crossing rivers and oceans, ranging mountains and alps. Continually crossing all rivers, I am finished off by droughts and showers. My charming figure they ravage; my body is exhausted and troubled for your sake.

*16ina puḫur ilāni kalāmi aqṭibi balāṭaka 17dannā rittāya lā urammâka ina pān ilāni 18naggalapāya ḫarruddā 19ittanaššāka ana kāša 20ina š[apt]ēya ētanarriš balāṭaka 21[...] balāṭaka balāṭu tušattar*

16In the assembly of all the gods I have spoken for your life.[c] My arms are strong and will not cast you off before the gods. My shoulders are always ready to carry you, you in particular. I keep desiring your life with my l[ip]s [...] your life, you increase life.

*22[...] Nabû liḫdâ šaptēka 23[ina puḫur ilāni] kalāmi 24[aqṭanab]bi damqātēka 25[balāṭaka eršā]kūma arappuda ṣer[u] 26[ina libbi ūʾa at]abbi ayyābka aṭa[bbaḫ] 27[...] ana mātīšu itūr[a]*

22[...] Nabû! May your lips rejoice! [In the assembly] of all [the gods I incessantly spe]ak for your good. [Desi]ring [your life] I roam the step[pe]. [In the midst of wailing[d] I will r]ise and slau[ghter] your enemy. [...] will retur[n] to his country.

[one unintelligible line; break of about twelve lines]
r. 1[*x Mul*]*lissu u Bēlet Arbail* 2[*ana*] *Aššūr-bāni-apli binūt qātīšina* 3*luballiṭā ana* [*d*]*ār*[*i*]

[break]

r. 1May Mullissu and the Lady of Arbela grant Assurbanipal, the creation of their hands, life for [e]ve[r]!

4*ša pî Dunnaša-āmur* 5[*mar'at Arba*]*il*
6*Nisannu* UD.18.KÁM *limmu Bēl-šadû'a* 7*šakin Ṣurri*

r. 4By the mouth of Dunnaša-amur,[e] [a woman from Arbe]la.
Nisan 18, eponymy of Bel-šaduʾa, governor of Tyre (650).[f]

[a] Restoration by Parpola 1997: 40 who translates the word *kidinnu* as a vocative: "O protégé..." I prefer to take it as a term for an oracle of protection, comparable to *šulmu* (see Parpola 1997: lxiii); this is suggested by the use of the word in a very similar context in ABL 186: "I have sent to the king, my lord, a *kidinnu* of Mullissu and the Lady of Kidmuri (i.e., Ištar), the mothers who love you."

[b] The goddesses, referred to in plural thus far, now merge together and speak as one divine person. For "roaming the steppe," see no. 75 (SAA 9 1.8), n. 2.

[c] Mullissu's interceding between Assurbanipal and the gods is reflected by SAA 13 139 (no. 112); cf. also Assurbanipal's Prism B v (no. 101) 39–40.

[d] For the restoration, cf. SAA 9 1.1 (no. 68) i 26; 2.5 iii 31.

[e] Possibly identical with Sinqiša-amur who uttered the oracles SAA 9 1.2 (no. 69) and, probably, 2.5 (no. 82); see Parpola 1997: il–l.

[f] The date indicates that the oracle was uttered while Assurbanipal was waging war against his elder brother Šamaš-šumu-ukin, the ruler of Babylonia. For this war, see Frame 1992: 131–90.

## 95. Fragment of a Report of a Prophecy Dunnaša-amur to Assurbanipal (?)

**Text:** SAA 9 10 (= CT 53 946 = 83-1-18,726).
**Photograph:** Parpola 1997: pl. XIII.
**Transliteration and translation:** Parpola 1997: 42.
**Discussion:** Parpola 1997: il–l, lxi, lxxi.

[beginning destroyed; obv. seven unintelligible lines; break of an unknown number of lines]
r. 1'[*... i*]*baš*[*ši* ...] 2'*ušēṣanni* [...] 3'*šarrūtu iddan* [...] 4'*ša mātāti gabb*[*u* ...] 5'*ūmu ša tap-*[...] 6'*u ša kēn*[*ūni* ...] 7'*lurr*[*ik* ...]

[beginning destroyed]

r.1'[...] there [will] be [...] will bring me out [...] will give the kingship [...] of all countries [...] the day when you/she [...] and the loy[al] ones [...] I shall length[en ...]

one unintelligible line; rest destroyed
s. 1 [. . .] *Dunnaša-āmur mā* [. . . 2 . . .] *mā raggintu ša ra*[*gim* . . .]

[break]

s.1 [. . .] the woman Dunnaša-amur[a] says: [. . .] the prophetess[b] who pro[phesies . . .]

[a] See no. 94 (SAA 9 9), note e.
[b] For the reading *raggintu* for MÍ.GUB.BA, see Parpola 1997: xlvi.

## 96. Fragment of a Report of a Prophecy NN to Assurbanipal

**Text:** SAA 9 11 (= CT 53 219 = K 1974).
**Photograph:** Parpola 1997: pl. XIII.
**Transliteration and translation:** Parpola 1997: 42–43.
**Discussion:** Parpola 1997: lxi–lxii, lxxi; Nissinen 1998b: 54, 59.

[obv. destroyed]
r. 1 [. . .] *ittal*[*ak* . . . 2 . . . *lā*] *tallīki an*[*a* . . . 3 *m*]*ā ūmē* [. . . 4 *n*]*akru akaššad ša Aššūr-bāni-apli* [. . . 5 *m*]*ā šibi mātāti utaqqa*[*n* . . .]

6 [*m*]*ā ina digilīya p*[*ānī* . . . 7 *a*]*danniš kakkabtu ša ḫurāṣi* [. . .] 8 *paššūru issēn qa kusāpu danni ina muḫ*[*ḫi* . . .] 9 *siḫḫāru sa'u* [. . . 10 . . .]*-māni ša šaddū*[*ni* . . . 11 *ša*]*pal kakkabtu ša* [*ḫurāṣi* . . . 12 *ina*] *rēšē-ya* [. . . 13 *ka*]*kkabā*[*ni* . . .]

[rest destroyed]

[beginning destroyed]
r. 1 [. . .] wen[t . . . but] you did [not] go t[o . . .] the days [. . .]
4 "I will vanquish the [e]nemy of Assurbanipal [. . .] Sit down! I will put the countries in orde[r . . .]"
6 In my pr[evious] vision [. . . g]reatly! A star-shaped emblem made of gold [. . .] a table, one liter of strong food up[on . . .] a bowl . . .[a] [. . .]s that are pull[ed . . . un]der the star emblem made of [gold . . . at] my head [. . .] stars [. . .]

[rest destroyed]

[a] The word *sa'u* is untranslatable.

# V

# Other Neo-Assyrian Documents

Apart from texts belonging to the genre of prophetic oracles, many other Neo-Assyrian sources mention prophets, refer to their activities or even quote prophetic words, thus amplifying substantially the evidence of prophecy from this period (Nissinen 1998a). The sources are both formally and thematically diverse, representing different genres and interests, and the references to prophets and prophecy in them are haphazard and entirely dependent on each writer's concerns and interpretations. While some texts give an account of an appearance of a prophet in a specific situation, only very few of them can be considered eye-witness reports (nos. 111, 113); indeed, some of them clearly indicate that this is not the case (nos. 109, 115). Some letter-writers are likely to quote from written sources, that is, from archival copies of prophetic oracles accessible to them (nos. 106, 107). This holds true for the inscriptions as well.

In spite of the fact that the non-prophetical texts only rarely present first-hand information of prophetic performances, they have the advantage of looking at prophecy from outside, thus demonstrating how prophecy was used and assessed by the prophets' contemporaries. Beside actual prophecies, these documents provide additional evidence of the socioreligious contexts of prophetic activity as well as of the position of the prophets within Neo-Assyrian society. Furthermore, they provide knowledge of themes and issues of prophetic concern not discernible in the actual oracles.

Within the huge corpus of Mesopotamian royal inscriptions, only a few of those of Kings Esarhaddon and Assurbanipal allude to prophecy, either as mere references to prophetic messages received by the king or as quotations of prophetic words. The historical contexts of these allusions are Esarhaddon's rise to power in the year 681 B.C.E. (nos. 97, 98) and Assurbanipal's wars against Mannea in approximately 660 (no. 100) and Elam in 653 (no. 101), as well as his restoration of the temple of Lady of Kidmuri (no. 99).

The technical term used for prophetic oracles in the inscriptions is *šipir maḫḫê* (lit. "message of prophets"), which is analogous to the divinatory terms *našparti ilāni u Ištār* "message of the gods and Ištar" (no. 97, line ii 6) and *šipir Ištar bēltīya ša lā innennū* "the unchanging message of Ištar, my lady" (no. 101, line v 79); the term thus reflects the role of the prophets as mediators of divine words. Noteworthy in this formulaic expression is the use of the word *maḫḫû;* in Neo-Assyrian, this word is otherwise used only in ritual texts and lexical lists, whereas the colloquial word for "prophet" is *raggimu*. The references to *šipir maḫḫê* appear in both military and cultic contexts and are always juxtaposed with other kinds of divination, such as dreams and astrological omens.

The two prophetic quotations are to be found in the inscriptions of Assurbanipal:

> Ištar, who dwells in Arbela, delivered Aḫšeri, who did not fear my lordship, up to his servants, according to the word that she had said in the very beginning: "I will, as I have said, take care of the execution of Aḫšeri, the king of Mannea." (no. 100)

> Ištar heard my desperate sighs and said to me: "Fear not!" She made my heart confident, saying: "Because of the prayer you said with your hand lifted up, your eyes being filled with tears, I have compassion for you." (no. 101)

Considering the divine speaker and clear affinities with the prophetic oracles, there is no reasonable doubt that these words are presented as prophetic ones, even though this is not explicitly mentioned. Especially number 101, which tells about Assurbanipal's participation in a festival of Ištar in Arbela and his prayer to the goddess, is more than any other passage in the Mesopotamian royal inscriptions concerned with divination, even alluding several times to prophecy.

That prophecy is mentioned in the inscriptions of Esarhaddon and Assurbanipal clearly coincides with the fact that the extant archival copies of prophecy were filed in the time of these two kings. This gave the craftsmen of the inscriptions the possibility of referring to prophecies in the same way as to other divinatory reports and even of quoting or paraphrasing their words. Especially the close parallelism of number 97 with the first and third collection of prophecies (nos. 68–77, 84–88), probably compiled by the same scribal circles who authored the inscription, provides clear evidence of the scribes' use of prophetic sources, the ideological focus of which was in line with their own and thus made them suitable for their purposes.

Prophets are acknowledged also in an ideological document of another kind, namely the Succession Treaty of Esarhaddon from the year

672. This treaty is historically related to number 97 and numbers 68–77, which were prepared for the same occasion, namely, the investiture of Assurbanipal as crown prince. One paragraph of the treaty deals with potential propagators of malevolence against Assurbanipal the crown prince designate (no. 102), among them prophets and other practitioners of divination of a noninductive kind, grouped together with terms *raggimu, maḫḫû,* and *šā'ilu amat ili,* the last designation meaning "inquirer of divine words" and usually connected with dream interpretation. The paragraph reckons with the possibility that prophecy, in contradiction to the royal ideology, may be used against the king. Such a case is indeed reported by Nabû-reḫtu-uṣur, who in his letters (nos. 115–117) informs the king of a conspiracy, manifest in a (pseudo)prophecy proclaimed near the city of Harran, according to which the seed of Sennacherib will be destroyed and a certain Sasî proclaimed the king.

In the Neo-Assyrian royal correspondence, prophecy is a recurrent theme. Mar-Issar, Esarhaddon's agent in Babylonia, reports a prophecy proclaimed on occasion of the substitute king ritual in 671 in Akkad (no. 109). Bel-ušezib, the only Babylonian scholar in Esarhaddon's inner circle, writes to the king soon after his enthronement, complaining about the favor the newly enthroned king has bestowed upon prophets and prophetesses instead of himself (no. 105). A few years later, however, he readily quotes a prophetic oracle, which between the lines corroborates the restoration of Babylon and the reestablishment of the cult of her main temple, Esaggil (no. 106). This quotation probably derives from a filed report of prophecy, and the same can be said of the prophetic quotation of Nabû-nadin-šumi, the chief exorcist also belonging to Esarhaddon's nearest men, who recommends the banishment of a person on the basis of a word of Ištar of Arbela and Nineveh (no. 107). The reference to prophecy made by another exorcist, Urad-Gula, has a totally different tone and motivation. Having served Esarhaddon for years, he has lost favor in Assurbanipal's eyes and describes his misery to him, trying to arouse his sympathy. As the last straw, he tells, he had even turned to a prophet, without avail (no. 108).

In addition to the correspondence of the king with his closest circle of scholars, there are a few relevant letters written by priests or temple officials. Two of them report an appearance of a prophetess. The first is by Nabû-reši-išši, who while giving account of sacrifices performed in a temple, most probably in that of Ištar in Arbela, cites the words of a prophetess, according to which some property belonging to the goddess has been given to Egyptians and should be returned (no. 113). In the second report (no. 111) Adad-aḫu-iddina writes to the king that a prophetess called Mullissu-abu-uṣri had proclaimed as a divine word that the royal throne should be transported to another place, probably to Akkad where it was needed on the occasion of the substitute king ritual mentioned in number 109. The demand for the throne implies that the temple in question is Ešarra, the temple of the god Aššur in the city Assur where the coronation of the Assyrian king took place. As for other texts, there is the tiny fragment number 114; its preserved text implies that the destroyed part of it contained a *šipirtu* of Ištar of Arbela for the king. The word *šipirtu* means a divine message normally written without a reference to the transmitter (Pongratz-Leisten 1999: 226–27), but in this case it is said to be spoken or reported by a votaress (*šēlūtu*) of the goddess (cf. no. 74). Such a *šipirtu* seems to be reported also by the temple official Aššur-hamatuʾa to Assurbanipal (no. 112). This letter begins with the divine self-representation without any introductory formula or greeting, and contains the word of Bel (Marduk) concerning his reconciliation with Mullissu and, through her intercession, with Assurbanipal. The language and the idea of the divine message fully concur with the extant prophecies, especially number 94.

The prophetic activities in temples are further documented by two ritual texts. The first is the so-called Marduk Ordeal, a commentary on a ritual in which Marduk is beaten and sent to prison (no. 103). This ritual is most probably to be associated with the return of the statue of Marduk to Babylon in the beginning of Assurbanipal's reign. It commiserates with Marduk and reflects the ideology of those who promoted the rebuilding of Babylon. Even prophets appear in this text as sympathizers of Marduk and Babylon, consistently with the prophetic oracles which are concerned for the reestablishment of the cult of Babylonian gods (nos. 78, 80, 106, etc.). In the Tammuz and Ištar text (no. 118), the prophets have a role to play in a healing ritual, together with "the shepherd boy of Dumuzi" (a cult functionary who intercedes on behalf of the people) and the "frenzied" men and women (*zabbu* and *zabbatu*), who are associated with prophets also in lexical lists (nos. 120, 126, 127).

Two administrative texts supplement the evidence of prophecy in Assyria from the cultic and military directions. The presence of the prophets in Ešarra is confirmed by the oldest Neo-Assyrian text in this collection, a long decree for the maintenance of this temple from the year 809 (no. 110). The text includes an expenditure of barley "for the presence of prophetesses" (*ša pān maḫḫâte*), who are placed under the paragraph concerning the divine council. This is compatible with the intercessory role of Ištar/Mullissu in the divine council reflected by prophecies (nos. 94, 112, etc.). The other text belonging to this category is a lodging list compiled on the occasion of some major event in Nineveh, originally consisting of about one hundred names (no. 104). One of the persons included in this document is Quqî, the prophet (*raggimu*), who is listed among high-ranking officials referred to as coming from Šadikanni.

## 97. Esarhaddon's Rise to Power

**Text:** Nin A i 1–ii 11 (= 1929-10-12, 1 and duplicates; see Borger 1956: 36–37; Porter 1993: 191–93).
**Copy:** Thompson 1931: pls. 1–13.
**Transliteration and translation:** Thompson 1931: 9–13; Bauer 1934: 170–81; Borger 1956: 39–45.
**Translation:** Oppenheim 1969: 289–90; Borger 1984: 393–95.
**Discussion:** Nötscher 1966: 177–78; Weippert 1972: 466–68; Tadmor 1983: 38–45; Porter 1993: 13–26, 106–9; Rowlett 1996: 109–10; Parpola 1997: lxxii–lxxiii; Nissinen 1998b: 14–34; Pongratz-Leisten 1999: 84–85.

[i 1] *ekal Aššūr-aḫu-iddina šarru rabû šarru dannu* [2] *šar kiššati šar māt Aššūr šakkanak Bābili* [3] *šar māt Šumeri u Akkadi šar kibrāt erbetti* [4] *rēʾûm kēnu migir ilāni rabûti* [5] *ša ultu ṣeḫerīšu Aššūr Šamaš Bēl u Nabû* [6] *Ištār ša Nīnua Ištār ša Arbail* [7] *ana šarrūti māt Aššūr ibbû zikiršu*

Property of Esarhaddon, the great king, the mighty king, king of the universe, king of Assyria, governor of Babylonia, king of Sumer and Akkad, king of the four regions,[a] the rightful shepherd, the beloved of the great gods, whom Aššur, Šamaš, Bel, Nabû, Ištar of Nineveh, and Ištar of Arbela called to the kingship of Assyria when he still was a baby.[b]

[8] *ša aḫḫēya rabûti aḫūšunu ṣeḫru anāku* [9] *ina qibīt Aššūr Sîn Šamaš Bēl u Nabû* [10] *Ištār ša Nīnua Ištār ša Arbail abu bānûa* [11] *ina puḫur aḫḫēya rēšēya kēniš ullīma* [12] *umma annû māru rēdûtīya* [13] *Šamaš u Adad ina bīri išālma annu kēnu* [14] *īpulūšu umma šū tēnûka*

[8] Even though I was younger than my big brothers, my father[c] who engendered me, justly elevated my head among my brothers, upon the command of Aššur, Sin, Šamaš, Bel, Nabû, Ištar of Nineveh, and Ištar of Arbela. He said: "This is my heir." By means of extispicy he consulted Šamaš and Adad who gave him a firm positive answer: "He is your successor."[d]

[15] *zikiršunu kabtu ittaʾidma nīšē māt Aššūr ṣeḫer rabi* [16] *aḫḫēya zēr bīt abīya ištēniš upaḫḫirma* [17] *maḫar Aššūr Sîn Šamaš Nabû u Marduk ilāni māt Aššūr* [18] *ilāni ašibūte šamê u qaqqari aššu naṣār rēdûtīya* [19] *zikiršun kabtu ušazkiršunūti*

[15] Respecting their solemn statement, he assembled the people of Assyria, young and old, as well as my brothers, the descendants of my father's house. To secure my succession, he made them swear a solemn oath before Aššur, Sin, Šamaš, Nabû, and Marduk, the gods of Assyria, the gods who inhabit heaven and earth.[e]

[20]*ina arḫi šalme ūme šemê kî qibītīšunu ṣirti* [21]*ina bīt rēdûti ašri šugludi ša šikin šarrūti* [22]*ina libbīšu bašû ḫadîš ērumma*

[20]In a favorable month, on an auspicious day, in accordance with their lofty command, I triumphantly entered the Palace of Succession, the formidable residence where the one to be appointed to kingship is located.[f]

[23]*riddu kēnu eli aḫḫēya ittabikma* [24]*ša ilāni umašširūma ana epšētīšunu šurruḫāti* [25]*ittaklūma ikappudū lemuttu* [26]*lišān lemuttim karṣī tašqirti kî lā libbi ilāni* [27]*elīya ušabšûma surrāti lā šalmāti* [28]*arkīya iddanabbubū zērāti*

[23]My brothers, though lavished with good education, forsook the gods and trusted in their own arrogant deeds, making devious schemes. They spoke evil of me and fabricated libellous rumors about me in a godless manner, they spread malevolent lies and hostility behind my back.[g]

[29]*pašru libbi abīya ša lā ilāni uzennû ittīya* [30]*šaplānu libbašu rēmu rašišūma* [31]*ana epēš šarrūtīya šitkunā ēnāšu*

[29]The gentle heart of my father they alienated from me against the will of the gods,[h] though in his heart he secretly commiserated with me and his eyes were set upon my kingship.

[32]*itti libbīya atammūma uštābila kabattī* [33]*umma epšētīšunu šurruḫāma ana ṭēme ramānīšunu* [34]*taklūma ša lā ilāni mīna ippušū* [35]*Aššūr šar ilāni rēmēnû Marduk ša nullâti ikkibšun* [36]*ina ikribi utninni u labān appi* [37]*uṣallišunūtima imgurū qibītī*

[32]I spoke with my heart and puzzled my head, asking myself: "Their deeds are haughty; they trust in their own decision. What will they bring about in their godlessness?" By means of prayers, lamentations and humble gestures I implored Aššur, the king of the gods, and the merciful Marduk, to whom treachery is an abomination, and they accepted my plea.[i]

[38]*kî ṭēm ilāni rabûti bēlēya lapān epšēt lemutti* [39]*ašar niṣirti ušēšibūnimma ṣulūlšunu ṭāba* [40]*elīya itruṣūma iṣṣurūʾinni ana šarrūti*

[38]In accordance with the will of the great gods, my lords, they transferred me away and made me dwell in a secure place, safe from their evil deeds.[j] Extending their sweet shade over me they preserved me for the kingship.

[41]*arkānu aḫḫēya immaḫûma mimma ša eli ilāni* [42]*u amelūti lā ṭāba ēpušūma ikpudū lemuttu*

[41]Afterwards my brothers went out of their senses doing everything that is displeasing to the gods and

[43]*issiḫūma kakkē ina qereb Nīnua balu ilāni* [44]*ana epēš šarrūti itti aḫāmeš ittakkipū lalā'iš* [45]*Aššūr Sîn Šamaš Bēl Nabû Ištār ša Nīnua Ištār ša Arbail* [46]*epšēt ḫammā'ē ša kî lā libbi ilāni innepšū* [47]*lemniš ittaṭlūma idāšun ul izzizū* [48]*emūqāšun lillūta ušālikūma* [49]*šaplānūa ušakmisūšunūti* [50]*nīšē māt Aššūr ša adê mamīt ilāni rabûti* [51]*ana naṣār šarrūtīya ina mê u šamni itmû* [52]*ul illikū rēṣūssun*

mankind. They planned evil and godlessly rose up in arms in Nineveh, butting each other like young goats to take over the kingship.[k] Aššur, Sîn, Šamaš, Bel, Nabû, Ištar of Nineveh, and Ištar of Arbela looked with displeasure upon the deeds of the rebels which were done against the will of the gods. They did not stand at their side, but turned their strength into weakness and made them bow under my feet. The people of Assyria, who had sworn the loyalty oath by the great gods with water and oil to secure my kingship, did not come to their assistance.

[53]*anāku Aššūr-aḫu-iddina ša ina tukulti ilāni rabûti bēlēšu* [54]*ina qereb tāḫāzi lā inī'u irassu* [55]*epšētīšunu lemnēti urruḫiš ašmēma* [56]*ū'a aqbīma ṣubāt rubûtīya ušarriṭma* [57]*ušaṣriḫa sipittu labbiš annadirma iṣṣariḫ kabattī* [58]*aššu epēš šarrūti bīt abīya arpisa rittīya* [59]*ana Aššūr Sîn Šamaš Bēl Nabû u Nergal Ištār ša Nīnua Ištār ša Arbail* [60]*qātī aššīma imgurū qibītī ina annīšunu kēni* [61]*šīr takilti ištapparūnimma alik lā kalâta* [62]*idāka nittallakma ninâra gārêka*

[53]I am Esarhaddon who, trusting in the great gods, his lords, never turns around in the tumult of the battle! I soon heard about their evil deeds. I cried out "Woe!";[l] I rent my princely garment and burst into lamentation.[m] I became enraged like a lion, my emotions were stirred up. I banged my hands together[n] for the sake of exercising the kingship of my father's house. With raised hands I prayed to Aššur, Sîn, Šamaš, Bel, Nabû, Nergal, Ištar of Nineveh, and Ištar of Arbela, and they accepted my words. Giving me their firm positive answer they constantly sent me this oracle of encouragement:[o] "Go ahead, do not hold back! We go constantly by your side; we annihilate your enemies."

[63]*ištēn ūmu šitta ūmāti ul uqqi pān ummānīya ul adgul* [64]*arkā ul āmur piqitti sīsê ṣimitti nīri* [65]*u unūt tāḫāzīya ul āšur ṣidīt girrīya ul ašpuk* [66]*šalgu kuṣṣu Šabāṭi dannat*

[63]I did not wait even for the next day, nor did I wait for my army. I did not secure the rear, I did not inspect my yoked horses or my combat equipment, I did not even

*kuṣṣi ul ādur* [67]*kīma urinni mupparši* [68]*ana sakāp zā'irīya aptâ idāya* [69]*ḫarrān Nīnua pašqiš u urruḫiš ardēma*

heap up provisions for my campaign. I was not afraid of the snow and the cold of the month of Shebat (IX),[p] the fierce cold, but spread my wings like a flying eagle[q] to repel my enemies and marched toward Nineveh quickly, despite the difficult obstacles along the way.

[70]*ellamūa ina erṣetim māt Ḫanigalbat gimir qurādīšun ṣīrūti* [71]*pān girrīya ṣabtūma uša''alū kakkēšun* [72]*puluḫti ilāni rabûti bēlēya isḫupšunūtīma* [73]*tīb tāḫāzīya danni ēmurūma ēmû maḫḫûtiš*

[70]In the territory of Ḫanigalbat,[r] their assembled elite troops blocked the advance of my troops and sharpened their weapons in front of me. However, fear of the great gods, my lords, befell them, and when they saw the attack of my strong battle array, they went out of their minds.

[74]*Ištār bēlet qabli u tāḫāzi rā'imat šangûtīya* [75]*idāya tazzizma qašassunu tašbir* [76]*tāḫāzāšunu raksu tapṭurma* [77]*ina puḫrīšunu iqbû umma annû šarrāni* [78]*ina qibītīša ṣīrti idāya ittanasḫarū tebû arkīya* [79]*kalūmeš idakkakū uṣallû bēlūti*

[74]Ištar, the Lady of warfare and battle who loves my priesthood, fell in beside me, broke their bows and disrupted their ranks. They said in their midst: "This is our king!" Upon her lofty command they came over to my side. Rising up after me and gamboling about like lambs they implored my sovereignty.

[80]*nīšē māt Aššūr ša adê nīš ilāni rabûti ina muḫḫīya izkurū* [81]*adi maḫrīya illikūnimma unaššiqū šēpēya* [82]*u šunu ḫammā'ē ēpiš sīḫi u bārti* [83]*ša alāk girrīya išmûma ṣābê tuklātēšunu ēzibūma* [84]*ana māt lā idû innabtū*

[80]The people of Assyria who had sworn loyalty to me before the great gods, came before me and kissed my feet. But when those rebels, who made conspiracy and insurrection, heard the approach of my campaign, they deserted the troops who had trusted in them and fled to an unknown land.[s]

*akšudamma ina kār Idiglat* [85]*ina qibīt Sîn u Šamaš ilāni bēl kāri* [86]*gimir ummānīya Idiglat rapaštum atappiš ušašḫiṭ* [87]*ina Addāri arḫi mitgāri* UD.8.KÁM *ūm eššēši ša Nabû* [ii 1]*ina qereb Nīnua āl bēlūtīya ḫadîš ērumma* [2]*ina kussi abīya ṭābiš ūšib*

[84]I reached the embankment of the Tigris and, upon the command of Sîn and Šamaš, the lords of the harbor, I let all my troops jump across the broad river Tigris as if it were nothing but a ditch.[t] In the month of Adar (XII), a favorable month, on the eighth day,[u] the day of

the festival of Nabû, I triumphantly entered Nineveh, the residence of my lordship, and happily ascended the throne of my father.

*[3]izīqamma šūtu mānit Ēa [4]šāru ša ana epēš šarrūti zâqšu ṭāba [5]ukkibānimma idāt dumqi ina šamāmē u qaqqari [6]šipir maḫḫê našparti ilāni u Ištār [7]kayyān usaddirūni ušarḫiṣūni libbu [8]ṣābē bēl ḫiṭṭi ša ana epēš šarrūti māt Aššūr [9]ana aḫḫēya ušakpidū lemuttu [10]puḫuršunu kīma ištēn aḫīṭma annu kabtu ēmissunūtīma [11]uḫalliqa zēršun*

ii [3]The Southwind, the breeze of Ea, was blowing—the wind whose blowing portends well for exercising the kingship. Favorable omens in the sky and on earth came to me. Oracles of prophets, messages of the gods and Ištar, were constantly sent to me and they encouraged my heart. The transgressors who had induced my brothers to the evil plans for taking over the kingship of Assyria I searched out, each and everyone of them, imposed a heavy punishment upon them, and destroyed their seed.[u]

[a] Cf. SAA 9 3.2 (no. 85) ii 3: "Aššur has given him the whole world [*kippat erbettim*]."

[b] Cf. SAA 9 1.4 (no. 71) ii 20–24.

[c] The father is Sennacherib, whereas one of the elder brothers is called Arda-Mullissi, who was ousted from his position as the crown prince. See Parpola 1980; Kwasman and Parpola 1991: xxvii–xxxiv.

[d] For a similar query to Šamaš, cf. SAA 4 149.

[e] The succession treaty of Sennacherib is partly preserved in SAA 2 3.

[f] The month in question is Nisan (I), 683. For the Palace of Succession, see no. 69 (SAA 9 1.2), n. 1. For *šikin šarrūti,* see *AHw* 1234 sub *šiknu* A 6.

[g] Cf. SAA 9 3.3 (no. 86) ii 10–12.

[h] Cf. SAA 9 1.8 (no. 75) v 15–20.

[i] Cf. SAA 9 3.3 (no. 86) ii 13–14.

[j] The "secure place" (lit. "secret place," *ašar niṣirti*) refers to the expatriation of Esarhaddon to the Western provinces (the territory of Ḫanigalbat, line i 70).

[k] The inscription does not mention that they even killed their father Sennacherib; see Parpola 1980.

[l] Cf. SAA 9 3.3 (no. 86) ii 13–14.

[m] Cf. *ina libbi ū'a* "in the midst of woe" SAA 9 1.1 (no. 68) i 26; 2.5 (above, no. 82) iii 31. Cf. also a similar passage in the Epic of Ninurta, or Lugale (van Dijk 1983: 61:70), in which Ninurta, upon hearing of Asakku's evil deeds, cries "Woe!" (*ū'a*). For commonalities between Lugale and Esarhaddon's inscription, see Parpola 2001: 185–86; Annus 2002: 100, and cf. the following notes.

[n] Or, "I wrenched my wrists," "I clenched my fists"; probably a gesture of exasperation. Cf. the Epic of Ninurta, which says that Ninurta "beat his thigh with his fist" (van Dijk 1983: 61:73).

[o] Rather than a prophetic oracle, the "oracle of encouragement" (*šīr takilti*) is the outcome of an extispicy; nevertheless, it is completely in line with the prophetic messages pertaining to the same situation. The wording of the oracle is reminiscent of the Epic of Ninurta (van Dijk 1983: 80:236): "Ninurta, warrior of Enlil: Go, do not hold back!" (*alik lā kalâta*).

[p] I.e., Shebat (IX), 681.

[q] Cf. the Epic of Ninurta (van Dijk 1983: 82:246), in which Ninurta spreads his wings towards the clouds to attack Asakku.

[r] Cf. above, note j.

[s] Cf. SAA 9 3.3 (no. 86) ii 20–21: "I drove them up to the mountain and let fire and brimstone rain upon them." Evidently, Esarhaddon did not manage to capture his brothers, since this is not explicitly mentioned and they are never heard of again. According to the biblical tradition (2 Kings 19:37 = Isa 37:38) they fled to "the land of Ararat," i.e., Urartu.

[t] Cf. SAA 9 1.6 (no. 73) iv 3–4; 3.3 (no. 86) ii 20.

[u] I.e., Adar (XII), 681. According to the chronicles of Esarhaddon (Grayson 1975: 82:38), the accession to the throne took place on the eighteenth or twenty-eighth, not on the eighth day.

[v] Cf. SAA 9 3.5 (no. 88) iv 25–30.

## 98. Esarhaddon's Ascending the Throne

**Text:** Ass A i 31–ii 26 (= VA 10130 + VA 8411 + UM 32-22-5 and duplicates; see Borger 1956: 1; Porter 1993: 184).
**Transliteration and translation:** Borger 1956: 2.
**Discussion:** Fales and Lanfranchi 1997: 108; Parpola 1997: lxxiv; Nissinen 1998b: 14–34; Pongratz-Leisten 1999: 85.

[i 31]*[Sîn Šam]aš ilāni maššūte* [32]*aš[šu d]ēn kitti* [33]*u mīšari* [34]*an[a māti] u nišē šarāku* [35]*arḫiš[a]mma ḫarrān kitti u* [36]*mīšari ṣabtūma* [37]UD.[x].KÁM UD.14.KÁM [38]*u[s]addirū tāmartu*

[i 31]The twin gods [Sin and Šam]aš, in or[der] to bestow a righteous and just [ju]dgement up[on the land] and the people, kept from month to month to the path of righteousness and justice, appearing regularly on the [xth] and fourteenth days.

[39]*Dilbat nabât kakkabāni* [40]*ina amurri* [ii 1]*[ina ḫarrān šū]t Ēa* [2]*inam-mirma ša kunnu* [3]*māte [ša] sulum* [4]*ilānīša niṣirtu* [5]*ikšudamma itbal* [6]*Ṣalbatānu pāris* [7]*pursê māt Amurri* [8]*ina ḫarrān šūt Ēa* [9]*ib'il ṣindašu* [10]*[š]a danān malki u mātīšu*

[39]Venus, the brightest of the stars, appeared in the west [in the path of] Ea and reached its hypsoma predicting the stabilization of the land and the reconciliation of its god; then it disappeared. Mars, who determines the decision for the

[11]*ukallim iskimbuš*

Westland, shone brightly in the path of Ea, and by his sign announced his decree that gives strength to the king and to his land.[a]

[12]*šipir maḫḫê* [13]*kayyān suddurā* [14]*ša išid kussī* [15]*šangûtīya* [16]*šuršudi ana ūmē ṣâti* [17]*iššaknānimma* [18]*idāt dumqi* [19]*ina šutti u gerrê* [20]*ša šuršudi karri* [21]*šulbur palêya* [22]*ittanabšā ēlīya* [23]*idāt dunqi* [24]*šuātina āmurma* [25]*libbī arḫuṣma* [26]*iṭṭīb kabattī*

[ii 12]Prophetic oracles concerning the establishment of the foundation of my priestly throne until far-off days were conveyed to me incessantly and regularly. Good omens kept occurring to me in dreams and speech omens[b] concerning the establishment of my throne[c] and the long life of my rule. When I saw these good signs, my heart turned confident and my mood became good.

[a] Parpola 1997: lxxiv gives the following dates for these celestial phenomena: Venus appears on the twenty-ninth of Tebet (X), 681; reaches its hypsoma on the fifteenth of Sivan (III), 680; and disappears on the eleventh of Tishri (VII), 680. The shining of Mars is dated to Ab (V) or Tishri (VII), 680.

[b] For *egerrû,* see no. 17, note c.

[c] The word used here is *karru,* which actually means a supporting structure of the throne; see *AHw* 450 sub *karru* II 4.

## 99. Assurbanipal's Establishment of the Cult of the Lady of Kidmuri

**Text:** Prism T ii 7-24 (= 1929-10-12, 2 and duplicates; see Borger 1996: 122–30) and Prism C i 53–66 (= Rm 3 and duplicates; see Borger 1996: 132–37).
**Copy:** Thompson 1931: pls. 14–15.
**Transliteration and translation:** Thompson 1931: 30–31; Borger 1996: 140–41, 206.
**Discussion:** Nissinen 1998b: 35–42.

[7]*Emašmaš Egašankalamma kaspu ḫurāṣu* [8]*uzaʾʾin lulê umalli* [9]*Šarrat Kidmūri ša ina uggat libbīša* [10]*atmanša ēzibu* [11]*ūšibu ašar lā simātīša* [12]*ina palêya damqi ša Aššūr išruka* [13]*taršâ salīmu* [14]*ana šuklul ilūtīša ṣīrti* [15]*šurruḫu mīsēša šūqurūti* [16]*ina šutti šipir maḫḫê*

[7]Emašmaš and Egašankalamma[a] I covered with silver and gold filled it with splendor. The Lady of Kidmuri, who in her anger had left her cella and taken residence in a place unworthy of her, relented during my reign made favorable to me by Aššur, and, to make perfect

[17]*ištanappara kayyāna*

her majestic divinity and glorify her precious rites, constantly sent me orders through dreams and prophetic oracles.

[18]*Šamaš Adad aš'alma* [19]*ēpulū'inni annu kēnu* [20]*simat ilūtīša rabûti ušarriḫ* [21]*ušēšibši ina parammāḫi* [22]*šubat darâti* [23]*parṣēša šūqurūti ukīnma* [24]*ušallima mīsēša*

[18]I consulted Šamaš and Adad by means of extispicy[b] and they gave me a firm positive answer. I made the insignia of her great godhead magnificent; I gave her an eternal seat in the inner sanctum.[c] I confirmed her precious rites and carried out her rituals properly.

[a] Temples of Ištar in Nineveh and Arbela.
[b] Literally, "I asked Šamaš and Adad."
[c] A conjectural translation; *para(m)māḫu* is used for cultic seats as well as for shrines (see *AHw* 829).

## 100. Assurbanipal's Mannean War

**Text:** Prism A ii 126–iii 26 (= Rm 1 and duplicates; see Borger 1996: 1–14).
**Transliteration and translation:** Streck 1916: 22–27; Borger 1996: 32–36.
**Discussion:** Weippert 1981: 98; Grayson 1991: 146–47; Laato 1996: 181; Nissinen 1998b: 43–44, 46–47, 52; Pongratz-Leisten 1999: 86.

[ii 126]*ina rebê girrīya adki ummānīya eli Aḫšēri* [127]*šar māt Mannāya uštēšera ḫarrānu ina qibīt Aššūr Sîn Šamaš* [128]*Adad Bēl Nabû Ištār ša Nīnua Bēlet Kidmūri Ištār ša Arbail* [129]*Ninurta Nergal Nusku qereb māt Mannāya ērub ittalak šalṭiš* [130]*ālānīšu dannūti adi ṣeḫrūti ša nība lā īšû* [131]*adi qereb Izirti akšud appul aqqur ina girri aqmu* [132]*nišē sīsê imārē alpē u ṣēni ultu qereb ālāni šâtunu* [133]*ušēṣamma šallatiš amnu*

[126]In my fourth campaign I mobilized my troops and took the straightest way against Aḫšeri, the king of Mannea. Upon the command of Aššur, Sin, Šamaš, Adad, Bel, Nabû, Ištar of Nineveh, the Lady of Kidmuri, Ištar of Arbela, Ninurta, Nergal, and Nusku I entered Mannea and triumphantly marched through it. I conquered, devastated, destroyed and burned with fire its fortified cities and its numberless small towns as far as Izirtu. The people, horses, donkeys, bulls and sheep I removed from these cities and counted them among the booty.

*Aḫšēri alāk girrīya* [134]*išmēma umaššir Izirtu āl šarrūtīšu* [iii 1]*ana Ištatti āl tukultīšu innabitma ēḫuz* [2]*marqītu nagû šuātu akšud mālak ešret ūmē ḫamšat ūmē* [3]*ušaḫribma šaqummatu atbuk*

[133]Aḫšeri, when he heard my troops coming, left Izirtu, his royal residence. He fled to Ištatti, his stronghold, and sought shelter there. I conquered this area, devastated a stretch of fifteen days' march and brought about a deathly silence.

[4]*Aḫšēri lā pāliḫ bēlūtīya ina amat Ištār* [5]*āšibat Arbail ša ultu rēši taqbû* [6]*umma anāku mītūtu Aḫšēri šar māt Mannāya* [7]*kî ša aqbû eppuš ina qāti ardānīšu tamnūšūma* [8]*nišē mātīšu sīḫu elīšu ušabšû ina sūq ālīšu šalamtašu* [9]*iddû indaššarū pagaršu* [10]*aḫḫēšu qinnūšu zēr bīt abīšu ušamqitū ina kakkē*

[4]Ištar, who dwells in Arbela, delivered Aḫšeri, who did not fear my lordship, up to his servants, according to the word that she had said in the very beginning: "I will, as I said, take care of the execution of Aḫšeri, the king of Mannea." The people of his country rose in rebellion against him, threw his corpse on the street of his city dragging his body to and fro. With weapons they beat his brothers, his family and his kinsmen down.

[11]*arkānu Ualli māršu ūšib ina kussīšu* [12]*danān Aššūr Sîn Šamaš Adad Bēl Nabû* [13]*Ištār ša Nīnua šarrat Kidmūri* [14]*Ištār ša Arbail Ninurta Nergal Nusku* [15]*ilāni rabûti bēlēya ēmurma* [16]*iknuša ana nīrīya* [17]*aššu balāṭ napištīšu upnāšu iptâ uṣallâ bēlūti* [18]*Erisinni mār rēdûtīšu* [19]*ana Nīnua išpuramma unaššiqa šēpēya* [20]*rēmu aršīšumma* [21]*mār šiprīya ša šulme umaʾʾir ṣēruššu* [22]*mārtu ṣīt libbīšu ušēbila ana epēš abarakkūti* [23]*maddattašu maḫrītu ša ina terṣi šarrê abbēya* [24]*ušabṭilu iššûni adi maḫrīya* [25]*šalāšā sīsê eli maddattīšu maḫrīti* [26]*uraddīma ēmissu*

[11]Afterward his son Ualli ascended his throne. He acknowledged the authority of Aššur, Sin, Šamaš, Adad, Bel, Nabû, Ištar of Nineveh, the Queen of Kidmuri, Ištar of Arbela, Ninurta, Nergal, Nusku, the great gods, my lords, and submitted to my yoke. For the sake of his life he opened his hands and implored my lordship. His crown prince Erisinni he sent to Nineveh where he kissed my feet. I was merciful to him and sent to him an envoy of peace. He had a daughter of his own offspring brought to me to be my housekeeper. His former tribute that he had interrupted in the time of the kings, my fathers, was brought to me again. I added thirty horses to his former tribute and imposed them on him.

## 101. Assurbanipal's War against Teumman, King of Elam

**Text:** Prism B v 15–vi 16 (= K 1775 + K 1847 + K 2732 + Sm 1712 and duplicates; see Borger 1996: 86-91).
**Transliteration and translation:** Streck 1916: 120-21; Piepkorn 1933: 64–71; Borger 1996: 99–105, 224–26.
**Translation:** Langdon 1914: 140–41; Talon 1994: 117–18.
**Discussion:** Nötscher 1966: 178, 184; Weippert 1972: 47; 1981: 97–98; Gerardi 1987: 122–34; Grayson 1991: 147–54; Sicre 1992: 240; Laato 1996: 180–81; Rowlett 1996: 118–19; Fales and Lanfranchi 1997: 109–10; Parpola 1997: xlvi–xlvii; Nissinen 1998b: 44–45, 47–51, 53–61; 2000a: 265–66; 2002b: 13; Butler 1998: 31–32, 155; Pongratz-Leisten 1999: 87, 120–22.

v 15 *ina Ābi araḫ nanmurti kakkab qašti* 16 *isinni šarrati kabitti mārat Illil* 17 *ana palāḫ ilūtīša rabûti ašbāk* 18 *ina Arbail āl narām libbīša* 19 *aššu tibût Elamê ša balu ilāni itbâ* 20 *ušannûni ṭēmu* 21 *umma Teumman kīam iqbi* 22 *ša Ištār ušannû milik ṭēmēšu* 23 *umma ul umaššar adi allaku* 24 *ittīšu eppušu mitḫuṣūtu*

15 In Ab (V), the month of the appearance of the Bow Star[a] and the festival of the Venerable Lady, the daughter of Enlil, when I was visiting Arbela, her beloved city, to worship her great divinity, an assault of the Elamites, which they made against the will of the gods was reported to me: "Thus spoke Teumman, whose power of discernment Ištar has confused: 'I shall not give up until I can go and wage war against him!'"

25 *šūt meriḫti annīti ša Teumman* 26 *iqbû amḫur šaqûtu Ištār* 27 *azziz ana tarṣīša akmis šapalša* 28 *ilūssa ušappâ illakā dimāya*

25 Because of this impudence uttered by Teumman, I approached Ištar, the most high. I placed myself before her, prostrated myself under her feet. My tears were flowing as I prayed to her divinity:

29 *umma Bēlet Arbail anāku Aššūr-bāni-apli* 30 *šar māt Aššūr binūt qātēki ša iḫšuḫūšu Aššūr* 31 *abu bānûki ana udduš ešrēti šullum parṣēšun* 32 *naṣar pirištīšun šuṭūb libbīšun imbû zikiršu* 33 *anāku ašrēki aštene''i* 34 *allika ana palāḫ ilūtīki u šullum parṣēki*

29 "O Lady of Arbela! I am Assurbanipal, king of Assyria, creation of your hands, whom Aššur, the father who made you, desired and whom he called by name to renovate shrines, to carry out the rituals of the gods,[b] to protect their secret lore and to delight their hearts. I am the one who visits regularly your dwellings, I come to worship you and take care of your rituals.

*[35]u šû Teumman šar māt Elamti lā mušāqir ilāni [36]kuṣṣur kali ana mitḫuṣi ummânīya [37]umma atti Bēlet bēlēti ilat qabli bēlet tāḫāzi [38]mālikat ilāni abbēša [39]ša ina maḫar Aššūr abi bānîki damiqtī taqbê [40]ina nīš ēnēšu ebbī iḫšuḫanni ana šarrūti*

[35]Now this Teumman, king of Elam, who does not respect the gods, has assembled all (his forces) to combat my troops. You are the lady of the ladies, the goddess of warfare, the lady of battle and the counsellor of the gods, your[c] fathers! You spoke good words for me before Aššur, the father who made you, so that he, raising his pure eyes, wished me to be the king.

*[41]aššu Teumman šar māt Elamti ša ana Aššūr [42]šar ilāni abi bānîki iḫtû biltu idkâ ummānšu [43]ikṣura tāḫāzu uša''ala kakkēšu [44]ana alāk māt Aššūr umma atti qaritti ilāni kīma bilti [45]ina qabal tamḫāri puṭṭirīšūma dikiššu meḫû [46]šāru lemnu*

[41]As to Teumman, king of Elam, he has become a burden[d] for Aššur, the king of the gods, the father who created you! He has assembled his troops and armed himself in preparation for war in order to march into Assyria. You are the most warlike among the gods! Scatter him like a load in the tumult of battle; raise against him a destructive wind and storm!"

*inḫēya šūnuḫūti Ištār išmēma [47]lā tapallaḫ iqbâ ušarḫiṣanni libbu [48]ana nīš qātēka ša taššâ ēnāka imlâ dimtu [49]artaši rēmu*

[46]Ištar heard my desperate sighs and said to me: "Fear not!" She made my heart confident, saying: "Because of the prayer you said with your hand lifted up, your eyes being filled with tears, I have compassion for you."[e]

*ina šāt mūši šuātu ša amḫurūši [50]ištēn šabrû utūlma inaṭṭal šuttu [51]iggiltīma tabrīt mūši ša Ištār ušabrûšu [52]ušannâ yâti umma Ištār āšibat Arbail [53]ērubamma imnu u šumēlu tullāta išpāti [54]tamḫat qaštu ina idīša [55]šalpat namṣāru zaqtu ša epēš tāḫāzi [56]maḫarša tazziz šî kīma ummi [57]ālitti itammâ ittīka [58]ilsīka Ištar šaqût ilāni išakkanka ṭēmu [59]umma tanaṭṭala ana epēš šašme [60]ašar pānūa šaknū tebâku anāku [61]atta taqabbīši umma ašar tallakī [62]ittīki lullik Bēlet bēlēti [63]šî*

[49]The very same night as I implored her, a visionary[f] lay down and had a dream. When he woke up, he reported to me the nocturnal vision shown to him by Ištar: "Ištar who dwells in Arbela entered, having quivers hanging from her right and left and holding a bow in her hand. She had drawn a sharp-pointed sword, ready for battle. You stood before her and she spoke to you like a mother who gave birth to you. Ištar, the highest of the gods, called to you and gave

*tušannakka umma atta akanna* [64]*lū ašbāta ašar maškanīka* [65]*akul akalu šiti kurunnu* [66]*ningûtu šukun nu''id ilūtī* [67]*adi allaku šipru šuātu eppušu* [68]*ušakšadu ṣummerāt lib-bīka* [69]*pānūka ul urraq ul inarruṭā šēpēka* [70]*ul tašammaṭ zūtka ina qabli tamḫāri* [71]*ina kir-immīša ṭâbi taḫṣinkāma* [72]*taḫtina gimir lānīka* [73]*pānušša girru innapiḫ* [74]*šamriš tattaṣi ana aḫâti* [75]*eli Teumman šar māt Elamti* [76]*ša uggugat pānušša taškun*

you the following order: 'You are prepared for war, and I am ready to carry out my plans.'[g] [61]You said to her: 'Wherever you go, I will go with you!' But the Lady of Ladies answered you: 'You stay here in your place! Eat food, drink beer, make merry and praise my godhead, until I go to accomplish that task, making you attain your heart's desire. You shall not make a wry face, your feet shall not tremble, you shall not even wipe the sweat in the tumult of war!'" [71]She sheltered you in her sweet embrace; she protected your entire body. Fire flashed in her face, and she went raging away, directing her anger[h] against Teumman, king of Elam, who had made her furious."

[77]*ina Elūli šipir ištārāti isinni Aššūr ṣīri* [78]*araḫ Sîn nannar šamê u erṣeti atkil ana purussê* [79]*nannari namri u šipir Ištār bēltīya ša lā innennū* [80]*adki ummānāt tāḫāzīya mun-daḫṣē ša ina qibīt Aššūr* [81]*Sîn u Ištār ittanašrabbiṭū ina qabli tamḫāri* [82]*eli Teumman šar māt Elamti urḫu aṣbatma* [83]*uštešsera ḫarrānu*

[77]In the month of Elul (VI), the month of the messages of the goddesses and the feast of the exalted Aššur, the month of Sin, the light of heaven and earth, I trusted in the decision of the bright Luminary and in the unchanging message of Ištar, my lady.[i] [80]I mobilized my combat forces, the fighters, who upon the command of Aššur, Sin, and Ištar dashed around into the heat of the fight. Against Teumman, the king of Elam, I made my way, taking the straightest route.

*ellamūa Teumman šar māt Elamti* [84]*ina Bīt-Imbî nadi madaktu erēb šarrūtīya* [85]*ša qereb Dēru išmēma iṣbassu ḫattu* [86]*Teumman iplaḫma ana arkīšu itūr ērub qereb Šūšan* [87]*kaspu ḫurāṣu ana šūzub napištīšu* [88]*uza''iz ana nišē mātīšu* [89]*rēṣēšu ālik idēšu pānuššu utirramma* [90]*ugdappiša ana maḫrīya* [91]*Ulāya*

[83]Teumman, the king of Elam, had encamped against me in Bit Imbi. When he heard that my kingship had entered Der,[j] he became horror-stricken. Teumman was afraid, turned around and withdrew to Susa. [87]To save his life he dispensed silver and gold to the people of his country. The henchmen who

*ana dannūtīšu iškun* [92]*iṣbat pān mašqê*

came to his rescue he returned to the front[k] and massed them in front of me. The river Ulaya he set up as his stronghold and blocked off the way to the watering place.

[93]*ina qibīt Aššūr Marduk ilāni rabûti bēlēya* [94]*ša utakkilū'inni* [95]*ina ittāti damqāti šutti egerrê šipir maḫḫê* [96]*ina qereb Til-Tuba abiktašunu aškun* [97]*ina pagrēšunu Ulāya askir* [98]*šalmātīšunu kīma balti u ašāgi* [99]*umallâ tamirti Šūšan*

[93]Upon the command of Aššur and Marduk, the great gods, my lords, who encouraged me with good omens, dreams, speech omens and prophetic messages, I defeated them in Tell Tuba.[l] With their bodies I stuffed up Ulaya. With their corpses, as if with thorn and thistle, I filled the outskirts of Susa.

[vi 1]*rēš Teumman šar māt Elamti* [2]*ina qibīt Aššūr u Marduk ilāni rabûti bēlēya* [3]*akkis ina puḫur ummānēšu* [4]*milammi Aššūr u Ištār māt Elamti* [5]*isḫupma iškunū ana nīrīya*

[vi 1]On the command of Aššur and Marduk, the great gods, my lords, I cut off the head of Teumman, the king of Elam, before his assembled troops.[m] The splendor of Aššur and Ištar beat the land of Elam down and they submitted to my yoke.

[6]*Ummanigaš ša innabtu* [7]*iṣbatu šēpēya ina kussîšu ušēšib* [8]*Tammarītu aḫūšu šalšāyu* [9]*ina Ḫîdalu ana šarrūti aškun* [10]*narkabāt ṣumbi sīsê parê* [11]*ṣimitti nīri tillê simat tāḫāzi* [12]*ša ina tukulti Aššūr Ištār ilāni rabûti bēlēya* [13]*birit Šūšan u Ulāya ikšudā qātāya* [14]*ina qibīt Aššūr u Marduk ilāni rabûti bēlēya* [15]*ultu qereb māt Elamti ḫadîš ūṣamma* [16]*ana gimir ummānātīya šalimtu šaknat*

[6]Ḫumban-nikaš, who had fled and grasped my feet, I seated upon his throne. Tammaritu, the third among his brothers, I placed in the kingship of Ḫidalu.[n] Chariots, wagons, horses, mules, harnessed animals, trappings fit for war which my hands, trusting in Aššur and Ištar, the great gods, my lords, captured between Susa and the Ulaya (I carried off as a booty[o]). Upon the command of Aššur, Marduk and the great gods I joyfully left Elam. My entire army was well.

[a] The year in question is 653. The Bow Star is Canis Maior, the "arrow" of which is Sirius; cf. Lewy 1965; Parpola 1997: xci–xcii, n. 114.

[b] Literally, "their rituals," which clearly refers to the gods; cf. "their secret lore" and "their hearts."

[c] Literally, "her."

[d] Literally, "who has bound (*ḫatû* III) a burden for Aššur"; cf. Borger 1996: 225: "der in bezug auf Assur … eine Last *auf sich geladen hat*" (italics original, indicating an uncertain translation).

[e] For similar prayers, cf., e.g., Esarhaddon Nin A (no. 97) i 53-62 and the inscription of Zakkur KAI 202 A (no. 136) 11–15; for the prophetic character of the divine answer, see Nissinen 1998b: 53.

[f] The word for "visionary" is *šabrû,* which denotes a person whose divinatory expertise is near to that of a prophet; see Huffmon 1992: 480; Nissinen 1998b: 56.

[g] Literally, "I am ready to go to where my face is directed."

[h] Literally, "her face."

[i] The "decision of the bright Luminary" and "the message of Ištar" (*nannari namri u šipir Ištar*) probably mean astrology and prophecy respectively; cf. "the messages of the goddesses" (*šipir ištārāti*), line v 77.

[j] The city of Der, located in the zone between Babylonia and Elam, had been under Assyrian control since the time of Sargon II, but was obviously invaded by Teumman.

[k] "Return to the front" is an attempt to understand the phrase, which is literally, "returned to his face."

[l] If the river Ulaya corresponds to the modern river Karkheh, on which Susa is located (see Dietrich 2001: 313), Tell Tuba cannot be far from Susa.

[m] According to Prism B vi 66–69 (cf. SAA 3 31 r. 8–9), Teumman's head was put on display in Nineveh.

[n] Ḫumban-nikaš and Tammaritu were sons of Urtaku, the king of Elam who reigned before Teumman. They had escaped the usurpation of Teumman in 674 and sought shelter in Assyria. Ḫidalu is an Elamite city east of Susa; its exact location is unknown.

[o] The syntax of the original text is incomplete.

## 102. Succession Treaty of Esarhaddon

**Text:** SAA 2 6 (ND 4327 and duplicates).
**Photograph:** Watanabe 1987: pls. 1, 8, 9 (ND 4327 etc.).
**Copy:** Wiseman 1958: pls. 2–3, 17, 18, 22.
**Transliteration and translation:** Wiseman 1958: 37–38; Watanabe 1987: 148–49, 180; Parpola and Watanabe 1988: 33; Nissinen 1998b: 156.
**Discussion:** Veijola 1995: 293–94; 2000: 121; Nissinen 1996: 176–82; 1998a: 159–63; 1998b: 121, 156–62; Otto 1998: 37–38; 1999: 3–4, 25, 54, 57–64; Huffmon 2000: 62.

### § 10, lines 108–22 (= ND 4327; 4345A/E; 4346E/I; 4349R; 4355F/I; 1959-4-14, 75; 1959-4-14, 76)

[108]*š[u]mma abutu lā ṭābtu lā deʾiqtu* [109]*lā banītu ina muḫḫi Aššūr-bāni-apli mār šarri rabû ša bēt rēdûti* [110]*mār Aššūr-aḫu-iddina šar māt*

[108]If you hear an evil, ill, and ugly word that is mendacious and harmful to Assurbanipal, the great crown prince of the Palace of

*Aššūr bēlkunu lā tarṣatūni* [111]*lā ṭābatūni lū ina pî nakrīšu* [112]*lū ina pî salmēšu* [113]*lū ina pî aḫḫēšu* [114]*aḫḫē abbēšu mār aḫḫē abbēšu* [115]*qinnīšu zara' bēt abīšu lū ina pî aḫḫēkunu* [116]*mar'ēkunu mar'ātē-kunu lū ina pî raggimi* [117]*maḫḫê mār šā'ili amat ili* [118]*lū ina pî napḫar ṣalmat kaqqadi mal bašû* [119]*tašammâni tupazzarāni* [120]*lā tal-lakāninni ana Aššūr-bāni-apli mār šarri rabû* [121]*ša bēt rēdûti mār Aššūr-aḫu-iddina šar māt Aššūr* [122]*lā taqabbâni*

Succession, son of Esarhaddon, king of Assyria, your lord, [111]may it come from the mouth of his enemy, from the mouth of his ally, from the mouth of his brothers, uncles, cousins, or his family, descendants of his father, [115]or from the mouth of your brothers, sons, or daughters, [116]or from the mouth of a *raggimu*, a *maḫḫû*, or an inquirer of divine words, [118]or from the mouth of any human being at all, [119]you must not conceal it but come and tell it to Assurbanipal, the great crown prince of the Palace of Succession, son of Esar-haddon, king of Assyria.

## 103. Marduk Ordeal (Assur and Nineveh Versions)

**Text:** SAA 3 34 (= VAT 9555, 9538 = *KAR* 143, 219); SAA 3 35 (= K 6333+ with duplicates).
**Photograph:** Livingstone 1989: pl. XII–XIV (SAA 3 35).
**Transliteration and translation:** Zimmern 1918: 14–21; von Soden 1955: 132–57; Frymer-Kensky 1983: 133–36; Livingstone 1986: 236; 1989: 82–91.
**Discussion:** von Soden 1955; Wohl 1970/71: 114; Frymer-Kensky 1983; Nissinen 2001a: 200–201.

### Lines SAA 3 34:28–29 and SAA 3 35:31:

*maḫḫû ša ina pān Bēlet-Bābili illakūni mupassiru šû ana irtīša ibakki illak*
*mā ana ḫursān ubbulūšu šî taṭarrad mā aḫūa aḫūa* [. . .]

The prophet who goes before the Lady of Babylon[a] is a bringer of news; weeping he goes toward her:
"They are taking him[b] to the *ḫursān*!"[c] She sends (the prophet)[d] away, saying: "My brother, my brother!" [. . .]

[a] I.e., Zarpanitu, the spouse of the god Marduk.
[b] I.e., Marduk.
[c] This word is interpreted as meaning the river ordeal, but Frymer-Kensky (1983: 138–39) shows that it rather means the cosmic location where Marduk is held captive.

[d] The implied object of the verb *ṭarādu* is without doubt the prophet.

## 104. List of Lodgings for Officials

**Text:** SAA 7 9 (= K 8143 + 80-7-19,105 = *ADD* 860).
**Photograph:** Fales and Postgate 1992: pl. II.
**Copy:** Johns 1901: nr. 860.
**Transliteration and translation:** Fales and Postgate 1992: 16–19.
**Discussion:** Nissinen 1998b: 64–65; Pongratz-Leisten 1999: 92.

### Lines r. i 20–24:

| | |
|---|---|
| *Nergal-mukīn-aḫi bēl mugirri* | Nergal-mukin-aḫi,[a] chariot owner; |
| *Nabû-šarru-uṣur rāb kiṣir mār šarri* | Nabû-šarru-uṣur, cohort commander of the crown prince; |
| *Wazāru ša-qurbūti ummi šarri* | Wazaru, bodyguard of the queen mother; |
| *Qūqî raggimu* | Quqî, prophet; |
| [blank space of one line] | [blank space of one line] |
| *gimir erbet mūšebī (Ša)dikannāya* | in all, four: the "residences" of the Šadikanneans.[b] |

[a] Or, Nergal-kenu-uṣur; see *PNA* 2/II: 949.
[b] The text has *di-ka-ni-a-a;* I follow the suggestion of Simo Parpola that this actually stands for people from Šadikanni, a city on the upper course of the River Ḫabur.

## 105. Bel-ušezib to Esarhaddon

**Text:** SAA 10 109 (= 82-5-22,105 = *ABL* 1216).
**Photograph:** Mattila (ed.) 1995: 133 (rev.).
**Copy:** Harper 1913 (XII): no. 1216.
**Transliteration and translation:** Peiser 1898: 34–39; Klauber 1914: 235–36; Waterman 1930 (I): 342–45; Parpola 1993: 86–88.
**Discussion:** Peiser 1898: 38–41; Waterman 1931 (III): 321–22; Labat 1959; Dietrich 1970: 64; Parpola 1980: 179–80; 1983: 50; Lanfranchi 1989: 112; Nissinen 1998b: 89–95; 2000b: 102; 2001a: 191; Huffmon 2000: 59.

[beginning destroyed; six unintelligible lines]

7' *[an]āku Bēl-ušēzib aradka ka[lab]ka u pāliḫka* [. . .] 8' *d[ib]bī ma'dūtu ibašši ša ina Nīnâ ašmû k[î ukallimu]* 9' *ammēni rēš raggimānu raggimātu* [. . . 10' *ša] āšipu ina pîya aprikūma ana šulmu mār šarri bēlīy[a* 11' *alli]ka la pāni dâku ušēzibamma ana ašīt[i aḫliqa]* 12' *ana muḫḫi dâkīya u dâku ša urdānīka ūmuss[u idbubū]* 13' *u ittu ša šarrūti ša Aššūr-aḫu-iddina mār šarri bēlī[ya]* 14' *ana Dadâ āšipi u ummi šarri aqbû umma Aššūr-aḫu-iddina* 15' *Bābili eppuš Esaggil ušaklal u yā[ši . . .]* 16' *ammēni adi muḫḫi ša enna šarru rēšā lā iššī u ina* [. . .] 17' *ašīti illikū šiknu šû babbanû ana mār [šarri bēlīya]* 18' *kî ša aqbû kî īpušū ana šarri bēlīya i[ddinū]* 19' *u kî nâri ina qātēšu dagil ilāni ša šar mātāti bēlīya lū i[dû kî]* 20' *šarru mātāti kalīšina ibellu u šanāti ma'dā[ti ilāni rabûti]* 21' *a[na]* UD [. . .] *inamdinū ana šarri bēlīya aqbû* [. . .]

22' *ešrā šan[āti ag]lâ ultu ša šalšīšu bilat kaspu nāmurāti* [. . .] 23' *addinu* [. . .] *ul iddinnūni u nāmurāti ma['dāti]* 24' *ḫarbanāt[i . . .] ana šarri lušēšib u ina pî šarri* [. . .]

[beginning destroyed]

7[I] am Bel-ušezib, your servant, your d[o]g and the one who fears you [. . .]. When I revealed the many w[or]ds that I heard in Nineveh, why, then [*did the king, my lord,* summ]on prophets and prophetesses, but until now has not summoned me?[a] [It was I who] muzzled the exorcist with my words and [we]nt to greet the crown prince, m[y] lord;[b] whose murder along with your servants' murder [was schemed] every day, who escaped from being killed only by [fleeing] to the tower;[c] and who told the omen of kingship of the crown prince Esarhaddon, my lord, to the exorcist Dadâ and the queen mother, saying: "Esarhaddon will restore Babylon, reestablish Esaggil and [. . .] me!" And when [. . .] went to the tower, this wonderful form, just as I had predicted it to the crown [prince, my lord], was made and g[iven] to the king, my lord, and it looked like a (figure of) a musician in his hands.[d] May the gods of the king of the lands, my lord, be wi[tness to what] I said to the king, my lord: "The king will rule all the countries and [the great gods] will give many years to . . . [. . .]."[e]

22All the pa[st] twenty yea[rs] since I gave [. . .] three talents of silver and audience gifts, [. . .] has not been given to me, in spite of the ab[undance of] audience gifts. Let me resettle for the king the wasted lands[f] [. . .], and by the king's command [. . .].

r. 1 *Kalbi māršu ša Nabû-ēṭir ana tarṣi šarri abīka riks[u itti]* 2 *ṭupšarrāni u bārâni ša lā ša šarri abīka ur[akkisu]* 3 *umma kî ittu lā banīti tattalku ana šarri n[iqabbi]* 4 *ummia ittu ešîti tattalka ṭuppi ana ṭuppi* [. . .] 5 *gabbīšunu idakkū kî ittu ša ina muḫḫīšu lā banâ[tu talliku]* 6 *u šû mimma ša lā banâ arkāniš alû kî illi[ka umma ittu]* 7 *ša ina muḫḫīya lā banâtu tallikamma lā taqbâni* [. . .] 8 *dibbī annûti ṭupšarrāni bārâni ina qātēšunu kî iṣbatū [ilāni ša šarri]* 9 *lū idû kî ittu mala ana tarṣi šarri abīka tal[lika lā iqbûma]* 10 *šarru abūka lā balṭūma u šarrūtu lā īpušūma*

r.1 Kalbu, son of Nabû-eṭir, ganged up [with] the scribes and haruspices in the reign of, the king, your father without his knowledge. He said: "If an inauspicious sign occurs, we just [say] to the king that an obscure sign has occurred." Report for report he censored all of them [. . .] when a sign [occurred] that was inauspicious to him. This was no good! Finally, then, when the demon appea[red, (the king) said: "If] there occurs a sign untoward to me and you do not report it to me, [. . .]!" These words were taken seriously indeed by the scribes and haruspices, and may [the gods of the king] witness that [they did report] every single sign that occ[urred] during the reign of your royal father who stayed alive and exercised the kingship!

*enn[a adû ittāti]* 11 *ana tarṣi šarri bēlīya ittalkāni ana muḫḫīšu mimma ša* [. . .] 12 *īziba ēkānu ittu babbanītu inamṣarū* [. . . 13 . . .] *ina qātēkunu tukallā lū* [. . .]

10 Even no[w], during the reign of the king, my lord, [signs] concerning him have occurred. Whatever there is [. . .] they have disregarded. Where is now the auspicious sign they are waiting for? [. . .] you keep to yourselves! May [. . .]

---

14 *[annītu ittu] ša šarrūte mār šarri ša ina āl pāṭi ašbu (ana abīšu bārtu ippušma kussâ lā iṣabbat)* 15 *[mār mammanāma uṣṣīma kussâ i]ṣabbat bītāti ilāni rabûti ana ašrīšunu u[tār] (sattukku ilāni ukān ekallāni iltēniš izannan)*

14 [This was the sign] of the kingship: (If a planet comes close to another planet,[g]) the son of the king who lives in a city on the frontier (will rebel against his father, but will not seize the throne). [A son of nobody will go forth and s]eize [the throne], rest[ore] the temples of the great gods, (establish the sacrifices of the gods and provide jointly for all the temples).

---

16 *[enna adû ittu ina] Ayyāri ana tarṣi šarri bēlīya tatt[alka* . . .]

16 [Now, then, a sign] has occu[rred] in the reign of the king,

[17][...] *šarrūti ša ūmē ṣâti ilsû* [...]
[18][...] *-bilu mār šarri ša iqbû* [...]

[six unintelligible lines]

my lord, [in] Iyyar (II) [...] called the kingship for far-off days [...] the crown prince, whom they said [...]

[rest too fragmentary for translation]

[a] The complicated sentence structure of the lines 8–16 is resolved in the translation by beginning the section with the crucial question, originally divided between the lines 9 and 16.

[b] I.e., Esarhaddon; Bel-ušezib refers to the time before his accession to the throne.

[c] The exact meaning of *ašītu* is not clear.

[d] It is difficult to understand what is meant with the "form" (*šiknu*) that looked like a "musician" (LÚ.NAR) in the king's hands.

[e] Parpola 1993: 87 restores: "t[o the king, my lord]"; the sign UD remains obscure.

[f] This probably means the restoration of Babylon, destroyed by Sennacherib in 689.

[g] The clauses in parentheses are not part of the original but are taken from *Enuma Anu Enlil* 56, an astrological series quoted here by Bel-ušezib in an abridged form (see Labat 1959; Parpola 1980: 179–80). The broken part of the tablet cannot have included all the restored text.

## 106. Bel-ušezib to Esarhaddon

**Text:** SAA 10 111 (= 83-1-18,1 = *ABL* 1237).
**Copy:** Waterman 1912: 3–4: Harper 1913 (XII): nr. 1237.
**Transliteration and translation:** Waterman 1912: 20–22; 1930 (I): 358–61; Pfeiffer 1935: 223–25; Parpola 1993: 89–90.
**Discussion:** Waterman 1912: 22–24; 1931 (III): 325–26; 1936 (IV): 269; Fales and Lanfranchi 1981; Lanfranchi 1989: 110–11; Ivantchik 1993a: 76–80, 189–94; Nissinen 1998b: 96–101; 2000a: 262–63; 2001: 198–99; Pongratz-Leisten 1999: 81–82.

*ana šar mātāti bēlīya aradka B[ēl-ušēzib]* [2]*Bēl Nabû u Šamaš ana šarri bēlīya likrub[u]*

To the king of the lands, my lord: your servant B[el-ušezib].[a]

May Bel, Nabû and Šamaš bless the king, my lord!

---

[3]*kakkubu kî dipāri ultu ṣīt Šamši iṣrurma* [4]*ina erēb Šamši irbi ṣāb nakri ina kabittīša imaqqut*

[3]If a star flashes like a torch from the east and sets in the west: the main army of the enemy will fall.

---

[5]*mišḫu* <*ina*> *šūti iškun iškunma* [6]*imṣur imṣurma izziz izzizma* [7]*ipruṭ ipruṭma ūmu sapiḫ* [8]*rubû ina*

[5]If a flash <in> the south appears and appears again, makes a circle and again makes a circle, then

*ḫarrān illaku mimma šumšu bušû qātīšu ikaššad*

stands still and again stands still, flickers and flickers again and disperses: a ruler who goes forth on a campaign will plunder property and possessions.

---

9 *kî šarru ana emūqīšu iltapru umma* 10 *ana libbi māt Mannāya erbā᾽ emūqa* 11 *gabbi lā errub ṣābu ša-pētḫallāti* 12 *u zukkû līrubū Gimirrāya* 13 *ša iqbû umma Mannāya ina pānīkunu šēpāni* 14 *niptarasu mindēma* 15 *pirṣatu šî zēr ḫalgatî šunu* 16 *[m]āmīti ša ili u adê ul idû* 17 *[nar]kabātu u ṣubbānu aḫīya aḫīya* 18 *[ina n]ērebi lū ušuzzū* 19 *[. . .] sissî u zukkû* 20 *[l]īrubūma ḫubut ṣēri ša māt Mannāya* 21 *[li]ḫbutūnu u lillikūnimma* 22 *[ina libbi] nērebi lū ušuzzū* 23 *[kî] iltēnšu šanîšu īterebūma* r. 1 *[ḫubut ṣēri] iḫtabtūnimma Gimirrāya* 2 *[ina muḫḫīšun]u lā ittalkūni emūqa* 3 *[gabbi lī]rubma ina muḫḫi ālāni ša Mannāya* 4 *[lidd]û Bēl ḫapû ša māt Mannāya* 5 *[iqtabi] ušannu ana qāt šarri bēlīya* 6 *[imanni k]î* UD.15.KÁM *agâ Sîn itti Šamaš* 7 *[innamr]u ina muḫḫīšunu šû šēp* 8 *[Gimi]rrāya la pānīšunu tattaprasu* 9 *[. . .] ikkaššadū*

9 As to what the king has written to his troops, saying:[b] "Enter the Mannean territory; however, not the whole army should enter. Let only the cavalry and the professional troops make their entry. What the Cimmerians have said, 'The Manneans are all yours; we shall keep aloof,' may be a lie! They are barbarians who recognize no oath taken before god and no treaty. [The cha]riots and wagons should stand side by side [in] the pass, [. . .] let the cavalry and the professional troops enter and plunder the Mannean countryside; then let them come back and take up position [in] the pass. [Only] after they have repeatedly entered and plundered [the countryside], and the Cimmerians have not fallen [upon them], the [whole] army may enter [and assault] the Mannean cities." — r. 4 Bel [has ordered] the destruction of Mannea and is now [delivering] them once more into the hands of the king, my lord. If the moon [is seen] together with the sun on the fifteenth day of this month,[c] it is on account of them, meaning that the [Cimm]erians will indeed keep aloof from them [. . .] will be conquered.

*anāku mūṣû u erēbi* 10 *ša māti [u]llīti ul īdi ana šarri bēlīya* 11 *altapra bēl šarrāni mūdê māti liš᾽al* 12 *u šarru akī ša ile᾽û ana emūqēšu* 13 *lišpur*

9 I have written to the king, my lord, without proper knowledge of the conditions in that country.[d] The lord of kings should consult an

*muštaḫalqūti ina muḫḫi mundaḫṣūti* [14]*ina nakri dannatu ina libbi tūmulūka* [15]*emūqa gabbi līrubu gudūdānu* [16]*lūṣûma ṣābīšunu ša ṣēri luṣabbitma* [17]*lišʾalū kî Indaruāya la pānīšunu irīqū* [18]*emūqu līrub ina muḫḫi ālāni liddū*

expert of the country and then write to his army as he deems best. Your advantage is, in any case, that there are more deserters than fighting soldiers among the enemy. When the whole army is entering, let patrols go and capture their men in the open country and then question them. If the Cimmerians[e] indeed stay away from them, let the whole army invade and assault the cities.

[19]*šar ilāni Marduk itti šarri bēlīya salim* [20]*mimma mala šarru bēlīya iqabbû ippuš* [21]*ina kussîka ašbāta nakrūtīka* [22]*takammu ayyābīka takaššad u māt nakrīka* [23]*tašallal*

[19]Marduk, the king of gods, is reconciled with the king, my lord. He does whatever the king, my lord, says. Sitting on your throne, you will vanquish your enemies, conquer your foes and plunder the land of your enemy.

*Bēl iqtabi umma akī* [24]*Marduk-šapik-zēri Aššūr-aḫu-iddina šar māt Ašš[ūr]* [25]*ina kussîšu lū ašib u māt[āti]* [26]*gabbi ana qātēšu amanni šarru bēlī[ya ...]* [27]*ḫadiš šarru akī ša ile[ʾū]* [28]*līpuš*

[23]Bel has said: "May Esarhaddon, king of Assyria, be seated on his throne[f] like Marduk-šapik-zeri![g] I will deliver all the countries into his hands!" The king, [my] lord [...].[h] The king may happily do as he deems best.

[a] Even though the name is almost completely broken, the identification is certain; see Dietrich 1970: 63 and Fales and Lanfranchi 1981: 9, 13.

[b] Following the suggestion of Fales and Lanfranchi 1981: 16–17, lines 9–r. 4 are interpreted here as a quotation from the king's earlier letter. Alternatively, if the quotation comprises only the words "Enter the Mannean territory" (thus Parpola 1993: 89), the continuation is to be understood as a personal opinion of the writer.

[c] Literally, "on this fifteenth day."

[d] Literally, "the exit and entry of that country."

[e] The text speaks of the Cimmerians here as "Indareans."

[f] Line 25 according to the collation of Manfried Dietrich (courtesy M. Dietrich): *ina* GIŠ.GU.ZA-*šú lu-ú a-ši-ib*.

[g] King of Babylonia (1081–1069) who restored the fortifications of Babylon and made a treaty with Aššur-bel-kala, the contemporary king of Assyria.

[h] The end of the line 26 following to the collation of Manfried Dietrich (courtesy M. Dietrich): LUGAL *be-lí-[a...]*.

### 107. Nabû-nadin-šumi to Esarhaddon

**Text:** SAA 10 284 (= K 1033 = *ABL* 58 = *LAS* 213).
**Copy:** Harper 1892 (I): no. 58.
**Transliteration and translation:** Waterman 1930 (I): 42–43; Parpola 1970: 158–59.
**Translation:** Talon 1994: 120.
**Discussion:** Waterman 1931 (III): 31; Parpola 1983: 208; Nissinen 1998b: 102–5; 2000a: 262; 2001: 191–92; Pongratz-Leisten 1999: 92; van der Toorn 2000: 76.

*ana šarri bēlīya* [2]*urdaka Nabû-[nādin]-šumi*
[3]*lū šulmu ana š[a]rri [bēlīy]a* [4]*Nabû u Marduk ana [šarri bēlīya]* [5]*addanniš adda[nniš likrubū]*
[break]
r. [1]*k[īm]a intara[ṣ]* [2]*pānī ammūte damqūti [ša šarri]* [3]*bēlīya issu pānīšu lis[ḫurū]* [4]*u kî ša Issār ša N[īnua]* [5]*Issār ša Arbail iqban[ni]* [6]*mā ša issi šarri bēlīn[i]* [7]*lā kēnūni mā issu māt Aššūr* [8]*ninassaḫšu kettumma* [9]*issu māt Aššūr linnis[iḫ]*

[10]*Aššūr Šamaš Bēl Nabû* [11]*šulmu ša šarri bēlīya* [12]*lišʾulū*

To the king, my lord: your servant Nabû-[nadin]-šumi.

[3]Good health to the king, m[y lord]! May Nabû and Marduk abundan[tly bless the king, my lord]!

[break]

r. [1]I[f] he turns out to be troublesome, let [the king], my lord, tu[rn] his gracious face away from him. According to what Ištar of N[ineveh] and Ištar of Arbela have said [to me]: "Those who are disloyal to the king our lord, we shall extinguish from Assyria,"[a] he should indeed be banished from Assyria!

[10]May Aššur, Šamaš, Bel, and Nabû take care of the well-being of the king, my lord!

[a] Cf. SAA 9 2.4 (no. 81) ii 29–33.

### 108. Urad-Gula to Assurbanipal

**Text:** SAA 10 294 (= K 4267 = *ABL* 1285).
**Photograph:** Parpola 1987: 266–67.
**Copy:** Harper 1913 (XII): no. 1285.
**Transliteration and translation:** Waterman 1930 (II): 392–95; Parpola 1987: 258–65; 1993: 231–34.
**Discussion:** Waterman 1931 (III): 338–39; Parpola 1987; Hurowitz 1993; Nissinen 1998b: 84–88; van der Toorn 1998c; Pongratz-Leisten 1999: 81; Huffmon 2000: 61.

*[ana šarri bēlīya urdaka Urdu-Gula*

[To the king, my lord: your servant Urad-Gula.[a]]

*[2]lū šulmu ana šarri bēlīya addanniš] Marduk [Zarpānītu [3]Nabû Tašmētu Issār ša Nīnua Issār] ša Arba[il Inurta Gula [4]Nērigal Lāṣ ana šarri bēlīya kē]nu addanniš addanniš likru[bū] [5][ūmē arkūti šanāti dārâ]ti an[a š]arri bēlīya ana širikti lišrukū*

[2][Very good health to the king,[b] my lord!] May Marduk [and Zarpanitu, Nabû and Tašmetu, Ištar of Nineveh and Ištar] of Arbe[la, Ninurta, Gula, Nergal and Laṣ] bless [the king, my righ]teous [lord] very, very much! May they grant the gift of [endless days and everla]sting [years] t[o the k]ing, my lord!

*[6][ilāni rabûti ša šamê kaqqiri li]ktarrabū šarrūtka nadīn zībīka [7][ellūti lirammū liḫšuḫ]ū sangûtka kibis šēpēka liṣ[ṣ]urū [8][lištēširū ḫūlka] naka-rūtēka liskipū lišamqitū ayyābīka [9][gārêka liṭa]rridū lilqutū biššašun [10]rāʾiūtka kīma ūlu u šamnu eli napḫar kiššat niš[ē l]iṭṭibbū [11]išdi kussi šarrūtīka kīma šipik šaddê lišaršidū ana ūmē ṣâti [12]Šamaš nūr šamê u kaqqiri ana dēn kittīka littaškan uznāšu [13]šarru bēlī ana dēni ša urdīšu liqūla dibbī gabbu šarru lēmur*

[6][May the great gods of heaven and earth] incessantly bless your kingship! [May they love the pure] sacrifices you offer and show their desire for] your priesthood! May they watch the steps you take [and make your road straight!] May they repel your assailants and cause the fall of your enemies! [May] they [dr]ive away [your adversaries] and take their property! [May] they continually make your shepherdhood as favorable to all manki[nd] as choicest oil; may they make the foundation of your royal throne steady as bedrock until far-off days! May Šamaš, the light of heaven and earth, lend an ear to your righteous judgment! May the king, my lord, heed the case of his servant;[c] may the king perceive his whole situation!

*[14]issu rēši ina libbi abīšu ša šarri amēlu lapnu mār lapni kalbu mītu [15][sakl]u u sukkuku anāku issu libbi kiqilliti intatḫanni [16][nāmu]rātēšu amaḫḫaršu issi ṣābi damqāti šumī [i]zzakkar [17][rē]ḫāti maʾdāti akkal ina birit ibašši kūdunu [18]alpu ittanna u šattīya ṣarpu issēn manû šina manê akaššad [19][ūmē] ša mār šarri bēlīya issi āšipīšu rēḫāti amaḫḫar [20][ina lib]bi aptāte attitiz*

[14]Originally, during the reign of the king's father, I was but a poor man, and a son of a poor man. A dead dog was I, a [simple]ton[d] of stunted ability. He lifted me from the dung heap! I received [audience g]ifts from him and my name was mentioned in high society.[e] What he abundantly left over, I would consume.[f] Now and then, he gave me a mule or an ox, and each year

*maṣṣartu [a]ttaṣṣar ūmu ammar ina pānīšu [21][a]zzizūni ikkibēšu attaṣṣar ina bēt ša-rēši u ša-ziqni [22]ša lā pîšu lā ērub ākil ukālāti nēši attadgil [23]ilka u[s]allima*

I earned a mina or two of silver. [When] my lord was crown prince, I received those leftovers together with his exorcists. Keeping watch I stood [at] the openings; every day that I spent in his service I kept to myself his private affairs.[g] I never went to the house of a eunuch or of a bearded courtier without his permission. I was considered one who is given the lion's share.[h] I appeased your god.

*ūmâ šarru bēlī iddāt abīšu urtaddi šumu damqu [24]ukta''in u anāku lā ina pitti epšētīya epšāk [25]kî [lā] ina pānītimma agduṣṣuṣ napšāti assakan [26]šumu lā damqu [l]iḫšu u šeṣṣû ša abiti izzī'ar [27]ik[k]ibē ša šarri bēlīya attaṣṣar bēlē ṭābti lā aṣbata [28]dibbī [. . .]-ūtu assaddad mazzassu nubattu [29][. . .] kanāšu kadāru u puluḫtu ša ekalli [30]urdāni ša-ziqni u ša-rēši ussammid mīnu ina libbi [31]aḫzāku*

[23]Now the king, my lord, has made even better the good name his father had established before him. I, however, have not been treated in accordance with what I have done. Never before have I suffered[i] like this, I have given up the ghost! Discrediting, whispering about and talebearing are hateful things! Discreet though I have been about the private affairs of the king, my lord, I have not found advocates. I endured[j] [. . .] words. My post [I made] my night's lodging; I taught the servants, whether bearded or eunuchs, submission, toil and fear of the palace—but how was I rewarded for all this?

*šumm[u] illaka ummânī dannūti u šaniūti [32]kūdinī inaššiū yāši issēn mūru liddi[n]ūni [33]iss[ēniš ina] Kanūni alpē uza''uzū anākūma issēn alpu [34]lū [. . .] ina libbi urḫi šanîšu šalšīšu [. . .] 3 4 ana [. . . iddu]nū [35][. . . š]amallû ša [āši]pi šanie [. . . iṣabba]t [36][u y]ābil[u . . .] ekkal u [anākūm]a [37][mīnu an]ašši ulâ dullu ana mī[ni epp]aš [38][. . . ]ṭū ša šarri lā adaggal lā [. . .]-pi [39][. . . ū]mu u mūšu ina pān gab'i ša nēši šarru uṣal[la]*

[31]If it is fit to the most prominent and even lesser scholars to be granted mules, I should be given at least one donkey! Lik[ewise], when oxes are distributed [in] Tebet (X), even I should be [granted] one ox. Within a month, two or three times [. . .] three or four [. . . are giv]en to [. . .]. [Even an ap]prentice of an [exor]cist [get]s two [. . . and] eats a [r]am [. . .]. As for [me], however, [what is my re]ward? Or wh[y am I wor]king at all? I cannot look at the

[40][. . .]*-ni ina libbi ukālāti lā sammūn[i]* [41][. . .] *libbī birti miḫrīya*
[six fragmentary or unreadable lines]

[. . .] of the king, nor [. . .]. Day and night I pra[y] to the king in front of the lion's den[k] [. . .] are not finicky[l] about the morsels [. . .] my heart amidst my colleagues [. . .]
[break]

r. [3]*egertu ina qāt Šarru-nūri ša-rēši ana šarri bēlīy[a* [4]*assapra] u muruṣ libbīya uktammera ana šarri bēlīya ašpur[a* [5]. . . *nubatt]u lā bēdat egertu šarru ana urdīšu issapra* [6]*[ma lā ū]da kî akannī šamruṣā-kāni mā anāku* [7][. . .]*-ad ātabakka abutu ša šarri bēlīya kî šadê ša[pšuqat]* [8]*e[gertu] issi kussî ša Nabû ina libbi tukulti assakanši kî mar'i ēd[i]* [9]*a[ttaṣ]arši issu maṣṣi sinqīya paṭrūni šarru bēlī addan-[niš]* [10]*[li]bb[āš]u lū ṭābšu urdušu lū iḫsusa mā ina dagālī[ya]* [11]*[l]iḫ-ḫura kišādī*

r. [3][I sent] a letter to the king, m[y] lord, through Šarru-nuri, the eunuch; but it only added to my bitter feelings that I wrote to the king, my lord. [. . .] Still in the same night, the king sent a letter to his servant, [saying: "I did not] know that you have got in such dire straits—I surely sent you [. . .]" The word of the king, my lord, is as diff[icult to take over] as a mountain! I put the l[etter] for safekeeping at the throne of Nabû, wa[tch]ing over it as if it were my only son. If my distress was relieved, let the king, my lord, be ov[er]joyed! If only he had remembered his servant and said: "[Let] him receive a necklace of mine in front of [my] eyes!"

*abutu šî šanītu mā ša ina kutal[līšu* [12]*m]aḫiṣṣūni pîšu lidbub u ša ina pîšu maḫiṣ[ūni* [13]*ina lib]bi mīni lidbub annurig šitta šanāti issu mar šinā um[āmēya]* [14]*[m]ēt[ū]ni šalšīšu ana Arbail mala ana Libbi-āli ina šēpīya at[talak]* [15]*[man]nu rā'imanni qātī iṣbat u lū ina pān šarri bēlīya u[šēribanni]* [16]*atâ ina libbi Ekallāti rēš āšipi šarru iššî u anāku ḫ[ūlu]* [17]*ša mudabbiri aṣṣabat issu pān ša nišē iša''ulūninni* [18]*mā atâ ina šēpēka ta[llak]a nišē bēti ettiqū dannūti ina kussî* [19]*šaniūti ina saparrāti ṣeḫrūti ina libbi kūdinī* [20]*anāku ina šēpēya i-*SAK-KUL *šarru iqabbi mā mār māti šû šarru liš'a[l]* [21]*abūa šeššet imār*

[11]There is also the saying: "The one who has been [st]abbed in the back can still speak with his mouth, but the one who has been stabb[ed] in the mouth, how can he speak?" It is two years now since [my] two draught an[imals d]ied. I have go[ne] three times to Arbela and once to Assur on foot; but was there [anybo]dy who would have been kind enough to grasp my hand and l[ead me] in front of the king, my lord? Why did the king summon an exorcist from Ekallate, while I had to take the desert r[oad] to avoid the people who would have been asking me: "You are go[in]g on foot, eh?" People pass

*eqlu issi Nabû-zēru-lēšir aḫīšu ibtatqa anāku u aḫūya* [22]*yāmuttu šalašat imār nittiši u šittā napšāti issēniš ina ṣilli šarri bēlīya* [23]*napšāti ḫamiš šeš aqṭunu*

my house, the nobles on palanquins, the lesser ones on carts and the low ones[m] on mules — and I go on foot. . . .[n] the king will say: "He is a citizen!" Let the king find out that my father and his brother Nabû-zeru-lešir parceled out six homers of field, while I myself and my brother got three homers each plus two servants.[o] With the consent of the king, my lord, I have purchased five or six servants.

*ina Bēt Kidmurri ētarab qarētu ētapaš* [24]*issī šî taddalḫanni ḫamiš šanāti lā muʾātu lā balāṭu* [25]*u maraʾī laššu šalaš issāti šattu annītu ittuqtanni u ikkāru* [26]*laššu bēt epinni eqlu laššu Anu Illil u Ēa ša ina kaqqadi* [27]*ša šarri bēlīya kunnūni šummu ammar mašʾenni ammar igrī* [28]*ša gallābi maṣṣākūni tēnû ša guzippīya ibaššûni* [29]*u šiqlē maṭṭi ana šeššet mana ṣarpu kaqqudu lā ḫabbulākūni*

[23]I entered the temple of Kidmuri to arrange a banquet there, yet that wife of mine disappointed me.[p] For five years she has been neither dead nor alive, and I still have no son. Three women have fallen to me this year, but I have no farmer, no tool shed, no farm.[q] By Anu, Enlil and Ea, who constantly dwell in the head of the king, my lord: I cannot afford a pair of sandals, I cannot pay the tailor, I do not even have a change of clothes! I have run up a debt of almost the capital of six minas of silver.

[30]*[u ina š]anātīya mā ana šībūti takšuda tukultaka lū mannu* [31]*[ina pān x l]ā maḫrāk elli ana ekalli lā tarṣāk raggimu* [32]*[assaʾal dum]qu lā āmur maḫḫur u diglu untaṭṭi* [33]*[ša šarru bēl]īya amārka dumqu nasḫurka mašrû* [34]*[libbu . . . ša ša]rri lēṭib lišpuranni ammar šinā umāmē* [35]*[. . .] -kē u tēnê ša guzippi u naṣāri* [36]*[. . .] -dāta ana mār šarrūti ša šarri bēlī[ya . . .]* [37]*[šarru bēlī issu libbi ṣeḫ]erīšu uddanni muk lā [. . .]*

[30]I am advanced [in y]ears already, and it is said: "Once you have reached old age, who will be your support?" [. . .] is not pleased with me; when I go to the palace, I am not good enough. [I consulted] a prophet without finding any [ho]pe. He was unresponsive, being unable to offer any vision. [O king], my [lord], mere seeing you is happiness and your attention is a fortune! May [the heart . . . of the k]ing soften so much that he will send me two draught animals, [. . .], and a spare suit of clothes. Guarding [. . .] for the crown-princehood of

| | |
|---|---|
| | the king, [my] lord [... The king, my lord] knows me [ever since] his [chi]ldhood [...] |
| [remaining three lines unintelligible] | [rest too fragmentary for translation] |

[a] The name of the author of the letter is not preserved, but the identification with Urad-Gula, one of Esarhaddon's chief exorcists and son of the exorcist Adad-šumu-uṣur, is certain; see Parpola 1987: 268–69. For the restorations of the rest of the letter, see Parpola 1987: 274–78.

[b] I.e., Assurbanipal.

[c] A clear allusion to the first lines of the Advice to a Prince, an admonitory work that the recipient of the letter was supposed to know: "If the king does not heed justice [*šarru ana dīni lā iqūl*], his people will be thrown to chaos, and his land will be devastated" (Lambert 1960: 112). The extant copy of this text belonged to Assurbanipal's library.

[d] For *saklu,* see no. 109 (SAA 10 352), n. 8. In fact, Urad-Gula was anything but a "simpleton" or a "common man"; cf. note h.

[e] Literally, "fortunate people," i.e., those belonging to the king's entourage.

[f] The "leftovers" belong to the author's hyperbolic language (cf. Mk 7:28; Lk 16:21), but they may also have a concrete point of reference in the surplus of the abundant cultic meals.

[g] The word *ikkibu* means things that are forbidden or taboo, in this case probably the king's private affairs or things concerning him that are not generally known.

[h] For *ukālāti* as a diminutive of *akālu* "food", see Parpola 1987: 275.

[i] For the translation, see Parpola 1987: 276.

[j] For the translation, see ibid.

[k] Lit.: "lion's pit" (*gabʾu;* cf. Aram. *gōb;* Heb. *gēb*); there is a clear contrast with the "lion's share" Urad-Gula used to enjoy earlier (line 22).

[l] For the translation, see van der Toorn 1998c: 632.

[m] Literally, "the small ones," referring to the social class rather than age.

[n] The text is clear but unintelligible; the word *issurri* "perhaps" would make sense.

[o] Literally, "living souls," referring to human beings.

[p] The point may be that the banquet was arranged in the temple of the Lady of Kidmuri (i.e., probably, the Ištar temple of Calah; cf. above, no. 99) to "cure" the supposed infertility of the wife, but it was not successful.

[q] Literally, "plough house," i.e., building for storing ploughs. Plough is a well-known euphemism for the male organ, and the context shows that the whole farming imagery refers to Urad-Gula's impotence.

## 109. Mar-Issar to Esarhaddon

**Text:** SAA 10 352 (= K 168 = *ABL* 437 = *LAS* 280).
**Copy:** Harper 1900 (IV): no. 437.
**Transliteration and translation:** Waterman 1930 (I): 302–5; Landsberger 1965: 46–51; Parpola 1970: 228–31; 1993: 288–89.
**Translation:** Moran 1969b: 625–26.
**Discussion:** Waterman 1931 (III): 162–63; Labat 1939: 359; Schott and Schaumberger 1941: 112–13; von Soden 1956: 103–4; Beek 1966: 25; Ramlot 1972: 881; Parpola 1983: 270–72; R. R. Wilson 1980: 112; Bottéro 1992: 147, 151–53; Nissinen 1998b: 68–77; 2001a: 202–3; Pongratz-Leisten 1999: 82–83; Villard 2001: 68–69.

*[ana šarri bēl]īya urdaka [Mār-Issār]* 2*[lū šulmu] ana šarri bēlīya [Nabû u Marduk* 3*ana šarri] bēlīya likrubū [ūmē arkūte]* 4*ṭūb šīri u ḫūd libbi [ilāni rabûti]* 5*ana šarri bēlīya lišrukū*

[To the king], my [lord]: your servant [Mar-Issar].

2[Good health] to the king, my lord! May [Nabû and Marduk] bless [the king], my lord! May [the great gods] grant [long life], physical health and cheerful mood to the king, my lord!

*[Damqî]* 6*mār šatammi ša Akka[d]* 7*ša māt Aššūr Bābili [u]* 8*mātāti kalīšina ibī[lūni šû]* 9*u sēgallīšu mūšu š[a* UD.X.KÁM *ana]* 10*dināni ša šarri bēlīya [u ana balāṭ na]pišti* 11*ša Šamaš-šumu-ukī[n imtū]tū* 12*ana pīdīšunu ana šīmti ittalak*

5[Damqî], the son of the chief administrator[a] of Akka[d],[b] who ru[led] Assyria, Babylonia [and] all the countries, [di]ed together with his queen on the night o[f the xth day as] a substitute for the king, my lord, [and to spare the li]fe of Šamaš-šumu-ukin.[c] He met his fate for their redemption.[d]

13*kimaḫḫu nētapaš šû u sēgallīšu* 14*dammuqū kannû taklittašunu* 15*kallumat qabrū bakiū* 16*šuruptu šarpat ittāti kalīšina* 17*paššā namburbê maʾdūte* 18*bēt rinki bēt šalāʾ mê nēpēšē* 19*ša āšipūtu eršaḫungê* 20*naqabâte ša ṭupšarrūtu* 21*ussallimū ētapšū šarru bēlī lū ūdi*

13We prepared the funerary chamber. He and his queen were made beautiful, treated with honor, displayed, buried and bewailed. The burnt-offering was made and all the omens were cancelled. A lot of apotropaic rituals, as well as ablution and purification rituals,[e] exorcisms, penitential psalms and scholarly litanies were completely performed. The king, my lord, should know this.

22*[a]sseme mā pānāt nēpēšē annūti* 23*ragginti tartugūmu* 24*ana Damqî*

22[I] have heard that, before these rituals, a prophetess had prophesied,

*mār šatammi taqṭi[bi]* 25*[m]ā šarrūtī tanašši* r. 1*[u] raggintu ina puḫri* 2*ša māti taqṭibaššu mā kakkišu* 3*šarriqtu ša bēlīya uktallim* 4*ina qāti assakanka namburbê* 5*annūti ša epšūni issalmū* 6*addanniš libbu ša šarri bēlīya lū ṭābšu*

saying to Damqî, the son of the chief administrator: "You will take over the kingship!"[f] [More-over], the prophetess had spoken to him in the assembly of the country: "I have revealed the thieving polecat[g] of my lord and placed it in your hands."—Those apotropaic rituals which were performed were extremely successful. The king, my lord, can be satisfied.

7*Akkadûʾa iptalḫū libbu nussaškinšunu* 8*ittūḫū u asseme mā šatammāni* 9*qēpāni ša māt Akkadî iptalḫūma*

r. 7The people of Akkad were frightened, but we cheered them up and they calmed down. I even heard that the chief administrators and delegates of Babylonia were frightened as well.

10*Bēl u Nabû ilāni kalīšunu ūmē* 11*ša šarri bēlīya ussārikū ina libbi dūri* 12*attalê Sîn ṭeḫê ilāni ibašši* 13*ana kaqqiri lā illak*

10Bel and Nabû and all the gods have given a long life to the king, my lord. However, as long as the period of the eclipse of the moon and the approach of the gods lasts, he should not go out into the open country.

*šumma pān* 14*šarri bēlīya maḫir kî ša pānīti* 15*saklu ana šatammūti lū* 16*paqīdi ina pān parakki ginû luqarrib* 17*ina ūm eššēši ina šalām bēti ina muḫḫi nidnakki* 18*[ana] Bēlet Akkadi lisrūqu*

13If the king, my lord, considers it appropriate, let a common man,[h] as before, be appointed to the office of the chief administrator. Let him perform the regular offerings before the dais, and let him burn incense [for] the Lady of Akkad on the censer on occasion of the *eššēšu* festival and the "Greeting of the Temple" ceremony.

*kīm[a* 19*attalû] issakan māt Akkadî ilta[pat* 20*šû ana] dināni šarri bēlīya lill[ik* 21*. . .]-uššu lizzizzi* 22*[. . .] ša šarri bēlīya lišlim[ū* 23*. . .] nišē lū nē[ḫū* 24*. . .]-šu aḫḫēš[u* 25*. . .] ibašši man[nu* 26*. . .] ša pān š[arri bēlīya* s. 1*m]aḫirūni ina kūmuššu šarru bēlī lipqīd[i]*

18When [an eclipse] takes place and afflicts Babylonia, let [him] be the substitute for the king, my lord, [. . .] let him stand. Let [the . . . s] of the king, my lord, be successful [. . .] let the people keep ca[lm]. Let the king, my lord, replace him with anyone [. . .] who is acceptable to the k[ing, my lord . . .] his [. . .]s, his brothers [and . . .].

[a] The modern languages have no exact equivalent for the word *šatammu;* translations such as "bishop" (Landsberger 1965) attempt to render the high religious authority of this position in modern terms, but the office of *šatammu* was not necessarily restricted to the realm of temples.

[b] The ancient Sargonid capital where the cult of Ištar, the Lady of Akkad, and the other gods of Akkad was reestablished three years earlier (674).

[c] Šamaš-šumu-ukin is mentioned here because the eclipse of the moon, on account of which the substitute king was chosen, afflicted Babylon and, hence, him personally as the crown prince of Babylon.

[d] This sentence puts in a nutshell the ideology of the substitution, for which see Parpola 1983: xxiv–xxv.

[e] The purpose of the *namburbi, bīt rimki,* and *bīt šalā᾽ mê* rituals was to purify the actual king from his sins, which were taken upon the substitute king.

[f] Cf., e.g., SAA 9 1.8 (no. 75) v 22–23: "Yours is the kingdom; yours is the power."

[g] For this reading and translation, see Nissinen 1998b: 74 and cf. SAA 9 1.7 (no. 74) and 9 4 (no. 89).

[h] The "common man" (*saklu*) means a person without a noble lineage, in this case a person not belonging to the powerful families of Babylonia.

## 110. Decree of Expenditures for Ceremonies in the Aššur Temple in Assur

**Text:** SAA 12 69 (= VAT 8920+ = NARGD 42+).
**Copy:** Weidner 1966: pl. 1–3.
**Transliteration and translation:** Postgate 1969: 84–90; Kataja and Whiting 1995: 71–77.
**Discussion:** Weidner 1966; Pongratz-Leisten 1999: 91–92; Nissinen 2000b: 99–100; 2001a: 188; 2002b: 16–17.

### Lines 27–31 (VAT 8920):

[blank space of one line with holes]

27 *nadbāku ša puḫur ilāni* 1 *sūt dišpu* 5 *qa šamnu* 4 *sât* [5 *qa šamaššammi k*]*arkadinnu inašši* 28 10 *emār kurummutu ana kusāpi* 5 *emār kibtu ana qa*[*duāti āpiāni inaššiū*] 29 1 *emār* 5 *sât ša pān maḫḫâte širāšê inašši*[*ū*] 30 *gimru* 1 *sūt* 4 *qa dišpu* 5 *qa šamnu* 4 *sât* 5 *qa šamaššammi* [11 *emār* 5 *sât kurummutu*] 31 5 *emār kibtu mimma*

[blank space of one line with holes]

27 The expenditure for the divine council: [The c]onfectioner tak[es] one seah of honey, five liters of oil, and four seahs [five liters of sesame. The bakers take] ten homers of barley for bread and five homers of wheat for *qa*[*dūtu*]-bread. The brewers tak[e] one homer five seahs of barley[a] for the prophetesses. 30 Total: one seah four

*anniu [nadbāku ša puḫur ilāni]*

liters of honey, five liters of oil, four seahs five liters of sesame, [eleven homers five seahs of barley], five homers of wheat. All this [is the expenditure for the divine council].

[blank space of one line with holes]

[blank space of one line with holes]

[a] There is no word for "barley" in the original, but this is what the context and the surrounding passages of the text suggest.

## 111. Adad-aḫu-iddina to Esarhaddon

**Text:** SAA 13 37 (= K 540 = *ABL* 149 = *LAS* 317).
**Copy:** Harper 1893 (II): no. 149.
**Transliteration and translation:** Waterman 1930 (I): 102–3; Landsberger 1965: 49; Parpola 1970: 271–72; Cole and Machinist 1999: 36–37.
**Discussion:** Waterman 1931 (III): 66; von Soden 1956; Parpola 1983: 329; Dietrich 1973: 39–40; Nissinen 1998b: 78–81, 99–100; 2000a: 260; 2000b: 93; Cole and Machinist 1998: xvii; Pongratz-Leisten 1999: 83–88; Huffmon 2000: 60.

*ana šarri bēlīya* [2]*urdaka Adad-aḫu-iddina*
[3]*lū šulmu ana šarri bēlīya* [4]*Aššūr Mullissu Nabû Marduk* [5]*ana šarri bēlīya* [6]*likrubū* [7]*Mullissu-abu-uṣri raggintu* [8]*ša kuzippī ša šarri* [9]*ana māt Akkadî tūbilūni* [10]*[ina] bēt ili tartug[u]m* [11]*[mā] kussiu issu bēt [i]li*

[five unreadable lines]
r. [6]*kussiu [l]ū tallik* [7]*mā nakarūti* [8]*ša šarrīya ina libbi* [9]*akaššad muk* [10]*ša lā šarri bēlīya* [11]*kussiu lā addan* [12]*kî ša šarru bēlī* [13]*iqabbûni* [14]*ina pitte nēpuš*

To the king, my lord: your servant Adad-aḫu-iddina.

[3]Good health to the king, my lord! May Aššur, Mullissu, Nabû, and Marduk bless the king, my lord! [7]Mullissu-abu-uṣri, the prophetess who conveyed the king's clothes to the land of Akkad,[a] prophesied [in] the temple: "[The] throne[b] from the te[mp]le [. . .]

[break]

r. [6]Let the throne go! I will catch the enemies of my king with it!" Now, without the authorization of the king, my lord, I shall not give the throne. We shall act according to what the king, my lord, orders.

[a] The land of Akkad designates Babylonia, as translated by Cole and Machinist 1998: 38. The destination of the king's clothes was probably the city of Akkad, where the substitute kings were enthroned; cf. SAA 10 352 (no. 109).

[b] The throne, as well as the king's clothes, were needed in the substitute king ritual; cf. SAA 10 189.

### 112. Aššur-ḫamatu'a to Assurbanipal

**Text:** 13 139 (= 83-1-18,361 = *ABL* 1249).
**Copy:** Harper 1913 (XII): nr. 1249.
**Transliteration and translation:** Klauber 1914: 260–61; Waterman 1930 (II): 370–71; Cole and Machinist 1999: 111.
**Discussion:** Waterman 1931 (III): 331–32; Cole and Machinist 1999: xvii; Nissinen 2000b: 97; 2002b: 11–12; Villard 2001: 71.

| | |
|---|---|
| [*anāku*] *Bēl ētarba* [2]*issi Mu*[*ll*]*issu assilim* [3]*Aššūr-bāni-apli šar māt Aššūr* [4]*ša turabbīni* [5][*l*]*ā tapallaḫ* [6][*anā*]*ku Bēl artēanki* [7]*Aššūr-bāni-apli ina māti ša kēnu/kēni* [8]*šû adi mātīšu* [9]*artēanki* | "[I] am Bel.[a] I have entered and reconciled with Mullissu. [3]Assurbanipal, king of Assyria, whom she raised: Fear not! [6]I am Bel, I have had mercy on you.[b] Assurbanipal is in a country which remains loyal to him. I have had mercy on you, together with his country. |
| [10]*ina šulmu šallimte* [11]*issu ālīki attūṣi* [12]*rēmu gimlu* [...] | [10]Safely and securely I departed from your city. Mercy and compassion [...]" |
| [break] [r.1']*ana Bēl atta*[*ḫar*] [2']*ussarrirri* [3']*Nabû-šarru-uṣur rādi kibsi* [4']*ša mūgīya assapar* | [break] [r. 1']I implored Bel and prayed to him. [3']Then I sent Nabû-šarru-uṣur, a tracker of my contingent.[c] |
| [5']*ana šarri bēlīya* [6']*urdaka Aššūr-ḫamātū'a* [7']*Aššūr Issār ana šarri* [8']*likrubbu* | [5']To the king, my lord, your servant Aššur-ḫamatu'a. May Aššur and Ištar bless the king. |

[a] The cuneiform script has only the sign EN, without the divine determinative, throughout the letter.

[b] The feminine suffix in *artēanki* indicates that Mullissu is addressed.

[c] "Contingent" is the conjectured translation of Cole and Machinist of the unclear word *mūgu*.

## 113. Nabû-reši-išši to Esarhaddon (?)

**Text:** SAA 13 144 (= Bu 91-5-9,145 = *CT* 53 969)
**Copy:** Parpola 1979: pl. 216.
**Transliteration and translation:** Cole and Machinist 1999: 116–17.
**Discussion:** Cole and Machinist 1999: xvii; Nissinen 2000a: 259–60; 2003: 6.

*ana šarri bēlīya* [2]*urdaka Nabû-rēšī-išši*
[3]*lū šulmu ana šarri* [4]*bēlīya*

[5]*Aššūr Issār Nabû* [6]*u Marduk* [7]*meat šanāti* [8]*ana šarri bēlīya* [9]*luballiṭū*

[10]*niqiāti ša šarri* [11][. . .] *epšāni* [12][UD.X].KÁM UD.16.KÁM [13][UD.X.KÁM] UD.20.KÁM [14][. . .]

[six lines too fragmentary for translation]
[r. 7]*tarrugu[m]* [8]*mā atâ* GIŠ.*ni-*[. . .] [9]*qablu . . .* [10]*ana muṣurāya* [11]*tādin*

[12]*mā pān šarri* [13]*qibia* [14]*lūsaḫḫirū* [15]*lidnūni* [16]*mā gabbi* [17]*nuḫšu* [18][...]-*šu* [s. 1]*addana*

To the king, my lord, your servant Nabû-reši-išši.

[3]Good health to the king, my lord.

[5]May Aššur, Ištar, Nabû, and Marduk let the king, my lord, live hundred years!

[10]The king's sacrifices [. . .] have been performed on the [xth] day and the sixteenth, the [xth], the twentieth, [. . .]

[break]

[. . .] [r. 7]she prophesied: "Why have you given the [. . .],[a] the grove and the . . .[b] to the Egyptians?

[12]Say to the king that they be returned to me, and I will give total abundance [to] his [. . .]."

[a] The word is broken away, but the determinative GIŠ indicates a wooden object.
[b] An unintelligible word.

## 114. NN to Esarhaddon (?)

**Text:** SAA 13 148 (= K 10865 = *CT* 53 413).
**Copy:** Parpola 1979: pl. 108.
**Transliteration and translation:** Cole and Machinist 1999: 119.
**Discussion:** Cole and Machinist 1999: xvii; Nissinen 2000b: 96.

[. . .]-*ia* [2][. . .] *šēlūtu [ša] Issār* [3]*[ša] Arbail ši[pirt]i* [4]*[ann]ītu ana š[arri . . .]* [5][. . .] *Issār* [. . .]
[rest destroyed]

[NN], votary [of] Ištar [of] Arbela [. . . th]is message for the k[ing . . .] Ištar [. . .]

[rest destroyed]

## 115. Nabû-reḫtu-uṣur to Esarhaddon

**Text:** SAA 16 59 (= *ABL* 1217 + *CT* 53 118 = 82-5-22,108 + K 13737).
**Copy:** Harper 1913 (XII): nr. 1217 (82-5-22,108); Parpola 1979: pl. 40 (K 13737).
**Transliteration and translation:** Klauber 1914: 236–39; Waterman 1930 (II): 344–47 (*ABL* 1217 only); Nissinen 1998b: 109–11; Luukko and Van Buylaere 2002: 52–53.
**Discussion:** Waterman 1931 (III): 322; Dietrich 1970: 160–61; 1973: 38–39; Brinkman 1977: 313–15; Parpola 1983: 239, 464; van der Toorn 1987: 89; Nissinen 1996: 182–93; 1998a: 163–70; 1998b: 108–54; 2000a: 261; 2001a: 203–6; Pongratz-Leisten 1999: 89–91; Huffmon 2000: 61–62.

*ana šarri [bēlīy]a* [2]*urdaka Nabû-rēḫtu-uṣur Bēl Bē[let Nabû Tašm]ētu* [3]*Issār ša Nīnua Issār ša Arbail ūmē [arkū]ti š[an]āti d[ār]âti* [4]*liddinū-nikka*

*ša ina libbi ṭābti ša abī[ka ina libbi adê ša abī]ka* [5]*u ina libbi adêka iḫṭûni Nikkal [... niš]ēšunu* [6]*šumšunu zara'šunu issu libbi ekallīka ḫallīqi ana [... lū]* [7]*takrur nišē ša issi Sāsî ūdû[ni arḫiš limuttū ...]* [8]*anīnu šarru bēlī dabābu ša Nikkal ū[da ... ...]* [9]*limūtū napšātīka napšāti ša qinnīka [šēzib ...]* [10]*abūka ummaka lū šunu limtu[ḫū ...]* [11]*napšātīka lā tuḫallāqa šarrūtu issu qātēk[a lā tušēli]* [12]*anīnu šarru bēlī [ina li]bbi dabābi Nik[kal annie]* [13]*lā tašī[aṭ ...]-ūnimma [...]* [14]*egertu [...]*

[break]

*CT* 53 118:4' *ina pānīšu izzazū [...]* 5'*pîšunu šakin [...]* 6'*kayyamānu ina muḫḫi Sās[î...]* 7'*mā ina pān šarri dammiq m[ā ...]* 8'*lēpušū issi Nabû-bēl-[...]* 9'*issi Ubru-Nabû [...]* 10'*issi rabiāni š[a ...]*

To the king, m[y lord], your servant Nabû-reḫtu-uṣur. May Bel and Be[let, Nabû and Tašme]tu, Ištar of Nineveh and Ištar of Arbela give you long days and ever[lasting years]!

[4]Nikkal [*has revealed*] those who sinned against [your] father's goodness and your [father's] and your own treaty. Destroy their name and seed from your palace! [May] she cast [...]! [May] the accomplices of Sasî [*die quickly*]. [8]Hear me,[a] O king, my lord! I k[now] the words of Nikkal. Let [the people] die! [Save] your life and the life of your family! Let [*the gods* ...] be your father and your mother, and let them li[ft up...]! Do not destroy your life, do not let the kingship [slip] from your hands! [12]Hear me, O king, my lord! Do not disregard [these] words of Ni[kkal! ...] a letter [...]

[break]

*CT* 53 118:4' ...are staying in his presence [...] are making common cause [*with* ...] 6'[They are] constantly [...] to Sas[î ...]: "Present yourselves in good light with the king! Let [...] do [...] with Nabû-belu-[...] with Ubru-Nabû [...] with the magnates w[ho...]

[break]

*ABL* 1217 r. 1' *issurri ibašši* [. . .] 2' *liš᾿ulū mā amtu ša Bēl-aḫu-uṣur ina q[an-n]i ša Ḫ[arrān] ina muḫ[ḫi. . .]* 3' *mā issu libbi Simāni sarḫat mā dabābu damqu ina muḫḫi* 4' *tadabbūbu mā abat Nušku šî mā šarrūtu ana Sāsî* 5' *mā šumu zar᾿u ša Sîn-aḫḫē-riba uḫallaqa*

[break]

*ABL* 1217 r. 1 Perhaps ther[e is . . .] let them ask [. . .]. "A slave girl of Bel-aḫu-uṣur [. . .] upon [. . .] on the ou[tski]rts of H[arran]; since Sivan (III) she has been enraptured[b] and speaks a good word about him: 'This is the word of Nusku: The kingship is for Sasî! I will destroy the name and seed of Sennacherib!'"

*rab mūgīka* 6' *ina šapla bābi rabie ša bēt Nabû bēt Bēl-aḫu-uṣur liš᾿al ša-šēpi [ša]* 7' *amtu ina bēt Sāsî ūbilūni lūbilūnišši dullu šarru* [. . .] 8' *ina muḫḫīša lēpūšu Bēl-aḫu-uṣur issu Ḫarrān lūbilūni Nušku* [. . .] 9' *šumu zar᾿u ša Sāsî ša Bēl-aḫu-uṣur ša nišē issīšunu ūdû[ni]* 10' *liḫliq šumu zar᾿u ša šarri bēlīya Bēl Nabû ana ṣāt [ūmē lūki]nnū*

6Let your squadron commander question the household of Bel-aḫu-uṣur under the main gate of the Nabû-temple. Let the *ša šēpi* guards who brought the slave girl into[c] the house of Sasî bring her here, and let the *king* [. . .] perform a(n extispicy) ritual on her (account). 8Let them bring Bel-aḫu-uṣur from Harran and [. . .] Nusku. May the name and seed of Sasî, Bel-aḫu-uṣur and their accomplices perish. May Bel and Nabû establish the name and seed of the king, my lord, until far-off days!

11' *issi Ardâ lidbubū mā* UD.27.KÁM *ina nubatti mā ana [Sā]sî* 12' *ša-muḫḫi-āli Issār-nādin-apli ṭupšarru mā simunu ḫa[nniu bēt]* 13' *illikūni issi Awiānu ša-rēši* [. . .] 14' *mā Issār-nādin-apli ṭupšarru mā Nabû-ēṭir annī[tu . . .]* 15' *mā* UD.28.KAM *mā Sāsî mīnu ina muḫḫi* [. . .] 16' *mā ana šanie ūme Sāsî issīka issi* [. . .] 17' *idbubū mā a[ṭ]â mīnu ša tām[u-rūni . . .]* 18' *rab mūgi* [. . .] *ṣābāni* [. . .] 19' *Issār-[nādin-apli] ṭupšar[ru . . .]* 20' *[. . . nišē š]a issīšunu issi Sāsî ūdûni [limuttū* 21' *. . . mar]᾿īka aḫḫē abbēka maṣṣartaka liṣṣurū* 22' *[. . . -k]a lupaḫḫir [. . . atta] tuqūnu ina ekallīka šībi* 23' *[. . .] adu bēt [. . .] [nišī limut]tū napšātīka šēzib*

11Let them speak with Ardâ as follows: "On the twenty-seventh, at night, [*when*] the scribe Issar-nadin-apli at this particular moment went to [Sa]sî, the city overseer,[d] [*did* . . .] with the eunuch Awyanu? [*Did*] the scribe Issar-nadin-apli [*say that*] Nabû-eṭir [. . .] thi[s]? What did Sasî [. . .] concerning it on the twenty-eighth? Did Sasî speak with you and with the [. . .] on the following day? Why have you [not reported] what you sa[w and heard]?" [*Let*] the squadron commander [. . .] men [. . .] the scrib[e] Issar-[nadin-apli . . .] 20The people w]ho conspire with them and with Sasî [should die! . . .]. Let your [son]s and uncles guard you. Let [*me*] gather your [. . . As for you,] stay in safety in your palace before [*they get ahead*] of you! [Let the people di]e! Save your life!

[a] The word *anīnu* is interpreted as an interjection similar to *anīna* or *annû* "behold" (cf. Heb. *hinnê*); cf. SAA 9 3.3 ii 13 (no. 86 n. 4) and *ABL* 1250 r. 7.

[b] The word *sarḫat* is interpreted as a G stat. of a verb corresponding to the Syriac *šrḥ* "to rage," the Aphʿel form of which has the meanings "to ravish, enrapture, fascinate, captivate."

[c] Or, "from."

[d] It is not clear whether the title "city overseer" (*ša-muḫḫi-āli*) belongs to Sasî or to another person. For Sasî, see *PNA* 3/I: 1093–95.

## 116. Nabû-reḫtu-uṣur to Esarhaddon

**Text:** SAA 16 60 (= *CT* 53 17 + *CT* 53 107 = K 1034 + 7395 + 9204 + 9821 + 10541 + 11021).
**Copy:** Parpola 1979: pl. 7, 38.
**Transliteration and translation:** Nissinen 1998b: 111–14; Luukko and Van Buylaere 2002: 54–56.
**Discussion:** Parpola 1983, 239; Nissinen 1998b: 108–53; 2001a: 203–6.

*ana šar*[*ri*] *bēlīya* [2]*urdaka Nabû-rēḫ*[*tu-uṣur*] [*Bēl*] *Bēlet Nabû Tašmētu* [3]*Issār ša Nī*[*nua Issār ša Arbail ilānī*]*ka ša* [4]*šumka* [*ana šarrūti izkurūni šunu luballiṭ*]*ūka* [5]*ša* [*ina li*]*bbi* [*ṭābti ša abīka ina libbi adê ša ab*]*īk*[*a*] [*u ina li*]*bbi adêka* [6]*iḫaṭṭūn*[*i ša ina muḫḫi napšātīk*]*a i*[*dabbabū*]*ni* [7]*šunu ina qātē*[*ka išakkanūšunu*] *šumšunu* [*issu māt Aš*]*šūr* [8]*issu libbi e*[*kallīka tuḫallaqa*] *dabābu anniu* [9]*ša Mullissu* [*šû šarru bēlī*] *ina libbi lū lā i*[*šīaṭ*]

To the ki[ng], my lord: your servant Nabû-re[ḫtu-uṣur. May Bel and] Belet, Nabû and Tašmetu, Ištar of Ni[neveh and Ištar of Arbela, your] gods who [called] you by name [to kingship, keep] you a[live]! Those who sinned against [your father's goodness, yo]ur fa[ther's and] your own treaty, and who p[lo]t [against yo]ur [life], they[a] shall [place] in [your] hands, [and you shall delete] their name [from As]syria and from [your pa]lace. This is the word of Mullissu; [the king, my lord,] should not be ne[glectful] about it.

[10]*ina* UD.6.KÁM *ša* [*Uraḫšamni diglu*] *a*[*dd*]*agal mā* [. . .] [11]*mā ina libb*[*i* . . . *bēl adê ša šarri bēlīya anāku*] [12]*lā mūqāya lā u*[*pazzar dibbī ša* . . .] [13]*kî ša āmurūni ina lib*[*bi* . . .]

[10]On the sixth of [*Marchesvan* (VIII)] I had a vi[sion]: "[. . .] in the midst [. . .]." [I am bound by the treaty of the king, my lord]; I cannot c[onceal the things that . . .].

14 *aktarar ana x urk*[*āti* . . .] 15 *šarru bēlī ūda akī bēt* [. . .] 16 *kî annî ina libbi egert*[*i šaṭir mā* . . .] 17 *lū iṣṣia mā* [. . .]

Just as I saw, in [. . .] I have put, *discree*[*tly*. . .] The king, my lord, knows that where [. . .] as [it is written] as follows in the lette[r: ". . .] should have ... [. . .]

[break]

CT 53 107:1' [. . . *m*]*ā mār š*[*arri* . . .] 2' *ana mār ša*[*rri* . . .] 3' *mā issi aḫēʾiš usamma*[*ḫūni* . . .] 4' *iqabbi mā annûti* [. . .] 5' *u mā ekallu gabbu issi* [. . .] 6' *memmēni mā marʾat Bambâ* [. . .] 7' *u ṣābāni ša Adad-šumu-uṣur Ar*[*dâ* . . .] 8' *iqṭibûni mā bārtu eppu*[*šū* . . .] 9' *mā šû ina libbi irtiḫi*[*ṣ* . . .] 10' *assakan mā ša Bēl Nabû Issār ša* [*Nīnua Issār ša Arbail* . . .] 11' *urtamme ša raminīšu* [. . .] 12' *Issār ša Nīnua mā* [. . .] 13' *ētapšū mā* [. . . 14' *m*]*ā* [*is*]*su libbi e*[*kalli* . . .]

[break]

CT 53 107:1' [. . .] the crown pr[ince . . .] to the crown prin[ce . . .] are in league with one another [. . .] he says: "These [. . .]" and: "The whole palace [is] with [. . .] anything; the daughter of Bambâ [. . .] and the men of Adad-šumu-uṣur and Ar[dâ. . .] have said to me: "They are making a rebellion [. . .]." He has become confident in (his) heart [and is saying:] "I have set [. . .]." He has rejected what Bel, Nabû, Ištar of Ni[neveh and Ištar of Arbela have . . .ed], and [. . .] of his own. Ištar of Nineveh says: "[. . .] have done [. . .] from the pal[ace. . .]

[break]

CT 53 107 r. 5 *kî annî q*[*ab*]*i mā ina Ḫarrān* [. . .] 6 *mā ina muḫḫīya akê ṭēmu iškun* [. . .] 7 *mā abūtu ša* [. . .] *addanniš tattaṣ*[*ra*] 8 *mā ekallu ana* [. . .] *tassakan mā ša* [. . .] 9 *mā* [*ṣāb*]*ānīya* [. . .] 10 *Sāsî* [. . .]

CT 53 107 r. 5 It w[as spo]ken as follows: "In Harran [. . .] What orders has he given [to you] about me? [. . .] The word of [. . .] *has become* very [. . .] You have turned the palace into a [. . .] My men [. . .] Sasî [. . .]"

[break]

CT 53 17 r. 9' [*ina p*]*ān ša-rēši* [. . .] 10' *napšātīka šēzib ar*[*ḫiš* . . .] 11' *šî Sāsî ana* [. . . 12' *Mi*]*lki-nūri Urdu-Issār iss*[*īšu* . . .] 13' *šaʾalšunu nišē a*[*mmar* . . .] *issīšunu ūdû*[*ni* 14 *l*]*iqbûnikka niš*[*ē annût*]*i limuttū lā tapallaḫ* 15' *Bēl Nabû Mullissu* [*issīka*] *izzazzū arḫiš nišē* 16' *limuttū napšātk*[*a šēzib*] *egertu annītu lū šiptu* 17' *ina muḫḫīka* [. . . *arḫi*]*š nišē limuttū* 18' *adu lā iḫarru*[*pūni*]

[break]

CT 53 17 r. 9' [in the pres]ence of the chief eunuch [. . .] Save your life! Qu[ickly ...] Sasî to [. . .] Milki-nuri and Urad-Issar [. . .] with [*him*]. 13' Interrogate them! Let them tell you the [. . .] people who conspi[red] with them, and let [these] people die! Have no fear; Bel, Nabû and Mullissu are standing [with you]. Let the people die quickly, and [save] your life! May this letter be a spell, it will [. . .] upon you! Let the

*anīnu šarru bēlī* [19'] *napšātīka ball[iṭ ṣābāni š]a Sāsî* [20] *šubtu u[ssēšibū] [mā] issinni* [21'] *idabbu[b mā adu lā iḫ]arrupūni* [22'] *mā anī[nu . . .]-šu* [s. 1] *anīnu šarru [bēlī] Bēl ana [. . .] ḫurāṣu abnāti ša kayyamānu [. . .]* [2] *lūbilū [atta tu]qūnu ana [x sarrir napš]ātīka lurrik ra[man]ka uṣur* KI.MIN KI.MIN [3] *napšātīka [napšāti ša] qinnīka [šēzib issu qāt] ša-rēšāni napšātīka šēzib* KI.MIN KI.MIN [4] *libbak[a ṣabt]a [. . . issīka l]izzizzū libbašunu gammurakka*

people die [quick]ly before they get ahe[ad] (of you).

[18'] Hear me, O king my lord! Sa[ve] your life! [The *men* o]f Sasî have [set] an ambush, [saying]: “The moment (the king) will speak with us, we shall [*kill*] him [before he gets ah]ead (of us).” [s. 1] Hear me, O king [my lord]! Bel [. . .] Let the [. . .] constantly bring gold and precious stones to [. . . As for you, ke]ep in safety, [pray] to [. . .] and let him prolong your life. Take care of your[se]lf, ditto ditto (= let the people die quickly)! [3] [Save] your life and [the life of] your family! Save your life [*from the hands of* the e]unuchs! Ditto ditto. Br[ace yo]urself! Let the [. . .] stand [with you], they are loyal to you.

[a] Scil. the gods.

## 117. Nabû-reḫtu-uṣur to Esarhaddon

**Text:** SAA 16 61 (= *CT* 53 938 = 82-1-18,508).
**Copy:** Parpola 1979: pl. 208.
**Transliteration and translation:** Nissinen 1998b: 114–15; Luukko and Van Buylaere 2002: 56–57.
**Discussion:** van der Toorn 1987: 78; Nissinen 1998b: 108–53.

*[ana šarri bēlīya* [2] *urdaka Nabû-rēḫtu-uṣur Bēl Bēlet Nabû Tašmētum* [3] *Issār ša] Nīnua Issār ša [Arbail ilānīka ša šumka* [4] *ana šarrū]ti izkurūni šun[u luballiṭūka]*

*[ša ina libbi* [5] *ṭābti] ša abīka ina libbi adê š[a abīka u ina libbi adêka* [6] *iḫaṭṭūni] ša ina muḫḫi napšātīka i[dabbabūni* [7] *šunu ina qātē]ka išakkanūšunu šum[šunu issu māt*

[To the king, my lord: your servant Nabû-reḫtu-uṣur. May Bel and Belet, Nabû and Tašmetu, Ištar of] Nineveh and Ištar of [Arbela, your gods who] called [you by name to kings]hip, [keep you alive]!

[4] [Those who sinned against] your father’s [goodness, your father’s and your own] treaty, and who p[lot] against your life, they shall place in yo[ur hands], and you shall delete

*Aššūr* 8 *issu libbi ekal*]*līka tuḫallaqa dabābu* [*anniu* 9 *ša Mullis*]*su šû šarru bēlī ina libbi lū l*[*ā išīaṭ*]

[their] name [from Assyria and from] your p[alace]. 8[This] is the word of [Mullis]su; the king, my lord, should not be ne[glectful] about it.

10[*ina* UD.X.KÁM *š*]*a Araḫšamna diglu addagal mā* [... 11 *mā ina libbi* ...] ... *bēl adê ša šar*[*ri bēlīya anāku* 12 *lā mūqāya lā upazz*]*ar dib*[*bī ša* ...]
[break]
r. 2′ *ša ina ekallīka epšūn*[*i* ...] 3 *lā išme lā ūda* [...] 4 *uznaka lū lā tasaḫḫur*[*a* ...] 5 *ḫalluqi ana* [...] 6′ *u Bambâ* [...]

[rest destroyed]

10[On the *sixth* o]f Marchesvan (VIII), I had a vision: "[...]." [I am] bound by the treaty of the ki[ng, my lord]; I cannot c[onceal] the thi[ngs that ...].
[break]
r. 2 ...which have been done in your palace [...] he has not heard, and does not know [...] Do not turn away your attention [...] to destroy [...] and Bambâ [...]
[rest destroyed]

## 118. Ritual of Ištar and Dumuzi

**Text:** Farber 1977 A II a (= K 2001+ and duplicates; see Farber 1977: 127).
**Copy:** Farber 1977: pl. 7–14.
**Transliteration and translation:** Farber 1977: 128–55.
**Discussion:** Farber 1977: 156–62; Nissinen 2000b: 93–94.

### Lines 1–33

*šumma amīlu eṭemmu iṣbassu lū sanḫulḫāzu iṣbassu* 2 *lū mimma lemnu iṣbassuma irteneddēšu*

If a man is seized by a spirit of a dead or a *sanḫulḫāzu* demon, or if any evil thing has seized him and afflicts him continually:

---

3 *epuštašu ina araḫ Duʾūzi enūma Ištār ana Dumuzi* 4 *ḫarmīša nīšī māti ušabkû* 5 *kimti amīli ašrānu paḫrat* 6 *Ištār izzazma pî nīšī iḫâra* 7 *murṣa ittabbal murṣa išakkan*

The ritual against it is the following: In the month of Tammuz, when Ištar makes the people of the land wail over Dumuzi, her beloved, and the family of the man[a] is gathered in a proper place, Ištar is there to attend to the people's concerns. She may take the sickness away, but she may cause sickness as well.

UD.28.KAM [8]*ūm tarbaṣi ūr uqnî kakkabti ḫurāṣi* [9]*ana Ištār taqâš šum marṣi tazakkar marṣa* [10]*šūzibī taqabbīma*

[7]On the twenty-eighth[b] day, the day of the pen, you shall give Ištar a vulva of lapis lazuli with a golden star.[c] You shall utter the name of the sick person and then say: "Save the sick one!"

*šinšeret akalī miḫḫa* [11]*ana bīt Ištār teleqqēma ana Ištār-rēṣūʾa* [12]*kaparri ša Dumuzi naṣrapta guḫaṣṣa* [13]*taqâš Ištār-rēṣūʾa ana Dumuzi* [14]*ṣabat abbūti annanna marṣi taqabbi*

[10]You shall take twelve loaves and *miḫḫu*-beer to the temple of Ištar and give Ištar-reṣuʾa, the shepherd boy of Dumuzi,[d] a crucible and a cord, saying: "Ištar-reṣuʾa, plead with Dumuzi on behalf of so-and-so, the sick one!"

*annâ* [15]*ina ūm tarbaṣi ina bīt Ištār teppuš*

[14]This is what you shall do on the day of the pen in the temple of Ištar.

---

[16]UD.29.KAM *ūm mayyāltu ana Dumuzi innaddû* [17]*ištēn qa qēma ša zikaru iṭēnu teleqqēma* [18]*ina rēš mayyāltīšu tumra tanappaḫ kamāna ina išāti tušabšal* [19]*ina šizbi damqi tamarras ina rēš mayyālti tašakkan* [20]*laḫan mê u šikari tukân*

[16]On the twenty-ninth[e] day, when the bed is prepared for Dumuzi, you shall take one liter of meal that a male person has ground up and place glowing embers at the head of the bed. Then you shall bake a *kamānu*-bread in the fire, baste it with good milk and place it at the head of the bed. You shall also place there a bowl with water and beer.

[21]*šappa sussulla ebbūba ṣinnata* [22]*ša ḫurāṣa aḫzā takša nāda* [23]*ana Dumuzi taqâš riksa ana Dumuzi tarakkas* [24]*nignak ballukki ina rēšīšu nignak burāši ina šēpītīšu tašakkan* [25]*ina šēpītīšu riksa ana Ištār tarakkas nignak burāši tašakkan* [26]*šikara tanaqqi šuluḫḫa tušallaḫ zidubdubbâ* [27]*tattanaddi ina imitti mayyālti ana eṭem kimti* [28]*ina šumēl mayyālti ana Anunnakī kispa takassip* [29]*mê kaṣûti u šikar lapti tanaqqi*

[21]You shall give Dumuzi a jug, a trough, a flute and a *ṣinnatu* pipe[f] covered with gold, a carrying rack and a skin bottle. Then you shall prepare the collection of offerings for Dumuzi, place a censer with *ballukku*-herbs at his head and another censer with juniper at his feet, after which you shall prepare the collection of offerings for Ištar at his feet. You shall place there a censer with juniper, libate beer and perform the sprinkling of water. Then you shall scatter the meal and perform on the right side of the

bed an offering for the spirits of the ancestors of the family, and on the left side of the bed a funerary offering for the Anunnaki.[g] You shall libate cold water and beer from oven-parched grain.

[30]*mirsa [ana k]aparrāti ša Dumuzi tašakkan* [31]*sebe kurummāti ana zabbi zabbati maḫḫê u maḫḫūti* [32]*tašakkan marṣa ana maḫar Ištār kīam tušadbabšu*

[30][For the s]hepherd boys of Dumuzi you shall place a confection;[h] for the frenzied men and women and for the prophets and prophetesses you shall place seven pieces of bread. Then let the sick person recite the following to Ištar:

---

[33]*rē'ītu Ištār ālikat pān būli . . .*

[33]O Ištar, shepherdess going before the cows (. . .)

[a] Or, "the family of each man."
[b] According to another manuscript, the twenty-seventh day.
[c] Vulvas of lapis lazuli are emblems of Ištar frequently used in different kinds of rituals.
[d] A cult functionary who intercedes on behalf of the people.
[e] According to another manuscript, the twenty-eighth day.
[f] A wind instrument of unknown type.
[g] The gods of the underworld.
[h] *CAD* M 108: "a confection made of dates, oil, butter etc."; cf. *AHw* 646: "Rührkuchen" (sub *mersu*).

# VI

# Miscellaneous Cuneiform Sources

The choice of sources collected in this chapter comprises texts of various places, ages, and genres. The sixteen texts of this selection are but an assortment, far from being an exhaustive collection of sources in which prophets and prophetesses—that is, usually *muḫḫûm/maḫḫû* or *muḫḫūtum/maḫḫūtu*—are mentioned (for a more nearly complete, but not fully exhaustive list, see *CAD* M 90–91, 176–77). They are gathered together to demonstrate both the chronological distribution of prophecy and the diversity of text types that contribute to our knowledge of ancient Near Eastern prophecy. To make the sample representative enough, at least one text from each main chronological period and text genre has been chosen as an example.

The oldest reference to a prophet can probably be found in a letter from the Ur III period (i.e., twenty-first century B.C.E.) in which the king of Ur orders an enormous amount of barley (18,000 liters!) to be delivered to an anonymous *maḫḫûm* of a deity who is a local manifestation of Ištar (no. 119). The affiliation of the prophets to the cult of Ištar and to the community of devotees of the goddess is further documented by the Middle Assyrian provisions list (no. 123), in which a considerably lesser amount of barley (ca. 645 liters) is delivered to prophets, prophetesses, and *assinnu*s of the Ištar temple in Kar-Tukulti-Ninurta. These people are listed among Kassite deportees, probably those captured by Tukulti-Ninurta I (1243–1207) during his victorious campaign against Kaštiliaš IV, the Kassite king of Babylonia. The institutional association between the prophets and the *assinnu*s and other gender-neutral persons such as the *kurgarrû* becomes clear also from the Neo-Babylonian list of regular offerings in Eanna, the Ištar temple of of Uruk (no. 130), which lists the portions of the king, the high priest, the scribe of Eanna, the temple administrator, *maḫḫû,* and *kurgarrû* in the same paragraph. The only literary text in this selection, the Middle Babylonian "Righteous Sufferer" from Ugarit (no. 122), after mentioning various kinds of divination, compares people who "bathe in their blood" to prophets, thus alluding to ecstatic self-mutilation, which is part of the image of the gender-neutral people as well.

Further associations between prophets and other classes of people are provided by lexical lists which, without being the result of a classification of people in any taxonomical or administrative sense, collect words which are either phonetically similar or otherwise associated, e.g., in terms of physical appearance or social function. In these lists (nos. 120, 124–126) prophets—*muḫḫû(tu)m/maḫḫû* or *raggimu*—regularly appear together with the "men-women" *assinnu* and *kurgarrû,* as well as with other cult functionaries, whose appearance and conduct were different from those of the average citizen: the "frenzied" people, wailers, lamentation singers, temple women, and the like; in number 126, *raggimu* is straightforwardly equated with *šabrû,* the visionary. Furthermore, prophets and prophetesses are included in the long list of persons whose physical or mental condition is conspicuous in one way or another in the city omen series *Šumma ālu* (no. 129). All these scattered occurences of prophets in different kinds of texts throw light on the behavior and social location of the Mesopotamian prophets.

The letter of the Hurrian king, Tušratta of Mitanni, to Amenophis III of Egypt (no. 121) is the only pertinent source within the El Amarna correspondence and one of the very few quotations of prophetic oracles outside Mari, Ešnunna, and Assyria. The letter is written just before the death of Amenophis III (1390–1352), to whom the statue of Ištar of Nineveh, believed to have curative power, had been sent even earlier during his illness as a sign of the goodwill of the Hurrian king. The oracle is presented as a word of Ištar/Šauška of Nineveh; hence it can be taken as a continuation of the Assyrian-Babylonian tradition of prophecy among the Hurrians. Another quotation of words of a person who is best characterized as a prophet comes from the Seleucid Babylonia. Two chronographic texts concerning the month of Tishri, 133 B.C.E., report the appearance of a man called Boatman (*mār Mallāḫi* "descendant of Boatman"), who comes to Babylon and Borsippa, evoking a response among the people. Even though presenting himself as a messenger of the goddess Nanaya, he speaks on behalf of "the strong, hitting God, your God," after which the temple council tries to silence him and warns the people against that madman and his words; it seems that this incident created a disturbance which may have caused the lives of some people (nos. 134–135).

The remaining texts, all Neo- or Late Babylonian, provide indirect references to prophets. The Late Babylonian *akītu* ritual from Hellenistic Uruk (no. 133) includes an oracle of Bel, which in every respect resembles the extant prophetic oracles, except that it is spoken by the high priest, not by a prophet. This may be taken as an example of a subsequent liturgical reuse of a (written) prophetic word (van der Toorn 2000: 77). The two Neo-Babylonian decrees (nos. 131, 132) concern the affairs of people who are designated as "descendant of Prophet" (*mār maḫḫê*). This designation is an ancestral name (see Lambert 1957; Frame 1992: 34), used as a kind of surname like the previously mentioned "son of Boatman", indicating that prophets could have descendants and/or inheritors who honored their anonymous prophetic ancestor by calling themselves "sons of Prophet."

### 119. King of Ur to Ur-Lisi

**Text:** TCS 1 369.
**Copy:** Scheil 1927: 44.
**Transliteration and translation:** Sollberger 1966: 90; Michalowski 1993: 55.
**Discussion:** Sollberger 1966: 191.

| | |
|---|---|
| *umma šarrumma* [2]*ana Ur-Lisina* [3]*qibīma* | Thus the king:[a] Say to Ur-Lisi:[b] |
| [4]60 *kur âm* [5]*ana maḫḫêm* [6]*ša Inanna* [7]*ša Girsu* [8]*idin* | [4]Give sixty kor barley to the prophet[c] of Inanna of Girsu. |

[a] The king in question is Amar-Sîn (2046–2038), the third king of the third dynasty of Ur; see Sollberger 1966: 12.

[b] Ur-Lisi was the governor of the city and district of Umma.

[c] The text reads LÚ.MAḪ-*em,* which could also be read as *lumaḫḫim,* referring to a *lumaḫḫu,* a purification priest (see no. 124 note d). This is how Michalowski 1993: 55 translates it, but note his explanation of *lumaḫḫum* in the glossary (p. 138): "A high-ranking priest, often translated 'ecstatic.'"

### 120. An Old Babylonian Lexical List (Lú Recension A)

**Text:** *MSL* 12 5.22 (= IM 58433+; see Civil et al. 1969: 157).
**Transliteration:** Civil et al. 1969: 158.

#### Lines 20–32

| | | |
|---|---|---|
| [20]lú-šim | = *sirāšû* | brewer |
| [21]lú-kurun-na | = *sābû* | innkeeper (man) |
| [22]mí-lú-kurun-na | = *sābītum* | innkeeper (woman) |

| | | |
|---|---|---|
| [23]lú-gub-ba | = *muḫḫûm* | prophet |
| [24]mí-lú-gub-ba | = *muḫḫūt[um]* | prophetess |
| [25]lú-tílla | = *wāṣû* | one who goes out (man)[a] |
| [26]mí-lú-tílla | = *wāṣītum* | one who goes out (woman) |
| [27]lú-giš-gi-sag-kéš | = *naqmu* | psoriatic (man)[b] |
| [28]mí-lú-giš-gi-sag-kéš | = *naqimtu[m]* | psoriatic (woman) |
| [29]lú-ní-su-ub-ba | = *zabbû* | frenzied man |
| [30]mí-lú-ní-su-ub-ba | = *zabbātum* | frenzied woman |
| [31]lú-ur-e | = *zabbû* | frenzied man |
| [32]lú-al-$e_{11}$-dè | = *maḫḫû* | prophet |

[a] When used of a human being, the word can mean any person going out; in this context it is noteworthy that it is sometimes used of a chanter (*kalû*); see *AHw* 1480 and cf. note b.

[b] The translation "psoriatic" comes from the commentary of *Ludlul bēl nēmeqi* (K 3291), line f (Lambert 1960: 54): *kīma naqimtu šūṣî uṣappira ṣupurāya* "He made my fingernails scratch like the rash of the one who has been sent away"; the word *šūṣû* is explained as the one "whom Ištar has sent to the fire" (*ša Ištar ana išāti ušēṣâ*). This not only creates a link to the ones "who go out" (lines 25–26) but refers to people whose appearance, obviously affected by a skin disease, is interpreted as being the divine ordinance. In another tablet of the Old Babylonian Lú-Series, *munaqqimum*, a word from the same root, is listed together with *musukkanum*, a sexually unclean person. See Lambert 1960: 299–300.

## 121. Tušratta of Mitanni to Amenophis III of Egypt

**Text:** EA 23 (= BM 29793 = *BB* 10).
**Photograph:** Bezold and Budge 1892: pl. 23; Waterman 1930: pl. 4.
**Copy:** Bezold and Budge 1892: 10.
**Transliteration and translation:** Knudtzon 1915: 178–81; Adler 1976: 170–73.
**Translation:** Ebeling in Greßmann 1926: 372–73; Moran 1992: 61–62.
**Discussion:** Adler 1976: 170–73; Kühne 1973: 37; Wegner 1981: 65; Wilhelm 1982: 41; Moran 1992: 62; Nissinen 2000a: 258–89.

*ana Nimmurīya šar Miṣrī* [2]*aḫīya ḫatanīya ša araʾʾamu* [3]*u ša iraʾʾa-manni qibīma* [4]*umma Tušratta šar Mitanni* [5]*ša iraʾʾamūka emūkāma*

Speak to Nimmuriya, the king of Egypt, my brother, my son-in-law whom I love and who loves me: Thus Tušratta, the king of Mitanni who loves you, your father-in-law:

[6]*ana yâši šulmu ana kāša lū šulmu* [7]*ana bītīka ana Tadu-Ḫeba mārtī-ya* [8]*ana aššatīka ša taraʾʾamu lū*

[6]I am well—may you be well, too! May all go well for your household and for Tadu-Ḫeba, my

*šulmu* [9]*ana aššātīka ana mārīka ana rabûtīka* [10]*ana narkabātīka ana sīsîka ana* [11]*ṣābīka ana mātīka u ana* [12]*mimmuka danniš danniš danniš lū šulmu*

daughter and your wife, whom you love. May all go very, very well for your wives and your sons, for your magnates, for your chariots, horses and troops, for your country and for anything that belongs to you!

---

[13]*umma Šauška ša Nīnâ bēlet mātāti* [14]*gabbīšināma ana Miṣrī* [15]*ina māti ša araʾʾamu lullikmāme* [16]*lussaḫḫirme anumma inanna* [17]*ultēbilma ittalka*

[13]Thus says Šauška[a] of Nineveh, the Lady of all countries: "I want to go to Egypt, the country that I love, and then return." Now I have sent her and she is on her way.

---

[18]*anumma ina tirṣi abiyāma* [19]*x x -tu ina māti šâši ittalka* [20]*u kīmē ina pānānum[m]a* [21]*ittašabma uktebbitūš[i* [22]*u] inanna aḫīya ana ešrīšu* [23]*eli ša pānānu likebbissi* [24]*aḫīya likebbissu ina ḫadê* [25]*limeššeršūma litūra*

[18]Now, during the reign of my father already, ...[b] went to that country. Just as she was honored when she dwelt there earlier, let my brother now honor her ten times more than before. Let my brother honor her and then joyfully let her go so that she may return.

---

[26]*Šauška bēlet šamê aḫūya u yâši* [27]*lissurrannâši meat līm šanāti* [28]*u ḫidûta rabīta bēltini* [29]*ana kilallīni liddinannāšīma* [30]*u kî ṭābi i nīpuš*

[26]May Šauška, the Lady of Heaven, protect my brother and me for 100,000 years! May our Lady bestow great joy on both of us! Let us act according to what is good.[c]

---

[31]*Šauška ana yâšimā ilī* [32]*u ana aḫīya lā ilšu*

[31]Is Šauška goddess for me alone; is she not goddess for my brother, too?

[a] Šauška is the main goddess of the Hurrians and the Hurrian equivalent to Ištar.
[b] An inexplicable word denoting the goddess.
[c] Or, "in all friendliness."

## 122. The Righteous Sufferer from Ugarit

**Text:** *Ugaritica* 5 162 (= RS 25460).
**Copy:** Nougayrol 1968a: 435.
**Transliteration and translation:** Nougayrol 1968a: 267-69.
**Discussion:** Nougayrol 1968a: 270-73; Roberts 1970; Huffmon 1992: 478–79; 2000: 64.

### Lines 2–12

[beginning broken away]
[2'] *šīrūʾa ittaʾdarā immâ kīma* [. . .] [3'] *ul itarraṣ bārû purussāya* [4'] *itta ul inamnan dayyānu*

[beginning broken away]
[. . .] My liver oracles remain obscure; they become like [. . .]. The haruspex cannot resolve my case; the judge does not give[a] any sign.

[5'] *dalḫā têrētum šutābulū šīrū* [6'] *muššakku šāʾilu bārû puḫādi* [7'] *igdamrū ummānū šaršubbâya* [8'] *uštammû ul iqbû adan murṣīya*

[5]The messages are confused;[b] the oracles discordant. The inquirer has run out of incense; the haruspex has no sheep left.[c] The scholars who deliberate on tablets[d] concerning my case do not tell me the time limit of my sickness.[e]

[9'] *ḫūrat kimti ana quddudi* <*u*>*lammadanni* [10'] *qerub salāti ana tukkulimma izzaz*

[9]The heads of my family tell me to humble myself, the immediate circle of my kin tries to inspire me with confidence.[f]

[11'] *aḫḫūʾa kīma maḫḫê* [*d*]*āmīšunu ramkū* [12'] *aššātūʾa šamna gilṣa raksa raḫâni*

[11]My brothers bathe in their [bl]ood like prophets, my wives anoint[g] my prepared (body) with choice oil.[h]

[a] Despite the reservations of Nougayrol 1968a: 270, the word *dayyānu* most probably refers to the god Šamaš, whose signs are interpreted by the the haruspices. The word *inamnan* is interpreted as G prs. of *nadānu* "to give" (= *inaddin*) with a Middle Babylonian nazalization of the geminate (see Aro 1955: 35–37) and an Assyrian vocalization.

[b] Written *dal-ḫat-e-re-tum;* cf. *Ludlul bēl nēmeqi* i 51 (Lambert 1960: 32).

[c] Cf. *Ludlul bēl nēmeqi* ii 6–7 (Lambert 1960: 38): "The haruspex (*bārû*) with his inspection has not got to the root of the matter, the inquirer (*šāʾilu*) with his incense (*maššakku*) has not elucidated my case."

[d] Written *ša-ar-šub-ba-*((*ša*))*-a-a,* where the last *ša* is probably erronoeously added (cf. *AHw* 1191); Nougayrol 1968a: 270 suggests a contamination from *šaršubbâ* (*mal*) *bašû* "(as many) tablets as there are", but the ending *-a-a* is better explained as a suffix sg. 1.

[e] Written *a-da-mur-ṣi-ia;* cf. *Ludlul bēl nēmeqi* ii 111 (Lambert 1960: 44): "The haruspex has not put a time limit on my illness."
[f] Written *a-na-at-ku-li-im-ma.*
[g] Written *ra-ḫa-ya-ni;* interpreted as G pl. 3. fem. vent. with suff. 1. sg. of *raḫû.*
[h] The two last lines probably describe mourning rites, as if the sufferer would already be dead; cf. *Ludlul bēl nēmeqi* ii 114–15 (Lambert 1960: 46): "My grave was waiting, and my funerary paraphernalia ready, Before I had died lamentation for me was finished." For *šamnu gilṣu* (= *ḫalṣu*), see Nougayrol 1968a: 271.

## 123. Middle Assyrian Food Rations List from Kar-Tukulti-Ninurta

**Text:** VS 19 1 (= VAT 17999).
**Copy:** Freydank 1976: pl. I–V.
**Transliteration and translation:** Freydank 1974: 58–73.
**Discussion:** Parpola 1997: xlvii, cv; Nissinen 2000b: 94; Lion 2000.

### Lines i 37'–39'

| | |
|---|---|
| 37' 10 *emār* 4 *sât* 5 *qa Aššūr-apla-iddina ina* UD.2.KÁM | Ten homers four seah five liters of barley[a] for Aššur-apla-iddina on the second day, |
| 38' *ana kurummat maḫḫu'ē maḫḫu-'āte u assinnē* 39' *ša bēt Iltār* | for the food rations of the prophets, prophetesses and the *assinnus*[b] of the Ištar temple. |
| *ṭuppušu lā ṣabtat* | His tablet has not been deposited. |

[a] The preceding paragraphs make it plain that the food to be delivered is barley.
[b] Freydank 1974: 60 has LÚ.*x*.MEŠ; however, the copy in Freydank 1976: pl. 1 shows a clear LÚ.⌜SAL⌝.MEŠ.

## 124. Neo-Assyrian Lexical List (Lú = *ša,* Tablet I, short recension I)

**Text:** *MSL* 12 4.212 (= *5 R* 40 3 = K 4142 etc.; see Civil et al. 1969: 92).
**Transliteration:** Civil et al. 1969: 102-3.
**Discussion:** Nissinen 2000b: 93.

### Lines 193–217

| | | |
|---|---|---|
| 193 gašan | = *bē[ltu]* | lady |
| 194 nin-dingir-ra | = *en[tu]* | high priestess |
| 195 nin-dingir-ra | = *ugbabtu* | priestess |
| 196 nu-gig | = *qadištu* | tabooed woman[a] |
| 197 nu-bar | = *kulmašītu* | temple woman[b] |
| 198 gudu$_4$-abzu | = *kurgarrû* | man-woman[c] |
| 199 [gu]du$_4$-síg-bar-ra | = *šu<sup></sup>ʾʾuru* | hairy one |
| 200 gudu$_4$-tur-ra | = *lumakku* | purification priest[d] |
| 201 nu-$^{\text{eš}}$èš | = *nēšakku* | cult functionary[e] |
| 202 susbu$^{\text{bu}}$ | = *ramku* | cult functionary |
| 203 sánga-mah | = *šangammāḫu* | high priest/exorcist |
| 204 [maš]-maš | = *mašmaššu* | exorcist |
| 205 nar-balag | = *āšipu* | exorcist |
| 206 ka-pirig | = MIN | (the same) |
| 207 muš-DU.$^{\text{la.la.ah}}$DU | = *mušlalaḫḫu* | snake-charmer |
| 208 lú-$^{\text{giš}}$gàm-šu-du$_7$ | = *muššipu* | exorcist |
| 209 la-bar | = *kalû* | chanter |
| 210 gala-mah | = *kalamāḫu* | chief chanter |
| 211 i-lu-di | = *munambû* | lamentation singer |
| 212 i-lu-a-li | = *lallaru* | wailer |
| 213 lú-gub-ba | = *maḫḫû* | prophet |
| 214 lú-ní-zu-ub | = *zabbu* | frenzied one |
| 215 kur-gar-ra | = *kurgarrû* | man-woman |
| 216 ur-sal | = *assinnu* | man-woman |
| 217 lú-$^{\text{giš}}$bala-šu-du$_7$ | = *nāš pilaqqi* | carrier of spindel[f] |

[a] The *qadištu* and the *kulmašītu* are female temple employees whose sacerdotal and sexual roles are disputed; they are involved, e.g., in childbirth, nursing and sorcery (see Leick 1994: 148–53, 229, 257–58). In the Epic of Gilgameš, *ugbabtum, qadištum,* and *kulmašītum* appear in sequence as "votaries of Gilgameš" (Gilg. iii 120–124).

[b] See note a.

[c] The role of the *kurgarrû* is analogous to that of the *assinnu,* who at Mari sometimers appears as prophet. Both groups have a permanent "third gender" role given by Ištar, whose devotees they are; see Leick 1994: 157–69; Nissinen 1998c: 28–36.

[d] The *lumakku/lumaḫḫu,* sometimes confused with *maḫḫû* (see Wohl 1970/71), is a priest of a high rank. Cf. no. 119 note c.

[e] For this class of cult functionaries, see Renger 1969: 138–43.

[f] The designation *nāš pilaqqi* is equal to *assinnu* and *kurgarrû.*

## 125. Neo-Assyrian Lexical List (Lú = *ša,* Tablet IV)

**Text:** *MSL* 12 4.222 (= VAT 9558).
**Transliteration:** Meissner 1940: 40; Civil et al. 1969: 132.

### Lines 116–123

| | | |
|---|---|---|
| 116 lú-ní-su-ub | = *maḫḫû* | prophet |
| 117 lú-gub-ba | = MIN | (as above) |
| 118 lú-al-è-dè | = MIN | (as above) |
| 119 mí-al-è-dè | = *maḫḫūtu* | prophetess |
| 120 lú-ní-zu-ub | = *zabb*[*u*] | frenzied man |
| 121 mí-ní-zu-ub | = *zabba*[*tu*] | frenzied woman |
| 122 lú-al-è-dè | = *ēl*[*û*] | the one who comes up[a] |
| 123 lú-zag-gír-lá | = *ša kak-k*[*a našû*] | sword-man[b] |

[a] Cf. line 118. Restoration by Simo Parpola.

[b] Restoration by Simo Parpola. This word denotes a servant of Ištar who is equipped with a sword and takes part in self-castration scenes (Parpola 1997: civ n. 232).

## 126. Neo-Assyrian Lexical List (ḪAR-gud B)

**Text:** *MSL* 12 6.2. (= *2 R* 51 2 = K 4344 etc.; see Civil et al. 1969: 225).
**Transliteration:** Civil et al. 1969: 225-26.
**Discussion:** von Weiher 1973: 107; Parpola 1997: ciii–civ n. 231; Nissinen 1998b: 10, 56.

### Lines 129-149

| | |
|---|---|
| 129 [lú]-eme-[tuku] = [*ša l*]*išāni* = [. . .] | interpreter |
| 130 [lú]-eme-nu-[tuku] = [*lā*] *išānû* = *šur*-[. . .] | poor |

| | |
|---|---|
| 131 [lú]-umuš-nu-tu[ku] = *[dunna]mû* = *sa[klu]* | one of lowly origin |
| 132 [lú]-zilulu = (blank) = *saḫ[ḫiru]* | one who prowls around |
| 133 [lú]-ur-sal = *[a]ssinnu* = *sinnišā[nu]* | man-woman |
| 134 lú-šabra = *šabrû* = *raggimu* | dreamer-prophet[a] |
| 135 lú-gub-ba = *a[p]illû* = *ašša-*[. . .] | prophet[b] |
| 136 lú-ú-bíl-la = *upillû* = *kuttimmu* | craftsman[c] |
| 137 lú-tibira = *gurgurru* = *kapšarru* | metalworker/engraver[d] |
| 138 lú-túg-tag-ga = *māḫiṣu ša sissikti* = *išpāru* | weaver |
| 139 lú-pan-tag-ga = (blank) = *māḫiṣu* | weaver[e] |
| 140 lú-kuš-tag-ga = *ēpiš ipši* = *paqqāyu* | maker of reed mats |
| 141 lú-ninni$_5$-tag-ga = *ēpiš [tuš]ši* = *ḫuppû* | weaver[f] |
| 142 lú-bára-tag-ga = *ēpiš ba[šā]mu* = *šabsû* | male midwife[g] |
| 143 lú-nu-bàndada = *laputt[û]* = *ḫa[za]nnu* | official |
| 144 lú-šar-rab-tu-ú = (blank) = *ṣuḫurtu* | young man[h] |
| 145 lú-ki-zu-ú = *tašlīšu* = *ḫanigalbatu* | chariot soldier[i] |
| 146 lú-ti-ru = *tīru* = *manzaz pāni* | courtier |
| 147 lú-an-né-ba-tu = *eššebû* = *maḫḫû* | prophet[j] |
| 148 lú-gidim-ma = *ša eṭimmu* = *manza[z]û* | necromancer |
| 149 lú-sag-bulug-ga = *mušēlû eṭimmu* = ÍD [. . .] | necromancer |

[a] For the difference between *šabrû* and *raggimu,* see Parpola 1997: xlvi–xlvii; Nissinen 1998b: 56.

[b] Note that *apillû* is equated with lú-gub.ba, the usual ideogram for *maḫḫû;* see below no. 129 note k.

[c] The word *upillû* means charcoal-burner, while *kuttimmu* is a designation of gold- or silversmith.

[d] Both *gurgurru* and *kapšarru* are designations of craftsmen, the latter possibly working with stones.

[e] Hence on the basis of the preceding line; other translations of *māḫiṣu* include "hunter," military scout," etc.; cf. *CAD* M/I 102–3.

[f] The word *ḫuppû* is here in a meaning different from that in the *Šumma ālu* omen where it means "cult dancer, acrobat."

[g] Thus *CAD* Š/I 16.

[h] Thus *AHw* 1109–10 (< *ṣeḫru* "young").

[i] The word *tašlīšu* is widely used for the third man in a chariot, whereas *ḫanigalbatu* relates to a special status in the Hurrian societies of the second millennium B.C.E., which involves the possession of a chariot; this appears to be more or less like the status of *mariyannu* in the same cultural milieu (Peter Machinist, private communication). Cf. von Weiher 1973.

[j] The word *eššebû* designates ecstatic cult functionaries who appear together with, e.g., exorcists; cf. next line.

## 127. Birth Omens
## (*Šumma izbu* xi)

**Text:** K 3998, K 4048, BE 36389 (see Leichty 1970: 130).
**Copy:** Wallis Budge 1910: pl. 37–38 (K 3998); 36 (K 4048); BE 36389 unpublished.
**Transliteration and translation:** Leichty 1970: 131.

### Lines 7–8

7 *šumma izbu uzun imittīšu ḫazmatma šāra napḫat māta maḫḫiātum iṣabbatū*
8 *šumma izbu uzun šumēlīšu ḫazmatma šāra napḫat māt nakri gabrû*

7 If an anomaly's right ear is cropped and inflated with wind: prophetesses will seize the land.
8 If an anomaly's left ear is cropped and inflated with wind: the same happens to the land of the enemy.

## 128. Commentary on the Birth Omens in Number 127

**Text:** K 1913.
**Copy:** Meek 1920: 120.
**Transliteration:** Leichty 1970: 230–31.

### Lines 365d–e

365d *māta maḫḫiātum iṣabbatū = māta šēḫu iṣabbat*
365e *maḫḫû = šēḫānu*

*maḫḫātus* will seize the land = possessed people will seize the land.
*maḫḫû* = possessed men.

## 129. City Omens

## (*Šumma ālu* i)

**Text:** K 6097; K 1367; BM 35582; BM 55550; BM 121041; Sm 797 (see Freedman 1998: 25, 51–54).
**Copy:** Gadd 1925: pl. 3–5.
**Transliteration and translation:** Nötscher 1928: 46–49; Freedman 1998: 32–35.
**Discussion:** Nötscher 1928: 56–57; 1929: 3; 1966: 174; Ramlot 1972: 881; Freedman 1998: 32–35.

**Lines 85–117**

85 *šumma ina āli pessûti ma᾿dū* [. . .]

If there are many limping men in a city, [. . .]

86 *šumma ina āli pessâti ma᾿dā ālu šuātu libbušu iṭâb*

If there are many limping women in a city, there is well-being in the city.

87 *šumma ina āli lillūti ma᾿dū libbi āli iṭâb*

If there are many crazy men in a city, the city is well.

88 *šumma ina āli lillāti ma᾿dā ālu šuātu* [*libbušu iṭâb*]

If there are many crazy women in a city, there is [well-being] in the city.

89 *šumma ina āli rabbūtu ma᾿dū nakrūti šarrāni*

If there are many weak men[a] in a city, there is hostility against the kings.

90 *šumma ina āli emqūti ma᾿dū nadê āli*

If there are many wise men in a city, the city will fall.

91 *šumma ina āli šullānū ma᾿dū sapāḫ* [*āli*]

If there are many pockmarked persons[b] in a city, [the city] will be destroyed.

92 *šumma ina āli sāmūti ma᾿dū libbi āli šuāti iṭâb*

If there are many red-skinned persons in a city, there is well-being in the city.

93 *šumma ina āli birdū ma᾿dū sapāḫ* [*āli*]

If there are many psoriatics[c] in a city, [the city] will be destroyed.

94 *šumma ina āli sukkukūti ma᾿dū sapāḫ* [*āli*]

If there are many deaf persons in a city, [the city] will be destroyed.

95 *šumma ina āli lā nāṭilūti ma᾿dū nazāk āli*

If there are many blind persons in a city, the city will fall.

96 *šumma ina āli kurgarrû ma᾿dū sapāḫ* [*āli*]

If there are many men-women in a city, [the city] will be destroyed.

97 *šumma ina āli pētû ma᾿dū nazāk* [*āli*]

If there are many bleeding persons[d] in a city, the city will fall.

98 *šumma ina āli ḫummurūti ma᾿dū nazāk* [*āli*]

If there are many cripples in a city, [the city] will fall.

99 *šumma ina āli kubbulū ma᾿dū sapāḫ* [*āli*]

If there are many disabled men[e] in a city, [the city] will be destroyed.

100 *šumma ina āli lāsimūti ma᾿dū sapāḫ* [*āli*]

If there are many runners[f] in a city, [the city] will be destroyed.

101 *šumma ina āli maḫḫû ma᾿dū nazāk* [*āli*]

If there are many prophets in a city, the city will fall.

102 *šumma ina āli maḫḫâti maʾdā nazāk* [*āli*]

If there are many prophetesses in a city, [the city] will fall.

103 *šumma ina āli akû maʾdū sapāḫ* [*āli*]

If there are many cripples in a city, [the city] will be destroyed.

104 *šumma ina āli lā išarūti maʾdū nazāk* [*āli*]

If there are many abnormally constituted persons[g] in a city, [the city] will fall.

105 *šumma ina āli šarrāqū maʾdū nazāk* [*āli*]

105 If there are many thieves in a city, [the city] will fall.

106 *šumma ina āli ēpiš balaggi maʾdū sapāḫ* [*āli*]

If there are many musicians who play the *balaggu*[h] in a city, [the city] will be destroyed.

107 *šumma ina āli šabrû maʾdū sapāḫ* [*āli*]

If there are many male dreamers in a city, [the city] will be destroyed.

108 *šumma ina āli šabrâtu maʾdā sapāḫ* [*āli*]

If there are many female dreamers in a city, [the city] will be destroyed.

109 *šumma ina āli* LÚ.DINGIR.RE.E.NE.MEŠ *maʾdū nazāk* [*āli*]

If there are many ...s[i] in a city, [the city] will fall.

110 *šumma ina āli muttaʾilūtu maʾdū nazāk* [*āli*]

110 If there are many performers of incubation[j] in a city, [the city] will fall.

111 *šumma ina āli ḫuppû maʾdū lib*[*bi āli iṭâb*]

If there are many cult dancers in a city, [there is well-being] in [the city].

112 *šumma ina āli bārûti maʾdū sapāḫ* [*āli*]

If there are many haruspices in a city, [the city] will be destroyed.

113 *šumma ina āli upillû maʾdū sapāḫ* [*āli*]

If there are many charcoal-burners in a city, [the city] will be destroyed.

114 *šumma ina āli apillû maʾdū sapāḫ* [*āli*]

If there are many *apillû*[k] in a city, [the city] will be destroyed.

115 *šumma ina āli zabbilū maʾdū nin* [. . .]

115 If there are many sheaf carriers[l] in a city, . . . [. . .]

116 *šumma ina āli tamkārūti maʾdū išātu* [. . .]

If there are many merchants in a city, fire [. . .]

117 *šumma ina āli ṭābiḫūti maʾdū murṣu* [. . .]

If there are many butchers in a city, the sickness [. . .]

[break]

[break]

[a] Freedman 1998: 33: "soft men" (cf. *AHw* 934). The word *rabbu* is derived from *rabābu* "to become weak."

[b] Or, "men with warts" (Freedman 1998: 33); cf. *AHw* 126; *CAD* Š/III 240–41.

[c] According to *CAD* B 246, the *birdu* has the same meaning as *šullānu* (line 91; cf. note b).

[d] Literally, "opener" (thus Freedman 1998: 33) or "opened" (< *petû*), interpreted here as persons with open wounds. *AHw* 861 suggests "wrestler" ("Klammer-Öffner").

[e] For this reading and translation of AD$_4$, see Leichty 1970: 176 n. 33.

[f] Rather than to sportsmen, this may refer to people with a distinctive walk.

[g] Thus *CAD* I/J 226; Freedman 1998: 33 translates "unrighteous men."

[h] Thus *CAD* E 238; Freedman 1998: 33 translates "mourners."

[i] An inexplicable word, probably meaning a class of temple servants; Freedman 1998: 35 translates "consecrated men."

[j] Thus *CAD* M/II 304 (< *utūlu*); Freedman 1998: 35: "habitual liers-down, lazy-bones"; this could connote sexual behavior. Another alternative would be *muttellu* (< *ne'ellû*), referring, e.g., to people with compulsive movements; cf. *AHw* 690.

[k] This word, phonetically close to the preceding *upillû,* cannot be translated with certainty. *AHw* 57 connects it with *assinnu* and *kurgarrû,* and one is tempted to ask whether A.PIL could stand for the prophetic designation *āpilu;* in a Neo-Assyrian lexical list (no. 126) *apillû* is equated with lú-gub.ba, which usually stands for *maḫḫû.*

[l] Thus *CAD* Z 7.

## 130. Neo-Babylonian List of Temple Offerings

**Text:** OECT 1 20-21 (= W-B 10).
**Copy:** Langdon 1923: pl. 20–21.
**Discussion:** Holma 1944: 223–33.

### Lines r. 35–46

| | |
|---|---|
| [r. 35] *[ša] qāti 3 bīt ḫimēti 3 urīṣē kurummat šarri* | [For] disbursement: three butter containers and three young goats, the ration of the king. |
| [36] [. . .] *aḫu rabû* [37] [. . .] *ša qāti ṭupšar Eanna* | [. . .]: the high priest. [. . .] portion of the scribe of Eanna. |
| [38] [. . . *libb*]*ē maḫḫû* [39] [. . .] *imittu qaqqadāti libbu kurgarrû* | [38] [. . . heart]s (for) the prophet. [. . .] right shoulder, heads, flanks, heart (for) the man-woman. |
| [40] [. . . *gi*]*nê kalēti ṭābiḫu* | [. . . of regul]ar offerings, kidneys (for) the butcher. |
| [41] [. . . *ša*] *qāti sāḫirti 3 parrāti 3 unīqāti ša šatammi* | [41] [. . . For] disbursement: a heifer, three ewes and three she-goats, of the temple administrator. |
| [42] [. . .] *aḫu rabû* [43] [. . .] *libbē maḫḫû* [44] [. . .] *šīrē qaqqadāti aḫē libbu kurgarrû* | [. . .] the high priest. [. . .] hearts (for) the prophet. [. . .] cuts of meat, heads, flanks, heart (for) the man-woman. |
| [45] [. . .] *ginê kalēti ṭābiḫu* | [. . . of] regular offerings, kidneys (for) the butcher. |

46*[kīma labīrīšu šaṭir]ma bari nakkūr Eanna*

[Written according to the original] and collated. Property of Eanna.

## 131. Neo-Babylonian Decree of Redemption of an Estate

**Text:** YOS 6 18.
**Copy:** Dougherty 1920: pl. VI.
**Transliteration and translation:** San Nicolò 1947: 297–98.
**Discussion:** San Nicolò 1947: 297–99.

*[bīt] Šamaš-šuma-ukīn māršu ša Nabû-zēra-ukīn mār maḫḫê* 2*[ṭeḫi bī]t Marduk-ēṭir rabû* 3*[ṭeḫi bī]t Šulâ māršu ša Nergal-ušallim* 4*mār mandidi ša Gimillu māršu ša Aplāya* 5*mār Šumāti* MU.16.KAM *Nabû-kudurrī-uṣur* 6*šar Bābili bītu ina qāt Šamaš-šuma-ukīn* 7*māršu ša Nabû-zēra-ukīn mār maḫḫê imḫurūma* 8*Iltār-aḫa-iddina māršu ša Rēmūt-Bēl mār maḫḫê* 9*ana Gimillu ubaqqiru Iltār-aḫa-iddina* 10*māršu ša Rēmūt-Bēl mār maḫḫê* 11TÚG.KUR.RA *ittaktim u ina ṭuppi* 12*ša Gimillu māršu ša Aplāya* 13*mār Šumāti ana mukinnūtu ašib*

[The house] of Šamaš-šuma-ukin, son of Nabû-zera-ukin, descendant of Prophet, [adjacent to[a] the] big [hou]se of Marduk-iṭir, [adjacent to the hou]se of Šulâ, son of Nergal-ušallim, son of a meter inspector, the house that Gimillu, son of Aplaya, son of Šumati, bought from Šamaš-šuma-ukin, son of Nabû-zera-ukin, descendant of Prophet, in the sixteenth year[b] of Nebuchadnezar, king of Babylonia, 8for which Iltar-aḫa-iddina, son of Remut-Bel, descendant of Prophet, made a claim against Gimillu: Iltar-aḫa-iddina, son of Remut-Bel, descendant of Prophet, covered himself with a KUR.RA garment,[c] and stands as a witness in the matter of the tablet of Gimillu, son of Aplaya, son of Šumati, to be witnessed.

14*mukinnū Nabû-tabni-uṣur māršu ša Bēl-īpuš* 15*mār Sîn-tabni*
*Šamaš-erība māršu ša Nergal-iddina* 16*mār Sîn-tabni*
*Nabû-bēl-šumāti māršu ša* 17*Zēru-Bābili mār Sîn-tabni*
18*Ibni-Iltār māršu ša Nergal-īpuš mār Kurî*
19*Iltār-ina-tēšê-ēṭir māršu ša Aplāya mār Kurî*

14Witnesses: Nabû-tabni-uṣur, son of Bel-ipuš, descendant of Sin-tabni;
Šamaš-eriba, son of Nergal-iddina, descendant of Sin-tabni;
Nabû-bel-šumati, son of Zeru-Babili, descendant of Sin-tabni;
Ibni-Iltar, son of Nergal-ipuš, descendant of Kurî;
Iltar-ina-teše-eṭir, son of Aplaya, descendant of Kurî;

20 *ina ašābi ša Nanāya-bēl-bīti mārassu* 21 *ša Nanāya-īpuš alti Rēmūt-Bēl* 22 *ummi ša Iltār-aḫa-iddina ṭupšarru Nabû-šumu-imbi* 23 *[māršu] ša Taqīš-Gula mār Ḫanbu* 24 *[Uru]k Šabāṭu* UD.8.KAM MU.1.KAM 25 *[Nab]û-na'id šar Bābili*

26 *Nabû-ēṭir-napšāti māršu ša* 27 *Nabû-šumu-ukīn mār bā[ʾiri]*

20 in the presence of Nanaya-bel-biti, daughter of Nanaya-ipuš, wife of Remut-Bel, mother of Iltar-aha-iddina.

Scribe: Nabû-šumu-imbi, [son] of Taqiš-Gula, descendant of Ḫanbu.

24 In [Ur]uk, month Shebat (IX), eighth day, first year of [Nab]onidus, king of Babylonia.

Nabû-eṭir-napšati, son of Nabû-šuma-ukin, descendant of Fis[herman[d]].

[a] Restorations by San Nicolò 1947: 297.

[b] I.e., in the year 589/88.

[c] A garment of unspecified kind; cf. Borger 1957: 7.

[d] Hence the restoration of San Nicolò 1947: 298 n. 1 (ŠU.[HA]).

## 132. Neo-Babylonian Decree of Delivery of Dates

**Text:** YOS 7 135.
**Copy:** Tremayne 1925: pl. LIII.
**Discussion:** Cocquerillat 1968: 118.

[6]0 *kur suluppī imitti eqli* 2 *ša nār Aššurīti ša Bulluṭâ* 3 *makkūr Iltār (ša) Uruk u Nanāya* 4 *ša sūti ša Ardīya māršu ša Nabû-bāni-aḫi* 5 *mār Rēmūt-Ēa ina muḫḫi Bēlšunu māršu* 6 *ša Nūrê mār Šamaš-bāni-apli māršu ša Damiq-Bēl mār maḫḫê* 7 *u Ilu-dannu-aḫḫēšu-ibni māršu ša Nabû-lēʾi*

*ina Duʾūzi ina ḫaṣāri* 8 *ina mašīḫu ša Bēlet Uruk* 9 *ina muḫḫi iltēt ritti itti* (1 *kur*) 10 *bilti tuḫallu liblibbi* 11 *mangāga sūtu* 4.5 *qû kiṣir esitti* 12 *u balāṭi ana Bēl inamdinū*

Sixty[a] homers of dates, tax of the field of the Aššuritu canal[b] of Bulluṭâ, property of Ištar of Uruk and Nanaya, which constitute the rent due to Ardiya, son of Nabû-bani-aḫi, descendant of Remut-Ea, owed by Belšunu, son of Nurê, son of Šamaš-bani-apli, son of Damiq-Bel, descendant of Prophet, and Ilu-dannu-ahhešu-ibni, son of Nabû-leʾi.

7 They will give it in the month of Tammuz (IV), in the place of delivery, applying the measure of the Lady of Uruk, in a single delivery, giving together with each kor[c] (of dates) a talent (of spadices from date-palms), a basket, date-palm

fronds and fibers, as well as one seah 4.5 liters as a tenancy and trade tax[d] for Bel.

*iltēn pūt šanê našû*

12 Each one bears the responsibility for the other.[e]

*13 mukinnū Marduk-šuma-iddin māršu 14 ša Nadīnu mār Sutīya 15 Arad-Bēl māršu ša Nabû-mušētiq-urri mār Egībi*
*16 ṭupšarru Nabû-bēlšunu māršu ša Iltār-šuma-ēreš 17 mār Ēa-ilūtu-ibni*

13 Witnesses: Marduk-šuma-iddin, son of Nadinu, descendant of Sutiya; Arad-Bel, son of Nabû-mušetiq-urri, descendant of Egibi.

Scribe: Nabû-belšunu, son of Iltar-šuma-ereš, descendant of Ea-ilutu-ibni.

*Bīt-Rēš Elūlu* 18 UD.9.KAM MU.2.KAM *Kambusīya* 19 *šar Bābili šar mātāti*

Bit-Nabû, month Elul (VI), ninth day, second year of Cambyses (527), king of Babylon, king of the lands.

l.e. 20 8 *kur suluppī siss[innu]* 21 *eṭrū*

l.e. 20 They have been paid eight homers of dates and spa[dices].

[a] Thus according to the collation of Cocquerillat 1968: 118.

[b] One of the irrigation canals in the environs of Uruk; see the map in Cocquerillat 1968: pl. 3a/3b.

[c] Sign GUR, which belongs to the standard formula (see Cocquerillat 1968: 57) is missing from the original.

[d] Literally, "fee of mortar and living," see Landsberger 1967: 56.

[e] I.e., all persons involved are jointly responsible for the delivery.

## 133. Late Babylonian *ākītū* Ritual

**Text:** *RAcc* 129–146 (= DT 15 + DT 114 + DT 109 = *4 R* 40 1 + *4 R* 40 2 + *ABRT* I 1)
**Copy:** Thureau-Dangin 1912: 149-52.
**Transliteration and translation:** Thureau-Dangin 1912: 129–46.
**Discussion:** Harner 1969: 421–22; van der Toorn 1987: 93; 2000: 77.

### Lines 434–452 (= DT 114 r. v 1'–7' + DT 109 r. i 1–12):

*lā tapallaḫ* [. . .] 435 *ša Bēl iqṭabi* [. . .] 436 *Bēl ikribka* [*ilteme* . . .] 437 *ušarbi bēlūtka* [. . .] 438 *ušaqqa šarrūtka* [. . .] 439 *ina ūm eššēši epu*[*š* . . .] 440 *ina pīt bābi ubbib qāt*[*ka* ...] 441 *urri u mūši lū* [. . .] 442 *ša Bābili*

"Fear not! [. . .] what Bel has said [. . .] Bel [has heard] your prayer [. . .] He has enlarged your rule[a] [. . .] He will exalt your kingship [. . .]! 439 On the day of the *eššēšu* festival, do [. . .]! Upon the opening

*ālšu* [. . .] [443]*ša Esaggil bīss*[*u* . . .] [444]*ša mārē Bābili ṣāb kidin*[*nīšu* . . .] [445]*Bēl ikarrabku* [. . . *an*]*a dāri*[*š*] [446]*uḫallaq nakarku ušamqat zā-mânku*

of the gate, purify [your] hands [. . .]! May [. . .] day and night! [442][You], whose city Babylon is, [. . .], whose temple Esaggil is, [. . .], whose [. . .] the people of Babylon, the privileged citizens, are: [445]Bel will bless you [. . . fo]r eve[r]! He will destroy your enemy, he will annihilate your adversary!"

[447]*enūma iqbû šarru kabāt appi ginûšu i*[*ppuš*] [448]*ḫaṭṭa kippata miṭṭa agâ ušeṣṣima ana šarri* [*inamdin*] [449]*lēt šarri imaḫḫaṣ enūma lēssu* [*imḫaṣu*] [450]*šumma dimātūšu illik Bēl sal*[*im*] [451]*šumma dimātūšu lā illakā Bēl ezzi*[*z*] [452]*nakru itebbamma išakkan miqissu*

[447]When he[b] has spoken (this), the king p[erforms] his regular offering in a dignified manner.[c] He[d] brings out the scepter, the ring, the divine weapon and the crown and [gives] them to the king. [449]He slaps the face of the king. If, when he [slaps] his face, his[e] tears flow, Bel is favor[able]; if his tears do not flow, Bel is angr[y], and an enemy will rise and cause his downfall.

---

[a] Or, "he has made your lordship great."
[b] I.e., *šešgallu,* the high priest.
[c] Literally, "with a weighty nose"; cf. *AHw* 416 sub *kabātu* 5 f.
[d] I.e., the high priest.
[e] I.e., the king's.

## 134. Late Babylonian Chronographic Text (Tishri, 133 B.C.E., Version B)

**Text:** *AD* 3 -132 B (= BM 35070 + BM 45699).
**Photograph:** Sachs and Hunger 1996: pl. 220–21.
**Copy:** Pinches in Sachs and Hunger 1996: pl. 218–19.
**Transliteration and translation:** Sachs and Hunger 1996: 216–19; del Monte 1997: 123–26; Nissinen 2002a: 64–66.
**Discussion:** del Monte 1997: 126–27; Nissinen 2002a.

### Lines B r. 25–u. e. 5

*arḫu šuātu iltēn mār Mallāḫi ittaṣb*[*atamm*]*a* [26]*ṭēnzu išnima iltēn parakku birīt bīt Sîn bīt Egišnugal u abulli* [. . .] [27]*nadû*

In that month, a man belonging to the Boatman family[a] became s[eiz]ed and went into a frenzy.[b] [. . .] A dais that lies between the

*nindabû ana muḫḫi iškunma ṭēmu ṭābu ana nišī iqbi umma Bēl ana Bābili īrub* [*nišū*] [28]*zikarū u sinnišāti illikūnimma nindabû ana muḫḫi parakki šuāti iškunū ana tarṣa* [*p*]*arakki šuāti* [29]*īkulū ištû iḫammū iruššū* 2 *kulūlū ḫi-ba-ṣu-x-x ana parakki šu*[*āti*]

[30]UD.11.KÁM *x* 2 LÚ.X X.MEŠ *ṣīrūtu x x x x*.MEŠ *našûnimma x x*.MEŠ *ultu nišē* (?) *māti ana* [...] [*mār Mallāḫi*] [31]*ṭēmu ana nišī šunūtu iqbi um*<*ma*> *Nanāya ana Barsip ana Ezida īterub ḫanṭiš mār Mallāḫi šu*[*āti*] [32]*u nišū ša ittīšu ana Barsip illikūnimma mārē Barsip ana pānīšunu iḫtamû iḫtadû dalāti abulli* [33]*ana pānīšunu iptetû mār Mallāḫi u nišū* [...] [34]*īpulū umma* [d]*x* [...] [35]*kulūlū šuāti* [...] [36][...] *Nanāya* [...]

[lo. e. 2][...] [3][...] *x x x x ina narkabti iškunū mār Mallāḫi šuāti x x x x x* [4][...] *x x x ina Bābili Barsip u* X.MEŠ [...] [5][... *inn*]*ammir u rigimšu ina sūqāti u berēti išemmû* [6][...] *x x x x* [...]

[l. e. 1][*umma mār*] *šip*[*r*]*i ša Nanāya a*[*nāku*] *ana muḫḫi ilu dannu māḫiṣu ilīkunu šaprāku kiništ*[*u*] *bīt ilī šuāti ana mār* [*Mallāḫi* ...] [2]*īpulū iḫsā ana* [*arkī*]*kunu tūrā ana ālānīkunu ālu ana ḫubti u šillat lā tanamdā ilī kīma ālu šillat lā tušēṣâ* [......]

temple of Sîn, Egišnugal, and the gate [of *Marduk*[c]...]

[27]He placed a food offering upon it and delivered a good message to the people: "Bel has entered Babylon!" The [people], men and women alike, came and placed food offerings on that dais and, opposite to that dais, ate and drank, rejoiced[d] and made merry. Two *luxuriant*[e] crowns ... for th[at] dais.

[30]On the eleventh day, two high-ranking *persons* were brought ... and ... from the *people*[f] of the land to [... *Boatman*] delivered a message to these people: "Nanaya has entered Borsippa and Ezida!"[g] Instantly, th[at] Boatman and the people with him went to Borsippa. The citizens of Borsippa rejoiced[h] and exulted in their presence and opened *the doors of the city gate*[i] in front of them. Boatman and the people [...]. They answered: "The god ... these crowns ... [...] Nanaya [...]"

[lo. e. 1][......] placed [...] in a chariot. That Boatman [......] in Babylon and Borsippa and [... he ap]peared, on the streets and squares they listened to his proclamation[j] [......]

[l. e. 1]"[I am] a mes[senger][k] of Nanaya! I have been sent on behalf of the strong, hitting god,[l] your God."[m] The council of that temple responded to [that] Boatman [*and to the people with him*], saying: "Retreat back, return to your cities! Do not deliver up the city to loot and plunder! Do not let the gods like the city be carried off as spoils! [...]"

[3][. . .] *īpulšunūtu umma mār [šip]ri ša Nanāya anākūma ālu ana ḫubti u šillat ul anamdin kīma qāt ili dannu māḫiṣu ana Ezida* UR [. . .]

[3][*Boatman*] responded to them, saying: "I am a [mes]senger of Nanaya; I will not deliver up the city to loot and plunder! As the hand of the strong, hitting God [. . . s] to Ezida [. . .]"

[4][. . . *kiništu*] *bīt ilī šuāti ana nišī ša it*[*ti mār Mal*]*lāḫi šuāti īpulū ša amat šābibannu lā tašemmânu* [*šēzib*]*ā napšātīkunu* [5][*uṣr*]*ā ramānīkunu*[. . . . . .] *nišū šanūtu qabêšunu ul imḫurū x iqbû* u. e. *umma* [. . .] [2]*ana Ezida* [. . .] [3]*ilu dannu māḫiṣ*[*u* . . .] [4][. . .] *mār Mallāḫi* [. . .] *šuāt*[*i*. . .]
[remaining lines unintelligible]

[4]The council of that temple responded to the people who were wi[th] that [Boatman]: "Do not listen to the words of that fanatic![n] [*Save*] your lives, [*protect*] yourselves! [. . . . . .]" The other people did not take up their words but said: "[. . .] to Ezida [. . .] the strong, hitting God [. . .] Boatman [. . .] this [. . .]"
[rest too fragmentary for translation]

[a] The man in question is called *mār Mallāḫi*, indicating that he belongs to a family of "descendants of Boatman;" cf. the descendants of Prophet in nos. 131-132. This by no means indicates that he himself is a boatman, since the ancestral names are often derived from an occupation (cf. Frame 1992: 34).

[b] Literally, "changed his consciousness."

[c] The traces of the destroyed signs in Pinches' copy exclude the reading dAMAR.UD (Marduk), but may indicate another name of the Marduk gate; see del Monte 1997: 125 n. 224 and cf. no. 135, line 26.

[d] Derived from *hamû*, as equivalent to *hadû* "to rejoice."

[e] Possible reading: *ḫi-ba-ṣu-ú-tú*.

[f] Reading UN.MEŠ.

[g] Cf. the note concerning the preceding month (VI) in the same text (line 29): "In that month, (this message) was in the mouth of people big and small: 'Nanaya has entered Borsippa and Ezida!'"

[h] Cf. note d.

[i] Adopting the uncertain reading GIŠ.IG.MEŠ KÁ.GAL; cf. del Monte1997: 124 n. 223.

[j] Possible reading *ri-gim-šú*.

[k] Reading [*um-ma* LÚ.DUMU] *šip-*[*r*]*i šă na-na-a-a a-*[*na-ku*]; cf. line l.e. 3.

[l] The epithet *māḫiṣu* "hitting" may refer to the arrow-shooting god common in Mesopotamian iconography and appearing, e.g., in the winged disc. The verb *maḫāṣu* means, among other things, "to strike," i.e., with an arrow.

[m] The text has a plural "your gods," i.e., "the totality of your gods"; cf. Hebrew *ʾĕlōhêkem*.

[n] Or, "hothead." The word *šābibannu* is derived from *šababu* "to glow."

## 135. Late Babylonian Chronographic Text (Tishri, 133 B.C.E., Version C)

**Text:** *AD* 3 -132 C (=BM 47748 + BM 47885).
**Photograph:** Sachs and Hunger 1996: pl. 221.
**Transliteration and translation:** Sachs and Hunger 1996: 224–25; del Monte 1997: 127; Nissinen 2002a: 66–67.
**Discussion:** del Monte 1997: 126–27; Nissinen 2002a.

### Lines 26–33

[26]*arḫu šuātu iltēn mār Mallāḫi parakkū ina birit abulli Marduk u* [. . . [27]. . .] *sinnišāti ana libbi ipḫurā u kusāpu ina libbi īkulā*

UD.11.[KAM . . . [28]. . .] *ṣīrūtu ultu Bābili u ultu ālāni šanûtu u*[. . . [29]. . . *ul*]*tu Barsip mār Mallāḫi šuāti ina nišē ṣīr*[*ūti* ...]

[30][. . .].MEŠ *nišē ultu āli x x x x x x* [. . . [31]. . .]-*tu ina libbīšunu idūkū u* [. . . [32]. . .] *ina Bābili u Barsip* [. . . [33]. . . *šipi*]*štu ša a*[*na* . . .]

[rest destroyed]

In that month, a man belonging to the Boatman family [. . .] the daises between the gate of Marduk and [. . .] women assembled in it and ate bread there.

[27]On the eleventh day, [. . .] high-ranking [. . .]s from Babylon and from other cities and [. . .] from Borsippa. That Boatman with the high-rank[ing] people . . .

[30][......]s the people from the city [......] they killed in their midst and [. . .] in Babylon and Borsippa [... the mes]sage that [was to be sent] t[o . . .]

[rest destroyed]

# VII

# West Semitic Sources

**Choon-Leong Seow**

In comparison to the cuneiform sources, there are few West Semitic texts that contain prophecies or reference to prophets and their activities, and none of them is complete. Arguably the most important of these is the plaster inscription uncovered at Tell Deir ʿAllā in the eastern Jordan Valley. Despite its fragmentary nature, it is clear that the inscription (no. 138) describes the visionary experience of the "seer" (*ḥzh,* corresponding to Heb. *ḥōzeh*), Balaam son of Beor, who is also known in the Bible (Num 22–24). Like the biblical prophets, the seer is given access to deliberations in the divine council, where a decision is made to bring about an eschatological catastrophe, and one of their members is dispatched to carry out the plan. Also fragmentary is an Ammonite inscription (no. 136) that records a prophetic oracle delivered to the king in the name of Milcom, the patron god of the Ammonites. The oracle bears some semblance to the genre of "salvation oracles" known from the Bible and elsewhere in the ancient Near East. Elements of such "salvation oracles" are also evident in the Aramaic Stela of Zakkur, king of Hamath—oracles that were delivered by prophetic figures known as *ḥzyn* (the Aramaic equivalent of Hebrew *ḥōzîm* "seers") and *ʿddn* "visionaries." Two Hebrew letters from Lachish (nos. 139, 141) mention prophets and their activities, thus providing a glimpse into their influence in the Judahite sociopolitical arena on the eve of the destruction of Jerusalem in the sixth century B.C.E. A third letter from the same group (no. 140) is included in this corpus because it is often thought to contain a reference to "the prophet" and, more importantly, because it gives some indication of the kinds of impact that prophetic utterances might have had in Judah. Apart from these six texts, there are no other West Semitic inscriptions that indisputably concern prophets and their activities.

## 136. Amman Citadel Inscription

This inscription, discovered in the Iron Age level of Jebel ed-Dalaʿah (ancient Rabbath-Ammon, the capital of the Ammonite kingdom), is dated on paleographic grounds to the ninth century B.C.E. It is fragmentary, being broken off at least on its left and right sides (and possibly also the bottom), so that it is unclear just how much of the original inscription has been lost. Nevertheless, it is evident from the extant portion that the inscription contains an oracle delivered in the name of Milcom, the patron deity of the Ammonites, presumably to the king who erected the commemorative monument of which the inscription is a part. The fragmentary text apparently records a word of divine assurance, no doubt delivered by a human intermediary, for the king's victory over his enemies. Elements of the text are reminiscent of the "salvation oracles" found in other ancient Near Eastern prophetic texts.

**Text:** Horn 1969: 8; Kutscher 1972: 27; Puech and Rofé 1973: 532; Aḥituv 1992: 219.
**Photograph:** Horn 1969: 3; Puech and Rofé 1973: 536– 37; Shea 1979: 18–19; Aḥituv 1992: 221.
**Copy:** Horn 1969: 5; Kutscher 1972: 27; Puech and Rofé 1973: 533; Fulco 1978: 40.
**Transliteration and translation:** Cross 1969: 17–19; Albright 1970: 38; Dion 1975: 32–33; Van Selms 1975: 5, 8; Fulco 1978: 39–41; V. Sasson 1979: 118; Shea 1979: 17–18; 1981: 105; Jackson 1983: 10; Aufrecht 1989: 155; Margalit 1995b: 201; 1998: 530–31; Lemaire 1997: 180.
**Translation:** Horn 1969: 8; Kutscher 1972: 27; Puech and Rofé 1973: 534; Aḥituv 1992: 219; Aufrecht 2000: 139.
**Discussion:** Cross 1969: 13–19; Horn 1969: 2–13; Albright 1970: 38–40; Kutscher 1972: 27–28; Puech and Rofé 1973: 531–46; Dion 1975: 24–33; Van Selms 1975: 5–8; Fulco 1978: 39–43; V. Sasson 1979: 117–25; Shea 1979: 18–25; 1981: 105–10; Jackson 1983: 9–33; Aufrecht 1989: 154–63; Aḥituv 1992: 219–23; Margalit 1995b: 200–210; 1998: 515–32; Lemaire 1997: 180–81; Aufrecht 2000: 139.

1. *m]lkm . bnh . lk . mbʾt sbbt[*
2. *] . kkl . msbb . ʿlk*[a] *. mt ymtn[*
3. *] kḥd . ʾkḥd [.] wkl . mʿr [.] b[*[b]
4. *] wbkl . s[d] rt ylnn ṣdq[m*
5. *d]l . tdl< > bdlt . bṭn kbh [tkbh*
6. *]h . tštʿ . bbn . ʾlm [*
7. *]wšlwh . wn[*
8. *š] lm . lk . wš[*

1. ] Milcom:[c] "Build entrances round about [
2. ] for all who besiege you shall surely die [
3. ] I will utterly annihilate, and anyone who agitates against [
4. ] but among all the columns, the legitimate ones will lodge [
5. ] you shall indeed hang on the innermost door.[d] You shall indeed [extinguish
6. ] you shall be feared among the gods.[e] [
7. ] and security and . . . [
8. ] peace to you and . . . [

[a] What immediately precedes *lk* is a matter of debate. There is a circle, which some take to be merely a chip in the stone. Fulco, who worked directly with the fragment, judges that it is "definitely" an *ʿayin* (1978: 41), and I accept that view. The *ʿayin* is here admittedly smaller than other *ʿayin*s in the inscription, yet there is no consistency in the sizes of letters in this inscription. In any case, *ʿl* is often used to indicate the object of the verb *sbb* (see Job 16:13; Judg 20:5; 2 Chr 18:31).

[b] This reading essentially follows Cross (1969: 17). Horn in the *editio princeps* (1969: 10–11), however, reads *mʿrb,* prompting Shea (1979: 24) to imagine troublesome Israelites coming "from the west."

[c] One may presume that the deity's name is cited in some formula introducing the oracle: "thus says Milcom," "oracle of Milcom," "word of Milcom," or the like.

[d] The sequence of letters—*l.tdlt bdlt*—is universally seen to be erroneous in some way. I assume that the final letter in *tdlt* is extraneous and propose that the word in question here is a verb from the root *dll* (to dangle).

[e] If the second-person subject is Milcom, the expression *bbn ʾlm* must mean "among the gods." If, however, the subject is the king, then one might interpret the *bn ʾlm* to refer to military rulers (compare Exod 15:5).

## 137. Zakkur Stela

This Aramaic inscription appears on three sides of the base of a stela that was found at Tell Afis (ancient Apish), some twenty-five miles southwest of Aleppo. A depiction of a god, presumably Iluwer (the patron deity of Apish), was originally set atop the base, but most of it has not survived. The inscription begins on the front face (A) and continues on the left side (B), which is, however, broken off so that about thirty lines of the inscription are missing. The right face (C) preserves only two lines, again with about thirty lines missing.

The monument was apparently commissioned by Zakkur, a usurper of the throne of the cities of Hamath and Luash in Syria. Ostensibly erected in honor of Iluwer, the stela celebrates Zakkur's victory over a coalition of Aramean and Anatolian states led by Bir-Hadad III of Damascus in the early eighth century B.C.E. Apart from its value for the reconstruction of the history of that region, this inscription provides a glimpse into the role of prophecy in ancient Syria. Threatened by hostile forces, Zakkur prayed to Baalshamayn ("the Lord of Heaven"), the patron deity of Hamath, and he claimed to have received a divine response through *ḥzyn* "seers" (A.12; biblical *ḥōzîm*) and divine intermediaries known as *ʿddn* "visionaries" (A.12).[a] The prophetic word includes elements reminiscent of the "salvation oracles" attested elsewhere in the ancient Near East.

**Text:** Pognon 1907: 173–75; Halévy 1908: 363–64, 366, 367, 370; Montgomery 1909: 58; Torrey 1915–17: 354–55; Ross 1970: 2; Tawil 1974: 51.
**Translation:** Pognon 1907: 175–76; Halévy 1908: 364–67, 370–71; Torrey 1915–17: 356–57; Black 1958: 246–47; Ross 1970: 3; Lipiński 1975: 22–23; Millard 1990: 273–74; Parker 1997: 107; Lemaire 2001: 94.
**Discussion:** Pognon 1907: 156–78; Halévy 1908: 357–76; Montgomery 1909: 57–70; Torrey 1915–17: 353–64; Black 1958: 242–50; Greenfield 1969: 174–91; 1987: 67–78; Jepsen 1969: 1–2; Ross 1970: 1–28; Zobel 1971: 91–99; Tawil 1974: 51–57; Lipiński 1975: 19–23; Millard 1989: 47–52; 1990: 261–75; Lemaire 1997: 184–86; 2001: 93–96; Parker 1997: 105–12; Nissinen 2000a: 264–65.

### A. Front

1. *[n]ṣbʾ . zy . šm . zkr . mlk [. ḥ]m[t] . wlʿš . lʾlwr [. ʾlh]*
2. *[ʾ]nh . zkr . mlk [.] ḥm[t] . wlʿš . ʾš . ʿnh . ʾnh . w[hwšʿ]*
3. *[n]y . bʿlšmyn . wqm [.] ʿmy . whmlkny . bʿlšm[yn . ʿl]*
4. *[ḥ]zrk . whwḥd . ʿly . brhdd . br . ḥzʾl . mlk . ʾrm . š*
5. *[bʿ] . ʿšr . mlk[n .] brhdd . wmḥnth . wbrgš . wmḥnth . w[m]*
6. *[lk . ] qwh . wmḥnth . wmlk . ʿmq . wmḥnth . wmlk . grg[m .]*
7. *[wmḥ]nth [.] wmlk . śmʾl . wm[ḥ]n[t]h . wmlk . mlz [. wm]ḥ[nth . wmlk]*
8. *[ . wmḥnth . wmlk . . w]m[ḥ]nt[h .] wšbʿ[t . ʿšr ]*
9. *[h]mw . wmḥnwt . hm . wśmw . kl [.] mlkyʾ [.] ʾl . mṣr . ʿl . ḥzr[k .]*
10. *whrmw . šr . mn [.] šr . ḥzr[k .] whʿmqw . ḥrṣ . mn . ḥr[ṣh .]*
11. *wʾśʾ . ydy . ʾl [.] bʿlš[my]n . wyʿnny [.] bʿlšmy[n . wym]*
12. *[ll ] . bʿlšmyn [.] ʾly . [b]yd . ḥzyn . wbyd . ʿddn [. wyʾm]*
13. *[r .] bʿlšmyn . ʾl [.] t[z]ḥl . ky . ʾnh . hml[ktk . wʾnh . ʾ]*
14. *[q]m . ʿm[k] . wʾnh [.] ʾḥṣlk . mn [.] kl . [mlkyʾ . ʾl . zy .]*
15. *mḥʾw . ʿlyk . mṣr [.] wyʾmr . l[y . bʿlšmyn . ]*
16. *[k]l [.] mlkyʾ . ʾl . zy . mḥʾw [. ʿlyk . mṣr . ]*
17. *[ .] wšwrʾ . znh . z[y . ]*

### B. Left

[Approximately thirty lines missing at the top.]
1. [ ] *ḥzrk* [.] *q*[ ]

2. [ ] *lrkb . [w]lprš .*
3. [ ] *mlkh . bgwh . ʾn*
4. [*h . bny*]*t . ḥzrk . whwsp*
5. [*t . lh*] *. ʾy*[*t .*] *kl mḥgt* [.]
6. [ ]ʾ *. wś*[*mt*]*h* [.] *mlk*[*t*]
7. [*y .* ]*th . ʾ*[ ]
8. [.] *ḥsnyʾ . ʾl* [.] *bkl . gb*[*l*]
9. [*y . wb*]*nyt* [.] *bty . ʾlhn . bk*[*l*]
10. [*gbl*]*y . wbnyt . ʾyt* [. ]
11. [ ʾ]*yt* [.] *ʾpš . w*[ ]
12. [ ]*yʾ* [.] *byt* [. ]
13. [ *w*]*śmt . qd*[*m . ʾl*]
14. [*wr .*] *nṣbʾ* [.] *znh . wk*[*tb*]
15. [*t . b*]*h . ʾyt* [.] *ʾšr . ydy* [*. wk*]
16. [*l .*] *mn . yhgʿ . ʾyt* [.] *ʾ*[*šr .*]
17. [*ydy .*] *zkr . mlk . ḥm*[*t . wl*]
18. *ʿš* [.] *mn . nṣbʾ* [.] *znh* [.] *wm*[*n .*]
19. [*y*]*hgʿ . nṣbʾ . znh . mn .* [*q*]
20. [*d*]*m . ʾlwr . wyhnsnh . m*
21. [*n . ʾš*]*rh . ʾw . mn* [.] *yšlḥ . b*
22. [ ]*th*[ ]
23. [ *. bʿ*]*lšmyn . wʾ*[*l*]
24. [*wr . w .*] *wšmš* [.] *wšhr* [.]
25. [ ]*. wʾl*[*hy .*] *šmy*[*n .*]
26. [*wʾlh*]*y . ʾrq* [.] *wbʿl* [.] *ʿ*
27. [ ] *ʾšʾ* [.] *wʾyt* [. ]
28. [ ]*š* [.] *šh .*

### C. Right

[Approximately thirty lines missing at the top.]
1. [ ]
2. [ .] *šm* [*. z*]*k*[*r .*] *wšm* [*. brh*]

### A. Front

1. The [st]ela that Zakkur, king of [Ha]ma[th] and Luash, set up for Iluwer, [his god.]
2. [I] am Zakkur, king of Hama[th] and Luash. I am a humble man, but
3. Baalshamayn [gave] me [victory] and stood with me. Baalsham[ayn] made me king [over]
4. [Ha]zrak.[b] Then Bir-Hadad the son of Hazael, the king of Aram, formed an alliance against me of

5. sev[en]teen king[s]: Bir-Hadad and his army, Bir-Gush and his army,
6. [the king] of Kue and his army, the king of Umq and his army, the king of Gurg[um
7. and] his [arm]y, the king of Samʾal and his army, the king of Miliz [and his army, the king of]
8. [. . . and his army, the king of . . . and his army—that is, seve[nteen]
9. of them with their armies. All these kings set up a siege against Hazr[ak].
10. They raised a wall higher than the wall of Hazr[ak]. They dug a moat deeper than [its] moa[t].
11. But I lifted my hands to Baalshamayn, and Baalshamay[n] answered me, [and]
12. Baalshamayn [spoke] to me [thr]ough seers and through visionaries, [and]
13. Baalshamayn [said], "F[e]ar not, for I have made [you] king, [and I who will
14. st]and with [you], and I will deliver you from all [these kings who]
15. have forced a siege against you!" Then Baalshamayn said to m[e . . . " ]
16. [a]ll these kings who have forced [a siege against you . . . ]
17. [ ] and this wall whi[ch . . . ]

**B. Left**

[Approximately thirty lines missing.]
1. [ ] Hazrak . . . [ ]
2. [ ] for the chariotry [and] the cavalry
3. [ ] its king in its midst. I
4. [built] Hazrak, and [I] added
5. [to it] the entire region of
6. [ ] and [I] es[tablish]ed [my] reign
7. [ ] . . . [ ]
8. these strongholds throughout [my] territ[ory].
9. [Then I reb]uilt the temples of the gods in a[ll]
10. my [territory], and I rebuilt [ ]
11. Apish and [ ]
12. [ ] . . . the temple of [ ]
13. [And] I set up befo[re Iluwer]
14. this stela, and [I] ins[cribed]
15. [on] it the accomplishment of my hands. [Anyone at all]
16. who removes the acc[omplishment of
17. the hands of] Zakkur, king of Hama[th and Lu]ash,
18. from this stela, and whoe[ver]
19. [re]moves this stela from

20. [befo]re Iluwer and takes it away fr[om]
21. its [pla]ce, or whosoever sends ...
22. [ ] ... [ ]
23. [ Baa]lshamayn and I[luwer ... ]
24. and Shamash and Shahar
25. [ ] and the go[ds] of heave[n]
26. [and the god]s of the earth and Baal ...
27. [ ] the man and [ ]
28. [ ] ....

### C. Right

[Approximately thirty lines missing at the top.]
1. [ ]
2. [ ] the name of [Za]kkur and the name of [his son ... ]

[a] The first of these terms corresponds with Biblical Hebrew *ḥōzeh* (pl. *ḥōzîm*), a term used of prophets as seers of visions (2 Kgs 17:13; Isa 28:15; Amos 7:12; etc.). The latter term is attested in Ugaritic ("herald") but not in Hebrew, although it may be related to the noun *ʿēd* "witness." See Lemaire 2001: 95.

[b] Biblical "Hadrach" (Zech 9:1); Assyrian "Hatarika."

## 138. Deir ʿAllā Plaster Texts

Found at Tell Deir ʿAllā, near the River Zerqa (biblical Jabbok) in the eastern Jordan Valley, these texts were apparently once displayed in a room of a building that is commonly believed to have been a sanctuary. Written in black and red ink on white plaster, fragments of the texts were found on the floor of that room when the building was destroyed by a violent earthquake—one of the many that plagued the region. As a result of that disaster, part of the plaster was burnt and the entire inscription fell to the ground, shattered in pieces, much of which was irretrievably lost. The fragments that remain were found in several groupings. J. Hoftijzer and G. van der Kooij, who were responsible for the *editio princeps* published in 1976, treated the two largest groupings (which they called "combinations") in considerable detail, but others have subsequently realigned the texts and succeeded in placing several other fragments, the most recent being the attempt of E. Lipiński in 1994. The texts have been dated to the eighth century B.C.E. on archaeological and paleographic grounds, as well as on the basis of radiocarbon testing. The inscription is clearly written in a Northwest Semitic language, but more precise classification of that language has eluded scholars. All in all, it appears to be a local Transjordanian dialect, with some features akin to Aramaic but other features closer to Hebrew and other "Canaanite" dialects.

Combination I clearly concerns the vision of Balaam son of Beor, "a seer of the gods," who is also known in the biblical tradition recorded in Num 22–24. Like the prophets of ancient Israel, Balaam in this account is privy to the deliberations of the divine council. The assembled deities—known in the account alternatively as "gods" and "Shaddayin" (a term related to the biblical divine epithet "Shaddai")—have ordained a catastrophe, and they charge a certain celestial being to execute the destruction on their behalf. Unfortunately, only the first letter of her name has been preserved (line 6), so her identity can only be a matter of conjecture. Like the deceiving spirit sent forth from the divine council witnessed by the prophet Micaiah the son on Imlah (1 Kgs 22:5-18) and like the adversary in the divine council who was permitted by God to set forth to harm Job (Job 1:6–12; 2:1–8), she plays a destructive role. The impending doom that she is to bring about is in many ways reminiscent of end-of-the-world scenarios that are often found in the Bible, notably in the preaching of the prophets. Creation will apparently be undone as the cosmic floods will be released upon the earth ("the bolts of heaven" will be broken), the dark rain clouds will cover the skies, and there will be pitch darkness and terror on earth. The second half of Combination I is exceedingly difficult, in large part because of the fragmentary nature of the text. Still, the scene described seems consonant with other depictions of divinely ordained catastrophes. The world is turned upside down as creatures of the earth act contrary to their nature. The mention of a number of unsavory creatures also echoes the oracles of doom in biblical prophetic eschatology.

Combination II is even more difficult to interpret. Its relationship to Combination I is by no means clear. Some scholars maintain that Combination II is somehow sequential to Combination I, in particular, that the two combinations may have represented the beginning and the end of the text, whether originally in a single column or in two columns. But others have denied that the two are related to one another in content, arguing that Combination II has nothing at all to do with the vision of Balaam son of Beor. However, there are clues within Combination II itself that suggest it has to do with prophecy, specifically, the mention of a "vision" (line 16). The allusion to the failure of someone (perhaps the king?) to seek counsel and advice (line 9) is also tantalizing, as is the invitation in line 17: "Come, let us judge and give a verdict."

**Photograph:** Hoftijzer 1976: 14; Hoftijzer and van der Kooij 1976: plates 1–15; Lemaire 1985a: 29, 32–33; Hackett 1986: 218, 221.

**Copy:** Hoftijzer and van der Kooij 1976: plates 23, 29–33; Weippert and Weippert 1982: 80; Lemaire 1985a: 33–34; 1985b: 319; 1985c: 278; Puech 1987: 16; Lipiński 1994: 114, 140.
**Transliteration and translation:** Hoftijzer and van der Kooij 1976: 173–82; Caquot and Lemaire 1977: 194–202; Garbini 1979: 171–72, 185–88; McCarter 1980: 51–52; Levine 1981: 196–97, 200–201; 1991: 61, 71; Weippert and Weippert 1982: 83, 103; Hackett 1984: 25–26, 29–30; 1986: 220; Lemaire 1985b: 318; 1997: 189–90; V. Sasson 1985: 103; 1986a: 287–89; 1986b: 149; Puech 1987: 17, 26–28; Wesselius 1987: 593–94; Weippert 1991: 153–58; Lipiński 1994: 115–17, 141–43; Dijkstra 1995: 47–51; Margalit 1995a: 282, 284–89.
**Transliteration:** Lemaire 1985c: 276–77, 280–81.
**Translation:** Ringgren 1983: 93–95; Smelik 1991: 83–84; Lemaire 2001: 97–98.
**Discussion:** Hoftijzer and van der Kooij 1976; Caquot and Lemaire 1977: 189–208; Garbini 1979: 166–88; McCarter 1980: 49–60; Delcor 1981: 52–73; 1989: 33–40; Levine 1981: 195–205; 1991: 58–72; Müller 1982: 56–67; 1978: 56–67; 1991: 185–205; Weippert and Weippert 1982: 77–103; Ringgren 1983: 93–98; Hackett 1984; 1986: 216–22; Lemaire 1985a: 26–39; 1985b: 313–25; 1985c: 270–85; 1997: 188–92; 2001: 96–101; V. Sasson 1985: 102–3; 1986a: 283–309; 1986b: 147–54; Puech 1986: 36–38; 1987: 13–30; Coogan 1987: 115–18; Wesselius 1987: 589–99; Hoftijzer 1991: 121–42; 1976: 11–17; Smelik 1991: 79–92; Weippert 1991: 151–84; Lipiński 1994: 103–70; Dijkstra 1995: 43–64; Margalit 1995a: 282–302; Nissinen 2002b: 6–7.

## Combination I

1. *ysr* [.] *spr* [. *blʿm* . *br bʿ*]*r* . *ʾl* . *ḥzh* . *ʾlhn* [.] *hʾ* [.] *wyʾtw* . *ʾlwh* . *ʾlhn* . *blylh* [. *wydbrw* . *l*]*h*
2. *km*[*ś*]*ʾ* . *ʾl* . *wyʾmrw* . *lb*[*lʿ*]*m* . *br bʿr* . *kh* . *ypʿl*[ ]*ʾ* . *ʾḥrʾh* . *ʾš* . *lr*[*ʾh* ]*ʿt*
3. *wyqm* . *blʿm mn* . *mḥr* . [*rph* .] *yd* . [*šp*]*l* . *ymn* . *w*[*ṣm* . *yṣm*. ] *lḥdrh* . *wlykl* [. *lyš*]*n* . *wbk*
4. *h* . *ybkh* . *wyʿl* . *ʿmh* . *ʾlwh* . *wy*[*ʾmrw* .] *lblʿm* . *br bʿr* . *lm* . *tṣm* [. *wl*]*m* . *tbkh* . *wyʾ*
5. *mr* . *lhm* . *šbw* . *ʾḥwkm* . *mh* . *šd*[*yn* . *pʿlw* .] *wlkw* . *rʾw* . *pʿlt* . *ʾlhn* . *ʾl*[*h*]*n* . *ʾtyḥdw*
6. *wnṣbw* . *šdyn* . *mwʿd* . *wʾmrw* . *lš*[ ] *tpry* . *skry* . *šmyn* . *bʿbky* . *šm* . *ḥšk* . *wʾl* . *n*
7. *gh* . *ʿṭm* . *wʾl* . *smrky* . *thby* . *ḥt* [. *bʿ*]*b* . *ḥšk* . *wʾl* [.] *thgy* . *ʿd* . *ʿlm* . *ky* . *ss ʿgr* . *ḥr*
8. *pt* . *nšr* . *wql* . *rḥmn* . *yʿnh* . *ḥ*[ ] *bny* . *nḥṣ* . *wṣrh* . *ʾprḥy* . *ʾnph* . *drr* . *nšrt* .

9. *ywn . wṣpr [ ]yn . w[bʾšr . yybl] . mṭh . bʾšr . rḥln . yybl . ḥṭr . ʾrnbn . ʾklw .*
10. *[ ]b . ḥpš[n . b]nzyt . ʾt[rwyw . ] štyw . ḥmr . wqbʿn . šmʿw . mwsr [.] gry . š*
11. *ʿ[l . ] ḥbṣn . hlkw . b[ ]l . ḥkmn . yqḥk . wʿnyh . rqḥt . mr . wkhnh .*
12. *[ ]tḥ[ ]lḥl[ ]lnšʾ . ʾzr . qrn . ḥšb . ḥšb . wḥšb . ḥ*
13. *[šb ]*
*wšmʿw . ḥršn . mn rḥq*
14. *[ ]wkl .*
*ḥzw . qqn . šgr . wʿštr . l*
15. *[ ]lnmr . ḥnyṣ*
*. hqrqt . bn*
16. *[y ]šn .*
*ʾ[ ]rn . wʿyn*

## Combination II

1. *[ ]*
2. *h.lš[ ]*
3. *rn . ʾkl[ byt]*
4. *ʿlmh . rwy . ddn . k[ ]*
5. *lh . lm . nqr . wmdr . kl . rṭb[ ]*
6. *yrwy . ʾl . yʿbr . ʾl . byt . ʿlmn . by[t ]*
7. *byt . lyʿl . hlk . wlyʿl . ḥtn . šm . byt[ ]*
8. *wrmh . mn . gdš . mn . pḥzy . bny . ʾš . wmn . šqy[ ]*
9. *[ ]ly . hlʿṣh . bk . lytʿṣ . ʾw lmlkh . lytmlk . yšb . [ ]*
10. *n . mš[ ]bn . tksn . lbš . ḥd . hn . tšnʾn . yʾnš . hn . t[ ]*
11. *ʾšm [ ]h . tḥt . rʾšk . tškb . mškby . ʿlmyk . lḥlq . ld[ ]*
12. *ʾh[ ]rk[ ]h . blbbm . nʾnḥ . nqr . blbbh . nʾnḥ . [ ]*
13. *bt . šmh . mlkn . yḥ[b]r . b[ ]t . lyšbm [.] yqḥ . mwt . ʿl . rḥm . wʿl[ ]*
14. *[ ]ʿl[ ]br . [ ]šmh . kbr . [ ]ḥ . y[ ] . lbb . nqr . šhh . ky . ʾth . l[ ]*
15. *lqṣh . šnt . h[ ]. wzlp . gdr [.] ṭš [. ]šʾlt . mlk . ssh . wš[ʾ]l[th ]*
16. *h . [ ]ḥzn . rḥq[ ʿ] mk . šʾltk . lm[ ]*
17. *ldʿt . spr . dbr . lʿmh . ʿl . lšn . lk . nšpṭ . wnlqh . ʾmr[ ]*
18. *wʿnšty . lmlk [ ]*

## Combination I

1. The warning of the Book of [Balaam, son of Beo]r, who was a seer of the gods. The gods came to him at night [and spoke to] him
2. according to the ora[cle] of El. They said to Ba[la]am, son of Beor, "Thus will [ ] do hereafter. No one [has seen ] ...
3. When Balaam arose on the morrow, (his) hand [was slack], (his) right

hand [hung] low. [He fasted continually] in his chamber, he could not [sleep], and he wept

4. continually. Then his people came up to him and [they said] to Balaam, son of Beor: "Why do you fast [and w]hy do you weep?" He
5. said to them: "Sit down and I shall tell you what the Shadda[yin have done]; come, see the acts of the gods! The gods gathered together;
6. the Shaddayin took their places in the assembly. And they said to the . . . [ ]:[a] "May you break the bolts of heaven, with your rain-cloud bringing about darkness and not
7. light, eeriness[b] and not your brightness.[c] May you bring terror [through the] dark [rain-clo]ud. May you never again be aglow.[d] For the *ssʿgr*(-bird) taunts
8. the eagle and the voice of the vultures resounds. . . . the young of the *nḥṣ*(-bird) and one rips the young of cormorants. The swallow mangles
9. the dove and the sparrow [ ] and [instead of ] it is the staff [that is led]; instead of ewes it is the rod that is led. The hares eat
10. [ ] the serf[s] are fi[lled with] beer, the [ ] are drunk with wine. Hyenas heed instruction; the whelps of
11. the fox [ ]. Multitudes go with [ ] laughs at the wise. The songstress mixes myrrh, while the priestess
12. [ ] to the one who wears a tattered girdle. The one who is esteemed esteems, and the one who esteems is esteemed.[e]
13. [ ] and the deaf hear from afar
14. [ ] and all see oppression of Shagar-wa-Ashtar . . .
15. [ ] to the leopard; the piglet chases the young
16. [of ] . . . and the eye

## Combination II

1. [ ]
2. . . . [ ]
3. . . . ate [ ]
4. his eternal [domicile], he fills with love like [ ]
5. to him/her, "Why are the sprout and the soil containing the moisture [ ]
6. El will be filled. Let him cross over to the eternal domicile, the house [ ]
7. the house where one who goes will not enter, and the bridegroom will not enter there, the house [ ]
8. and the vermin from the tomb, from the thighs of men and from the legs of [ ]

9. [ ] has he not sought counsel from you, or has he not sought the advice of one who sits [ ]
10. ....you will cover with a single garment. If you hate him, he will be weak, if you [ ]
11. I will put [ ] under your head. You will lie down on your eternal bed to be destroyed [ ]
12. ....[ ] in their heart. The scion sighs to himself, he sighs [ ]
13. ... his name. Our king will join with [ ] he will not bring them back. Death will take the suckling of the womb and the suckling of [ ]
14. [ ] suckling [ ] his mighty name [ ] the heart of the scion is weak, even though he has come to [ ]
15. at the end of the year [ ] and he who approaches[f] the plastered wall [ ] the request of the king for his horse, and his request [ ]
16. [ ] a distant vision [ ] your [peo]ple. Your request for ...[ ]
17. to know the account that he spoke to his people orally. Come let us judge and give verdict. Say [ ]
18. I have punished the king [ ]

[a] Only the first letter of the divine name is preserved. Scholars usually restore the name Shamash (corresponding to the sun-goddess Shapshu in Ugaritic) or Shagar (presumably a short form of Shagar-wa-Ashtar in line 14). Less plausibly, the city name Shomeron (Samaria) has been proposed.

[b] Assuming a relation to Akkadian *eṭemmu*.

[c] Cf. Arabic *samaru* (used of the radiance of the moon), but also Akkadian *samaru,* a term used of ornaments.

[d] Cf. Arabic *wahaja* (to glow, glisten).

[e] I am at a loss here and simply follow McCarter's conjecture.

[f] Assuming the G participle form of the root *zlp,* attested in Arabic with the meaning "to approach, draw near."

## 139. Lachish Ostracon 3

Among the important finds discovered at Tell ed-Duweir (ancient Lachish) are a group of over thirty Hebrew inscriptions, twelve of which are letters written in ink on ostraca (potsherds) from the last days of Judah in the sixth century B.C.E. The fortress was destroyed by Nebuchadnezzar's Babylonian army in 586, and these letters represent the desperate military communication around that strategic stronghold before its collapse.

Ostracon 3 originates from a certain Hoshaiah, a junior officer at an unknown outpost, to Yaush, the military commander at Lachish. The former wrote in response to an earlier communication from his superior, who, dissatisfied with Hoshaiah's failure to comply satisfactorily with an order, apparently suggested that if Hoshaiah could not read, then he should get a scribe to do so for him. After a fairly typical epistolary introduction, Hoshaiah indignantly protests the implication that he might be illiterate. Then he gets to the substance of his communiqué, namely, the transfer of a detachment under his command and the status of a report about an oracle by "the prophet" (*hnbʾ*). Through the messengers who had come to effect the transfer, Hoshaiah learns that Coniah son of Elnathan, the commander of the army, had gone down to Egypt. Some scholars have read this mission to Egypt in light of the relations between the kingdom of Judah and Egypt at this time (see Jer 37:7; Ezek 17:15) and have occasionally cited the Aramaic papyrus of Saqqara as a parallel example of a message that might have been relayed to the pharaoh of Egypt by the group referred to in this letter. Moreover, it appears that Tobiah, a high official in the royal palace in Jerusalem, had issued a report of an oracle by the unnamed prophet that began—as many oracles recorded in the Bible do—with the word: "Beware!" The identity of this unnamed prophet has been the subject of a great deal of speculation. Jeremiah, who was active at the time, has often been suggested. However, there were many other prophets active in Jerusalem, some supportive of Jeremiah's message (e.g., Uriah, Jer 26:20–24) and some in direct opposition to it (e.g., Hananiah, Jer 28:1). In any case, one may deduce that the identity of the prophet must have been known to Yaush, since Hoshaiah uses the definite article: "the prophet." The allusion to the prophet's message is frustratingly laconic. One knows nothing about its content beyond its first word. It is not even clear at whom the oracle was directed. Nevertheless, it is evident the message was of grave concern to the military establishment, perhaps because they feared that it might have a demoralizing effect on the citizenry.

**Text:** Dussaud 1938: 263–66; Dupont-Sommer 1948: 44; Thomas 1948: 131; de Vaux 1967: 465–66; Cassuto 1975: 230–31; Aḥituv 1992: 36; Barstad 1993b: 8*; Renz and Röllig 1995: 416–19.
**Photograph:** Dupont-Sommer 1948: 68; Aḥituv 1992: 38–39.
**Copy:** Cross 1985: 44; Smelik 1991: 122.
**Transliteration and translation:** Albright 1939: 17–19; 1941: 19; Michaud 1941: 48; Pardee 1982: 84–85; Cross 1985: 41–43; Smelik 1990: 133, 135–36; Parker 1994: 69.
**Transliteration:** Richter 1987: 74–75.
**Translation:** Albright 1936b: 12–13; 1938: 13; 1941: 20–21; Dussaud 1938: 263–65, 267; Dupont-Sommer 1948: 44–45; Thomas 1948: 131; de Vaux 1967: 466; Müller 1970: 238–40; Cassuto 1975: 231; Lemaire 1977: 100–101; Smelik 1991: 121; Aḥituv 1992: 37; Renz and Röllig 1995: 416–19; Rüterswörden 2001: 184–85.
**Discussion:** Albright 1936b: 10–16; 1938: 11–17; 1939: 16–21; 1941: 18–24; Joüon 1936: 88; Dussaud 1938: 258–60, 263–68; Michaud 1941: 48–57;

Dupont-Sommer 1948: 43–68; Thomas 1948: 131–36; de Vaux 1967: 457–84; Müller 1970: 237–42; Cassuto 1975: 229–35; Lemaire 1977: 100–109, 141–43; Pardee 1982: 81–89, 242; Cross 1985: 41–47; Richter 1987: 73–103; Smelik 1990: 133–38; 1991: 121–25; Aḥituv 1992: 36–41; Barstad 1993b: 8*–12*; Parker 1994: 65–78; Renz and Röllig 1995: 412–19; Rüterswörden 2001: 184–88.

**Obverse**

1. *ʿbdk . hwšʿyhw . šlḥ . l*
2. *hg*[*d*] *l*[*ʾd*]*ny* [*yʾwš*] *. yšmʿ .*
3. *yhwh* [ʾ]*t ʾdny . šmʿt . šlm*
4. *w*[*š*]*m*[*ʿt*] *ṭb . wʿt . hpqḥ*
5. *nʾ . ʾt ʾzn* [.] *ʿbdk . lspr . ʾšr*
6. *šlḥth* [.] *ʾl ʿbdk . ʾmš . ky . lb*
7. [ʿ]*bdk . dwh . mʾz . šlḥk . ʾl . ʿbd*
8. *k . wky* [.] *ʾmr . ʾdny . lʾ . ydʿth .*
9. *qrʾ . spr . ḥyhwh . ʾm . nsh . ʾ*
10. *yš lqrʾ ly . spr lnṣḥ . wgm .*
11. *kl . spr* [.] *ʾšr ybʾ . ʾly* [.] *ʾm .*
12. *qrʾty . ʾth w*[*ʾḥ*]*r ʾtnnhw*
13. *ʾl . mʾwm*[*h*] *wlʿbdk . hgd .*
14. *lʾmr . yrd śr . hṣbʾ .*
15. *knyhw bn ʾlntn lbʾ .*
16. *mṣrymh . wʾt*

**Reverse**

1. *hwdwyhw bn ʾḥyhw w*
2. *ʾnšw šlḥ . lqḥt . mzh .*
3. *wspr . ṭbyhw ʿbd . hmlk . hbʾ*
4. *ʾl . šlm . bn ydʿ . mʾt . hnbʾ . lʾm*
5. *r . hšmr . šlḥh . ʿbʾdʿk . ʾl . ʾdny .*

1. Your servant, Hoshaiah, has sent (this document)
2. to info[rm] my lord, [Yaush.] May YHW[H] cause
3. my lord to hear tidings of peace
4. and [ti]dings of good. Now, open
5. the ear of your servant regarding the letter that
6. you sent to your servant yesterday evening. For the heart of
7. your [ser]vant has been sick ever since you sent (it) to your servant,
8. and because my lord said: “You did not understand it![a]
9. Call a scribe!” As YHWH lives, no one has ever tried

10. to read a letter for me! Moreover,
11. any letter that comes to me, if
12. I have read it, I can afterwards repeat it
13. to the last detail! Now it has been told to your servant,
14. saying, "The commander of the army,
15. Coniah the son of Elnathan, has gone down
16. to Egypt, and he has sent (orders)

**Reverse**

1. to take Hodaviah the son of Ahijah
2. and his men from here."
3. As for the letter of Tobiah the servant of the king,[b] which came
4. to Shallum the son of Jaddua from the prophet, saying,
5. "Beware!"—your serv<ant> has sent it to my lord.

[a] The final *h* on *ydʿth* is ambiguous. Some construe it as a vowel marker. Given the general paucity in Epigraphic Hebrew of forms of the 2ms perfect that are unambiguously spelled with plene orthography, however, I prefer to take it as a 3ms suffix referring back to the "letter" mentioned in line 5.

[b] It appears that Tobiah, a high official in the royal palace, had issued a report of an oracle by the unnamed prophet that began—as many oracles recorded in the Bible do—with the word: "Beware!" One can only presume that the rest of that oracle would have been spelled out in Tobiah's report that somehow came into the hands of Shallum the son of Jaddua.

## 140. Lachish Ostracon 6

This letter echoes some of the issues touched upon in Ostracon 3. It is also written to Yaush, the commander of the fortress at Lachish, by an unnamed officer, possibly Hoshaiah, who wrote the letter in Ostracon 3. It is included in this corpus because of the supposed reference to "the prophet" in line 5, which, if correctly restored, finds tantalizing echoes of the prophet Jeremiah (38:4). In any case, some scholars see evidence in this letter of the kinds of impact that prophetic utterances might have had in Judah.

**Text:** Dussaud 1938: 262; Torczyner 1938: 105, 117; de Vaux 1967: 474; Aḥituv 1992: 48; Renz and Röllig 1995: 426–27.
**Photograph:** Torczyner 1938: 102; Aḥituv 1992: 49.
**Copy:** Torczyner 1938: 103–4.
**Transliteration and translation:** Albright 1939: 19–20; 1941: 22–23; Michaud 1941: 57; Parker 1994: 69.

**Translation:** Albright 1938: 16; Dussaud 1938: 262; Torczyner 1938: 117; de Vaux 1967: 474; Lemaire 1977: 120–21; Aḥituv 1992: 48; Renz and Röllig 1995: 426–27; Rüterswörden 2001: 179–80.
**Discussion:** Albright 1936a: 31–33; 1938: 11–17; 1939: 16–21 (notes only); 1941: 18–24; Dussaud 1938: 256–71; Torczyner 1938: 101–19; Michaud 1941: 42–60; 1957: 39–60; Thomas 1946: 7–9, 13; 1958: 244–45; de Vaux 1967: 457–84; Lemaire 1977; Aḥituv 1992: 48–50; Parker 1994: 65–78; Renz and Röllig 1995: 425–27; Rüterswörden 2001: 179–81.

1. *ʾl ʾdny yʾwš . yrʾ . yhwh ʾ*
2. *t ʾdny ʾt hʿt hzh . šlm my*
3. *ʿbdk klb ky . šlḥ . ʾdny ʾ[t sp]*
4. *r hmlk wʾt spry hśr[m lʾm]*
5. *r qrʾ nʾ whnh . dbry . h[ ]*
6. *lʾ ṭbm lrpt ydyk[ . wlhš]*
7. *qṭ ydy hʾ[nšm . h]ydʿ[m h]*
8. *hm wʾnk[y ]ʾdny hlʾ tk*
9. *tb ʾlhm lʾ[mr] lmh tʿśw*
10. *kzʾt w[byr]šlm h[n]h l*
11. *mlk [w]l[byt]h [t]ʿśw hd[br]*
12. *hz[h w]ḥy . yhwh ʾlh*
13. *yk ky [m]ʾz qrʾ ʿb*
14. *dk ʾ[t] hsprm l[ʾ] hyh*
15. *lʿb[dk šlm]*

1. To my lord, Yaush. May YHWH cause my lord to see
2. this period (in) peace. Who is
3. your servant, a mere dog, that my lord has sent [the letter]
4. of the king and the letters of the official[s, saying,]
5. "Read!"?[a] Now the words of the [ ][b]
6. are not good, weakening your hands [and slackening]
7. the hands of the m[en] who [are in]for[med about]
8. them. As for me ... my lord, will you not write
9. t[o them], say[ing,] "Why do you act
10. like this, even [in Jeru]salem? Now, against
11. the king [and] his [house you] are doing this th[ing].
12. By the life of YHWH, your God,
13. (I swear) that since your servant read
14. the letters there has been no
15. [peace] for [your] serv[ant ]

[a] The writer of the letter had apparently been reprimanded earlier for failure to read (and obey) the commander's written orders.

[b] On the basis of the remarkable parallel in Jer 38:4, a number of scholars read here *h*[*nbʾym*] (the prophets) or *h*[*nbʾ*] (the prophet). Albright (1938: 15–16) and de Vaux (1939: 198), however, read the letter *š* after *h,* thus *hś*[*rym*] (the officials).

## 141. Lachish Ostracon 16

This ostracon, written on both sides, is fragmentary; only the middle of the letter it contained is preserved, and one cannot be certain how much of the original text has been lost. Still, there is a clear reference to a prophet (*hnbʾ* in obv. line 5), whose name, even though only partially preserved, is clearly Yahwistic. Together with Ostracon 3 (and possibly Ostracon 6?), this letter indicates concerns in official circles with the popular impact of prophetic utterances as Judah faced mortal danger from without during her last days.[a]

**Text:** Torczyner 1938: 173; Renz and Röllig 1995: 433–34.
**Photograph:** Torczyner 1938: 170.
**Copy:** Torczyner 1938: 171–72; Michaud 1957: 55.
**Transliteration and translation:** Michaud 1957: 55–56; Parker 1994: 75;
**Translation:** Renz and Röllig 1995: 433–34.
**Discussion:** Torczyner 1938: 169–73; Thomas 1946: 7–9, 13; 1958: 244–45; Michaud 1957: 39–60; Parker 1994: 65–78.

### Obverse

1. [ ]*ḥmh*[ ]
2. [ ]*hhy*[ ]
3. [ ]*šlḥh ʿ*[*bdk* ]
4. [ *s*]*pr bny*[ ]
5. [ *y*]*hw hnbʾ* [ ]
6. [ ]*m* [ ]

### Reverse

1. [ ] *ʾt* [ ]
2. [ ] *ʿ*[ ]
3. [ ]*šlḥ ʾ*[ ]
4. [ ]*dbr wḥ* [ ]

**Obverse**

1. ] . . . [
2. ] . . . [
3. your] se[rvant] sent it/him [
4. the l]etter of the sons of[b] [
5. -ya]hu, the prophet [
6. ] . . . [

**Reverse**

1. ] . . . [
2. ] . . . [
3. ] he has sent . . . [
4. ] word and . . . [

[a] See Parker 1994: 65–78.

[b] The most obvious reading of *bny* is "the sons of," but the possibility of a personal name here cannot be ruled out, namely, *bny*[*hw*] (Benaiah).

# VIII

# Report of Wenamon

**Robert K. Ritner**

## 142. Ecstatic Episode from "The Report of Wenamon" (col. 1/34–43)

**Text:** Möller 1909: 29; Gardiner 1932: 61–76.
**Transliteration and Translation:** Ritner forthcoming.[a]
**Translation:** Wilson 1969; Wente 1973; Lichtheim 1973–80: 2:224–30.
**Discussion:** Helck 1986; Winand 1987.

Composed in the nonliterary vernacular of genuine administrative reports, but with obvious rhetorical flourishes, the narrative of Wenamon is a disputed work of Egyptian literature and has been considered either a factual report or an unusually accurate historical romance. The tale and the surviving copy date to the final years of Ramses XI (ca. 1080–1070 B.C.E.),[b] the last ruler of Dynasty Twenty, during the de facto political division of Egypt that would characterize the succeeding dynasty. Dispatched by the theocratic state of Thebes to obtain timber for the sacred bark of Amon, the priest Wenamon is robbed, stranded, and arrives in Byblos on a stolen ship with only his portable image of the god Amon. After much delay and verbal abuse, Wenamon is successful in his mission only when his god possesses a medium at the court of Byblos and demands an audience.

The term for "medium" is written as the common Egyptian word for "youth," further qualified as "big/great." On the basis of context, it has been suggested that this term represents a Semitic word for "seer" (perhaps related to Aramaic *ʿddn;* cf. no. 137).[c] Context need not exclude the literal Egyptian meaning, however. The use of child mediums is well-attested in Hellenistic Egyptian texts,[d] and the ecstatic of Wenamon may represent an antecedent of the later practice. The addition of "great" to terms for "youths" is not unusual in Egyptian.[e]

*ỉw pꜣ [wr] n Kpn hꜣb n=ỉ r ḏd i-r[wiꜣ tw]k [m (1/35) tꜣy=ỉ ] mr.(t) ỉw=ỉ hꜣb n=f r ḏd i-ỉr[=ỉ šm n=ỉ r] tn(w) [. . .] n=ỉ(?) šm[ỉ (1/36) . . .] ỉr [. . .] r ẖnw.t ỉmy ṯꜣ[y](1/37).tw=(ỉ) r Km.t [ʿ]n [ỉ]w=ỉ ỉr hrw 29 n tꜣy=f m[r.t ỉw i-ỉr]=f nw hꜣb n=ỉ m mn.t r ḏd i-rw(1/38)iꜣ twk (m) tꜣy=ỉ mr.(t)*

*ḫr ỉr sw wdn (n) nꜣy=f nṯr.w [ỉ]w pꜣ nṯr ṯꜣy wʿ ʿḏdi ʿꜣ (n) nꜣy=f (1/39) ʿḏdi.w ʿꜣy.w ỉw=f di.t=f ḫꜣwt ỉw=f ḏd n=f*

*ỉny [pꜣ] nṯr r ḥr(y) ỉny pꜣ ỉpw.ty nty ẖr-r=f (1/40) (ỉ)n ꜣImn i-wḏ sw mntf i-di ỉw=f*

*ỉw i-ỉr pꜣ ḫꜣwt ḫꜣwt m pꜣy grḥ ỉw gm(1/41)=ỉ wʿ bꜣr ỉw ḥr=s r Km.t ỉw ꜣtp=ỉ pꜣy=ỉ ỉnk nb r=s ỉw i-ỉr=ỉ nw (1/42) r pꜣ kkw r ḏd hꜣy=f ꜣtp=ỉ pꜣ nṯr r tm di.t ptri sw k.t ỉr.t*

*ỉw pꜣ (1/43) ỉmy-rꜣ mr.(t) ỉy n=ỉ r ḏd smn tw šꜣʿ dwꜣ ḫr=f n pꜣ wr*

The [prince] of Byblos sent to me, saying: "Get [out of my] harbor!" And I sent to him saying, "Where should [I go? . . .] I(?) go [. . .] If [you can find a ship] to transport me, let me be taken back to Egypt." I spent twenty-nine days in his ha[rbor, even though] he spent time sending to me daily, saying: "Get out of my harbor!"

Now when he offered to his gods, the god (Amon) seized a great seer from among his great seers, and he caused him to be in an ecstatic state, and he[f] said to him:

"Bring up the god!
    Bring the messenger who bears him!
It is Amon who has sent him.
    He is the one who has caused that he come."

But the ecstatic became ecstatic on that night only after I had found a ship heading for Egypt, and I had loaded all my belongings onto it, and I had watched for darkness to fall so that I might put the god on board in order to prevent another eye from seeing him.

And the harbor master came to me to say: "Stay until tomorrow; so says the prince."

[a] The current translation is derived from Ritner forthcoming.

[b] The date of the manuscript generally has been considered terminal Twentieth–early Twenty-First Dynasty; see Gardiner 1932: xi; J. A. Wilson 1969: 25; Lichtheim 1973–80: 2:224; and Caminos 1977: 3–4. A date in early Dynasty XXII, originally suggested by Möller 1909: 29, is accepted by Helck 1986: 1215–16.

[c] For discussion and bibliography, see Hoch 1994: 86–87.

[d] For examples, see Betz 1992: 196–99.

[e] Cf. *ḫr ʿꜣ* "big/great boy" (Coptic ϩⲗⲗⲟ).

[f] The seer speaks to the prince of Byblos.

# Concordances

| A. | WAW |
|---|---|
| 15 | 38 |
| 100 | 23 |
| 122 | 43 |
| 222 | 36 |
| 368 | 11 |
| 428 | 47 |
| 431 | 48 |
| 455 | 25 |
| 671 | 24 |
| 907 | 37 |
| 925 | 9 |
| 963 | 13 |
| 994 | 42 |
| 996 | 17 |
| 1047 | 7 |
| 1121 | 1 |
| 1249b | 52 |
| 1968 | 2 |
| 2030 | 31 |
| 2050 | 9 |
| 2209 | 26 |
| 2233 | 18 |
| 2264 | 14 |
| 2437 | 41 |
| 2731 | 1 |
| 2858 | 44 |
| 3165 | 51 |
| 3178 | 21 |
| 3217 | 22 |
| 3420 | 5 |
| 3424 | 45 |

| A. | WAW |
|---|---|
| 3719 | 6 |
| 3724 | 33 |
| 3760 | 3 |
| 3796 | 53 |
| 3893 | 16 |
| 3912 | 8 |
| 4260 | 4 |
| 4400 | 46 |
| 4674 | 61 |
| 4675 | 60 |
| 4865 | 30 |
| 4883 | 48 |
| 4934 | 32 |
| 4996 | 19 |

| *ABL* | WAW |
|---|---|
| 58 | 107 |
| 149 | 111 |
| 437 | 109 |
| 1216 | 105 |
| 1217 | 115 |
| 1237 | 106 |
| 1249 | 112 |
| 1280 | 93 |
| 1285 | 108 |

| ARM | WAW |
|---|---|
| 2 90 | 30 |
| 2 108 | 48 |
| 3 40 | 31 |
| 3 78 | 32 |
| 6 45 | 11 |
| 9 22 | 54 |
| 10 4 | 17 |
| 10 6 | 22 |
| 10 7 | 23 |
| 10 8 | 24 |
| 10 9 | 18 |
| 10 10 | 41 |
| 10 50 | 42 |
| 10 51 | 43 |
| 10 53 | 5 |
| 10 80 | 7 |
| 10 81 | 14 |
| 10 100 | 37 |
| 10 106 | 33 |
| 10 117 | 45 |
| 13 23 | 19 |
| 13 112 | 39 |
| 13 113 | 40 |
| 13 114 | 20 |
| 21 333 | 55 |
| 22 167 | 56 |
| 22 326 | 58 |
| 23 446 | 59 |
| 25 15 | 60 |
| 25 142 | 61 |
| 25 816 | 15 |
| 26 194 | 4 |
| 26 195 | 5 |
| 26 196 | 6 |
| 26 197 | 7 |

| **ARM** | **WAW** |
|---|---|
| 26 198 | 8 |
| 26 199 | 9 |
| 26 200 | 10 |
| 26 201 | 11 |
| 26 202 | 12 |
| 26 203 | 13 |
| 26 204 | 14 |
| 26 205 | 15 |
| 26 206 | 16 |
| 26 207 | 17 |
| 26 208 | 18 |
| 26 209 | 19 |
| 26 210 | 20 |
| 26 211 | 21 |
| 26 212 | 22 |
| 26 213 | 23 |
| 26 214 | 24 |
| 26 215 | 25 |
| 26 216 | 26 |
| 26 217 | 27 |
| 26 218 | 28 |
| 26 219 | 29 |
| 26 220 | 30 |
| 26 221 | 31 |
| 26 221bis | 32 |
| 26 222 | 33 |
| 26 223 | 34 |
| 26 227 | 35 |
| 26 229 | 36 |
| 26 232 | 37 |
| 26 233 | 38 |
| 26 234 | 39 |
| 26 235 | 40 |
| 26 236 | 41 |
| 26 237 | 42 |
| 26 238 | 43 |
| 26 239 | 44 |
| 26 240 | 45 |
| 26 243 | 46 |
| 26 371 | 47 |
| 26 414 | 48 |
| 27 32 | 49 |

| ***CT*** | **WAW** |
|---|---|
| 53 17 | 116 |
| 53 107 | 116 |
| 53 118 | 115 |
| 53 219 | 96 |
| 53 413 | 114 |
| 53 938 | 117 |
| 53 946 | 95 |
| 53 969 | 113 |

| **FLP** | **WAW** |
|---|---|
| 1674 | 66 |
| 2064 | 67 |

| **K** | **WAW** |
|---|---|
| 168 | 109 |
| 216 | 127 |
| 540 | 111 |
| 883 | 91 |
| 1033 | 107 |
| 1034 | 115 |
| 1367 | 129 |
| 1292 | 94 |
| 1545 | 93 |
| 1775 | 101 |
| 1847 | 101 |
| 1913 | 128 |
| 1974 | 96 |
| 2001 | 118 |
| 2401 | 84-88 |
| 2732 | 101 |
| 3998 | 127 |
| 4142 | 124 |
| 4267 | 108 |
| 4310 | 68-77 |
| 4344 | 126 |
| 6097 | 129 |
| 6259 | 90 |
| 6333 | 103 |
| 6693 | 129 |
| 7395 | 116 |
| 8143 | 104 |
| 9204 | 116 |
| 9821 | 116 |
| 10541 | 116 |
| 11021 | 116 |
| 10865 | 114 |
| 12033 | 78-83 |
| 13737 | 115 |

| **M.** | **WAW** |
|---|---|
| 6188 | 10 |
| 7306 | 15 |
| 8071 | 27 |
| 9451 | 50 |
| 9576 | 35 |
| 9601 | 34 |
| 9717 | 65 |
| 11046 | 12 |
| 11436 | 62 |
| 13741 | 49 |
| 13841 | 39 |
| 13842 | 40 |
| 13843 | 20 |
| 13496 | 29 |
| 14836 | 28 |
| 15299 | 27 |

| **SAA** | **WAW** |
|---|---|
| 2 6 | 101 |
| 3 34 | 103 |
| 3 35 | 103 |
| 7 9 | 104 |
| 9 1 | 68-77 |
| 9 2 | 78-83 |
| 9 3 | 84-88 |
| 9 4 | 89 |
| 9 5 | 90 |
| 9 6 | 91 |
| 9 7 | 92 |
| 9 8 | 93 |
| 9 9 | 94 |
| 9 10 | 95 |
| 9 11 | 96 |
| 10 109 | 105 |
| 10 111 | 106 |
| 10 284 | 107 |
| 10 294 | 108 |
| 10 352 | 109 |
| 12 69 | 110 |
| 13 37 | 111 |
| 13 139 | 112 |
| 13 144 | 113 |
| 13 148 | 114 |
| 16 59 | 115 |
| 16 60 | 116 |
| 16 61 | 117 |

# Bibliography


Adler, Hans-Peter

1976 *Das Akkadische des Königs Tušratta von Mitanni.* AOAT 201. Kevelaer: Butzon & Bercker; Neukirchen-Vluyn: Neukirchener Verlag.

Aḥituv, S.

1992 *Handbook of Ancient Hebrew Inscriptions: From the Period of the First Commonwealth and the Beginning of the Second Commonwealth (Hebrew, Philistine, Edomite, Moabite, Ammonite, and the Bileam Inscription)* [Hebrew]. Biblical Encyclopedia Library 7. Jerusalem: Bialik.

Albright, William Foxwell

1936a "News of the Schools." *BASOR* 62: 31–33.

1936b "A Supplement to Jeremiah: The Lachish Ostraca." *BASOR* 61: 10–16.

1938 "The Oldest Hebrew Letters: The Lachish Ostraca." *BASOR* 70: 11–17.

1939 "A Reexamination of the Lachish Letters." *BASOR* 73: 16–21.

1941 "The Lachish Letters after Five Years." *BASOR* 82: 18–24.

1970 "Some Comments on the Amman Citadel Inscription." *BASOR* 198: 38–40.

Alster, Bendt, ed.

1980 *Death in Mesopotamia.* Mesopotamia 8 [= CRRAI 26]. Copenhagen: Akademisk Forlag.

Anbar, Moshe

1974 "L'activité divinatoire de l'*āpilum,* le 'répondant,' d'après une lettre de Mari." *RA* 75: 91.

1975 "Aspect moral dans un discours 'prophetique' de Mari." *UF* 7: 517–18.

1979 "La durée du règne de Zimri-Lim." *Israel Oriental Studies* 9: 1–8.

1991 *Les tribus amurrites de Mari*. OBO 108. Fribourg: Universitätverlag; Göttingen: Vandenhoeck & Ruprecht.

1993a "Mari and the Origin of Prophecy." Pp. 1–5 in *kinattūtu ša dārâti: Raphael Kutscher Memorial Volume*. Edited by A. F. Rainey. Tel Aviv Occasional Publications 1. Tel Aviv: Tel Aviv University, Institute of Archaeology.

1993b "'Below the Strow the Water Flow'. Prophet's Opposition to the Treaty between Mari and Eshnunna" [Hebrew]. *Bet Mikra* 136: 21–27.

1993c "Un *āpilum* cite le mythe de Atram-ḫasis?" *NABU* 1993: 53 (§67).

1994 "'Thou Shalt Make No Covenant with Them' (Exodus 23:32)." Pp. 41–48 in *Politics and Theopolitics in the Bible and Postbiblical Literature*. Edited by H. G. Reventlow, Y. Hoffman, and B. Uffenheimer. JSOTSup 171. Sheffield: Sheffield Academic Press.

1997 "Les tromperies d'Elam et d'Ešnunna." *NABU* 1997: 17 (§15).

Annus, Amar

2002 *The God Ninurta in the Mythology and Royal Ideology of Ancient Mesopotamia*. SAAS 14. Helsinki: Neo-Assyrian Text Corpus Project.

Aro, Jussi

1955 *Studien zur mittelbabylonischen Grammatik*. StudOr 20. Helsinki: Societas Orientalis Fennica.

Artzi, Pinhas, and Abraham Malamat

1971 "The Correspondence of Šibtu, Queen of Mari in *ARM* X." *Or* 40: 75–89 (= Malamat 1998: 175–91).

Astour, Michael C.

1992 "Sparagmos, Omophagia, and Ecstatic Prophecy at Mari." *UF* 24: 1–2.

Asurmendi, Jesús, Jean-Marie Durand, René Lebrun, Émile Puech, and Philippe Talon

1994 *Prophéties et oracles 1: dans le Proche-Orient ancien*. Supplément au Cahier Evangile 88. Paris: Cerf.

Asurmendi, Jesús, Didier Devauchelle, René Lebrun, André Motte, and Charles Perrot

1994 *Prophéties et oracles 2: en Égypte et en Grèce*. Supplément au Cahier Evangile 89. Paris: Cerf.

Aufrecht, W. E.

1989 *A Corpus of Ammonite Inscriptions*. Ancient Near Eastern Texts and Studies 4. Lewiston, N.Y.: Mellen, 1989.

2000 "The Amman Citadel Inscription. *COS* 2:139.

Banks, Edgar James

1898 "Eight Oracular Responses to Esarhaddon." *AJSL* 14: 267–77.

Bardet, Guillaume, Francis Joannès, Bertrand Lafont, Denis Soubeyran, and Pierre Villard

1984 *Archives administratives de Mari I.* ARM 23. Paris: Editions Recherche sur les Civilisations.

Barstad, Hans

1993a "No Prophets? Recent Developments in Biblical Prophetic Research and Ancient Near Eastern Prophecy." *JSOT* 57: 39–60 (= pp. 106–26 in *The Prophets: A Sheffield Reader.* Edited by Philip R. Davies. Biblical Seminar 42. Sheffield: Sheffield Academic Press, 1996).

1993b "Lachish Ostrakon III and Ancient Israelite Prophecy." *ErIsr* 24: 8*–12*.

2000 "*Comparare necesse est?* Ancient Israelite and Ancient Near Eastern Prophecy in a Comparative Perspective." Pp. 3–12 in Nissinen, ed., 2000.

2001 "Den gammeltestamentliga profetismen belyst ved paralleller fra Mari." *TTKi* 72: 51–67.

Bauer, Theo

1934 Review of T. R. Campbell, *The Prisms of Esarhaddon and Assurbanipal,* B. Meissner, *Neue Nachrichten über die Ermordung Sanheribs und die Nachfolge Asarhaddons,* and H. Hirschberg, *Studien zur Geschichte Esarhaddons. ZA* 42: 170–84.

Bauks, Michaela

2001 "'Chaos' als Metapher für die Gefährdung der Weltordnung." Pp. 431–64 in *Das biblische Weltbild und seine altorientalischen Kontexte.* Edited by B. Janowski and B. Ego. FAT 32. Tübingen: Mohr Siebeck.

Beck, P.

1993 "A Note on 'Battering-ram' and 'Towers' in ARMT XXVI.199.1–57." *NABU* 1993: 53 (§68).

Beek, M. A.

1966 "Der Ersatzkönig als Erzählungsmotiv in der altisraelitischen Literatur." Pp. 24–32 in *Volume du Congrès: Genève, 1965.* Edited by P. A. H. de Boer. VTSup 15. Leiden: Brill.

Ben Zvi, Ehud, and Michael H. Floyd, eds.

2000 *Writings and Speech in Biblical and Ancient Near Eastern Prophecy.* SBLSymS 10. Atlanta: Society of Biblical Literature.

Berger, P.-R.
1969 "Einige Bemerkungen zu Friedrich Ellermeier: Prophetie in Mari und Israel (Herzberg, 1968)." *UF* 1: 209.
Betz, Hans Dieter, ed.
1992 *The Greek Magical Papyri in Translation Including the Demotic Spells*. Chicago: University of Chicago Press.
Bezold, Carl, and E. A. Wallis Budge
1892 *The Tell el-Amarna Tablets in the British Museum with Autotype Facsimiles*. London: British Museum.
Biggs, Robert D.
1969 "Akkadian Oracles and Prophecies." *ANET* 604–5.
Birot, Maurice
1960a *Archives royales de Mari 9: Textes administratifs de la salle 5*. TCL 30. Paris: Paul Geuthner.
1960b *Textes administratifs de la salle 5 du palais*. ARM 9. Paris: Concours des relations culturelles.
1964 *Textes administratifs de la salle 5 du palais (2e partie). ARM 12*. Paris: Concours de la direction générale des affaires culturelles.
1972 "Simaḫlânê, roi de Kurda." *RA* 66: 131–39.
1975 *Lettres de Yaqqim-Addu, gouverneur de Sagarâtum*. ARM 14. Paris: Geuthner.
1978 "Données nouvelles sur la chronologie du règne de Zimri-Lim." *Syria* 55: 333–43.
1980 "Fragment du rituel de Mari relatif au *kispum*." Pp. 139–50 in Alster, ed., 1980.
1993 *Correspondance des gouverneurs de Qaṭṭunân*. ARM 27. Paris: Editions Recherche sur les Civilisations.
Birot, Maurice, Jean-Robert Kupper, and Olivier Rouault
1979 *Répertoire analytique des Archives royales de Mari (2e volume) des tomes I–XIV, XVIII et des textes divers hors-collection: Première partie: noms propres*. ARM 16/1. Paris: Geuthner.
Black, M.
1958 "The Zakir Stele," Pp. 242–50 in *Documents from Old Testament Times*. Edited by D. W. Thomas. London: Thomas Nelson & Sons.
Bodi, Daniel
1991 *The Book of Ezekiel and the Poem of Erra*. OBO 104. Fribourg: Universitätsverlag; Göttingen: Vandenhoeck & Ruprecht.
Bordreuil, Pierre, and Dennis Pardee
1993a "Le combat de *Ba'lu* avec *Yammu* d'après les textes ougaritiques." *MARI* 7: 63–70.

1993b "Textes ougaritiques oubliés et 'transfuges.'" *Sem* 41–42: 23–58.

Borger, Rykle

1956 *Die Inschriften Asarhaddons, Königs von Assyrien*. AfOB 9. Graz: self-published.

1957 "Assyriologische und altarabische Miszellen." *Or* 26: 1–11.

1984 "Historische Texte in akkadischer Sprache aus Babylonien und Assyrien." *TUAT* 1.4: 354–410.

1996 *Beiträge zum Inschriftenwerk Assurbanipals: Die Prismenklassen A, B, C = K, D, E, F, G, H, J und T sowie andere Inschriften*. Wiesbaden: Harrassowitz.

Bottéro, Jean

1992 *Mesopotamia: Writing, Reasoning, and the Gods*. Translated by Z. Bahrani and M. van de Mieroop. Chicago: University of Chicago Press.

Brinkman, J. A.

1977 "Notes on Arameans and Chaldeans in Southern Mesopotamia in the Early Seventh Century B.C." *Or* 46: 304–25.

Budge, E. A. Wallis

1910 *Cuneiform Texts from Babylonian Tablets in the British Museum*. Part 27. CT 27. London: British Museum.

Buss, Martin J.

1969 "Mari Prophecy and Hosea." *JBL* 88: 338.

Butler, Sally A. L.

1998 *Mesopotamian Conceptions of Dreams and Dream Rituals*. AOAT 258. Münster: Ugarit-Verlag.

Caminos, Ricardo A.

1977 *A Tale of Woe: From a Hieratic Papyrus in the A. S. Pushkin Museum of Fine Arts in Moscow*. Oxford: Griffith Institute, Ashmolean Museum.

Caquot, André, and André Lemaire

1977 "Les textes araméens de Deir ʿAlla." *Syria* 54: 189–208.

Cassuto, Umberto

1975 "The Lachish Ostraca (1939)." Pp. 229–35 in idem., *Biblical and Oriental Studies*. Jerusalem: Magnes.

Charpin, Dominique

1987 "Les décrets royaux à l'époque Paleo-Babylonienne, à propos d'un ouvrage récent." *AfO* 34: 36–44.

1988 Pp. 7–232 in *Archives épistolaires de Mari I/2*. Edited by D. Charpin, F. Joannès, S. Lackenbacher, and B. Lafont. ARM 26/2. Paris: Editions Recherche sur les Civilisations.

1990 "L'*andurârum* à Mari." *MARI* 6: 253–270.

1991 "Un traité entre Zimri-Lim de Mari et Ibâl-pî-El II d'Ešnunna." Pp. 139–66 in *Marchands, Diplomates et Empereurs: Études sur la civilisation mésopotamienne offertes à Paul Garelli*. Edited by D. Charpin and F. Joannès. Paris: Editions Recherche sur les Civilisations.

1992 "Le contexte historique et géographique des prophéties dans les textes retrouvés à Mari." *BCSMS* 23: 21–31.

1993 "Un souverain éphémère en Ida-maraṣ: Išme-Addu of Ašnakkum." *MARI* 7: 185–87.

1993–94 "Compte rendu du CAD volume S (1984)." *AfO* 40–41: 1–23.

1998a "L'évocation du passé dans les lettres de Mari." Pp. 91–110 in *Intellectual Life of the Ancient Near East: Papers Presented at the Forty-Third Rencontre Assyriologique Internationale Prague, July 1–5, 1996*. [CRRAI 43.] Edited by J. Prosečký. Prague: Oriental Institute.

1998b "Toponymies amorrite et biblique: La ville de Ṣîbat/Ṣobah." *RA* 92: 79–92.

2001 "Prophètes et rois dans le Proche-Orient amorrite." Pp. 21–53 in Lemaire, ed., 2001.

2002 "Prophètes et rois dans le Proche-Orient amorrite: Nouvelles données, nouvelles perspectives." Pp. 7–38 in Charpin and Durand, eds., 2002.

Charpin, Dominique, and Jean-Marie Durand

1985 "La prise du pouvoir par Zimri-Lim." *MARI* 4: 297–343.

1986 "'Fils de Sim'al': les origines tribales des Rois de Mari." *RA* 80: 141–83.

1991 "La suzeraineté de l'empereur (Sukkalmah) d'Elam sur la Mésopotamie et le 'nationalisme' amorrite." Pp. 59–66 in *Mésopotamie et Elam: Actes de la XXXVIe Rencontre Assyriologique Internationale, Gand, 10–14 juillet 1989*. [CRRAI 36.] Mesopotamian History and Environment Occasional Publications 1. Ghent: University of Ghent and Oriental Institute of the University of Chicago.

1997 "Aššur avant l'Assyrie." *MARI* 8: 367–391.

———, eds.

1997 *Florilegium marianum III. Recueil d'études à la mémoire de Marie-Thérèse Barrelet*. Mémoires de NABU 4. Paris: SEPOA.

2002 *Florilegium marianum VI: Recueil d'études à la mémoire d' André Parrot*. Mémoires de NABU 7. Paris: SEPOA.

Charpin, Dominique, and N. Ziegler

2002 *Florilegium marianum V: Mari et le Proche-Orient à l'époque amorrite: essai d' histoire politique*. Mémoires de NABU 6. Paris: SEPOA (forthcoming).

Civil, Miguel

1974 "Notes brèves 12." *RA* 68, 95.

Civil, M. et al

1969 *Materials for Sumerian Lexicon 12: The Series lú* = ša *and Related Texts*. Rome: Pontificium Institutum Biblicum.

Cocquerillat, Denise

1968 *Palmeraies et cultures de l'Eanna d'Uruk (559–520)*. Ausgrabungen der Deutschen Forschungsgemeinschaft in Uruk-Warka 8. Berlin: Gebr. Mann.

Cole, Steven W.

1997 "The Destruction of Orchards in Assyrian Warfare." Pp. 29–40 in *Assyria 1995: Proceedings of the Tenth Anniversary Symposium of the Neo-Assyrian Text Corpus Project, Helsinki, September 7–11, 1995*. Edited by S. Parpola and R. M. Whiting. Helsinki: Neo-Assyrian Text Corpus Project.

Cole, Steven W., and Peter Machinist

1998 *Letters from Priests to the Kings Esarhaddon and Assurbanipal*. SAA 13. Helsinki: Neo-Assyrian Text Corpus Project.

Conrad, Diethelm

1960 "Samuel und die Mari-'Propheten': Bemerkungen zu 1 Sam 15:27." Pp. 273–280 in *XVII. Deutscher Orientalistentag vom 21. bis 27. Juli 1968 in Würzburg. Vorträge, Teil 1*. Edited by W. Voigt. ZDMGSup 1:1. Wiesbaden: Steiner.

Coogan, Michael D.

1987 "Canaanite Origins and Lineage: Reflections on the Religion of Ancient Israel." Pp. 115–18 in Miller, Hanson, and McBride, eds., 1987.

Craghan, John F.

1974 "The ARM X 'Prophetic' Texts: Their Media, Style, and Structure." *JANESCU* 6: 39–57.

1975 "Mari and Its Prophets: The Contributions of Mari to the Understanding of Biblical Prophecy." *BTB* 5: 42–44.

Cross, Frank Moore

1969 "Epigraphic Notes on the Ammān Citadel Inscription." *BASOR* 193: 13–19.

1985 "A Literate Soldier: Lachish Letter III." Pp. 41–47 in *Biblical and Related Studies Presented to Samuel Iwry*. Edited by A. Kort and S. Morschauer. Winona Lake, Ind.: Eisenbrauns.

Cryer, Frederick H.

1994 *Divination in Ancient Israel and Its Near Eastern Environment: A Socio-Historical Investigation*. JSOTSup 142. Sheffield: Sheffield Academic Press.

Delattre, A.

1889 "The Oracles Given in Favour of Esarhaddon." *Babylonian and Oriental Record* 3: 25–31.

Delcor, Mathias

1981 "Le texte de Deir ʿAlla et les oracles bibliques de Balaʿam." Pp. 52–73 in *Congress Volume, Vienna*. Edited by J. Emerton. VTSup 32. Leiden: Brill.

1989 "Des inscriptions de Deir ʿAlla aux traditions bibliques, à propos des šdyn, des šedim et de šadday." Pp. 33–40 in *Die Väter Israels: Beiträge zur Theologie der Patriarchenüberlieferungen im Alten Testament*. Edited by J. Scharbert, A. R. Müller, and M. Görg. Stuttgart: Katholisches Bibelwerk.

Deller, Karlheinz

1983 "STT 366: Deutungsversuch 1982." *Assur* 3: 139–53.

Del Monte, Giuseppe F.

1997 *Testi Cronografici*. Vol. 1 of *Testi dalla Babylonia Ellenistica*. Studi Ellenistici 9. Pisa: Istituti editoriali e poligrafici internazionali.

Devauchelle, Didier

1994 "Les prophéties en Égypte ancienne." Pp. 6–30 in Asurmendi, Devauchelle, Lebrun, Motte, and Perrot 1994.

Dietrich, Manfried

1970 *Die Aramäer Südbabyloniens in der Sargonidenzeit (700–648)*. AOAT 7. Kevelaer: Butzon & Bercker; Neukirchen-Vluyn: Neukirchener Verlag.

1973 "Prophetie in den Keilschrifttexten." *JARG* 1: 15–44.

1979 Neo-Babylonian Letters from the Kuyunjik Collection. CT 54. London: British Museum Publications.

1986 "Prophetenbriefe aus Mari." *TUAT* II/1: 83–93.

2001 "Das biblische Paradies und der babylonische Tempelgarten: Überlegungen zur Lage des Gartens Eden." Pp. 281–323 in *Das biblische Weltbild und seine altorientalischen Kontexte*. Edited by B. Janowski and B. Ego. FAT 32. Tübingen: Mohr Siebeck.

Dietrich, Manfried, and Ingo Kottsieper, eds.

1998 *"Und Mose schrieb dieses Lied auf": Studien zum Alten Testament und zum Alten Orient. Festschrift für Oswald Loretz zur Vollendung seines 70. Lebensjahres mit Beiträgen von Freunden, Schülern und Kollegen*. AOAT 250. Münster: Ugarit-Verlag.

Dietrich, Manfried, and Oswald Loretz

1980 "Totenverehrung in Mari (12803) und Ugarit (KTU 1.161)." *UF* 12: 381–82.

Dijk, J. van

1983 Introduction, texte composité, traduction. Vol. 1 of LUGAL UD ME-LÁM-bi NIR-ĞÁL: *Le récit épique et didactique des Travaux de Ninurta du Déluge et de la Nouvelle Création*. Leiden: Brill.

Dijkstra, Meindert

1980 *Gods voorstelling: Predikatieve expressie van zelfopenbaring in Oudoosterse teksten en Deutero-Jesaja*. Dissertationes Neerlandicae, Series Theologica 2. Kampen: Kok.

1995 "Is Balaam Also among the Prophets?" *JBL* 114: 43–64.

Dion, Paul-Eugène

1970 "The 'Fear Not' Formula and Holy War." *CBQ* 32: 565–70.

1975 "Notes d'épigraphie Ammonite." *RB* 82: 24–33.

Dossin, Georges

1938 "Un rituel du culte d'Ištar provenant de Mari." *RA* 35: 1–13.

1948 "Une révélation du dieu Dagan à Terqa." *RA* 42: 125–34.

1966 "Sur le prophétisme a Mari." Pp. 77–86 in *La divination en Mésopotamie ancienne et dans les régions voisines*. CRRAI 14. Paris: Presses universitaires de France.

1967 *Archives royales de Mari X: La correspondance féminine*. TCL 31. Paris: Geuthner.

1975 "Tablettes de Mari." *RA* 69: 23–30.

1978 *Correspondance féminine*. With the collaboration of André Finet. ARM 10. Paris: Geuthner.

Dossin, Georges, Jean Bottéro, Maurice Birot, M. L. Burke, Jean-Robert Kupper, and André Finet

1964 *Textes divers offerts à André Parrot à l'occasion du XXX^e^ anniversaire de la découverte de Mari*. ARM 13. Paris: Concours de la Commission des Fouilles.

Dougherty, Raymond Philip

1920 *Records from Erech, Time of Nabonidus (555–538 B.C.)*. YOS 6. New Haven: Yale University Press.

Dupont-Sommer, A.

1948 "Un papyrus araméen d'époque saïte découvert à Saqqara." *Sem* 1: 43-68.

Durand, Jean-Marie

1982a *Archives royales de Mari XXI: Textes administratifs des salles 134 et 160 du Palais de Mari*. TCM 5. Paris: Geuthner.

1982b "In Vino Veritas." *RA* 76: 43–50.

1983a *Textes administratifs des salles 134 et 160 du Palais de Mari*. ARM 21. Paris: Geuthner.

1983b "Relectures d'ARMT XIII, 1: La correspondance de *Mukannišum*." *MARI* 2: 141–49.

1984 "Trois études sur Mari." *MARI* 3: 127–80.

1985 "La situation historique des Šakkanakku: nouvelle approche." *MARI* 4: 147–72.

1987a "Documents pour l'histoire du royaume de Haute-Mésopotamie, I." *MARI* 5: 155–98.

1987b "L'organisation de l'espace dans le palais de Mari: le témoignage des textes." Pp. 39–110 in *Le système palatial en Orient, en Grèce et à Rome: Actes du colloque de Strasbourg 19–22 Juin 1985*. Edited by E. Lévy. Université des Sciences Humaines de Strasbourg, Travaux du Centre de Recherche sur le Proche-Orient et la Grèce antiques 9. Leiden: Brill.

1988 *Archives épistolaires de Mari I/1*. ARM 26/1. Paris: Editions Recherche sur les Civilisations.

1990 "La cité-état d'Imâr à l'époque des rois de Mari." *MARI* 6, 39–92.

1992 "Mari: Texts." *ABD* 4: 529–36.

1993a "Le mythologème du combat entre le Dieu de l'Orage et la Mer en Mésopotamie." *MARI* 7: 41–61.

1993b "*rakâbum* 'triompher de.'" *NABU* 1993: 96 (§113).

1994 "Les 'déclarations prophétiques' dans les lettres de Mari." Pp. 8–74 in Asurmendi, Durand, Lebrun, Puech, and Talon 1994.

1995 "La religión en Siria durante la época de los reinos amorreos según la documentación de Mari." Pp. 125–533 in P. Mander and J.-M. Durand, *Semitas occidentales*. Vol. 2/1 of *Mitología y religión del Oriente Antiguo*. Estudios Orientales 8. Sabadell: AUSA.

1997a "Les prophéties de Mari." Pp. 115–34 in Heintz, ed., 1997.

1997b "La divination par les oiseaux." *MARI* 8: 273–82.

1998a "Travaux sur Mari." *NABU* 1998: 86–87 (§94).

1998b *Les documents épistolaires du palais de Mari*. Vol. 2. LAPO 17. Paris: Cerf.

2000 *Les documents épistolaires du palais de Mari*. Vol. 3. LAPO 18. Paris: Cerf.

2002 *Florilegium marianum VII: Le culte d'Addu d'Alep et l'affaire d'Alahtum*. Mémoires de NABU 4. Paris: SEPOA.

Durand, Jean-Marie, and Michaël Guichard

1997 "Les rituels de Mari." Pp. 19–78 in Charpin and Durand, eds., 1997.

Dussaud, René

1938 "Le prophète Jérémie et les lettres de Lakish." *Syria* 19: 258–60, 263–68.

Ellermeier, F.

1968 *Prophetie in Mari und Israel*. Theologische und orientalistische Arbeiten 1. Herzberg: Jungfer.

Ellis, Maria deJong

1987 "The Goddess Kititum Speaks to King Ibalpiel: Oracle Texts from Ishchali." *MARI* 5: 235–66.

1989 "Observations on Mesopotamian Oracles and Prophetic Texts: Literary and Historiographic Considerations." *JCS* 41: 127–86.

Fales, Frederick Mario, ed.

1981 *Assyrian Royal Inscriptions: New Horizons in Literary, Ideological and Historical Analysis.* OAC 17. Roma: Istituto per l'Oriente.

Fales, Frederick Mario, and Giovanni B. Lanfranchi

1981 "ABL 1237: The Role of the Cimmerians in a Letter to Esarhaddon." *East and West* 31: 9–33.

1997 "The Impact of Oracular Material on the Political Utterances and Political Action in the Royal Inscriptions of the Sargonid Dynasty." Pp. 99–114 in Heintz, ed., 1997.

Fales, Frederick Mario, and J. N. Postgate

1992 *Palace and Temple Administration.* Part 1 of *Imperial Administrative Records.* SAA 7. Helsinki: Helsinki University Press.

1994 *Provincial and Military Administration.* Part 2 of *Imperial Administrative Records.* SAA 11. Helsinki: Helsinki University Press.

Finet, André

1966 "Adalšenni, roi de Burundum." *RA* 60: 17–28.

1982 "Un cas de clédomancie à Mari." Pp. 48–53 in *Zikir Šumim: Assyriological Studies Presented to F. R. Kraus on the Occasion of His Seventieth Birthday.* Edited by G. van Driel, D. J. H. Krispijn, M. Stol, and K. R. Veenhof. Nederlands Instituut voor het Nabije Oosten Studia Francisci Scholten Memoriae Dicata 5. Leiden: Brill.

Fleming, Daniel E.

1993a "The Etymological Origins of the Hebrew *nābîʾ*: The One Who Invokes God." *CBQ* 55: 217–24.

1993b "*nābû* and *munabbiātu:* Two New Syrian Religious Personnel." *JAOS* 113: 175–83.

1993c "LÚ and MEŠ in [lú]*na-bi-i*[MEŠ] and Its Mari Brethren." *NABU* 1993: 2–4 (§4).

1998 "Mari and the Possibilities of Biblical Memory." *RA* 92: 41–78.

2000 *Time at Emar: The Cultic Calendar and the Rituals from the Diviner's House.* Winona Lake, Ind.: Eisenbrauns.

Frame, Grant

1992 *Babylonia 689–627 B.C.: A Political History.* Istanbul: Nederlands Historisch-Archaeologisch Instituut te Istanbul.

Freedman, Sally

1998 *Tablets 1–21.* Vol. 1 of *If a City Is Set on a Height: The Akkadian Omen Series Šumma alu ina mēlê šakin.* Occasional

Publications of the Samuel Noah Kramer Fund 17. Philadelphia: University of Pennsylvania Museum.

Freydank, Helmut
1974 "Zwei Verpflegungstexte aus Kār-Tukultī-Ninurta." *AOF* 1: 55–89.
1976 *Mittelassyrische Rechtsurkunden und Verwaltungstexte*. VS 19. Berlin: Akademie-Verlag.

Fronzaroli, Pelio
1997 "Les combats de Hadda dans les textes d'Ébla." *MARI* 8: 283–90.

Frymer-Kensky, Tikva
1982 "The Tribulations of Marduk: The So-called 'Marduk Ordeal Text.'" *JAOS* 103: 131–41.

Fulco, William J.
1978 "The ʿAmman Citadel Inscription: A New Collation." *BASOR* 230: 39–43.

Gadd, C. J.
1925 *Cuneiform Texts from Babylonian Tablets, &c., in the British Museum, Part XXXVIII* [CT 38]. London: British Museum.

Garbini, Giovanni
1979 "L'Iscrizione di Balaam Bar-Beor." *Henoch* 1: 166–88.

Gardiner, Alan H.
1932 *Late Egyptian Stories*. Brussels: Fondation Égyptologique Reine Élisabeth.

Gerardi, Pamela deHart
1987 "Assurbanipal's Elamite Campaigns: A Literary and Political Study." Ph.D. diss. University of Pennsylvania.

Ginsberg, H. L.
1948 "An Aramaic Contemporary of the Lachish Letters." *BASOR* 111: 24–27.

Gitay, Yehoshua, ed.
1997 *Prophecy and Prophets: The Diversity of Contemporary Issues in Scholarship*. SemeiaSt. Atlanta: Scholars Press.

Gordon, R. P.
1993 "From Mari to Moses: Prophecy at Mari and in Ancient Israel." Pp. 63–79 in *Of Prophets' Visions and the Wisdom of Sages: Essays in Honour of R. Norman Whybray on His Seventieth Birthday*. Edited by H. A. McKay and D. J. A. Clines. JSOTSup 162. Sheffield: Sheffield Academic Press.

Grabbe, Lester L.
1995 *Priests, Prophets, Diviners, Sages: A Socio-Historical Study of Religious Specialists in Ancient Israel*. Valley Forge, Pa.: Trinity Press International.

2000 "Ancient Near Eastern Prophecy from an Anthropological Perspective." Pp. 13–32 in Nissinen, ed., 2000.

Grayson, A. K.

1975 *Assyrian and Babylonian Chronicles.* TCS 5. Locust Valley, N.Y.: Augustin.

Graziani, Simonetta, ed.

2000 *Studi sul Vicino Oriente antico dedicati alla memoria di Luigi Cagni.* Istituto Universitario Orientale, Dipartimento di Studi Asiatici, Series Minor 61. Napoli: Istituto Universitario Orientale.

Greenfield, Jonas C.

1969 "The Zakir Inscription and the Danklied." Pp. 174–91 in *Proceedings of the Fifth World Congress of Jewish Studies.* Vol. 1. Internationaler Kongreß für Studien zum Judentum. Jerusalem: World Union of Jewish Studies.

1987 "Aspects of Aramean Religion." Pp. 67–78 in Miller, Hanson, and McBride, eds., 1987.

Greßmann, Hugo

1914 "Die literarische Analyse Deuterojesajas." *ZAW* 34: 254–97.

———, ed.

1926 *Altorientalische Texte zum Alten Testament.* 2d ed. Berlin: de Gruyter.

Groneberg, Brigitte

1986 "Die sumerisch-akkadische Inanna/Ištar: Hermaphroditos?" *WO* 17: 25–46.

1997 *Lob der Ištar: Gebet und Ritual an die altbabylonische Venusgöttin.* Cuneiform Monographs 8. Groningen: Styx.

Guichard, Michaël

1999 "Les aspects religieux de la guerre à Mari." *RA* 93: 27–48.

Hackett, Jo Ann

1984 *The Balaam Text from Deir ʿAlla.* HSM 31. Chico, Calif.; Scholars Press.

1986 "Some Observations on the Balaam Tradition at Deir ʿAllā." *BA* 49: 216–22.

Haldar, Alfred

1945 *Associations of Cult Prophets among the Semites.* Uppsala: Almqvist & Wiksell.

Hämeen-Anttila, Jaakko

2000a *A Sketch of Neo-Assyrian Grammar.* SAAS 13. Helsinki: Neo-Assyrian Text Corpus Project.

2000b "Arabian Prophecy." Pp. 115–46 in Nissinen, ed., 2000.

Harner, Philip B.

1969 "The Salvation Oracle in Second Isaiah." *JBL* 88: 418–34

Harper, Robert Francis, ed.

1892–1914 *Assyrian and Babylonian Letters Belonging to the Koyunjik Collection of the British Museum*. Vols. 1–14. Chicago: University of Chicago Press.

Hayes, John H.

1967 "Prophetism at Mari and Old Testament Parallels." *AThR* 49: 397–409.

1968 "The Usage of Oracles against Foreign Nations in Ancient Israel." *JBL* 87: 81–92.

Heimpel, Wolfgang

1999 "Minding an Oath." *NABU* 1999: 41 (§ 42).

Heintz, Jean-Georges

1969 "Oracles prophétiques et 'guerre sainte' selon les archives royales de Mari et l'Ancien Testament." Pp. 112–38 in *Congress Volume: Rome, 1968*. VTSup 17. Leiden: Brill.

1971a "Prophetie in Mari und Israel." *Bib* 52: 543–55.

1971b "Aux origines d'une expression biblique: *ūmūšu qerbū* in A.R.M. X/6, 8'?" *VT* 21: 528–40.

1972 "Langage prophétique et 'style du cour', selon Archives royales de Mari X et l'Ancien Testament." *Sem* 22: 5–12.

1979 "De l'absence de la statue divine au 'Dieu qui se cache' (Ésaïe, 45/15): aux origines d'un thème biblique." *RHPhR* 59: 427–37.

1990 *Bibliographie de Mari—Archéologie et Textes (1933–1988)*. Travaux du Groupe de Recherches et d'Études Sémitiques Anciennes [G.R.E.S.A.], Université des Sciences Humaines de Strasbourg 3. Wiesbaden: Harrassowitz.

1992 "Supplément I (1989–1990)." *Akkadica* 77: 1–37.

1993 "Supplément II (1991–1992)—[Addenda and Corrigenda. Édition du 31 Déc. 1992]." *Akkadica* 81: 1–22.

1994 "Bibliographie de Mari: Supplément III (1992–1993)." *Akkadica* 86: 1–23.

1995 "Supplément IV (1993–1994) [Addenda and Corrigenda. Edition du 31 Déc. 1994]." *Akkadica* 91: 1–22.

1996 "Supplément V (1994–1995)." *Akkadica* 96: 1–22.

1997a "La 'fin' des prophétes bibliques? Nouvelles théories et documents sémitiques anciens." Pp. 195–214 in Heintz, ed., 1997.

1997b "Des textes sémitiques anciens à la Bible hébraïque: un comparatisme légitime?" Pp. 127–56 in *Le comparatisme en histoire des religions: pour un état de la question. Actes du Colloque international du Centre de Recherches d'Histoire des Religions, Université des Sciences Humaines de Strasbourg, 18–20 Septembre 1996*. Edited by F. Bœspflug and F. Dunand. Paris: Cerf.

1997c "Supplément VI (1995–1996)." *Akkadica* 104–5: 1–23.

1998 "Supplément VII (1996–1997)." *Akkadica* 109–10: 1–21.

2000 "Bibliographie de Mari: Supplément VIII (1997–1999)." *Akkadica* 118: 20–45.

———, ed.

1997 *Oracles et prophéties dans l'antiquité. Actes du Colloque de Strasbourg 15–17 Juin 1995*. Université des sciences humaines de Strasbourg, Travaux du Centre de recherche sur le Proche-Orient et la Grèce antiques 15. Paris: de Boccard.

Helck, W.

1986 "Wenamun." *LÄ* 6: 1215–17.

Heltzer, M.

1999 "On the Origin of the Near Eastern Archaeological Amber." Pp. 169–76 in *Languages and Cultures in Contact: At the Crossroads of Civilizations in the Syro-Mesopotamian Realm*. [CRRAI 42.] Edited by K. van Lerberghe and G. Voet. OLA 96. Leuven: Peeters.

Hoch, James E.

1994 *Semitic Words in Egyptian Texts of the New Kingdom and Third Intermediate Period*. Princeton, N.J.: Princeton University Press.

Hoffner, Harry A., Jr.

1967 "Second Millennium Antecedents to the Hebrew *ʾôb*." *JBL* 86: 385–401.

Hoftijzer, Jacob

1976 "The Prophet Balaam in a Sixth Century Aramaic Inscription." *BA* 39: 11–17.

1991 "What Did the Gods Say? Remarks on the First Combination of the Deir ʿAlla Plaster Texts." Pp. 121–42 in Hoftijzer and van der Kooij, eds., 1991.

Hoftijzer, Jacob, and Gerrit van der Kooij

1976 *Aramaic Texts from Deir ʿAlla*. DMOA 19. Leiden: Brill.

———, eds.

1991 *The Balaam Text from Deir ʿAlla Re-evaluated: Proceedings of the International Symposium Held at Leiden 21–24 August 1989*. Leiden: Brill.

Holma, Harri

1944 "Zum akkadischen Wörterbuch. 9–10." *Or* 13: 223–35.

Hölscher, Gustav

1914 *Die Propheten: Untersuchungen zur Religionsgeschichte Israels*. Leipzig: Hinrichs.

Horn, S. H.

1969 "The Amman Citadel Inscription." *BASOR* 193: 2–13.

Huehnergard, John
1999 "On the Etymology and Meaning of Hebrew *nābîʾ*." *ErIsr* 26: 88*–93*.
Huffmon, Herbert B.
1968 "Prophecy in the Mari Letters." *BA* 31: 101–24. Repr. as pp. 199–224 of vol. 3 in *The Biblical Archaeologist Reader*. Edited by E. F. Campbell Jr. and D. N. Freedman. Garden City, N.Y.: Doubleday, 1970.
1976a "The Origins of Prophecy." Pp. 171–86 in *Magnalia Dei. The Mighty Acts of God: Essays on the Bible and Archaeology in Memory of G. Ernest Wright*. Edited by F. M. Cross, W. E. Lemke, and P. D. Miller. Garden City, N.Y.: Doubleday.
1976b "Prophecy in the Ancient Near East." *IDBSup* 697–700.
1992 "Ancient Near Eastern Prophecy." *ABD* 5: 477–82.
1997 "The Expansion of Prophecy in the Mari Archives: New Texts, New Readings, New Information." Pp. 7–22 in Gitay, ed., 1997.
2000 "A Company of Prophets: Mari, Assyria, Israel." Pp. 47–70 in Nissinen, ed., 2000.
Hurowitz, Victor Avigdor
1993 "ABL 1285 and the Hebrew Bible: Literary Topoi in Urad Gula's Letter of Petition to Assurbanipal." *SAAB* 7: 9–17.
Ishida, Tomoo
1977 *Royal Dynasties in Ancient Israel: A Study on the Formation and Development of Royal-Dynastic Ideology*. BZAW 142. Berlin: de Gruyter.
Ivantchik, Askold I.
1993a *Les Cimmériens au Proche-Orient*. OBO 127. Fribourg: Editions Universitaires; Göttingen: Vandenhoeck & Ruprecht.
1993b "Corrigenda aux textes akkadiens mentionnant les Cimmériens. 2. Oracle de la déesse Mullissu à Assourbanipal." *NABU* 1993: 39–41 (§49).
Jack, J. W.
1938 "The Lachish Leters: Their Date and Import." *PEQ* 70: 180.
Jackson, K. P.
1983 *The Ammonite Language of the Iron Age*. HSM 27. Chico, Calif.: Scholars Press.
Jacquet, A.
2002 "LUGAL-MEŠ et *malikum:* nouvel examen du *kispum* à Mari." Pp. 51–68 in Charpin and Durand, eds., 2002.
Jastrow, Morris, Jr.
1912 *Die Religion Babyloniens und Assyriens*. Vol. 2. Gießen: Töpelmann.

Jean, Charles-François
1941 *Archives royales de Mari 2*. TCL 23. Paris: Geuthner.
1950 *Lettres diverses*. ARM 2. Paris: Concours du Centre National de la Recherche Scientifique.
Jepsen, Alfred
1969 "Kleine Bemerkungen zu drei westsemitischen Inschriften." *MIOF* 15: 1–2.
Joannès, Francis
1988 Pp. 233–355 in *Archives épistolaires de Mari I/2*. Edited by D. Charpin, F. Joannès, S. Lackenbacher, and B. Lafont. ARM 26/2. Paris: Editions Recherche sur les Civilisations.
Johns, C. H. W.
1901 *Additional Cuneiform Texts, Introduction, Officials, Metrology*. Vol. 2 of *Assyrian Deeds and Documents*. Cambridge: Bell.
Joüon, Paul
1936 "Sur les ostraca hébraïques de Lachish." *RES* 17: 88.
Kataja, Laura, and Robert M. Whiting
1995 *Grants, Decrees and Gifts of the Neo-Assyrian Period*. SAA 12. Helsinki: Helsinki University Press.
Klauber, Ernst Georg
1914 "Zur Politik und Kultur der Sargonidenzeit." *AJSL* 30: 233–87.
Klengel, Horst
1965 "Der Wettergott von Ḫalab." *JCS* 19: 87–93.
Knudtzon, J. A.
1915 *Die Texte*. Vol. 1 of *Die El-Amarna-Tafeln mit Einleitung und Erläuterungen*. VAB 2. Leipzig: Hinrichs.
Köckert, Matthias
2001 "Die Theophanie des Wettergottes Jahwe in Psalm 18." Pp. 209–26 in *Kulturgeschichten: Altorientalische Studien für Volkert Haas zum 65. Geburtstag*. Edited by T. Richter, D. Prechel, and J. Klinger. Saarbrücken: Saarbrücker Druckerei und Verlag.
Koppen, F. van
2002 "Seized by the Royal Order: The Households of Sammêtar and Other Magnates at Mari." Pp. 289–372 in Charpin and Durand, eds., 2002.
Kraus, F. R.
1971 "Akkadische Wörter und Ausdrücke VIII: *zikir šumim, šumam zakāru*." *RA* 65: 99–112.
Kühne, Cord
1973 *Die Chronologie der internationalen Korrespondenz von El-Amarna*. AOAT 17. Kevelaer: Butzon & Bercker; Neukirchen-Vluyn: Neukirchener Verlag.

Kupper, Jean-Robert
1950 *Correspondance de Kibri-Dagan, gouverneur de Terqa*. ARM 3. Paris: Concours du Centre National de la Recherche Scientifique.
1948 *Archives royales de Mari 3: Lettres*. TCL 24. Paris: Geuthner.
1953 *Archives royales de Mari 6: Lettres*. TCL 27. Paris: Geuthner.
1954 *Correspondance de Baḫdi-Lim, préfet du palais de Mari*. ARM 6. Paris: Concours de la Commission des Fouilles.
1957 *Les nomades en Mésopotamie au temps des rois de Mari*. Bibliothèque de la Faculté de Philosophie et Lettres de l'Université de Liége 142. Paris: Belles Lettres.
1964 "Correspondance de Kibri-Dagan." *Syria* 41, 105–16.
1971 "La date des *Šakkanakku* de Mari." *RA* 65: 113–18.
1983 *Documents administratifs de la salle 135 du Palais de Mari*. ARM 22/1–2. Paris: Editions Recherche sur les Civilisations.

Kutscher, R.
1972 "A New Inscription from ʿAmman" [Hebrew]. *Qad* 2: 27–28.

Kwasman, Theodore, and Simo Parpola
1991 *Tiglath-Pileser III through Esarhaddon*. Part 1 of *Legal Transactions of the Royal Court of Nineveh*. SAA 6. Helsinki: Helsinki University Press.

Laato, Antti
1992 *The Servant of YHWH and Cyrus: A Reinterpretation of the Exilic Messianic Programme in Isaiah 40–55*. ConBOT 35. Stockholm: Almqvist & Wiksell.
1996 *History and Ideology in the Old Testament Prophetic Literature: A Semiotic Approach to the Reconstruction of the Proclamation of the Historical Prophets*. ConBOT 41. Stockholm: Almqvist & Wiksell.
1998 "The Royal Covenant Ideology in Judah." Pp. 93–100 in Schunck and Augustin, eds., 1998.

Labat, René
1939 *Le caractère religieux de la royauté assyro-babylonienne*. Paris: Librairie d'Amérique et d'Orient.
1959 "Asarhaddon et la ville de Zaqqap." *RA* 53: 113–18.

Labat, René, André Caquot, Maurice Sznyzer, and Maurice Vieyra, eds.
1970 *Les religions du Proche-Orient asiatique: Textes babyloniens, ougaritiques, hittites*. Le trésor spirituel de l'humanité. Paris: Librairie Arthème Fayard et Éditions Denoël.

Lafont, Bertrand
1984 "Le roi de Mari et les prophètes du dieu Adad." *RA* 78: 7–18.

1988 Pp. 461–541 in *Archives épistolaires de Mari I/2*. Edited by D. Charpin, F. Joannès, S. Lackenbacher, and B. Lafont. ARM 26/2. Paris: Editions Recherche sur les Civilisations.

1999 "Sacrifices et rituals à Mari et dans le Bible." *RA* 93: 57–77.

2001 "Relations internationales, alliances et diplomatie au temps des rois de Mari." *Amurru* 2: 213–328.

2002 "La correspondance de Mukannišum trouvée dans le palais de Mari: nouvelles pièces et essai d'évaluation." Pp. 373–412 in Charpin and Durand, eds., 2002.

Lambert, Wilfred George

1957 "Ancestors, Authors and Canonicity." *JCS* 11: 1–14.

1963 *Babylonian Wisdom Literature*. Oxford: Clarendon.

1978 *The Background of Jewish Apocalyptic*. London: Athlone.

1985 "The Pantheon of Mari." *MARI* 4: 525–39.

Lambert, Wilfred George, and A. Millard

1969 *Atra-ḫasīs: The Babylonian Story of the Flood*. Oxford: Clarendon.

Landsberger, Benno

1965 *Brief des Bischofs von Esagila an König Asarhaddon*. Mededelingen der Koninklijke Nederlandse Akademie van Wetenschappen, afd. Letterkunde. Nieuwe Reeks 28/6. Amsterdam: Noord-Hollandsche Uitgevers Maatschappij.

1967 *The Date Palm and Its By-products according to the Cuneiform Sources*. AfOB 17. Graz: self-published.

Lanfranchi, Giovanni B.

1989 "Scholars and Scholarly Tradition in Neo-Assyrian Times: A Case Study." *SAAB* 3: 99–114.

1990 *I Cimmeri: Emergenza delle élites militari iraniche nel Vicino Oriente (VIII–VII sec. a.C.)*. History of the Ancient Near East, Studies 2bis. Padova: Sargon.

Langdon, Stephen

1914 *Tammuz and Ishtar: A Monograph upon Babylonian Religion and Theology Containing Extensive Extracts from the Tammuz Liturgies and All of the Arbela Oracles*. Oxford: Clarendon.

1916 "A Ritual of Atonement Addressed to Tammuz and Ishtar." *RA* 13: 105–17.

1923 *Sumerian and Semitic Religious and Historical Texts*. Vol. 1 of *The H. Weld-Blundell Collection in the Ashmolean Museum*. OECT 1. Oxford: Oxford University Press.

Lebrun, René

1994 "Le prophétisme en pays Hittite et en Syrie au IIe millénaire." Pp. 79–84 in Asurmendi, Durand, Lebrun, Puech, and Talon 1994.

Leichty, Erle
1970 *The Omen Series Šumma izbu.* TCS 4. Locust Valley, N.Y.: Augustin.
Leick, Gwendolyn
1994 *Sex and Eroticism in Mesopotamian Literature.* London: Routledge.
Lemaire, André
1977 *Les ostraca.* Vol. 1 of *Inscriptions Hébraïques.* Paris: Cerf.
1985a "Fragments from the Book of Balaam Found at Deir Alla." *BAR* 11: 26–39.
1985b "L'inscription de Balaam trouvée à Deir ʿAlla: épigraphie." Pp. 313–25 in *Biblical Archaeology Today: Proceedings of the International Congress on Biblical Archaeology, Jerusalem, April 1984.* Edited by J. Amitai. Jerusalem: Israel Exploration Society and Israel Academy of Sciences and Humanities.
1985c "Les inscriptions de Deir ʿAlla et la littérature araméenne antique." *CRAI:* 270–85.
1993 "Les groupes prophétiques dans l'ancien Israël." Pp. 39–55 in *L'Ancien Proche-Orient et les Indes: Parallélismes interculturels religieux. Colloque franco-finlandais les 10 et 11 novembre 1990 à l'Institut finlandais, Paris.* StudOr 70. Helsinki: Finnish Oriental Society.
1996 "Les textes prophétiques de Mari dans leurs relations avec l'Ouest." Pp. 427–38 in *Mari, Ébla et les Hourrites: dix ans de travaux.* Edited by J.-M. Durand. Amurru 1. Paris: Recherche sur les Civilisations.
1997 "Oracles, politique et littérature dans les royaumes araméens et transjordaniens (IX$^{e}$–VIII$^{e}$ s. av. n.è.)." Pp. 171–93 in Heintz, ed., 1997.
1999 "Traditions amorrites et Bible: le prophétisme." *RA* 93: 49–56.
2001 "Prophètes et rois dans les inscriptions ouest-sémitiques (IX$^{e}$–VI$^{e}$ siècle av. J. C.)." Pp. 85–115 in Lemaire, ed., 2001.
———, ed.
2001 *Prophètes et rois: Bible et Proche-Orient.* Paris: Cerf.
Levine, Baruch A.
1981 "The Deir ʿAlla Plaster Inscriptions." *JAOS* 101: 195–205.
1991 "The Plaster Inscriptions from Deir ʿAlla: General Interpretation." Pp. 58–72 in Hoftijzer and van der Kooij, eds., 1991.
2000 "The Deir ʿAlla Plaster Inscriptions." *COS* 2: 140–45.
Lewy, Hildegard
1965 "Ištar-ṣâd and the Bow-Star." Pp. 273–81 in *Studies in Honor of Benno Landsberger on His Seventy-Fifth Birthday, April*

*21, 1965*. Edited by H. G. Güterbock and T. Jacobsen. AS 16. Chicago: University of Chicago Press.

Lichtheim, Miriam

1973–80 *Ancient Egyptian Literature: A Book of Readings*. 3 vols. Berkeley and Los Angeles: University of California Press.

Limet, Henri

1986 *Textes administratifs relatifs aux métaux*. ARM 25. Paris: Éditions Recherche sur les Civilisations.

Lindblom, Johannes

1962 *Prophecy in Ancient Israel*. Philadelphia: Fortress.

Lindenberger, James M.

1994 *Ancient Aramaic and Hebrew Letters*. SBLWAW 4. Atlanta: Scholars Press.

Lion, Brigitte

2000 "Les mentions de 'prophètes' dans la seconde moitié du II$^{e}$ millénaire av. J.-C." *RA* 94: 21–32.

Lion, Brigitte, and Cécile Michel

1997 "Criquets et autres insectes à Mari." *MARI* 8: 707–24.

Lipiński, Edward

1975 *Studies in Aramaic Inscriptions and Onomastics*. OLA 1. Leuven: Leuven University Press.

1994 *Studies in Aramaic Inscriptions and Onomastics II*. OLA 57. Leuven: Peeters.

Livingstone, Alasdair

1986 *Mystical and Mythological Explanatory Works of Assyrian and Babylonian Scholars*. Oxford: Clarendon.

1989 *Court Poetry and Literary Miscellanea*. SAA 3. Helsinki: Helsinki University Press.

Lods, A., and Georges Dossin

1950 "Une tablette inédite de Mari, intéressante pour l'histoire ancienne du prophetisme sémitique." Pp. 103–10 in *Studies in Old Testament Prophecy Presented to Prof. Theodore H. Robinson by the Society for Old Testament Study on His Sixty-Fifth Birthday, August 9th 1946*. Edited by H. H. Rowley. Edinburgh: T&T Clark.

Loretz, Oswald

2000 "Sparagmos und Omophagie in Māri und Ugarit." Pp. 1719–30 in Graziani, ed., 2000.

Lucas, E. C.

2000 "Daniel: Resolving the Enigma." *VT* 50: 66–80.

Luckenbill, Daniel David

1927 *From Sargon to the End*. Vol. 2 of *Ancient Records of Assyria and Babylonia*. Chicago: University of Chicago Press.

Luukko, Mikko, and Greta Van Buylaere
2002 *The Political Correspondence of Esarhaddon*. SAA 16. Helsinki: Helsinki University Press.
Malamat, Abraham
1956 "'Prophecy' in the Mari Documents" [Hebrew]. *ErIsr* 4: 74–84.
1958 "History and Prophetic Vision in a Mari Letter" [Hebrew]. *ErIsr* 5: 67–73.
1962 "Mari and the Bible: Some Patterns of Tribal Organization and Institutions." *JAOS* 82: 143–50.
1966 "Prophetic Revelations in New Documents from Mari and Their Relation to the Bible." Pp. 207–27 in *Volume du congrès: Genève, 1965*. VTSup 15. Leiden: Brill (cf. Malamat 1998: 82–101).
1980 "A Mari Prophecy and Nathan's Dynastic Oracle." Pp. 68–82 in *Prophecy: Essays Presented to Georg Fohrer*. Edited by J. A. Emerton. BZAW 150. Berlin: de Gruyter (= Malamat 1998: 106–21).
1987 "A Forerunner of Biblical Prophecy: The Mari Documents." Pp. 33–52 in Miller, Hanson, and McBride, eds., 1987.
1989a *Mari and the Early Israelite Experience*. Oxford: Oxford University Press for the British Academy.
1989b "Parallels between the New Prophecies from Mari and Biblical Prophecy." *NABU* 4: 61–64 (= Malamat 1998: 122–27).
1991a "The Secret Council and Prophetic Involvement in Mari and Israel." Pp. 231–36 in *Prophetie und geschichtliche Wirklichkeit im alten Israel: Festschrift für Siegfried Herrmann zum 65. Geburtstag*. Edited by R. Liwak and S. Wagner. Stuttgart: Kohlhammer (= Malamat 1998: 134–41).
1991b "New Light from Mari (ARM XXVI) on Biblical Prophecy." Pp. 185–90 in *Storia e tradizioni di Israele: Scritti in onore di J. Alberto Soggin*. Edited by D. Garrone and F. Israel. Brescia: Paideia (= Malamat 1998: 128–33).
1993 "A New Prophetic Message from Aleppo and Its Biblical Counterparts." Pp. 236–41 in *Understanding Poets and Prophets: Essays in Honour of George Wishart Anderson*. Edited by A. G. Auld. JSOTSup 152. Sheffield: Sheffield Academic Press (= Malamat 1998: 151–56).
1997 "The Cultural Impact of the West (Syria-Palestine) on Mesopotamia in the Old Babylonian Period." *AOF* 24: 312–19 (= Malamat 1998: 13–23).
1998 *Mari and the Bible*. Studies in the History and Culture of the Ancient Near East 12. Leiden: Brill.
2000 "Addendum to Luigi Cagni's Collection of Mari Prophecies." Pp. 631–34 in Graziani, ed., 2000.

Margalit, Baruch
1995a "The 'Balaam' Inscription from Deir ʿAlla (DAPT)," *UF* 26: 282–302.
1995b "Studies in NWSemitic Inscriptions." *UF* 27: 200–210.
1998 "Ninth-Century Israelite Prophecy in the Light of Contemporary NWSemitic Epigraphs." Pp. 515–32 in Dietrich and Kottsieper, eds., 1998.

Martin, François
1902 *Textes réligieux assyriens et babyloniens*. Bibliothèque de l'École des Hautes Études 130. Paris: Bouillon.

Mattila, Raija, ed.
1995 *Nineveh, 612 BC: The Glory and Fall of the Assyrian Empire*. Catalogue of the Tenth Anniversary Exhibition of the Neo-Assyrian Text Corpus Project. Helsinki: Helsinki University Press.

Mauer, Gerlinde, and Ursula Magen, eds.
1988 *Ad bene et fideliter seminandum: Festgabe für Karlheinz Deller*. AOAT 220. Kevelaer: Butzon & Bercker; Neukirchen-Vluyn: Neukirchener Verlag.

Mayer, Walter
1978 *Die Archive des Palastes und die Prosopographie der Berufe*. Vol. 1 of *Nuzi-Studien*. AOAT 205. Kevelaer: Butzon & Bercker; Neukirchen-Vluyn: Neukirchener Verlag.

McCarter, P. Kyle
1980 "The Balaam Texts from Deir ʿAllā: The First Combination." *BASOR* 239: 49–60.

McCarthy, Dennis J.
1978 *Treaty and Covenant: A Study in Form in the Ancient Oriental Documents and in the Old Testament*. 2d ed. AnBib 21A. Rome: Pontificio Istituto Biblico.

Meek, Theophile James
1920 "Some Explanatory Lists and Grammatical Texts." *RA* 17: 117–206.

Meissner, Bruno
1940 *Studien zur assyrischen Lexikographie IV*. MAOG 13/2. Leipzig: Harrassowitz.

Michalowski, Piotr
1993 *Letters from Early Mesopotamia*. SBLWAW 3. Atlanta: Scholars Press.

Michaud, Henri
1941 "Le témoignage des ostraca de Tell Douweir concernant le prophète Jérémie." *Revue des études sémitiques et babyloniaca* 1941: 48–57.

1957 “Les ostraca de Lakiš conservés à Londres.” *Syria* 43: 39–60.

Millard, A.

1989 “The Homeland of Zakkur.” *Sem* 39: 47–52.

1990 “Israelite and Aramean History in the Light of Inscriptions.” *TynBul* 41: 261–75.

Miller, Patrick D., Paul D. Hanson, and S. Dean McBride, eds.

1987 *Ancient Israelite Religion: Essays in Honor of Frank Moore Cross*. Philadelphia: Fortress.

Möller, Georg

1909 *Literarische Texte des neuen Reiches*. Vol. 2 of *Hieratische Lesestücken für den akademischen Gebrauch*. Leipzig: Hinrichs.

Montgomery, J. A.

1909 “Some Gleanings from Pognon's ZKR Inscription.” *JBL* 28: 57–70.

Moran, William L.

1969a “New Evidence from Mari on the History of Prophecy.” *Bib* 50: 15–56.

1969b “Akkadian Letters.” *ANET*, 623–32.

1992 *The Amarna Letters*. Baltimore: Johns Hopkins University Press.

1993 “An Ancient Prophetic Oracle.” Pp. 252–59 in *Biblische Theologie und gesellschaftlicher Wandel: Für Norbert Lohfink*. Edited by G. Braulik, W. Groß, and S. McEvenue. Freiburg: Herder.

Müller, Hans-Peter

1970 “Notizen zu althebräischen Inschriften I.” *UF* 2: 237–42.

1978 “Einige alttestamentliche Probleme zur aramäischen Inschrift von Dēr ʿAllā.” *ZDPV* 94: 56–67.

1982 “Die aramäische Inschrift von Dēr ʿAllā und die älteren Bileamsprüche.” *ZAW* 94: 214–44.

1991 “Die Funktion divinatorischen Redens und die Tierbezeichnungen der Inschrift von Tell Deir ʿAllā.” Pp. 185–205 in Hoftijzer and van der Kooij, eds., 1991.

———, ed.

1991 *Babylonien und Israel: Historische, religiöse und sprachliche Beziehungen*. WdF 633. Darmstadt: Wissenschaftliche Buchgesellschaft.

Nakata, Ichiro

1974 “Deities in the Mari Texts.” Ph.D. diss. Columbia University. Ann Arbor: University Microfilms.

1982 “Two Remarks on the So-Called Prophetic Texts from Mari.” *ASJ* 4: 143–48.

Nissinen, Martti

1991 *Prophetie, Redaktion und Fortschreibung im Hoseabuch: Studien zum Werdegang eines Prophetenbuches im Lichte von Hos 4 und 11*. AOAT 231. Kevelaer: Butzon & Bercker; Neukirchen-Vluyn: Neukirchener Verlag.

1993 "Die Relevanz der neuassyrischen Prophetie für die alttestamentliche Forschung." Pp. 217–58 in *Mesopotamica–Ugaritica–Biblica: Festschrift für Kurt Bergerhof*. Edited by M. Dietrich and O. Loretz. AOAT 232. Kevelaer: Butzon & Bercker; Neukirchen-Vluyn: Neukirchener Verlag.

1996 "Falsche Prophetie in neuassyrischer und deuteronomistischer Darstellung." Pp. 172–95 in *Das Deuteronomium und seine Querbeziehungen*. Edited by T. Veijola. SFES 62. Helsinki: Finnische Exegetische Gesellschaft; Göttingen: Vandenhoeck & Ruprecht.

1998a "Prophecy against the King in Neo-Assyrian Sources." Pp. 157–70 in Schunck and Augustin, eds., 1998.

1998b *References to Prophecy in Neo-Assyrian Sources*. SAAS 7. Helsinki: Neo-Assyrian Text Corpus Project.

1998c *Homoeroticism in the Biblical World: A Historical Perspective*. Minneapolis: Fortress.

2000a "Spoken, Written, Quoted and Invented: Orality and Writtenness in Ancient Near Eastern Prophecy." Pp. 235–71 in Ben Zvi and Floyd, eds., 2000.

2000b "The Socioreligious Role of the Neo-Assyrian Prophets." Pp. 89–114 in Nissinen, ed., 2000.

2001a "City As Lofty As Heaven: Arbela and Other Cities in Neo-Assyrian Prophecy." Pp. 172–209 in *"Every City Shall Be Forsaken": Urbanism and Prophecy in Ancient Israel and the Near East*. Edited by L. L. Grabbe and R. D. Haak. JSOTSup 330. Sheffield: Sheffield Academic Press.

2001b "Neither Prophecies Nor Apocalypses: The Akkadian Literary Predictive Texts." Paper read at the 2001 Annual Meeting of the Society of Biblical Literature in Denver, November 18, 2001. Forthcoming in *Knowing the End from the Beginning: The Prophetic, The Apocalyptic, and their Relationships*. Edited by L. L. Grabbe and R. D. Haak. JSPSup.

2002a "A Prophetic Riot in Seleucid Babylonia." Pp. 62–74 in *"Wer darf hinaufsteigen zum Berg YHWHs?" Beiträge zu Prophetie und Poesie des Alten Testaments, Festschrift für Sigurdur Örn Steingrímsson zum 70. Geburtstag*. Edited by H. Irsigler. Arbeiten zu Text und Sprache im Alten Testament 72. St. Ottilien: EOS Verlag.

2002b "Prophets and the Divine Council." Pp. 4–19 in *Kein Land für sich allein: Studien zum Kulturkontakt in Kanaan, Israel/ Palästina und Ebirnâri für Manfred Weippert zum 65. Geburtstag*. Edited by U. Hübner and E. A. Knauf. OBO 186. Fribourg: Universitätsverlag; Göttingen: Vandenhoeck & Ruprecht.

2003 "Das kritische Potential in der altorientalischen Prophetie." Pp. 1–33 in *Propheten in Mari, Assyrien und Israel*. Edited by M. Köckert and M. Nissinen. FRLANT. Göttingen: Vandenhoeck & Ruprecht.

———, ed.

2000 *Prophecy in Its Ancient Near Eastern Context: Mesopotamian, Biblical, and Arabian Perspectives*. SBLSymS 13. Atlanta: Society of Biblical Literature.

Noort, Eduard

1977 *Untersuchungen zum Gottesbescheid in Mari: Die "Mariprophetie" in der alttestamentlichen Forschung*. AOAT 202. Kevelaer: Butzon & Bercker; Neukirchen-Vluyn: Neukirchener Verlag.

Nötscher, Friedrich

1928 "Haus- und Stadtomina der Serie *šumma âlu ina mêlê šakin*." *Or* 31:1–78.

1929 "Die Omen-Serie *šumma âlu ina mêlê šakin* (CT 38–40)." *Or* 39–42: 1–247.

1966 "Prophetie im Umkreis des alten Israel." *BZ* NS 10: 161–97 (= pp. 214–58 in Müller, ed., 1991).

Nougayrol, Jean

1956 "Asarhaddon et Naqi'a sur un bronze du Louvre (AO 20.185): II." *Syria* 33: 151–60.

1968a "Textes suméro-accadiens des archives et bibliothèques privées d'Ugarit." *Ugaritica* 5: 1–446.

1968b "La divination babylonienne." Pp. 25–81 in vol. 1 of *La Divination*. Edited by A. Caquot and M. Leibovici. Paris: Presses Universitaires de France.

Oliva, Juan

1994 "Seeking an Identity for Diritum." *NABU* 1994: 16–17 (§15).

Oppenheim, A. Leo

1952 "The Archives of the Palace of Mari." *JNES* 11: 129–39.

1954/56 "Sumerian: inim.gar, Akkadian: *egirrû*, Greek: *kledon*." *AfO* 17: 49–55.

1956 *The Interpretation of Dreams in the Ancient Near East*. Transactions of the American Philosophical Society NS 46/3. Philadelphia: American Philosophical Society.

1966 "Perspectives on Mesopotamian Divination." Pp. 35–43 in *La divination en Mésopotamie ancienne et dans les régions voisines*. CRRAI 14. Paris: Presses universitaires de France.
1969 "Babylonian and Assyrian Historical Texts." *ANET,* 556–67.

Otto, Eckart
1998 "Die Ursprünge der Bundestheologie im Alten Testament und im Alten Orient." *ZABR* 4: 1–84.
1999 *Das Deuteronomium: Politische Theologie und Rechtsreform in Juda und Assyrien*. BZAW 284. Berlin: de Gruyter.
2000 "Political Theology in Judah and Assyria: The Beginning of the Hebrew Bible as Literature." *SEÅ* 65: 59–76.

Overholt, Thomas W.
1986 *Prophecy in Cross-Cultural Perspective: A Sourcebook for Biblical Research*. SBLSBS. Atlanta: Scholars Press.
1989 *Channels of Prophecy: The Social Dynamics of Prophetic Activity*. Minneapolis: Fortress.

Ozan, Grégoire
1997 "Les Lettres de Manatân." Pp. 291–305 in Charpin and Durand, eds. 1997.

Pardee, Dennis
1982 *Handbook of Ancient Hebrew Letters*. Chico, Calif.: Scholars Press.

Parker, Simon B.
1993 "Official Attitudes toward Prophecy at Mari and in Israel." *VT* 43: 50–68.
1994 "The Lachish Letters and Official Reactions to Prophecies." Pp. 65–78 in *Uncovering Ancient Stones: Essays in Memory of H. Neil Richardson*. Edited by L. M. Hopfe. Winona Lake, Ind.: Eisenbrauns.
1997 *Stories in Scripture and Inscriptions: Comparative Studies on Narratives in Northwest Semitic Inscriptions and the Hebrew Bible*. Oxford: Oxford University Press.

Parpola, Simo
1970 *Texts*. Part 1 of *Letters from Assyrian Scholars to the Kings Esarhaddon and Assurbanipal*. AOAT 5/1. Kevelaer: Butzon & Bercker; Neukirchen-Vluyn: Neukirchener Verlag.
1979 *Neo-Assyrian Letters from the Kuyunjik Collection*. CT 53. London: British Museum.
1980 "The Murderer of Sennacherib." Pp. 171–82 in Alster, ed., 1980.
1983 *Commentary and Appendices*. Part 2 of *Letters from Assyrian Scholars to the Kings Esarhaddon and Assurbanipal*. AOAT 5/2. Kevelaer: Butzon & Bercker; Neukirchen-Vluyn: Neukirchener Verlag.

1987 "The Forlorn Scholar." Pp. 257–78 in *Language, Literature and History: Philological and Historical Studies Presented to Erica Reiner.* Edited by F. Rochberg-Halton. AOS 67. New Haven: American Oriental Society.

1993 *Letters from Assyrian and Babylonian Scholars.* SAA 10. Helsinki: Helsinki University Press.

1995 "The Imperial Archives of Nineveh." Pp. 15–25 in Mattila, ed., 1995.

1997 *Assyrian Prophecies.* SAA 9. Helsinki: Helsinki University Press.

2000 "Monotheism in Ancient Assyria." Pp. 165–209 in *One God or Many? Concepts of Divinity in the Ancient World.* Edited by B. N. Porter. Transactions of the Casco Bay Assyriological Institute 1. Casco Bay, Maine: Casco Bay Assyriological Institute.

2001 "Mesopotamian Precursos of the Hymn of Pearl." Pp. 181–93 in *Mythology and Mythologies: Methodological Approaches to Intercultural Influences.* Edited by R. M. Whiting. Melammu 2. Helsinki: Neo-Assyrian Text Corpus Project.

Parpola, Simo, and Kazuko Watanabe

1988 *Neo-Assyrian Treaties and Loyalty Oaths.* SAA 2. Helsinki: Helsinki University Press.

Peiser, F. E.

1898 *Studien zur orientalischen Altertumskunde.* Part 2. MVAG 3/6. Berlin: Wolf Peiser.

Perroudon, Marie-Claire

1993 "An Angry Goddess." *SAAB* 6: 41–44.

Petersen, David L.

1997 "Rethinking the Nature of Prophetic Literature." Pp. 23–40 in Gitay, ed., 1997.

2000 "Defining Prophecy and Prophetic Literature." Pp. 33–44 in Nissinen, ed., 2000.

Pfeiffer, Robert H.

1935 *State Letters of Assyria: A Transliteration and Translation of 355 Official Assyrian Letters Dating from the Sargonid Period (722–625 B.C.).* AOS 6. New Haven: American Oriental Society.

1955 "Akkadian Oracles and Prophecies." *ANET,* 449–52.

Pognon, H.

1907 *Inscriptions sémitiques de la Syrie, de la Mésopotamie et de la region de Mossoul.* Paris: Gabalda.

Pongratz-Leisten, Beate

1999 *Herrschaftswissen in Mesopotamien: Formen der Kommunikation zwischen Gott und König im 2. und 1. Jahrtausend v.Chr.* SAAS 10. Helsinki: Neo-Assyrian Text Corpus Project.

Porter, Barbara Newling
1993 *Image, Power, and Politics: Figurative Aspects of Esarhaddon's Babylonian Policy*. Philadelphia: American Philosophical Society.

Postgate, J. N.
1969 *Neo-Assyrian Royal Grants and Decrees*. Studia Pohl, Series Major 1. Rome: Pontificial Biblical Institute.

Puech, Émile
1986 "Admonitions de Balaam, l'homme qui voit les dieux." *MdB* 46: 36–38.
1987 "Le texte 'ammonite' de Deir ʿAlla: les admonitions de Balaam (première partie)." Pp. 13– 30 in *La vie de la Parole, de l'Ancien au Nouveau Testament: Études d'exégèse et d'herme-neutique biblique offertes à Pierre Grelot*. Paris: Desclee.

Puech, Émile, and Alexander Rofé
1973 "L'inscription de la citadelle d'Amman." *RB* 80: 531–46.

Radner, Karen
1995 "The Relation between Format and Content of Neo-Assyrian Texts." Pp. 63–78 in Mattila, ed., 1995.

Ramlot, Léon
1972 "Prophétisme." *DBSup* 8: 812–1222.

Rawlinson, Henry C., ed.
1875 *The Cuneiform Inscriptions of Western Asia*. Vol. 4. London: Trustees of the British Museum.
1891 *The Cuneiform Inscriptions of Western Asia*. Vol. 4. 2d. ed. London: Trustees of the British Museum.

Renger, Johannes
1969 "Untersuchungen zum Priestertum der altbabylonischen Zeit: 2. Teil." *ZA* 59: 104–230.

Renz, Johannes, and Wolfgang Röllig
1995 *Handbuch der althebräischen Epigraphik*. Vol. 1. Darmstadt: Wissenschaftliche Buchgesellschaft.

Richter, W.
1987 "Lakiš 3—Vorschlag zur Konstitution eines Textes." *BN* 37: 73–103.

Ringgren, H.
1983 "Balaam and the Deir ʿAlla Inscription." Pp. 93–98 in *Isaac Leo Seeligmann Volume: Essays on the Bible and the Ancient World*. Ed. A. Rofé and Y. Zakovitch. Vol. 3. Jerusalem: Rubenstein's.

Ritner, Robert K.
forthcoming *The Libyan Anarchy: Documents from Egypt's Third Intermediate Period*. SBLWAW.

Roberts, J. J. M.
1970 "A New Parallel to 1 Kings 18:28–29." *JBL* 89: 76–77.
Römer, W. H. Ph.
1971 *Frauenbriefe über Religion, Politik und Privatleben in Māri. Untersuchungen zu G. Dossin, Archives Royales de Mari X (Paris 1967).* AOAT 12. Kevelaer: Butzon & Bercker; Neukirchen-Vluyn: Neukirchener Verlag.
Ross, James F.
1970 "Prophecy in Hamath, Israel, and Mari." *HTR* 63: 1–28.
Rouault, Olivier
1977 *Mukannišum: L'administration et l'économie palatiales à Mari.* ARM 18. Paris: Geuthner.
Rowlett, Lori L.
1996 *Joshua and the Rhetoric of Violence: A New Historicist Analysis.* JSOTSup 226. Sheffield: Sheffield Academic Press.
Rüterswörden, Udo
2001 "Der Prophet in den Lachish-Ostraka." Pp. 179–92 in *Steine–Bilder–Texte: Historische Evidenz außerbiblischer und biblischer Quellen.* Edited by C. Hardmeier. ABG 5. Leipzig: Evangelische Verlagsanstalt.
Sachs, Abraham J., and Hermann Hunger
1996 *Diaries from 164 B.C. to 61 B.C.* Vol. 3 of *Astronomical Diaries and Related Texts from Babylonia.* Österreichische Akademie der Wissenschaften, Philologisch-historische Klasse, Denkschriften 247. Vienna: Österreichische Akademie der Wissenschaften.
Salonen, Armas
1969 *Die Fußbekleidung der Alten Mesopotamier nach sumerisch-akkadischen Quellen.* AASF B 157. Helsinki: Suomalainen tiedeakatemia.
1970 *Die Fischerei im Alten Mesopotamien nach sumerisch-akkadischen Quellen.* AASF B 166. Helsinki: Suomalainen tiedeakatemia.
San Nicolò, Mariano
1947 "Zum *atru* und anderen Nebenleistungen des Käufers beim neubabylonischen Immobiliarkauf." *Or* 16: 273–302.
Sasson, Jack M.
1973a "The Worship of the Golden Calf." Pp. 151–59 in *Orient and Occident: Essays Presented to Cyrus H. Gordon on the Occasion of His Sixty-Fifth Birthday.* Edited by H. A. Hoffner Jr. AOAT 22. Kevelaer: Butzon & Bercker; Neukirchen-Vluyn: Neukirchener Verlag.

1973b "Biographical Notices on Some Royal Ladies from Mari." *JCS* 25: 59–78.

1974 "Reflections on an Unusual Practice Reported in ARM X:4." *Or* 43: 404–10.

1979 "The Calendar and Festivals of Mari during the Reign of Zimri-Lim." Pp. 119–41 in *Studies in Honor of Tom B. Jones*. Edited by M. A. Powell Jr. and R. H. Sack. AOAT 203. Kevelaer: Butzon & Bercker; Neukirchen-Vluyn: Neukirchener Verlag.

1980 "Two Recent Works on Mari." *AfO* 27: 127–35.

1982 "An Apocalyptic Vision from Mari? Speculations on ARM X:9." *MARI* 1: 151–67.

1983 "Mari Dreams." *JAOS* 103: 283–93.

1984a "Thoughts of Zimri-Lim." *BA* 47: 110–20.

1984b "Zimri-Lim Takes the Grand Tour." *BA* 47: 246–51.

1993 "Mariage entre grandes familles." *NABU* 1993: 43–44 (§52).

1994 "The Posting of Letters with Divine Messages." Pp. 299–316 in *Florilegium Marianum II: Recueil d'études à la mémoire de Maurice Birot*. Edited by D. Charpin and J.-M. Durand. Mémoires de NABU 3. Paris: SEPOA.

1995a "Mari Apocalypticism Revisited." Pp. 285–98 in *Immigration and Emigration within the Ancient Near East: Festschrift E. Lipiński*. Edited by K. van Lerberghe and A. Schoors. OLA 65. Leuven: Peeters.

1995b "Water beneath Straw: Adventures of a Prophetic Phrase in the Mari Archives." Pp. 599–608 in *Solving Riddles and Untying Knots: Biblical, Epigraphic, and Semitic Studies in Honor of Jonas C. Greenfield*. Edited by Z. Zevit, S. Gitin, and M. Sokoloff. Winona Lake, Ind.: Eisenbrauns.

1998 "About 'Mari and the Bible.'" *RA* 92: 97–123.

Sasson, Victor

1979 "The ʿAmman Citadel Inscription As an Oracle Promising Divine Protection: Philological and Literary Comments." *PEQ* 111: 117–25.

1985 "Two Unrecognized Terms in the Plaster Texts from Deir ʿAlla." *PEQ* 115: 102–3.

1986a "The Book of Oracular Visions of Balaam from Deir ʿAlla." *UF* 17: 283–309.

1986b "The Language of Rebellion in Psalm 2 and the Plaster Texts from Deir ʿAlla," *AUSS* 24: 147–54.

Sayce, Archibald H., ed.

1891 *Records of the Past: New Series being English Translations of the Ancient Monuments of Egypt and Western Asia*. Vol. 5. London: Bagster & Sons.

Schart, Aaron
1995 "Combining Prophetic Oracles in Mari Letters and Jeremiah 36." *JANESCU* 23: 75–93.
Scheil, V.
1897 "Choix de textes réligieux assyriens." *RHR* 36: 197–207.
1927 "Tablettes anciennes." *RA* 24: 43–45.
Schmidt, Brian B.
1994 *Israel's Beneficent Dead: Ancestor Cult and Necromancy in Ancient Israelite Religion and Tradition.* FAT 11. Tübingen: Mohr Siebeck.
Schmidtke, Friedrich
1916 *Asarhaddons Statthalterschaft in Babylonien und seine Thronbesteigung in Assyrien 681 v.Chr.* Leiden: Brill.
Schmitt, Armin
1982 *Prophetischer Gottesbescheid in Mari und Israel.* BWANT 6/14. Stuttgart: Kohlhammer.
Schott, Albert, and Joh. Schaumberger
1941 "Vier Briefe Mar-Ištars an Asarhaddon über die Himmelserscheinungen der Jahre 670/668." *ZA* 47: 89–130.
Schult, Hermann
1966 "Vier weitere Mari-Briefe 'prophetischen' Inhalts." *ZDPV* 82: 228–32.
Schunck, Klaus-Dietrich, and Matthias Augustin, eds.
1998 *"Lasset uns Brücken bauen. . . ": Collected Communications to the XVth Congress of the International Organization for the Study of the Old Testament, Cambridge 1995.* BEATAJ 42. Frankfurt am Main: Lang.
Shea, W. H.
1979 "Milkom As the Architect of Rabbath-Ammon's Natural Defences in the Amman Citadel Inscription." *PEQ* 111: 18–25.
1981 "The Amman Citadel Inscription Again." *PEQ* 113: 105–10.
Sicre, José Luis
1992 *Profetismo en Israel: El Profeta. Los Profetas. El Mensaje.* Estella (Navarra): Verbo Divino.
Simpson, W. K., ed.
1973 *The Literature of Ancient Egypt: An Anthology of Stories, Instructions, and Poetry.* New Haven: Yale University Press.
Smelik, Klaas A. D.
1990 "The Riddle of Tobiah's Document: Difficulties in the Interpretation of Lachish III, 19– 21." *PEQ* 122: 133–38.
1991 *Writings from Ancient Israel.* Translated by G. I. Davies. Louisville: Westminster John Knox.

Soden, Wolfram von

1950 "Verkündigung des Gotteswillens durch prophetisches Wort in den altbabylonischen Briefen aus Mâri." *WO* 1: 397–403 (= pp. 19–31 in *Bibel und Alter Orient: Altorientalische Beiträge zum Alten Testament*. Edited by H.-P. Müller. BZAW 162. Berlin: de Gruyter 1985 = pp. 201–13 in Müller, ed., 1991).

1955 "Gibt es ein Zeugnis dafür, daß die Babylonier an die Wiederauferstehung Marduks geglaubt haben?" *ZA* 51: 132–66.

1956 "Beiträge zum Verständnis der neuassyrischen Briefe über die Ersatzkönigriten." In *Vorderasiatische Studien: Festschrift für Prof. Dr. Viktor Christian, gewidmet von Kollegen und Schülern zum 70. Geburtstag*. Edited by K. Schubert. Vienna: Notring der wissenschaftlichen Verbände Österreichs.

1968 "Aramäische Wörter in neuassyrischen und neu- und spätbabylonischen Texten. Ein Vorbericht. II (*n-z* und Nachträge)." *Or* 37: 261–71.

1969 "Einige Bemerkungen zu den von Fr. Ellermeier in 'Prophetie in Mari und Israel' erstmalig bearbeiteten Briefen aus ARM 10." *UF* 1: 199.

1977 "Aramäische Wörter in neuassyrischen und neu- und spätbabylonischen Texten. Ein Vorbericht. III." *Or* 46: 183–97.

Sollberger, Edmond

1966 *The Business and Administrative Correspondence under the Kings of Ur*. TCS 1. Locust Valley, N.Y.: Augustin.

Spieckermann, Hermann

1982 *Juda unter Assur in der Sargonidenzeit*. FRLANT 129. Göttingen: Vandenhoeck & Ruprecht.

Starr, Ivan

1990 *Queries to the Sungod: Divination and Politics in Sargonid Assyria*. SAA 4. Helsinki: Helsinki University Press.

Steiner, Richard C.

1997 "The Aramaic Text in Demotic Script." *COS* 1: 309–27.

Steymans, Hans Ulrich

2002 "'Deinen Thron hab ich unter den großen Himmeln festgemacht.' Die formgeschichtliche Nähe von Ps 89,4–5.20–38 zu Texten vom neuassyrischen Hof." Pp. 184–251 in *"Mein Sohn bist du" (Ps 2,7): Studien zu den Königspsalmen*. Edited by E. Otto and E. Zenger. SBS 192. Stuttgart: Katholisches Bibelwerk.

Stol, M.

1991 Review of Durand 1988 and Charpin et al. 1988. *JAOS* 111: 626–28.

Streck, Maximilian
1916 *Assurbanipal und die letzten assyrischen Könige bis zum Untergange Niniveh's.* Vols. 1–3. VAB 7. Leipzig: Hinrichs.

Strong, S. Arthur
1893 "On Some Oracles to Esarhaddon and Ašurbanipal." *BA* 2: 627–645.

Tadmor, Hayim
1982 "The Aramaization of Assyria: Aspects of Western Impact." Pp. 449–70 in *Mesopotamien und seine Nachbarn: Politische und kulturelle Wechselbeziehungen im Alten Vorderasien vom 4. bis 1. Jahrtausend v. Chr.* Edited by H.-J. Nissen and J. Renger. Berliner Beiträge zum vorderen Orient 1. [CRRAI 25.] Berlin: Reimer.
1983 "Autobiographical Apology in the Royal Assyrian Literature." Pp. 36–57 in *History, Historiography and Interpretation: Studies in Biblical and Cuneiform Literatures.* Edited by H. Tadmor and M. Weinfeld. Jerusalem: Magnes; Leiden: Brill.

Talon, Philippe
1980 "Un nouveau panthéon de Mari." *Akkadica* 20: 12–17.
1994 "Les textes prophétiques du premier millénaire en Mésopotamie." Pp. 97–125 in Asurmendi, Durand, Lebrun, Puech, and Talon 1994.

Tawil, H.
1974 "Some Literary Elements in the Opening Sections of the Hadad, Zākir, and the Nērab II Inscriptions in the Light of East and West Semitic Royal Inscriptions." *Or* 43: 51–57.

Thomas, D. Winton
1946 *"The Prophet" in the Lachish Ostraca.* London: Tyndale.
1948 "Ostracon III: 13-18 from Tell ed-Duweir." *PEQ* 80: 131–36.
1958 "Again: The 'Prophet' in the Lachish Ostraca." Pp. 244–45 in *Von Ugarit nach Qumran.* Edited by J. Hempel and L. Rost. BZAW 77. Berlin: Töpelmann.

Thompson, R. Campbell
1931 *The Prisms of Esarhaddon and Ashurbanipal found at Nineveh, 1927–8.* London: Trustees of the British Museum.

Thureau-Dangin, F.
1921 *Rituels accadiens.* Paris: Leroux.

Toorn, Karel van der
1987 "L'oracle de victoire comme expression prophétique au Proche-Orient ancien." *RB* 94: 63–97.
1998a "A Prophetic Role-Play Mistaken for an Apocalyptic Vision (ARM XXVI no. 196)." *NABU* 1998/1: 3–4.

1998b "Old Babylonian Prophecy between the Oral and the Written." *JNSL* 24: 55–70 (= pp. 219–34 in Ben Zvi and Floyd, eds. 2000).

1998c "In the Lion's Den: The Babylonian Background of a Biblical Motif." *CBQ* 60: 626–40.

2000 "Mesopotamian Prophecy between Immanence and Transcendence: A Comparison of Old Babylonian and Neo-Assyrian Prophecy." Pp. 70–87 in Nissinen, ed., 2000.

Torczyner, H.

1938 *Lachish I: The Lachish Letters*. The Wellcome Archaeological Research Expedition to the Near East. London: Oxford University Press.

Torrey, C. C.

1915–17 "Zakar and Kalamu Inscriptions." *JAOS* 35: 353–64.

Tremayne, Arch

1925 *Records from Erech: Time of Cyrus and Cambyses (538–521 B.C.)*. YOS 7. New Haven: Yale University Press.

Tsukimoto, Akio

1985 *Untersuchungen zur Totenpflege* (kispum) *im alten Mesopotamien*. AOAT 216. Kevelaer: Butzon & Bercker; Neukirchen-Vluyn: Neukirchener Verlag.

Uehlinger, Christoph

1992 "Audienz in der Götterwelt: Anthropomorphismus un soziomorphismus in der Ikonographie eines altsyrischen Zylindersiegels." *UF* 24: 339–59.

van Selms, A.

1975 "Some Remarks on the ʿAmmān Citadel Inscription." *BO* 32: 5–8.

Vaux, Roland de

1939 "Les Ostraka de Lachis." *RB* 48: 189–206.

Veenhof, K. R.

1982 "Observations on Some Letters from Mari (ARM 2, 124; 10,4; 43; 84; 114) with a Note on *tillatum*." *RA* 76: 119–40.

Veijola, Timo

1995 "Wahrheit und Intoleranz nach Deuteronomium 13." *ZTK* 92: 287–314.

2000 *Moses Erben: Studien zum Dekalog, zum Deuteronomismus und zum Schriftgelehrtentum*. BWANT 149. Stuttgart: Kohlhammer.

Villard, Pierre

2001 "Les prophéties à l'époque néo-assyrienne." Pp. 55–84 in Lemaire, ed., 2001.

Waterman, Leroy

1912 "Some Koyunjik Letters and Related Texts." *AJSL* 29: 1–36.

1930–36 *Royal Correspondence of the Assyrian Empire: Translated into English, with a Transliteration of the Text and a Commentary.* 4 vols. University of Michigan Studies, Humanistic Series 17–20. Ann Arbor: University of Michigan Press.

Wegner, Ilse

1981 *Gestalt und Kult der Ištar-Šawuška in Kleinasien.* AOAT 36. Kevelaer: Butzon & Bercker; Neukirchen-Vluyn: Neukirchener Verlag.

Weidner, Ernst

1966 "Assyrische Erlasse aus der Zeit Adadnirâris III." *AfO* 21: 35–41.

Weiher, E. von

1973 "Ḫanigalbat." *RlA* 4: 105–7.

Weinfeld, Moshe

1995 *Social Justice in Ancient Israel and in the Ancient Near East.* Publications of the Perry Foundation for Biblical Research in the Hebrew University of Jerusalem. Jerusalem: Magnes; Minneapolis: Fortress.

Weippert, Manfred

1967 *Die Landnahme der israelitischen Stämme in der neueren wissenschaftlichen Diskussion.* FRLANT 92. Göttingen: Vandenhoeck & Ruprecht.

1972 "'Heiliger Krieg' in Israel und Assyrien: Kritische Anmerkungen zu Gerhard von Rads Konzept des 'Heiligen Krieges im alten Israel.'" *ZAW* 84: 460–93 (= pp. 259–300 in Müller, ed., 1991; = pp. 71–97 in Weippert 1997c).

1981 "Assyrische Prophetien der Zeit Asarhaddons und Assurbanipals." Pp. 71–115 in Fales, ed., 1981.

1985 "Die Bildsprache der neuassyrischen Prophetie." Pp. 55–93 in H. Weippert, K. Seybold, and M. Weippert, *Beiträge zur prophetischen Bildsprache in Israel und Assyrien.* OBO 64. Fribourg: Universitätsverlag; Göttingen: Vandenhoeck & Ruprecht.

1988 "Aspekte israelitischer Prophetie im Lichte verwandter Erscheinungen des Alten Orients." Pp. 287–319 in Mauer and Magen, eds., 1988.

1991 "The Balaam Text from Deir ʿAlla and the Study of the Old Testament." Pp. 151–84 in Hoftijzer and van der Kooij, eds., 1991 (= "Der 'Bileam'-Text von *Tell Dēr ʿAllā* und das Alte Testament." Pp. 163–88 in Weippert 1997c).

1997a "'Das frühere, siehe, ist eingetroffen. . .': Über Selbstzitate im Prophetenspruch." Pp. 147–69 in Heintz, ed., 1997.

1997b "Prophetie im Alten Orient." *NBL* 3: 196–200.

1997c *Jahwe und die anderen Götter: Studien zur Religionsgeschichte des antiken Israel in ihrem syrisch-palestinischen Kontext*. FAT 18. Tübingen: Mohr Siebeck.

2001 "'Ich bin Jahwe'—'Ich bin Ištar von Arbela.' Deuterojesaja im Lichte der neuassyrischen Prophetie." Pp. 31–59 in *Prophetie und Psalmen: Festschrift für Klaus Seybold zum 65. Geburtstag*. Edited by. B. Huwyler, H.-P. Mathys, and B. Weber. AOAT 280. Münster: Ugarit-Verlag.

2002 "'König, fürchte dich nicht!' Assyrische Prophetie im 7. Jahrhundert v. Chr." *Or* 71: 1–54.

Weippert, Helga, and Manfred Weippert

1982 "Die 'Bileam'-Inschrift von *Tell Dēr ʿAllā*." *ZDPV* 98: 77–103 (= pp. 131–61 in Weippert 1997c).

Wente, Edward F.

1973 "The Report of Wenamon." Pp. 142–55 in *The Literature of Ancient Egypt*. Edited by W. K. Simpson. New Haven: Yale University Press.

Wesselius, J. W.

1987 "Thoughts about Balaam: The Historical Background of the Deir Alla Inscription on Plaster." *BO* 44: 589–99.

Westermann, Claus

1960 *Grundformen prophetischer Rede*. BEvTh 31. Munich: Kaiser Verlag.

1964 "Das Heilswort bei Deuterojesaja." *EvT* 24: 355–73.

Wilhelm, Gernot

1982 *Grundzüge der Geschichte und Kultur der Hurriter*. Darmstadt: Wissenschaftliche Buchgesellschaft.

Wilcke, Claus

1979 "Truppen von Mari in Kurda." *RA* 73: 37–50.

1983 "*ittātim ašqi aštāl:* Medien in Mari¿" *RA* 77: 93.

Wilson, John A.

1969 "The Journey of Wen-Amon to Phoenicia." *ANET*, 25–29.

Wilson, Robert R.

1980 *Prophecy and Society in Ancient Israel*. Philadelphia: Fortress.

Winand, Jean.

1987 *Le voyage d'Ounamon*. Aegyptiaca Leodiensia 1. Liege: C. I. P. L.

Wohl, Howard

1970/71 "The Problem of the *maḫḫû*." *JANESCU* 3: 112–18.

Wolff, Hans Walter

1961 *Dodekapropheton 1: Hosea*. BKAT 14/1. Neukirchen: Neukirchener Verlag.

Wyatt, N.
1998 "Arms and the King: The Earliest Allusions to the Chaoskampf Motif and their Implications for the Interpretation of the Ugaritic and Biblical Traditions." Pp. 833–82 in Dietrich and Kottsieper, eds., 1998.

Ziegler, N.
1999 *Florilegium marianum IV: Le Harem de Zimri-Lim*. Mémoires de NABU 5. Paris: SEPOA.

Zimmerli, Walther
1953 "Ich bin Jahwe." Pp. 179–209 in *Geschichte und Altes Testament: Albrecht Alt zum 70. Geburtstag*. BHT 16. Tübingen: Mohr Siebeck (= pp. 11–40 in Walther Zimmerli, *Gottes Offenbarung: Gesammelte Aufsätze*. TB 19. Munich: Kaiser, 1963).

Zimmern, Heinrich
1918 *Zum babylonischen Neujahrsfest*. Zweiter Beitrag. Berichte über die Verhandlungen der Sächsichen Gesellschaft der Wissenschaften zu Leipzig, Phil.-hist. Klasse 70/5. Leipzig: Teubner.

Zobel, Hans-Jürgen
1971 "Das Gebet um Abwendung der Not und seine Erhörung in den Klageliedern des Alten Testaments und in der Inschrift des Königs Zakir von Hamath." *VT* 21: 91–99.

# Glossary

All dates are B.C.E.

***ʿddỉ ʿ3.*** A child-medium; literally a "great youth/seer."

**Adad (Addu).** Weather god, especially worshiped in northern Babylonia and Syria; city god of Aleppo; one of his manifestations was called the Lord of Kallassu.

**Adad-aḫu-iddina.** Assyrian temple official at the time of Esarhaddon.

**Addu-duri.** One of the most influential women of Mari; probably member of the royal family, possibly mother of Zimri-Lim.

**Aḫšeri.** King of Mannea at the time of Assurbanipal.

**Aḫum.** Priest of the temple of Annunitum at Mari.

**Akkad.** City in northern Babylonia, founded by Sargon I; capital of the kings of Agade in twenty-fourth to twenty-second centuries. "The land of Akkad" (*māt Akkadî*) is the traditional designation of all Babylonia.

**Alaḫtum.** City in northern Syria, probably identical with Alalaḫ; mandate of Mari in the time of Zimri-Lim.

**Aleppo (Ḫalab).** Modern Ḫalab. City in northern Syria; capital of the kingdom Yamḫad and native city of Šibtu, queen of Mari.

**Amenophis III.** Pharaoh of Egypt (1391–1353); husband of Tadu-Ḫeba, daughter of the Hurrian king Tušratta.

**Amon.** The state god of Egypt and the chief of the Egyptian pantheon.

**Andarig.** City-state south of the Sinjar mountain and east of the River Habur.

**Annunitum.** A manifestation of Ištar at Mari and the most important female deity in prophetic oracles form Mari; also worshiped at Akkad and Sippar.

***āpilūm*** fem. ***āpiltūm*** "Answerer," i.e., transmitter of divine answers to human inquiries; besides *muḫḫûm,* the main designation of a person transmitting divine words at Mari.

**Arbela.** Modern Irbīl. One of the principal cities in the Assyrian heartland; center of Ištar cult and prophecy in the Neo-Assyrian era.

***assinnu.*** "Man-woman," a person whose gender role, analogous to that of the *kurgarrû,* is permanently changed by Ištar and who lived as a devotee of the goddess.

**Aššur.** Initially the eponymous deity of the city of Assur, later the Assyrian supreme god and the totality of all gods, whose main priest the king of Assyria was; in the Neo-Assyrian era, Mullissu (equated with Ištar of Nineveh) appears as his wife. The rise of Aššur to his elevated position is analogous to the rise in the status of Marduk in Babylonia.

**Assur.** Modern Qalʿat aš-Širqāṭ. Political capital of Assyria from Assur-uballit I (fourteenth century) through Assurnasirpal II (ninth century); after that religious capital of Assyria and center of worship of Aššur, the supreme god of Assyria. Also called Libbi-āli, "Inner City."

**Assurbanipal.** King of Assyria (668–627), son of Esarhaddon.

**Aššur-ḫamatu'a.** Temple official in Arbela.

**Baalshamayn.** "The Lord of Heaven," Syro-Palestinian supreme god, venerated throughout the Semitic cultural sphere during the first millennium B.C.E.

**Babylon.** Modern Bābil. Capital of Babylonia and cradle of Mesopotamian scholarship, site of the Esaggil temple for Marduk and seat of the Hammurabi dynasty; destroyed by Sennacherib in 689 and rebuilt by Esarhaddon and Assubanipal in the 670s and 660s.

**Baḫdi-Lim.** Prefect of the royal palace at Mari.

**Bel.** See Marduk.

**Belet-biri.** "The Lady of Divination," or "the Lady of the Wells," a hypostasis of Ištar at Mari.

**Belet-ekallim.** "The Lady of the Palace," the patroness of the royal family of Mari, whose temple occupied a large area in the royal palace of Mari; also worshiped in Babylonia.

**Bel-ušezib.** Babylonian astrologer in Esarhaddon's court.

**Borsippa.** Modern Birs Nimrūd. One of the principal cities of Babylonia, site of the Ezida temple of Nabû.

**Byblos.** Principal seaport on the coast of Lebanon, one of the most important Phoenician cities.

**Calah (Kalḫu).** Modern Tell Nimrūd. Principal capital of Assyria from Assurnasirpal II through Sargon II (ca. 864–707), center of worship of Ninurta and Ištar.

**Cimmerians.** People of Caucasian or Central Asian origin who invaded large areas in Urartu and Asia Minor in the Neo-Assyrian era.

**Dagan.** One of the principal West Semitic deities, head of the pantheon of Ebla, main god of the Philistines, second in rank after El at Ugarit and member of the Sumerian pantheon; very prominent at Mari, where his temple, source of many prophecies, was located next to the royal palace.

**Dašran.** Locality in the district of Terqa.

**Dir.** Provincial town, not far away from Mari to the south; center of worship of Diritum.

**Diritum.** Goddess of Dir.

***egerrû (m).*** Portentous speech or otherwise ominous auditory experience; one of the terms for prophetic discourse at Mari and juxtaposed with dreams and prophecies in Assyria.

**Ekallatum.** Modern Haikal. City in Assyria, north of Assur; capital of Išme-Dagan.

**Elam.** Kingdom in southwestern Iran.

**Esaggil.** Temple of Marduk at Babylon; one of the biggest sanctuaries in Mesopotamia and principal temple of Babylonia; incorporated the ziggurat Etemenanki (inspiration for "the tower of Babel"), which was regarded as the center of the universe.

**Esarhaddon.** King of Assyria (681–669), son of Sennacherib.

**Ešarra.** Temple of Aššur at Assur; housed the throne of the Assyrian kings who were enthroned and buried in this sanctuary.

**Ešnunna.** Modern Tell Asmar. Early second-millennium city and state between the River Tigris and the Zagros mountains, on the course of the River Diyala.

***eššēšu.*** A festival, the exact nature of which is still to be clarified. Behind the word there is the verb *edēšu* "to be, become new, rejuvenate" as well as the adjective *eššu* "new"; cf. *ūmu eššu* "new day." This "rejuvenation festival" is mentioned in a variety of contexts and its placement in the cultic calendar is unclear.

**Gaššum.** Locality in the western part of Ida-maraṣ on the upper course of the River Ḫabur.

**Hamath.** Modern Ḥamā. City-state in Syria, on the middle course of the Orontes River.

**Hammurabi.** King of Babylonia (1792–1750).

**Hammurabi.** King of Kurdâ at the time of Zimri-Lim of Mari.

**Ḫanat.** Goddess of the town Ḫanat on the Euphrates.

**Haneans.** The common designation of Simʾalites and Yaminites, nomadic population of the kingdom of Mari.

**Ḫišamitum.** Goddess of Ḫišamta, a town in the district of Terqa; she had a temple even at Mari.

**Ḫubšalum.** An oasis on the fringes of the desert south of the Sinjar mountain.

**Ibalpiel II.** King of Ešnunna at the time of Hammurabi of Babylonia and Zimri-Lim of Mari (ca. 1779–1765).

**Ida-maraṣ.** Area under the control of Zimri-Lim of Mari, west of the River Ḫabur.

**Ikrub-El.** See Yakrub-El.

**Ilan-ṣura.** Kingdom of Ḫaya-Sumu, vassal of Zimri-Lim.
**Ili-ḫaznaya.** *assinnu* of the temple of Annunitum at Mari.
**Inib-šina.** Sister of Zimri-Lim, king of Mari; possibly high priestess of Adad.
**Išme-Dagan.** King of Ekallatum (Assyria), son of Šamši-Adad, king of Assyria, and brother of Yasmaḫ-Addu, king of Mari.
**Itur-Asdu.** Governor of the district of Mari, later governor of Naḫur at the time of Zimri-Lim.
**Itur-Mer.** Protective god of Mari, hypostasis of the weather-god Mer.
**Ištar (Inanna).** The most important Mesopotamian goddess, embodiment of opposites as virgin, whore, and mother, involved in love and war and capable of transforming gender roles; worshiped in her various aspects all over ancient Near East, including Mari where her main manifestation was Annunitum. In Assyria, Ištar of Arbela was the principal speaker of prophetic words and patroness of the prophets, and Ištar of Nineveh was equated with Mullissu, the spouse of the supreme god Aššur.
**Izirtu.** Capital of Mannea, exact location unknown.
**Kanisan.** Son of Kibri-Dagan.
**Kar-Tukulti-Ninurta.** Modern Telūl al-ʿAqār. City on the east bank of the River Tigris, about 3 km north of Assur; founded by Tukulti-Ninurta I in the late thirteenth century.
**Kibri-Dagan.** Governor of Terqa at the time of Zimri-Lim.
**Kititum.** Ištar of Ešnunna.
**Kurdâ.** City and kingdom north of the Sinjar mountain between the upper courses of the Rivers Ḫabur and Tigris.
**Lachish.** Modern Tell ed-Duwēr. City in Judaea, destroyed by Nebuchadnezzar in 586.
**Lady of Akkad.** Ištar of Akkad.
**Lady of Babylon.** Designation of Zarpanitu, the spouse of Marduk.
**Lady of Kidmuri.** Ištar of Calah.
**Lanasûm.** Representative of Mari at Tuttul at the time of Zimri-Lim.
**Libbi-ali.** See Assur.
***maḫḫû,*** fem. ***maḫḫūtu.*** Assyrian literary equivalent of *muḫḫûm/ muḫḫūtum.*
**Mannea.** Kingdom in northwestern Iran, east of the Zagros mountains and south of the lake Urmia.
**Marduk.** The patron deity of the city of Babylon who was elevated to the status of the Babylonian supreme god, absorbing functions of many other deities; also called Bel ("the Lord"). The center of the worship of Marduk was his temple Esaggil at Babylon.
**Mari.** Modern Tell Ḥarīrī. City and kingdom that in the second half of the third and first half of the second millennium occupied large areas on the middle Euphrates and the River Ḫabur; center of worship of Dagan and

site of one of the biggest royal archives excavated in the ancient Near East.
**Mar-Issar.** Esarhaddon's agent in Babylonia.
**Milcom.** The state god of the Ammonites.
**Mitanni.** Empire of the Hurrians in the fifteenth/fourteenth century; the principal rival of Egypt controlling large areas in Assyria, Syria and Cilicia.
***muḫḫûm,*** fem. ***muḫḫūtum.*** The commonest designation of a prophet at Mari, where the *muḫḫûm/muḫḫūtum* belonged to the personnel of temples of different deities. In other sources from the Ur III (late third millennium) to the Neo-Babylonian period (sixth century), people called *muḫḫûm/muḫḫūtum* appear as prophets and cult functionaries, more often than not in the worship of Ištar.
**Mukannišum.** High official at Mari at the time of Zimri-Lim.
**Mullissu (Ninlil).** Initially the spouse of the god Enlil; in Assyria, wife of Aššur and a manifestation of Ištar, equated with Ištar of Nineveh. Speaks frequently in prophetic oracles, more often than not as united with Ištar of Arbela.
**Nabû.** Patron of Mesopotamian scribes, keeper of the tablet of destiny; son of Marduk in the Babylonian pantheon and patron god of the city of Borsippa; assumed a high status in the Neo-Assyrian and Neo-Babylonian era.
**Nabû-nadin-šumi.** Chief exorcist of Esarhaddon and Assurbanipal.
**Nabû-reḫtu-uṣur.** Assyrian citizen, possibly in the service of the queen mother.
**Nabû-reši-išši.** Temple official in Arbela.
**Naḫur.** City and religious center under the control of Mari on the upper course of the River Ḫabur.
**Nanaya.** Sumerian goddess, often appearing as another aspect of Inanna/Ištar, spouse of the god Nabû; worshiped especially at Uruk.
**Naqia.** Mother of Esarhaddon, king of Assyria.
**Nikkal (Ningal).** Sumerian goddess, mother of Šamaš and Inanna, later one of the manifestations of Ištar. Goddess of dream interpretation and spouse of the moon-god Sîn, worshiped especially at Harran.
**Nineveh.** Modern Tell Qūyunğiq. Principal capital of Assyria from the reign of Sennacherib until the collapse of the Assyrian Empire (704–612); site of the Emašmaš temple of Ištar and of royal palaces housing the most prolific royal archives known from the ancient Near East.
**Ninḫursag.** "Lady of the Mountain," one of the Mesopotamian mother goddesses, mother of Ninurta; merges together with Mullissu.
**Ninurta.** Son of Enlil and Mullissu/Ninḫursag; the heavenly crown prince, warrior, and farmer. For the Assyrian kings, Ninurta's defeat of the demon Asakku was the prototype of their victory over their enemies. The center of his worship in Neo-Assyrian period was Calah.
**Nur-Sîn.** Zimri-Lim's representative in Alaḫtum.

**Nusku.** Initially son of Enlil, god of fire and light; in the Neo-Assyrian period, worshiped at Harran as the son of Sîn; virtually equated with Nabû.
***qammatum.*** A designation of unclear derivation of a female transmitter of divine words; the only preserved message of the *qammatum* of Dagan of Terqa is reported twice in the letters from Mari.
**Qaṭṭunan.** City under the control of Mari on the upper course of the River Ḫabur.
***raggimu,*** fem. ***raggintu.*** "Proclaimer," Neo-Assyrian designation of a prophet, colloquial equivalent of *muḫḫûm/muḫḫūtum*.
***šabrû.*** Neo-Assyrian word for a visionary and dream interpreter.
**Šadikanni.** Modern Tell ʿAğāğa. City in the Neo-Assyrian Empire on the upper course of the River Ḫabur.
**Saggaratum.** City in the kingdom of Mari, north of Terqa, near the confluence of the Rivers Euphrates and Ḫabur.
**Šakkâ.** Locality in the district of Mari.
**Šamaš.** Sun-god and the god of justice and truth, "Lord of Heaven and Earth," invoked in extispicy rituals.
**Šamaš-naṣir.** Zimri-Lim's officer at Terqa.
**Šamaš-šumu-ukin.** Son of Esarhaddon and the elder brother of Assurbanipal; crown prince of Babylonia until Esarhaddon defeated him in a civil war (672–648).
**Sammetar.** Majordomo of the palace of Mari and one of the most influental officers during the first years of Zimri-Lim's reign.
**Šamši-Adad.** King of Assyria (ca. 1835/30–1777); seized control of Mari after Yaḫdun-Lim, installed his sons Yasmaḫ-Addu at Mari and Išme-Dagan at Ekallatum.
***šārtum u sissiktum.*** "Hair and garment fringe," which, when attached to a letter, personalized the person, e.g., a prophet, whose message was reported; this was done for the purpose of authenticating the message by extispicy.
**Sasî.** A high official (major or city overseer) in Nineveh (c. 675–665).
**Šauška.** The main goddess of the Hurrians, also worshiped by the Hittites; the Hurrian equivalent of Ištar of Nineveh.
**Šelebum.** *assinnu* of the temple of Annunitum at Mari.
**Šibtu.** Queen of Mari, wife of Zimri-Lim and daughter of Yarim-Lim, king of Aleppo.
**Šimatum.** Daughter of Zimri-Lim and wife of Ḫaya-Sumu, king of Ilan-ṣura.
**Sim'alites.** A designation for tribal groups living on the left (i.e., northern) side of the Euphrates.
**Sippar.** Modern Tell Abu-Ḥabba. City in northern Babylonia on the lower course of the River Euphrates, center of the worship of Šamaš.
***šulmu.*** "Peace, well-being, greeting of peace": in the Neo-Assyrian prophecies, a term for a salvation oracle.

**Susa.** Capital of Elam.
**Tebi-gerišu.** High official at Mari in the beginning of Zimri-Lim's reign.
**Terqa.** Modern Tell ʿAšāra. Religious center and the most important city after Mari in Zimri-Lim's kingdom.
***têrtum.*** Oracle; result of different kinds of divination, including extispicy and prophecy.
**Teumman.** King of Elam (674–653).
**Tišpak.** Deity especially worshiped in Ešnunna.
**Tušratta.** King of Mitanni, the Hurrian Empire (1365–1335/22).
**Tuttul.** Modern Tell Bīʿa. City on the upper course of the River Euphrates at the junction with the River Baliḫ; seat of a sanctuary of Dagan. Also identified with the modern Hīt on the middle course of the River Euphrates between Mari and Sippar.
**Urad-Gula.** Exorcist in Esarhaddon's court.
**Ur-lisi.** Governor of Umma, a major Sumerian city in the Ur III period.
**Yaḫdun-Lim.** King of Mari (ca. 1810–1795), father of Zimri-Lim.
**Yakrub-El.** Possibly a manifestation of the god Adad or a divinized ancestor worshiped at Terqa.
**Yaminites.** Designation for tribal groups living on the right (i.e., southern) side of the Euphrates.
**Yamutbal.** Area east of Tigris, probably south of Ešnunna.
**Yaqqim-Addu.** Governor of Saggaratum at the time of Zimri-Lim.
**Yasim-El.** Military commander at Andarig at the time of Zimri-Lim.
**Yasmaḫ-Addu.** King of Mari (ca. 1793–1775), son of Šamši-Adad, king of Assyria, and brother of Išme-Dagan, king of Ekallatum (Assyria).
**Zakira-Ḫammû.** Governor of Qaṭṭunan at the time of Zimri-Lim.
**Zakkur.** King of the Aramean city-states Hamath and Luash in the early eighth century.
**Zimri-Lim.** King of Mari (ca. 1775–1761), son of Yaḫdun-Lim.

# Indexes

The numbers refer to the numbers of the texts. Underlined numbers indicate that the deity is presented as the speaker of an oracle or as the patron deity of the prophet.

### 1. Names of Deities and Other Extraordinary Beings


Abba 35
Adad 1, 2, 4, 17, 50, 61, 64, 97, 99, 100
Admu 55, 59
Amon 142
Amu of Ḫubšalum 49
Anunnaki 118
Annunitum 8, 10, 22, 23, 24, 26, 37, 42, 58
Anu 66, 108
Aššur 71, 83, 84, 85, 86, 97, 99, 100, 101, 107, 111, 112, 113
Asumûm 18
Baalshamayn 137
Banitu (cf. Ištar) 78
Bel (cf. Marduk) 71, 97, 100, 106, 107, 109, 112, 115, 116, 117, 132, 133
Belet 115, 116, 117
Belet-biri 43
Belet-ekallim 9, 17, 19, 21, 24, 42, 45
Bel-Tarbaṣi 85
Dagan 3, 4, 6, 7, 9, 12, 15, 16, 17, 19, 20, 25, 30, 31, 32, 34, 37, 38, 39, 40, 42, 46, 53, 60, 62, 63, 64
Diritum 9, 18
Dumuzi 118
Ea 18, 97, 98, 108
El 138
Enlil 101, 108
Erra 64
Gula 108
Ḫanat 6
Ḫišamitum 5
The "Hitting God" 134
Ikrub-El 6, 30, 31, 32, 39, 40
Iluwer 137
Inanna (cf. Ištar) 119
Ištar 51, 112, 113, 118, 123
—of Arbela 68, 69, 70, 72, 74, 75, 76, 79, 81, 87, 88, 90, 91, 92, 94, 97, 100, 101, 107, 108, 114, 115, 116, 117
—of Bišra 42
—of Kidmuri 99, 100, 108
—of Nineveh (cf. Mullissu, Šauška) 97, 100, 107, 108, 115, 116, 117
—of Uruk 132
Itur-Mer 17, 41, 43, 55, 59, 64
Kititum (cf. Ištar) 66, 67
Lady
—of Akkad 109

## 2. Names of Prophets



## 3. Designations of Prophets

## 4. Personal Names (Other Than Prophets)

## 5. Names of Peoples and Tribes

## 6. Place Names